D0943785

HISTORICAL DICTIONARIES OF PEOPLES AND CULTURES
Jon Woronoff, Series Editor

1. *The Kurds*, by Michael M. Gunter, 2004.
2. *The Inuit*, by Pamela R. Stern, 2004.
3. *The Druzes*, by Samy Swayd, 2006.
4. *Southeast Asian Massif*, by Jean Michaud, 2006.

Historical Dictionary of the Peoples of the Southeast Asian Massif

Jean Michaud

*Historical Dictionaries of
Peoples and Cultures, No. 4*

The Scarecrow Press, Inc.
Lanham, Maryland • Toronto • Oxford
2006

SCARECROW PRESS, INC.

Published in the United States of America
by Scarecrow Press, Inc.
A wholly owned subsidary of
The Rowman & Littlefield Publishing Group, Inc.
4501 Forbes Boulevard, Suite 200, Lanham, Maryland 20706
www.scarecrowpress.com

PO Box 317
Oxford
OX2 9RU, UK

British Library Cataloguing in Publication Information Available

Library of Congress Cataloging-in-Publication Data
Michaud, Jean, 1957–
 Historical dictionary of the peoples of the Southeast Asian massif / Jean
Michaud.
  p. cm. — (Historical dictionaries of peoples and cultures ; no. 4)
 Includes bibliographical references.
 ISBN 0-8108-5466-X (hardcover : alk. paper)
 ISBN 978-0-8108-5466-6
 1. Southeast Asia–History–Dictionaries. 2. Ethnology–Southeast
Asia–Dictionaries. I. Title. II. Series: Historical dictionaries of people and cultures;
no. 4.
 DS524.M54 2006
 959.003–dc22   2005028438

Contents

List of Illustrations

TABLES

FIGURES

MAPS

Editor's Foreword

Dwelling in the more mountainous parts of the Southeast Asian massif, in the present-day states of Cambodia, Laos, Vietnam, Thailand, Burma (Myanmar) and southwest China, there are more than a thousand "peoples." They often do not have very much in common. Some groups number in the hundreds, others in the millions. They belong to different ethnicities, speak different languages, practice different religions, have different customs, and wear different attire. Some were always self-governing, others feudal fiefs. Most live from agriculture, often quite poorly, and not all have been dragged fully into the modern economy. Yet, despite any differences and lack of contact, they do share certain bonds. Many came from somewhere else and were chased—sometimes repeatedly—farther up the highlands while their enemies occupied the more fertile lowlands. Even today, they are regarded as intolerably backward and in need of advice, or orders, from the central authorities, which designate and treat them as "minorities." And their relations with lowland neighbors are often strained. Actually, despite having survived for many centuries, at present they are again at risk and their fate as distinct peoples hangs in the balance.

Clearly, something must be done. But just what is hard to say. Indeed, when dealing with millions of people, divided among hundreds of distinct if sometimes related groups, living in half-a-dozen countries, some of them not very forthcoming about internal conditions, it is even hard enough to get a handle on the situation. This makes the *Historical Dictionary of the Peoples of the Southeast Asian Massif* particularly welcome. It brings together in a handy format a wealth of information that is otherwise widely dispersed and not readily accessible. The introduction covers the field broadly and explains past and present problems. The dictionary includes entries on about 200 specific groups, on the circumstances in each of the six states, and on topics of more general interest

ix

regarding the polity, society, and economy. There are even entries on some of their leaders. The rather extensive bibliography points to other sources for readers interested in specific groups, periods, or fields. For this book, more than most other historical dictionaries, it was necessary for the author to sort through masses of information (much of it erroneous) and clarify the situation for several states and many peoples. That was the far from simple task taken on by Jean Michaud, a social anthropologist who fortunately knows the region well and is also fluent in French, an asset when dealing with the history of Laos, Cambodia, and Vietnam. Having graduated from the Université de Montréal, he worked as a lecturer at the Centre for South-East Asian Studies of the University of Hull in England for seven years before returning to his alma mater. Dr. Michaud has also served as visiting lecturer and researcher at the Université de Paris-X and the University of Otago in New Zealand. Over comparatively few years he has produced an impressive number of papers, chapters, and books, and organized panels and seminars. The same energy, and an obvious concern for the fate of the highland peoples, motivated this book, which should help the rest of us see things more clearly in a field where confusion is almost inevitable.

Jon Woronoff

Preface

Demographic evidence alone suffices to justify devoting a book to the highland societies of the southeastern portion of the Asian landmass, with a total population of about 80 million, in an area generally known in English as Mainland Southeast Asia, sometimes also as the Indochina Peninsula, the upland portion of which I opted to call in this dictionary the Mainland Southeast Asian massif.

Beyond the demographic argument, there are also compelling motives to want to know more about these groups. Through what was popularized in the West as the "Vietnam War," recent history has brought several of them, such as the Montagnards and the Hmong, to the forefront of the region's political stage, sometimes into Western daily news. Less widely known is the fact that before that major Asian civil wars of the 19th and early 20th centuries involved highland groups—one can think of the Panthay and the Miao rebellions in southwest China, or the Black Flags incursions into French Indochina—highlighting the role several of these minority groups played in shaping the region politically as we know it today. Nearly all modern regional borders are now located in mountainous terrain, and highland groups have been entwined in the geostrategic struggles for national security.

In economic terms, the all-important opium production and trade, which from the 1840s onward was instrumental in making possible the successful establishment of France and Britain in Asia and served, later, to finance revolutionary and counterrevolutionary efforts, relied on highland groups for the production and transport of the lucrative narcotic. Today, a fresh motive to keep the highland minorities at the top of the political agenda in the whole Southeast Asian massif is their impact on the delicate highland ecosystem. Under international impetus, heads of watersheds have become eco-strategic systems which, when neglected, can have a harmful impact, through deforestation and highland erosion, on life in the heavily populated lowlands. The highlands and their populations have become inevitable partners of the local governments in managing the common future of all in the Peninsula and in southwest China.

It is very difficult to select significant persons from the ethnic minorities about whom to write individual entries because although a few have made it onto the world stage, such as White Thai leader Deo Van Tri, Hmong General Vang Pao, or Shan drug baron Khun Sa, most have only been declared local heroes—or villains, depending on which side they stood for. Indeed, cultural and political marginality are not conducive to yielding many "historical figures," history being written, as everyone knows, by the victors. Reflecting this relative anonymity for an international readership, the biographical portion of this dictionary remains comparatively modest. Yet it also includes nonminority explorers, missionaries, colonial administrators, and scholars whose works on peoples of the Southeast Asian massif have become classics.

Acknowledgments

I am indebted to Vanina Bouté, Bénédicte Brac de la Perrière, Candice Cornet, Steeve Daviau, Rodolphe De Koninck, Yves Goudineau, Stéphane Gros, John McKinnon, Jean-Claude Neveu, Jan Ovesen, Vatthana Pholsena, and Sarah Turner for sharing with me their expertise; Daphné Marion and Diana Mok for their assistance on Chinese terminology; Candice Cornet, Peter Foggin, and François Robinne for graciously providing original photographs; graduate students François Fortin-Deschênes, Caroline Goulet, Marise Lachapelle, Geneviève Polèse, and Laura Schoenberger for aptly sorting out and putting together the maps, chronology, tables, and bibliography; and Stéphane Bernard and Bruno Thibert for cartographic backing. Jon Woronoff, the series editor, has been extremely helpful all along.

And especially, I wish to thank Sarah Turner and Desmond Manderson for their intellectual companionship and unfailing encouragement while writing this book.

Reader's Note

In this book, a standardized, English-friendly Romanization is used instead of the vernacular scripts, that is, the Pali-based scripts of Burma, Thailand, Laos, and Cambodia (generally transposed in the Romanized form promoted by the respective national authorities). Standard *pinyin* is used for Chinese, which is officially accepted in China as an alternative to customary ideographic writing. Next door, the Romanized Vietnamese script, *quốc ngữ*, which does represent tones with specific diacritics, has officially dethroned ideographic *chữ nôm* for nearly a century now. Using it integrally would be tempting. However, due to phonetic specificities in the pronunciation of several Roman letters or clusters of letters (đ, â, ê, o·, u·, or tr, gi, nh, for instance), which differ from English or even do not exist in this language as specific sounds, its use could prove confusing to the general reader (see, for example, the Dao entry). For the English-speaking readers, this means that official ethnonyms of groups in Vietnam as reproduced here, that is, written closest to the original but without diacritics, may still pronounce differently than they are read. Whenever possible, the appropriate pronunciation is given in brackets.

In all cases, however, tones are lost in transcription. Tonal languages differ structurally from nontonal, Western languages. To dispense with writing tones is as puzzling to the tonal-language speakers as randomly dispensing with half the consonants when writing English. Romanization, clearly, is used here as a compromise.

In China, Burma, Cambodia, and Vietnam the surname normally comes first, which explains why a comma is unnecessary, as in Chairman Deng Xiaoping, where Deng is the surname, or Vietnamese historian Nguyen The Anh, with Nguyen the surname. In Thailand and Laos, the order of name and surname is the same as in English. However, the given name is usually the one used in public, in place of the surname as would be the case in English. For instance, Thailand's Prime Minister Thaksin Shinawatra, where Shinawatra is indeed the surname, is routinely and appropriately called Prime Minister Thaksin in the media. As an entry or in a bibliography, his name should be written "Thaksin Shinawatra," not "Shinawatra, Thaksin."

Boldface type within each dictionary entry indicates cross-referencing to another entry. To avoid cluttering the text unnecessarily, terms referring to that entry are only bolded the first time they appear. The names of the six countries sharing the Southeast Asian massif are not boldfaced, and frequently used terms such as "minority" are not normally boldfaced, as it should be evident that these entries exist.

Acronyms and Abbreviations

CASS	Chinese Academy of Social Sciences
CIA	Central Intelligence Agency
CUN	Central University for Nationalities of China
DRV	Democratic Republic of Vietnam
EFEO	*Ecole Française d'Extrême-Orient*
FULRO	*Front Unifié pour la Libération des Races Opprimées*
GZAR	Guangxi Zhuang Autonomous Region
LPDR	Lao People's Democratic Republic
MEP	*Société des Missions Étrangères de Paris*
NEZ	New Economic Zones (Vietnam)
PMSI	*Pays Montagnard du Sud-Indochinois*
PRC	People's Republic of China
RPA	Romanized Popular Alphabet
RVN	Republic of Vietnam
SLORC	State Law and Order Restoration Council (Myanmar/ Burma)
SRV	Socialist Republic of Vietnam
SSCT	*Sip Song Chau Tai*
SSPN	*Sip Song Phan Na*
UNESCO	United Nations Educational, Scientific, and Cultural Organization
UWSA	United Wa State Army (Myanmar/Burma)

Chronology

Only events having significance for the history of the Southeast Asian massif are listed. For the general history of the six countries sharing the massif, see the respective Scarecrow Press historical dictionaries.

B.C.

3000–2000   Neolithic cultures, probably Austroasiatic-speaking population.

ca. 2500   Proto-Malay migration from China into the Peninsula.

2000–500   Early bronze age settled communities in the central Mekong region.

ca. 300   Deutero-Malay migration into the Peninsula from China.

A.D.

8th to 13th centuries   Nan Chao Kingdom in western Yunnan. Slow spread of Tai peoples west and south of their area of origin in China, into the Tai highlands of northwest Vietnam, northeast Laos, northern Thailand, and northeastern Burma.

13th century, 2d half, Mongol (Yuan) dynasty in China takes over Nan Chao Thai kingdom, from where Chinese troups descend on Dai Viet, and Pagan in Burma. Important migration into China of Middle Eastern Muslims, who will form the core of the Hui minority.

1292   Marco Polo travels to the Southeast Asian massif.

1405–1433   Over a 28-year period, pioneer Hui navigator Zheng He leads massive Chinese fleets to dozens of Asian and African countries.

16th c.   Maize from Spanish America introduced to China, allowing easier Han colonization of the southwest mid- and highlands.

18th c. Major highland rebellions and imperial repressions in southwest China. Presumably the time of the first migrations to the Peninsula of the Miao-Yao groups.

1838–1842 First Opium War between China and European colonial powers.

1851–1864 Taiping Rebellion in southwest China.

1854–1873 Miao Rebellion in Southern China involving, in addition to the Miao, important numbers from other minorities.

1855–1872 Panthay Rebellion chiefly involving the Hui minority in southwest China.

1856–1858 Second Opium War between China and European colonial powers.

1858 Start of French military conquest of Indochina.

1860s–1890s Substantial migration of various minority representatives from China into the Peninsula in connection with social unrest in China and Flag Armies activity in the Peninsula.

1866 Foundation of the China Inland Mission.

1866–1868 First European colonial exploration of the Mekong River along its entire course, by Ernest Doudart de Lagrée and Francis Garnier.

1867 French colonial protectorate over Cambodia.

1873 Siege of Hanoi by White Thai leader Deo Van Tri and the Black Flags.

1875–1901 Kha revolt in the Laotian province of Huaphanh.

1879–1895 Pavie Mission, a major French scientific and diplomatic mission across the Indochina Peninsula and active over 16 years.

1884–1895 French military "pacification" of Red River delta and Tonkin's highlands.

1885 Official recognition by China of French supremacy over Annam and Tonkin.

1886 Start of British rule in Burma.

1889 Official recognition of the hereditary lordship of the Deo family over the White Thai domain of the Sip Song Chau Thai in Tonkin.

1891 Creation of the Military Territories Administration in Upper Tonkin.

1893 French colonial protectorate over Laos.

1894–1896 Official demarcations of the Sino-Tonkinese borders agreed between China and French colonial power in Indochina.

1895 Laos divided for administrative purposes into Upper and Lower Laos. **June 30:** Sino-French treaty transfers two Lue principalities of the Sip Song Phan Na (Meuang Sing and Phongsaly) to French Laos.

1896 **January 15:** Anglo-French Convention defines British and French spheres of influence in Mainland Southeast Asia.

1898–1903 First comprehensive ethnographic survey of the north Tonkin highland minorities by the French military.

1899 Foundation in Hanoi of the Ecole Française d'Extrême-Orient.

1901–1907 Phu Mi Bun Revolt on the Boloven Plateau in Laos, led by Bak Mi and Ong Kommadam.

1904 Introduction of the Pollard Script in Yunnan.

1908–1910 Insurrection of Tai Lue chief Vannaphum in Phongsaly ends with his death.

1909 Death of Deo Van Tri, succeeded by his son as Lord of the Sip Song Chau Tai. Completion of the Haiphong-Kunming rail link.

1911 Promulgation of the Republic of China.

1914–1916 Lue revolt in Luangnamtha and Chinese-Tai revolt in Xam Neua and Phongsaly.

1916 Formation of the French colonial Fifth Military Territory covering the province of Phongsaly in Laos.

1918–1921 The Ba Chay ("Mad Man's") Hmong rebellion in Tonkin and Laos.

c1920 Acknowledgment by the Kuomintang of the existence of only four non-Han minorities in the Republic of China (Mongols, Manchus, Tibetans, Tatars), none of which represents the southwest minorities.

1925 Ong Kommadam circulates anti-French call to arms on the Boloven Plateau.

1925–1928 French missionary François Savina commissioned by the Chinese and the French colonial authorities to investigate native languages of Hainan.

1930–1931 Nghe An uprising in Vietnam.

1931 Last comprehensive national census of Burma that included detailed figures on highland minorities.

1934–1936 New outbreak of unrest on the Boloven elicits strong French retaliation, ends with death of Ong Kommadam.

1935 First promise of minority self-determination rights by Communist Party of Vietnam. **April–May:** Communist Long March dwells in Yunnan among minorities.

1942–1945 Japan occupies Mainland Southeast Asia and some of its highlands. Hmong leader Touby Lyfoung supports French armed resistance against Japan in Laos.

1945 Start of enmity between the Ly and Lo clans among the Hmong in Laos, leading to the former siding with the Royal Lao government and the latter with the Pathet Lao.

1945–1946 Republican Chinese troops occupy Tonkin and its highlands at the request of the Allies, to disarm the Japanese.

1946–1954 First Indochina War.

1947 Ho Chi Minh and communist followers take refuge among Tay ethnic minority in the Thai Nguyen highlands. Setting up of the Kachin State and the Shan State in Burma. Creation of the Karen National Union of Burma.

1948 Independence of Burma, and Karen rebellion. The French, concerned with winning the war against the nationalist Vietnamese, create the Tai Federation in northern Tonkin, dissolved in 1954.

1949 Birth of the People's Republic of China (PRC) and abolition of ancient feudal states such as Sip Song Phan Na.

1950–1958 Seminal ethnographic research on "minority nationalities" (*shaoshu minzu*) in China and promotion of Romanized scripts for minorities.

1951 Establishment in Beijing of the Central Institute of Nationalities, renamed The central University for Nationalities in 1993.

1952 Setting up of the Karen State in Burma.

1953 Viet Minh offensive in northern Laos. French forces occupy military outpost at Dien Bien Phu to hinder Viet Minh movement into Laos. Independence of Cambodia. First post-revolution national census in China announcing that 6 percent of the population belongs to non-Han ethnicities.

1954 White Thai leader Deo Van Long flown out of Tonkin. **March 13:** Viet Minh siege of the French at Dien Bien Phu; the French are overwhelmed and surrender on May 6. **July 21:** Geneva Agreements and partition of Vietnam between North (Democratic Republic of Vietnam, DRV) and South (Republic of Vietnam, RVN). Important migration from North Vietnam to Laos and South Vietnam of minority partisans of the French colonial government.

1954–1975 Second Indochina War.

1954–ca. 1980 Implementation of the New Economic Zones scheme sending lowland Vietnamese to live in the highlands, first in DRV, then in the South after reunification.

1955–1956 Creation of the Viet Bac and Tay Bac Autonomous Regions in the highlands of the DRV.

1957 Establishment of the Guangxi Zhuang Autonomous Region in China.

1958–1961 Great Leap Forward in the PRC generalizing the commune system and collectivization.

1958–1960 Adoption by the DRV of a three-year plan launching collectivization in the North.

1959–1975 Active, though secret, air support to anticommunist fighters in highland Laos via "Air America."

1959 The *shaoshu minzu* of China are officially declared to number 51. Chinese invasion of Tibet. Abolition of opium poppy growing in Thailand.

1961 Buddhism made state religion in Burma. Creation of the Kachin Independence Organization in Burma. Establishment by Gordon Young of the first official list of "hill tribes" in Thailand.

1961–1963 "Strategic hamlets" relocation policy in the Central Highlands of the RVN.

1962 First census in independent Cambodia.

1964 Start of communist-supported insurrection in Thailand. Creation of the "United Struggle Front for the Oppressed Races" (FULRO) in southern Vietnam.

1964–1973 American-led heavy bombing of the Laotian eastern highlands along the Ho Chi Minh trails.

1966–1976 Cultural Revolution in the PRC.

1968 Establishment in Hanoi of the Institute of Ethnology of Vietnam. Most active phase of "Air America" operations in Laos, with over 200 aircraft.

1970s First implementation of national programs of sedentarization of "hill tribes" and substitution crops to replace opium poppy cultivation in Thailand.

1974 Burmese Constitution establishing the seven highland *pyi ne*, or states.

1975 Khmer Rouge victory in Cambodia followed by Pol Pot regime (1975–1977), takeover of South Vietnam by North Vietnamese Communist forces, communist Pathet Lao victory in Laos. Important migration from Laos to Thailand of minority partisans of the Royal Lao Government; General Vang Pao seeks refuge in Thailand. The Committee of Nationalities is set up in Laos.

1976 Creation of a unified Socialist Republic of Vietnam (SRV). End of the Autonomous Regions in the northern highlands of Vietnam. First waves of lowland migrants to the Vietnamese Central Highlands under the New Economic Zones scheme applied to the south.

1977   Center for Nationalities Research of China established within the Academy of Social Sciences. Death of revolutionary leader Sithon Kommadam.

1978   In Laos, decision to undertake rapid program of agricultural collectivization. Deng Xiaoping in power in the PRC: "Four Modernizations," Open Door policy, and end of rural collectivization. Death of Hmong anticommunist leader of Laos, Touby Lyfoung, in a reeducation camp in Sam Neua.

1978–1989   Vietnam invades and occupies Cambodia; China retaliates by invading a section of the northern Vietnamese highlands for one month.

1979   Production of the definitive list of 54 Nationalities (*cac dan toc*) in Vietnam.

1981   Production of the definitive list of 55 *shaoshu minzu* in China.

1982   End of state monopoly on opium in Vietnam.

1983   Last known national census in Burma.

1985   First national census in the Lao People's Democratic Republic. National census in Thailand.

1986   Economic Renovation (*Doi Moi*) decided in Vietnam. Launch of the New Economic Mechanisms in Laos. Hmong procommunist leader of Laos, Faydang Lobliayao, dies.

1987   End of hostilities between the Hmong communists and the military in Thailand. Buddhism is declared state religion in Cambodia. General Vang Pao, based in the United States, announces formation of a Revolutionary Government of Laos in exile.

1988   Hainan Island becomes a province in China. Signature by all countries sharing the massif of the UN Drug Convention.

1989   National census in Vietnam.

1990   Installation of the State Law and Order Restoration Council (SLORC) junta in Burma (Myanmar), taking a hard line toward minorities.

1990s Massive state-led programs of sedentarization and adoption of cash crops among highland societies in all countries sharing the massif (except Burma). Lowland Viet encouraged by the state to seek economic opportunities in the highlands. Intensification of the relocation policy in highland Laos.

1992 Definitive list of 47 ethnic groups (*sonsat*) promulgated in Laos.

1992–1993 Adoption of new land and forest law in Vietnam, including a ban on opium poppy cultivation and tree felling in protected forests.

1993 Opening up of Vietnam's highlands to international tourism.

1995 National census held in Laos, Thailand, Cambodia. Setting up of the Vietnam Museum of Ethnology in Hanoi.

1995–2004 UN International Decade of the World's Indigenous People, in which socialist China, Vietnam, and Laos as well as junta-led Burma refuse to participate.

1996 Shan drug baron Khun Sa surrenders and settles in Rangoon.

1997 State Peace and Development Council replaces SLORC in Burma.

1999 Close to 300 million methamphetamine pills produced in highland Burma. National census in Vietnam.

2000 National census in the PRC. National census in the United States yielding the figure of 186,310 Hmong in that country.

2001 Selection of Nong Duc Manh, from the Tay minority, as general secretary of the Executive Committee of the Communist Party of Vietnam.

2001, 2003 Civil unrest on Vietnam's Central Highland plateau involving highlanders, repressed by the army.

2001 The three-tiered ethnic classification in Laos (Lao Loum, Theung, and Sung) is quietly abandoned.

2004 Total ban on opium poppy cultivation in Laos.

2005 National census in Laos, Cambodia, and Thailand.

F. Fortin-Deschesnes & J. Michaud

Map 1. Area of Interest

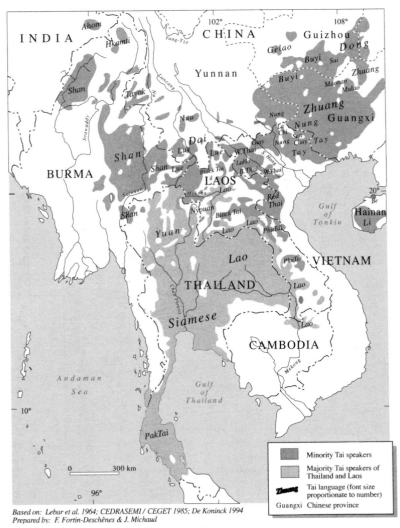

Based on: Lebar et al. 1964; CEDRASEMI / CEGET 1985; De Koninck 1994
Prepared by: F. Fortin-Deschênes & J. Michaud

Map 2.   Distribution of Tai-Kadai Speakers

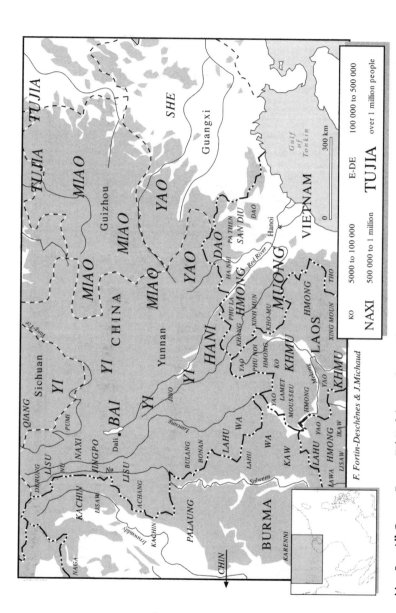

Map 3. All Groups Except Tai-Kadai—North Massif

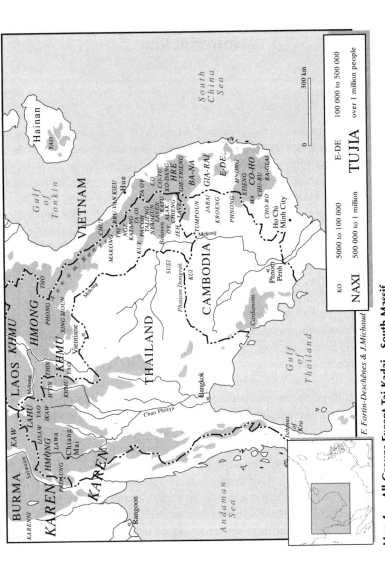

Map 4. All Groups Except Tai-Kadai—South Massif

F. Fortin-Deschênes & J.Michaud

NAXI	KO	5000 to 100 000	E-DE	100 000 to 500 000
		500 000 to 1 million		over 1 million people
			TUJIA	

0 300 km

Introduction

The main purpose of this book is to bring to the attention of the general public an important, though little-known, cluster of societies of Asia. Lowland majorities that occupy fertile plains and coastal areas of the southeast section of the Asian landmass are well known in the West; namely the Han Chinese, the Viet, the Thai, the Burmans, the Khmer, the Lao. But how many, in the broader international community, have heard of the Yi or the Tujia, with a population of 8 million each? Or the Dong, the Buyi, and the Yao, each weighing 3 million on the demographic scale? In fact, even the massive Zhuang, with 16 million, have constantly failed to make the news outside China.

Like the Kurds, who were addressed in the first volume published in the Historical Dictionaries of Peoples and Cultures series of Scarecrow Press, the Asian societies dealt with here spread over several countries. Like the Kurds, each of these constitutes a minority. However, their total number is about three times that of the Kurds. Moreover, they show drastic linguistic and cultural differences among themselves. These groups, living in the highlands at a distance from the densely populated deltas, are in fact geographically dispersed and politically fragmented. Among them, they speak hundreds of languages from five language families. Their economic systems range from hunting and gathering, to forest horticulture, rice growing agriculture—for the majority—and, for a growing proportion, to wage work in the most modern and technologically advanced urban areas of East and Southeast Asia.

Indeed, the highland societies of the mainland Southeast Asian massif offer so much cultural originality that they have become prized targets for the international industry of ethnic tourism, a new economic lifeline that may—but perhaps only may—prove crucial to the preservation of their distinct identities in the face of persistent pressures toward national cultural integration, and the imperatives of the market economy threatening to turn them into little more than commodities.

1

THE HIGHLAND PEOPLES

Attempting to summarize competently the staggering cultural diversity found in the highlands of mainland Southeast Asia is a daunting task. The latest census data on Burma (Myanmar), Thailand, Laos, Cambodia, Vietnam, and China, the six countries under consideration here, yield the figure of approximately 130 million individuals belonging to one or another of what each of these countries calls, in its own way, its "ethnic minorities." Of particular interest to this dictionary, 80 million of these people live in the Asian highlands extending east from the Himalayas. This is, in demographic terms, equal to the population of Vietnam, the most populous country in mainland Southeast Asia. Or one can also calculate that it is 15 million more than the population of Thailand, nearly twice the population of Burma, and five times the combined population of Laos and Cambodia.

Across these six countries, the official numbers of different highland ethnic minority groups accounting for the 80 millions are 49 in Vietnam, 46 in Laos, 29 in China, 11 in Thailand, and an estimated 21 in Burma and 14 in Cambodia. However, given the overlap between these national lists, linked to the fact that several ethnic denominations straddle borders, merely adding up these numbers cannot get to the essence of the matter. In reality, the possible number of distinct ethnic identities in the highlands can be over a thousand when taking into account the array of local names and language variations within each group. Such is the linguistic and cultural variety in these mountains that, combined with the incomplete state of scientific knowledge about these peoples, no authoritative figures can be obtained about how many groups there are.

Generically, the mainland Southeast Asian massif's peoples are variously called, when official vernacular terms are translated into English, mountain people, highlanders, hill tribes, Nations, Nationalities, minorities, Minority Nationalities, or National Minorities. Across time, countries, and political regimes, agreement has never been reached about which ethnonyms (ethnic names) should be assigned to most highland groups, in particular those found in more than one country. The truth of the matter is that most names used officially are exonyms, names groups are given by their neighbors regardless of what they themselves might prefer to be called. The problem with exonyms is that they are often misleading. If a certain proportion can be considered appropriate, some are outright derogatory or offensive. For instance, highlanders in the southern Annam Range were for a long time generically called *Moi*, "savages," encapsulating their cultural subordination. The generic terms *Kha* in Laos, and *Man*, *Miao*, and *Lolo* in China were used for a long time with similar negative connotations. Other exonyms are simply faulty, too broad, or applied to the wrong people. In China, the Miao, Tujia, and Zhuang all number 8 million or more. Surely subgroups could be meaningfully acknowledged and labeled with different, more suitable names. Another very common and rather rudimentary practice in assigning exonyms consists of using colors of the attire to differentiate subgroups, such as Red, White, and Striped Miao; White, Black, and Red Thai; and many more. Overall, studies have shown that exonyms are often terms of marginalization, and as such, they tell us more about the preconceptions of the naming groups than anything useful about the peoples being named.

In search of a solution to the naming dilemma, one could also take into account autonyms, or names members of a society assign to themselves regardless of what their neighbors might call them. Taking popular examples in the West, the Sioux prefer to call themselves Lakota, the Eskimos are in reality Inuit, the Laps are Saami, etc. As a rule, it is widely accepted that autonyms are more suitable and more respectful than exonyms. Unfortunately, on the ground autonyms show such a degree of diversity and inconsistency, often with no rational justification, that a logical mind might find it impossible to manage at the macrolevel. Regionalisms prevail even from one watershed to the next, clan names are sometimes swapped with group names, local topographical features become part of names, and variations show up even within the smallest groups, all such discrepancies being most often due to an all-too-human desire to distinguish oneself—often in spite of logic. And even when a name is shared by a significant number of persons, local pronunciation often drifts in ways that can sometimes prove perplexing to the outside observer. The utmost care is thus required when assigning and using ethnonyms in the high region, disparity being far more prevalent than regularity. Popular, supposedly definitive terminology, such as that printed in coffee table books and tourist guidebooks, or indeed in the official discourse of several countries in the Peninsula, should be kept in check.

For this dictionary, a compromise solution has been adopted, which was to accept official national ethnonyms but correct mistakes whenever possible and cross-reference to alternative names. Close to 200 ethnonyms thus have their own entries, which is the largest number the relatively humble format of this series allows.

Other dilemmas remain. The deceptively simple notion of "national minority group" itself masks potential pitfalls. First, the bulk of the groups in the mainland Southeast Asian massif are not national. They are in fact transnational, meaning that they are found on both sides of many of the massif's borders. The Karen, Hani, Lolo, Yao, Kachin, Khmu, Tay, Katu, and Lamet, to name a few, all spread over the massif in two countries or more. Representatives of the Tai linguistic family, the most widespread highland language group, with 33 million speakers, are established in considerable numbers in all six countries.

Second, the term "minority" is only conceptually valid when looking at the situation from within the borders of a single state. With around 5 million Hmong in Asia, equal to the population of Laos, a legitimate and internationally acknowledged sovereign nation, the notion of "minority" is intellectually less than satisfactory when labeling such a numerous group.

Finally, even the word "group" is contentious, as it suggests a sense of community and social cohesion that groups in the region do not all feel or share.

There is another problem: Since they in fact present more differences among themselves than similarities, do the highland societies dwelling in the mainland Southeast Asian massif form a "people"—the explicit object of this series? Is their apparent social and cultural resemblance merely an illusion, because all that they really share, beyond the use of a common ecosystem, is to *not be* one of the dominant lowland majorities that have ruled the region for centuries? The position in this dictionary is that, clearly, no, these dozens of diverse groups do not form a "people." They constitute instead many "peoples," a notion that, in this case, must not be defined strictly as a homogeneous, essential entity. What these peoples actually share is a sense of being different from the majorities, a sense of geographical remoteness, and a state of marginality connected to a degree of political and economic distance from the seats of regional power. Geographical remoteness becomes a metaphor for political isolation, and for the subordination of those who are most likely to have been classified by the powers-that-be, through history, as "savages." In cultural terms, "peoples," here, is truly plural and multiple, producing a cultural mosaic with contrasting colors rather than an integrated picture in harmonized shades. Yet when observing from the necessary distance, that mosaic becomes a distinctive and relatable picture, a legitimate subject for a "Dictionary of People," though clearly an unusual one.

GEOGRAPHICAL AREA

At their maximum extension, the highland groups considered here are scattered over a transnational domain most of the time situated above an elevation of 500 meters (see map 1), an area of approximately 2.5 million square kilometers, approximately the size of Western Europe. From north to south, it includes southern and western Sichuan, all of Guizhou and Yunnan, western and northern Guangxi, western Guangdong, most of northern Burma with an adjacent segment of extreme eastern India, the north and west of Thailand, practically all of Laos above the Mekong Valley, northern and central Vietnam along the Annam Cordillera, and the north and east fringes of Cambodia. It constitutes one immense massif; it is also a terrain of remarkable physical and climatic diversity. Stretching from the temperate Yangtze River system, which roughly demarcates its northern boundary, it moves south to encompass the high ranges extending southeast from the Himalayas and the Tibetan Plateau, and all the monsoon high country drained by the Irrawaddy, Salween, Chao Phraya, Mekong, and Red Rivers.

In more ways than one, China's southwest uplands form a world of their own, with a specific logic and an extremely complex, little-known history. The region has political, linguistic, and biophysical particularities, and to address all of these in one book, one has to remain humble and accept that ultimately it may be necessary to devote an individual dictionary only to these peoples. However, it is plainly impossible to address the Peninsula's highland societies in a satisfactory manner without tapping the source of Chinese history, where the ancestry of so many among them is deeply rooted. The chief drawback of this unavoidable choice is that the large highland population in southwest China is inversely proportional to the ethnological detail available to distinguish peoples there from one another. Politics in China have dictated the agenda on minorities, and as a consequence, cultural definition is left wanting.

Malaya, beyond the extreme south of the massif, falls outside our scope, as does the Tibetan plateau on the massif's northwestern periphery. In the first case, academics agree that physically and culturally, Malaya, which is disconnected form the massif by the Isthmus of Kra, is also better associated in cultural, linguistic, and historical terms with the Malay world that forms the bulk of the peoples of Maritime Southeast Asia. As for Tibet and its cultural periphery, despite its irrefutable minority status within China, it is more appropriately conceived of as a distinct cultural entity, a centralized and religiously harmonized historical kingdom with a long political existence. Likewise, it would be tempting to try to include in this survey the "Scheduled Tribes" located in the far-eastern portion of northern India, such as those found in the states of Assam, Manipur, Mizoram, and Nagaland. These groups are indeed marginal and subsidiary in their country and share many similarities with a number of groups in the Peninsula, particularly regarding social organization, cosmology, and agricultural practices. However, their historical and political center of gravity leans more toward the subcontinent than the Peninsula, and consequently, our study area has been limited to the western Burma border.

LANGUAGES AND SCRIPTS

Linguistic classification in the massif, which one would assume could offer an appropriate apparatus to discriminate ethnic entities into logical categories, is still unsure and tentative. The mixture of languages spoken in those highlands—dozens of them, though again, no exact figure can be ascertained—cover five major language families: Austronesian, Austro-Asiatic, Sino-Tibetan, Tai-Kadai, and Miao-Yao. The first family includes, for instance, Malay as spoken in Maritime Southeast Asia and by a handful of groups dwelling in the southern Annam Cordillera. The second comprises Vietnamese as well as the major Mon-Khmer cluster. The third includes, in addition to the huge branch constituted by Chinese languages, the Tibeto-Burman galaxy. Tai-Kadai, although not the largest, is the most widespread family, with native speakers all over the massif. Finally, there is Miao-Yao, which is rather specific, yet geographically very dispersed.

This fivefold classification is still debated among linguists. Proto-languages, the common stems of languages, which are today sometimes drastically distinct from one another, are being explored as we speak and as a consequence, particular languages are still being shifted from one family to the other, becoming new subfamilies, or being merged with another related language. Yet with all its flaws language remains one of the safest structural elements for clustering ethnic identities. It constitutes the backbone of the ethnic division used in this dictionary.

The six countries covered here each have a different national language. More problematic is the fact that they also have six different and mutually unintelligible scripts—with the arguable exception of the Thai and Lao scripts, which are related. This lack of homogeneity precludes, in this modest publication, doing justice to the suitable national scripts in entries that would ideally require their use.

HISTORY AND SOURCES

Except for relatively recent Han (Chinese) migrants, most of today's inhabitants of China's southwest highlands are believed to be aboriginal to that region; that is, they were the first human settlers there. Whether they initially settled there of their own will, in response to demographic pressure or political adversity in the lowlands, and whether they were indigenous to another area in the massif than the one they currently occupy, has not been ascertained, and perhaps never will be due to the lack of evidence. In the continuation of the massif into the Peninsula, it is believed that most of the current inhabitants, whatever their ethnicity and nationality today, are migrants from elsewhere on the Asian continent. The most ancient migrations, generally called Proto- and Deutero-Malay, predate the Christian era. A variety of Austronesian and Austro-Asiatic clusters still visible today were part of that ancient movement, as well as some lowland groups still present, such as the Cham, the Khmer, and the Mon. Roughly during the last millennium B.C. and the first millennium A.D., later migration flows, following land routes, brought new groups from the north, who went on to establish their own kingdoms in the fertile and hospitable lowlands. These include the Viet, the Thai, and the Burman, who either eliminated, assimilated, or pushed farther away or higher up a number of their predecessors. Scholars think that this process is the most likely reason why numerous earlier groups—those Austronesian and Austro-Asiatic speakers—found themselves moving up into the hills and highlands of the massif, such as the Annam Cordillera.

Thus, over time, various kingdoms and empires—Chinese dynasties, Tibetans, the kingdoms of Funan, Chenla, Champa, Angkor, Dai Viet, and Dvaravati, to name a few—claimed sections of the fertile lowland deltas and floodplains surrounding the massif, stamping a definitive political supremacy on specific territories still prevailing to this day: the Han in southern China, the Tibetans on the Tibet plateau, the Viet (Kinh) in northern Vietnam, who went on to snatch south Vietnam from the Cham and the Khmer; the Khmer in Cambodia; the Thai in Siam; and the Burman in Burma (Myanmar). In the process, remnants of an array of earlier groups were displaced to the highlands, where they did their best to survive the new lowland masters, sometimes standing their ground successfully, as did the Tai, Bai, Naxi, and Yi kingdoms in the central massif, but more often merging, acculturating, sometimes plainly assimilating to these predatory lowland neighbors.

Starting in the sixteenth century A.D., within Southwest China and between China and the Peninsula were set in motion a series of smaller, more discrete migration waves. The Han's continuous progress into the southwest highlands of the Middle Empire, accelerated by the import from the Americas of maize suitable for the highland climate, motivated some of the groups that had long lived or found refuge there to get moving again to escape subordination, assimilation, or annihilation. This time, Han occupation of virtually all of the surrounding fertile valleys meant that the only remaining uninhabited zones open to migration were situated farther south and west in the massif's uplands. Starting roughly 500 years ago and peaking at times of major political turmoil in southwest China in the nineteenth century, a more or less constant flow of mountain dwellers left their homes in southern China—and perhaps also far-eastern India—to push south into the nearly vacant high grounds in the south of Yunnan and the northern parts of Burma, Thailand, Laos, and Vietnam (they did not reach Cambodia), where they now form a significant portion of the total national highland population. While all the states in the Peninsula have now passed regulations to curb such unwarranted flow of migrants, it is likely that a fair number of illegal migrants still pour out of China, following family connections and trade networks. The era of massive migration into the Peninsula's highlands, however, is definitely over.

A review of the highland minorities' migrations in the region would not be complete without mention of the most recent migratory wave that took highlanders outside Asia, when the First and Second Indochina Wars in the second half of the 20th century drove several hundred thousand of them onto the road to such faraway destinations as the United States, France, Australia, and Canada. These migrations outside Asia, however, are not covered in any detail by this dictionary.

In terms of archaeological heritage, the longer human groups dwell in one location, the more material evidence they are likely to have left behind. Southwest China, the source of most highland groups in the massif, and northern Burma seem to be the zones where such evidence is the most likely to be unearthed, thanks to the earlier sedimentation of human groups in these highlands. For instance, the Naxi in the Lijiang region, the Dai around the Erh Hai Lake, the Yi in central Yunnan, the Lue of the Sip Song Phan Na, the Zhuang, Kam, and Tujia of Guangxi and Guizhou, and the Shan in eastern Burma have long built their dwellings with lasting material, carved sizeable water works, and erected temples and pagodas. But elsewhere, the picture is less promising. Of the peoples under scrutiny here, particularly in the Peninsula, where many arrived as nomadic or seminomadic migrants, a large number only produced temporary shelters made of biological materials, clothes processed from hemp, and shallow graves that have quickly disappeared. Animism, their chief religious system, did not necessitate the building of lasting worship buildings. The occasional grinding stone and, later, metal tools are for many all they left behind. Even their signature on the landscape—swiddens, foot and horse paths, graveyards, village sites—has been largely reclaimed by the forest or erased by later occupants. In brief, archaeology is of limited assistance in the highlands of the Peninsula compared to the wealth of baked brick and stone buildings, deep foundations, temples, cities and citadels, carved steles, clay or metal artifacts, jewelry, impressive graves, and even libraries left by the surrounding civilizations.

When lacking solid material evidence, historians can opt for working from text. Here again, the harvest for the massif is relatively sparse.

Only a small number of highland groups have fashioned lasting indigenous scripts. The pictographic script of the Naxi in western Yunnan, for example, is an entirely indigenous invention. As a handy substitute, Chinese ideograms were adopted by the Yao, who could thus register their genealogies in colorful codexes. The Tai groups in the Sip Song Chau Tai used variations of the Pali-based Siamese script to write the occasional annals, as did some of their Tai-speaking neighbors in upland Laos. These particular cases aside, it is predominantly when Western Christian missionaries came in contact with local groups in the 19th and early 20th centuries, bringing with them Romanized and syllabic alphabets to translate the Bible into the vernaculars, that most of the massif's languages were for the first time put on paper. The Pollard script, a syllabic assemblage, thus became popular among certain Miao groups in China, while Barney and Smalley's Romanized Popular Alphabet for Hmong is now widely used by the Hmong refugees from Laos living in the West. In the second half of the 20th century, the process of alphabetization of minority languages was pursued and completed by the local governments.

Still, if most highlanders in the Peninsula have not written about themselves before the immediate past, their literate neighbors have been more prolific. Chinese, Vietnamese, Thai, Lao, and Burmese official annals yield some information on the identity, cultures, and whereabouts of numerous highland groups on the periphery of their domains. Most of the time, this information takes the form of administrative reports filed by passing officials and traders, or by military officers leading parties sent to pacify the uplands. These reports routinely contained a few lines, most often derogatory, about "barbarians" met on those journeys and expeditions. Rampant bigotry, a forceful discourse of exclusion of the "savage" unfavorably compared to the civilized self, lowers the value of these texts for learning about the mountain dwellers in the more distant past. Nevertheless, though modest, imprecise, and distorted, the harvest they yield is priceless.

It was with the arrival of European observers in the massif, toward the middle of the 19th century, that text of a more solid ethnographic nature increased. Up until the end of European colonial rule in the region, Western missionaries and explorers in Southwest China and Thailand, British officials in Burma, and French representatives in French Indochina collected crucial elements of oral history, completed with their own observations. Hundreds of such reports can be consulted in archives and in old colonial journal issues, which also include photographs, drawings, hand-made and ordinance maps, artifacts, etc. Except in wartime, ethnological, linguistic, and historical research has been growing since then. Today, an army of international scholars issues new publications on one or another of the highland groups every day. These three types of sources—Asian annals, colonial archives, and modern scientific works—are used by academics around the world in combination with field investigations to support the works they produce.

It is also worthwhile to bear in mind that the notion of text can embrace oral text. Oral tradition in the highlands is rich and lively. It can be mined for historical evidence, though great care must be exercised when interpreting such material. One classical form of oral tradition, the myth, embeds information on the creation of the world, the appearance of humans, and the distinctions between male and female seen from within a given tradition. However, poetic license is granted to the storytellers, and myths cannot be assimilated with historical facts. But oral history, unlike mythology, is more reliable. It is composed of events set in the memory of living elders who can testify to their veracity—or lie about them. When collected with care and cross-checked for error or distortion, oral history yields valuable pictures painted with what the subjects have themselves experienced firsthand. On a longer time scale, oral history can include information passed across a few generations, though in such cases additional confirmation is needed from other sources. Thus, when no archaeological evidence can be found or used to confirm, for example, the moment a given group actually entered a region for the first time, and the written records are mute or nonexistent, oral history can generally give a relatively dependable account.

RELIGION AND RELATIONSHIP TO NATURE

The variety of religious beliefs and practices in the highlands ranges from early forms of animism to shamanism, ancestor worship, geomancy, and ultimately local syncretism, feeding on constituted world religions such as Buddhism, Hinduism, Islam, Christianity, and philosophies like Confucianism and Taoism. Such diversity cannot be addressed here. Instead, a broad picture of how religious combinations materialized among the highland groups is drawn.

Perhaps half of the highland minorities in the mainland Southeast Asian massif do not follow, at least not in full, one of the dominant world religions mentioned above. Among a significant proportion of the ones who do, it is actually a syncretic version that they practice. At any rate, many of the highland societies still are, or were until recently, what anthropologists call generically "animists." The notion of animism is a broad and convenient umbrella created to cover the variety of original religious systems of all human societies, based on the veneration of various elements of nature, hence the term "animism," that is, the practice of assigning a "soul" (*anima*) to objects or natural phenomena. It refers to a world of benevolent and malevolent spirits, ghosts of deceased ancestors, a universe that constantly needs to be actively dealt with as its influence reaches everything from the newborn's health to house location and shape, agricultural practices, food restrictions, migration patterns, or the final resting place of the dead. To propitiate these otherworldly spirits, to cure illnesses, defeat bad luck, or simply negotiate for a better living, a range of intercessors are needed, both men and women, who are generally called in the vernaculars "spirit doctors" or, more commonly in the West, priests and shamans.

No so-called pure forms of animism exist today in these highlands, as total isolation is a thing of the past—if indeed it ever existed. Over time, intergroup contacts and human movement caused original forms of religious beliefs and accompanying rituals to be altered by neighboring or competing belief systems and practices. Before European involvement, diverse types of syncretism gradually occurred among varieties of animistic beliefs and practices inside the region, which were further blended later when Confucianism and Taoism spread in China; Hinduism in western Burma and around the ancient Khmer and Cham kingdoms in the lower Mekong basin; Buddhism expanded virtually all over the Peninsula, taking over Hinduism; and when Muslim merchants and craftspeople migrated from northern to Southwest China and eventually into the extreme north and south of the Peninsula. Then with European colonists came forms of Christianity, which were proposed to lowlanders and highlanders alike, often playing into a political strategy of divide-and-rule that still sets apart today's Christianized highland groups in Burma and Vietnam from the overwhelmingly Buddhist lowland majorities.

This religious distinction between highlanders and national majorities is one of the most serious sources of ill-feeling in the Peninsula at the moment. A case in point is provided by those inhabitants of the Central Highlands in southern Vietnam. A colonial religious conversion to Catholicism of many groups there played a central role in ensuring that they would support the anticommunist forces during the Indochina Wars. Defeated in 1975, these groups are now being monitored closely by a Vietnamese state that distrusts them. Not helping their cause is the fact that these Christianized groups keep in touch with some of their fighting representatives who took refuge in the United States and elsewhere at the end of the war. Some among these refugees have obtained the support of fundamentalist Christian groups and use this alliance to vigorously lobby the United States government to maintain a hard line on socialist Vietnam regarding what they allege to be religious repression of highland Christians. For the Vietnamese security services, a strong and unfortunate connection is thus made between the cultural distinction of the Central Highlanders, the Christian faith, and their resistance to socialism.

Religion and Ecology

The tenacity of ancient animistic practices even when syncretism has occurred is, however, cause for some recurrent behavior throughout highland groups, notably in their relationship to nature. Generally speaking, highland groups in the Peninsula still perceive themselves as being *part of* nature, as embedded in it, as opposed to being "environed" by it, as in the modern notion of "environment." The evolution of the space they live in is an inseparable element of their individual and collective well-being. Countless forms of rituals underscore this refusal to conceive of humans as set apart from nature: rites to select a village site that intend to reassure and compensate the local spirit of the soil; prohibition against cutting down forests along watercourses because these are inhabited by friendly ghosts; assigning a soul to certain species of trees, which means that no one should cut them down; prayers and offerings before and after an animal has been killed to ensure its freed spirit will be at peace; complex shamanistic symbolic cavalcades in the outer-world to visit the Gods in their homeland and convince them to put an end to a streak of bad harvests or soil depletion.

It has been observed that such apparently solely religious beliefs and practices often carry very practical wisdom, such as enforcing a certain minimum length of time for fields to be left fallow or forbidding tree felling at certain times of year. As opposed to modern agronomy and forestry science, these practices represent the sediments of hundreds of years of intimate and, more often than not, balanced interaction with nature. It has been demonstrated that before cash cropping became the norm in the Peninsula's highlands, as elsewhere, the ancient and common practice of swiddening (slash-and-burn) in small settlements had proved to be highly sustainable in the long term. It is only with the intensification of agriculture and the imposition of monocultures and plantations that forests started to shrink severely and the demographic increase went beyond sustainable thresholds, breaking the previous ecological balance. A recent trend in highland development is thus to actively reassess the value of this ancient indigenous knowledge in an effort to reconnect nature and human societies, and again make the highlanders the competent custodians of the highland forests and ecosystems they have inhabited for centuries, even millennia.

RELATIONSHIP WITH THE LOWLANDS

Historically, the political relationship between highland and lowland societies has been a complex and often strained one, clearly more for the former than for the latter. Before European colonization and the resulting adoption of the principle of national territories bounded by definitive and secured borders, peoples on the Peninsula's highland fringes were generally of limited interest to the lowland rulers. Politically as much as economically, these fringes acted in the vast majority of cases as mere buffer zones. Keeping the inhabitants of these buffer zones in an obedient position through feudal tributary relationships was, most of the time, considered a good enough strategy, better than to conquer, populate, and police these marches at high cost. Such was the situation in, for instance, the buffer zones between China and Tibet (the Naxi domain); China, Laos, and Burma (the Sip Song Phan Na, the Kachin, and the Shan states); northern Vietnam and Laos (the Sip Song Chau Tai); and Vietnam and Cambodia (the Montagnard kingdoms). Only occasionally would a lowland power actually invade and permanently occupy such highland fringes, usually when land was badly needed to support an excess population of farmers, or in times of local uprisings such as the numerous rebellions in Southwest China in the 18th and 19th centuries, triggered at least in part by the foray of Han settlers from the plains taking over fertile high valleys in the southwest.

On the economic front, exchanges were, if not intense, regular and complementary. Highlanders have long been providers of forest produce to the lowlands through a complex and hierarchical system of matching demand and supply. On the highest grounds, semimobile groups such as the Chin, Yao, Hmong, or Khmu collected rare timber—in particular coffin wood—medicinal plants, game, and various parts of animals considered essential in the Chinese, Siamese, or Vietnamese pharmacopeias. Mid-elevation groups such as the Yi, the Bai, and the many Tai-speaking groups, all long sedentarized wet-rice cultivators settled in valleys and in control of the road and river systems, then controlled the circulation of these goods toward the lowland markets. In the opposite direction, they channeled other merchandise necessary to themselves such as cloth, precious metals, and tools, and to the highlanders, in particular, salt, metals, arms, and gunpowder, which they traded for a robust fee. Another product that was channeled from the highlands to the lowlands was the highly profitable raw opium. Limestone-based soils, common in the massif, combined with cooler temperatures, were perfect for opium poppy cultivation, which thus became the monarch of highland cash crops from the mid-19th century until roughly the 1980s, when most countries in the massif gave in to international pressure to ban the henceforth unwanted narcotic.

Relationship to the State: Then and Now

Official positions toward mid- and highlanders vary across countries in the massif. It can generally be asserted that two main trends exist: a paternalistic one in socialist states—China, Vietnam, and Laos—and a pragmatic one under capitalist governments—Thailand, Cambodia, and, to a degree, Burma.

During times of war, communist ideology in the massif was strongly influenced by the Soviet Union (USSR). Communism posited as a basic principle that everyone was equal within the socialist republic. At the source of this apparently egalitarian rhetoric was the need, during independence/revolutionary struggles in Vietnam, Laos, and China, for nationalist/socialist forces to win the allegiance of the largest possible numbers in the local peasantry and workforce. This political strategy was largely responsible for the initial leniency and wide-open promises made during the early years of the struggle, which routinely included cultural and political independence once victory was achieved. The wars once over and socialist rule in place, virtually all promises for minority self-rule were forgotten or replaced with watered-down substitutes guaranteeing that priority was given to the one and indivisible socialist nation and national territory. Next, the new socialist states set out to "help" the highland comrades long kept in a state of cultural and economic subordination by the "feudal" agents of the past. They were thus "supported" to catch up with the enlightened industrial socialist masses by joining the proletariat working in mines, dams, or factories, while benefiting from increased educational and health services. All national minorities were granted full-fledged national citizenship, but this apparently favorable status also required that in return for this recognition and for help modernizing from their "big brothers," the "little brothers" were to "progress," that is, to leave behind their "backward" ways and think and behave like socialist nationals. Cultural, religious, economic, and especially political distinctions in the highlands were only to be tolerated if they did not stand in the way of integration into the socialist nation. In practice, this policy boiled down to cultural, economic, and political absorption into the majority, with only the most benign expressions of material cultural being allowed to persist in set formats (in particular, house architecture and clothing, dance, and music expressed during annual "minority culture days"), keeping only the picturesque and inoffensive as a token contribution to national ethnic variety. This policy has been euphemistically called "selective cultural preservation."

In the opposite camp, in the capitalist sphere, the highlanders' legal position appears markedly weaker, as many have not even been granted national citizenship. In Thailand, just about half of the "hill tribes" are currently full citizens despite most of them having lived for several generations on that soil. In Cambodia, a country still in a state of political and economic turmoil, leaders simply cannot at this stage afford to pay much attention to the highland groups' rights. In Burma (Myanmar), armed confrontation and repression is the only policy of the Burman-centered junta. In practice, however, beyond the legal quandary or the lack of means, capitalist countries sharing the massif have taken a very pragmatic approach to their national minorities. In a nutshell, if they can take care of themselves without being a burden on or a threat to the nation, and even contribute to increasing the national wealth, they are welcome to remain as different from "us" as they wish—or can. Advocates of this liberal position perceive lowland civilization as superior to highland "tribalism," but no systematic action is taken to impose "cultural progress" on these lesser cultures if they do not so wish. The end result appears to be a fast cultural assimilation with the majority through market integration and national education.

Over the last 25 years, with the general introduction of the market economy in China, Vietnam, and Laos, the socialist position has become more and more indistinguishable from that of the capitalists. Pragmatism, the key stance in a free market economy, is gradually eroding security concerns, which, even in strongly centralized states, are slowly disappearing. Only Burma still constitutes a sad exception.

This general lack of cultural sensitivity to highland ethnic difference among lowland majorities surrounding the massif can be explained by the fact that the highland/lowland cultural dichotomy has long been fueled by an age-old and all too human discrimination by lowland farmers against heavily forested highlands, considered to be the domain of malevolent spirits and, perhaps more important, of little-known and poorly controlled nomads and sometimes rebels. For sedentary lowlanders, the highlands and the forests are allocated to the barbarians and the "raw" civilizations. All across the massif, groups dwelling higher up have been systematically associated with this derogatory categorization, while those living in regions of moderate altitude, with thinner forest cover and in closer proximity to the dominant lowland civilizations, are deemed more palatable, yet still to be treated with some caution.

Over the past 20 years, despite their ridiculously small numbers compared to the national majorities—with the notable exception of Laos—highlanders have been persistently blamed by their respective governments for most, if not all, of the deforestation, land erosion, and chemical poisoning of land and waterways that affect virtually every watershed. Highlanders' agricultural behavior is publicly decried by state officials everywhere, especially swiddening, which is depicted as highly detrimental to the environment. To discourage its practice, isolated populations are brought into the open and relocated along national road networks, and crop substitution programs are implemented to enforce sedentarization and commercial agriculture. But the real picture is not that black and white. Swiddening has been practiced all over the world for tens of thousands of years. It has proved to be highly sustainable provided that circumstances remain favorable. However, in several areas in the massif nowadays, increased demography, decreased availability of forested land, and the spreading of sedentarized cash cropping and the concomitant use of chemicals all contribute to reducing the duration of fallows to a level where natural regeneration is severely impaired. Such deterioration is a fact. But what officials fail to publicly acknowledge is that other factors have an even more definitive impact on highland forest and land erosion: massive illegal logging done right in front of lenient state agents, who turn a blind eye; the migration of millions of lowlanders to the uplands, sponsored by the national governments; and the ill-adapted agricultural practices of these migrants, who know little about farming the highlands.

Today, in the massif, highlanders are generally facing governments lacking reliable cultural information about them, lacking often even the interest to learn more about them. However, this does not stop these governments from vigorously implementing policies of cultural integration and economic standardization. Education, in principle a tool for emancipation, is geared toward Sinization, Thai-ization, Lao-ization, or Vietnamization of minorities. Only perhaps in southwestern China and northeastern Burma, where critical masses are reached by certain groups, can cultural resistance be successful—be it only thanks to their sheer demographic inertia. Tourism, the new gold rush in the massif, is a crucial factor in this equation, bringing to the world's attention these exotic minority cultures much sought after by cultural and adventure tourist wholesalers. There is hardly a travel agency in the West today that does not have on display one or several brochures advertising the smile of a colorful highland Southeast Asian minority man, woman, or child. Even national tourists increasingly crave the "little brothers," often more in connection with the sexual fantasies nurtured by the dominant cultures than for what these hosts really are. Nevertheless, this increased visibility does contribute to curbing the states' enthusiasm for processing their minorities into the national mold, which they would do more ruthlessly if there were no witnesses to their project.

CUSTOMARY SOCIAL STRUCTURES AND THE ECONOMY

To better understand the social distinctiveness of highland societies as well as the influence this uniqueness has on their modes of adaptation today, it is useful to picture them as they appeared to the outside world at the time of European contact, roughly a century ago. That is, just before the rapid pace of modernization they have since been subjected to made many among them take drastically different routes than the ones they had followed previously.

Feudal Groups

In political terms, the highland societies that dwelled at medium altitudes in the mainland Southeast Asian massif were in regular contact with each other, and with the major lowland kingdoms and empires. Thus, a degree of diffusion among midland societies and from the cultural, political, and economic lowland cores toward the periphery occurred, causing, among other things, these groups to adopt a feudal social organization. A review of colonial writings in the late 19th century paints a portrait of such widespread feudalism among the peoples met in the midregion at that time. At the time of European contact, the Shan of northeastern Burma were highly differentiated between a dominant elite controlling the land and the means of production and a mass of peasants laboring for them and supporting the whole system. In Yunnan, the Naxi, the Bai, and the Yi operated on the same pattern, as did the Tujia in Guizhou. The Tai Lue had a feudal realm in the Sip Song Phan Na, the White Thai theirs in the Sip Song Chau Tai in northern Vietnam, the Zhuang in Guangxi, and the Dong in Guizhou.

Acephalous Groups

At that time, either in the marginal uplands at the periphery of these feudal kingdoms, or more often at higher reaches within them, in a kind of archipelago of mountaintops where feudal monarchs had not installed their own peasants, was a mosaic of "tribes" that had in common the type of ecosystem they had colonized and their political subordination to the feudal lords. Among themselves, these "tribal" groups' social organizations were all kinship-based, even household-based in some cases; that is, their highest form of political formalization was determined by, and limited to, kinship ties. In short, they were without a centralized form of political authority, without a state. Wherever this form of simple political structure has been observed around the world, it has been known as stateless or acephalous.

In social terms, groups in this category showed an integrated organization, meaning that the political, the economic, and the religious constantly overlapped in all matters of daily life. Each of these dimensions could not be detached from the others; social ties were most commonly based on lineage (the known genealogy) or clan (the known and the assumed genealogy as expressed in a common surname).

In cultural terms, much as feudal societies were nearly all Tai and Tibeto-Burman and showed a degree of cultural connectivity, conversely, practically all the Austronesian, Mon-Khmer, Miao-Yao, and the remaining portion of the Tibeto-Burman groups belonged to the acephalous category. An exception was in the highlands at the south of the Annam Cordillera, where several groups had developed local chiefdoms of an intermediary type, more complex than the purely acephalous groups, yet falling somewhat short of developing fully fledged feudal kingdoms.

The Economy

At the time of European contact, the upland economy was structured in two ways: socially, along the lines of feudalism and acephality; and geographically, by inclusion in the three-tiered structure encompassing the lowlands, midregion, and highlands.

The economic rationale of feudalism is well known and need not be repeated here. The important fact is that an elite in control of the land and the agricultural surpluses used a variety of forms of coercion to extract wealth from the labor of its peasantry, for which in return they provided access to the land as tenants as well as varying degrees of economic and political stability. Outside the strict perimeter of the kingdom, trade relationships allowed the elites to use surpluses in elaborate exchange systems with the surrounding region, from which additional profits were derived. Tribute could also be extorted from weaker neighbors, whose local masters paid a price to safeguard their political liberty; tribute also had to be paid to more powerful monarchs.

In economic terms, acephalous societies were one of three possible economic systems: hunting-gathering, horticulture, or a simple form of peasantry, a "prefeudal" one. In all cases, the household (a group of individuals linked by blood or alliance and living under the same roof) was the fundamental building block; it also constituted the smallest economic and ritual unit. Subsistence agriculture was the norm, with various degrees of dependency on the market for the provision of indispensable commodities that could not be grown, gathered, or produced locally.

Hunters-gatherers, such as the Mlabri of Thailand and Laos, were in a state of continual nomadism and only took from nature what it provided naturally. They lived in small bands of no more than a few dozen individuals. Horticulturalists, on the other hand, constituted the bulk of the acephalous groups, with the ubiquitous practice of swiddening as the principal form of food production. Pioneering swiddening, with very short or no fallows at all, the most aggressive and damaging form of "slash-and-burn," was limited to groups sticking to active nomadism or to those heavily involved in the land-exhausting culture of the opium poppy. Rotational swiddening, with long fallows, was a more finely balanced activity with little long-term impact on the environment, and was practiced by groups willing to stay in a given vicinity, such as the Karen on the Burma-Thailand border or most groups in the Central Highlands. Finally, early forms of peasantry chiefly involved the groups closer to the feudal clusters and denoted a gradual attraction toward these strong gravitational cores, falling just short of being a constitutive part of those systems. The Kachin of upper Burma, in the orbit of feudal Shan, were a good example of this.

It is through elaborate trade networks that a three-tiered geographical division—highlands, midregion, and lowlands—was tied together. Different ecological niches and variations in the degree of industrialization, diffused chiefly from the lowlands, ensured that inhabitants of each tier could provide the others with a number of exclusive produce, goods, and services. From the high and midregions came opium, maize alcohol, timber, medicinal and decorative plants, and rare animal parts, which were traded for indispensable processed goods common in the lowlands but often absent in the highlands, such as those listed earlier. Midregion groups could channel either way their specific production of rice and fruit, clothes, jewelry, or troops and labor, graciously made available to lowland powers within the framework of tributary dependency. There are many known occurrences of the midregion groups extorting this same privilege from the less solidly organized highland groups dwelling in the upper reaches of their domains. While the populations at both ends of this trade system were the main producers/gatherers of the merchandise put into circulation, the midregion groups, in addition to providing additional merchandise, crucially acted as people cashing in on this two-way circulation.

THE HIGHLAND ECONOMY TODAY

In the second half of the 20th century, rapid and sometimes drastic changes affected the highlands. The end of European colonialism and the establishment of socialist regimes in China (1949), Vietnam (1954 in the north, 1975 in the south), Burma (the Ne Win regime from 1962 to 1989), Laos (1975), and Cambodia (under Khmer Rouge rule 1975–1979, then under Vietnamese occupation until 1989), followed by the political implosion of Burma (Myanmar) and Cambodia and the opening up to the market economy virtually everywhere since the 1980s, all contributed to modifying the local economic equilibrium, not to mention U.S.-backed, capital-intensive Thailand, occupying de facto the coveted position of most economically developed country, sharing the massif. Opium production and trade were officially phased out after the end of the second Indochina War (1954–1975), and substitution crops were actively implemented. The groups in the midregion saw their strategic advantage as trade intermediaries vanish at the same rate that the road infrastructures extended into the highlands, while their feudal political organizations were deemed unsuitable to the modern world, socialist and capitalist alike, and had to be brought down, ending a centuries-old social and economic domination. As mentioned earlier, subsistence agriculture, adjusted to the household's needs and often based on swiddening, was branded economically unsound and environmentally unsuitable, and was replaced over the last decades of the century with cash cropping and plantations geared to market demand, thus exposing inadequately literate highlanders to the hazards of brutal market shifts most of them were not yet equipped to fully understand and swiftly adjust to.

The switch to commercial agriculture in the mountains was made possible in large part thanks to the new hegemony of Western discourse on environmental protection, conveyed to the local level via an array of development projects conceived and implemented by countless international agencies and nongovernmental organizations (NGOs) funded by the industrialized world. For highland agriculturalists, hand in hand with the environmental concerns and the spreading of cash cropping came the forced relocation of villages closer to the road grid—particularly in Laos—and the sedentarization of mobile or semimobile groups by clustering them in permanent village sites. Such drastic changes concluded the final monetarization of highland exchanges, relegating payment in nature and barter to the narrow circle of close kin. The increasing recourse to the market also entailed useful consequences, such as bringing to the mountains goods and commodities that were not available before and adding opportunities for the sale of local agricultural produce. In particular, it opened channels for the provision of the necessary implements of cash cropping, that is, seeds, fertilizers, pesticides, and so on. However, with rampant illiteracy and without the necessary level of technical information, the use of these industrial inputs by highlanders caused many ecological problems downstream, where dangerously high amounts of chemicals are washed down by the monsoon rains that the ever-shrinking forest cover cannot hold back as effectively as before.

Current Issues

The region's state programs are attuned to economic "growth" and cultural "progress." The dominant rhetoric, after decades of applied social evolutionism inherited from Marxism and capitalism alike, has been superseded by the language of "development." With countless agencies from the affluent world knocking at the door to offer their services—and the loans in hard currency that will help pay for these—the techniques and technology of the international development industry are relentlessly applied to minority health, education, and customary agricultural practices that are labeled obsolete and harmful. Ensuring "better" gender balance is also on the agenda. All these initiatives play directly into the local governments' strategy of integrating minorities into the nation. In the process, cultural dimensions are paid only subsidiary attention, other issues being judged more urgent. One must recognize, however, that the general indicators of health and education do show a clear improvement in the highlands.

China clearly has a strong central policy of controlling and integrating its southwestern *shaoshu minzu*, or minority nationalities. The region is politically sensitive because it touches several international borders, is rich in natural resources important to the national development, provides a substantial portion of the country's diet through intensive agriculture, and is a land of migration for the surplus lowland population. Han immigration to the southwest, much as in Tibet, does not really mask a desire to eventually outnumber locals and take final political, economic, and cultural control of these margins. If organized resistance to this "invasion" is fomented locally at all, no news of it seems to filter out. Tourism, which could constitute a means to preserve local cultures by showing them to the outside world, as alluded to earlier, is controlled and formatted by the state so that only specific areas, nonthreatening groups, and selected cultural practices can be easily consumed by the tourists. Many nationally famous places fit this picture, such as Lijiang, Dali, and Lugu Lake in western Yunnan or clusters of Miao villages in southwest Guizhou. These destinations have been totally converted by the central government into mass-tourism resorts exhibiting the beauties of nature and the highly sanitized elements of minority cultures deemed suitable for public display by the authorities.

Burma (Myanmar), most prominently, has a history of using its military to crush internal opposition. The Karen, some of whom harbor a desire for political autonomy, have been fighting the central Burmese government for decades. The Shan and Wa control large sections of their semiautonomous state thanks to armed resistance financed by drug trafficking. There, resistance is waged not so much on grounds of a will for political autonomy as on a strong involvement in very profitable smuggling operations centered on the transformation of opium into morphine, heroin, and amphetamines. Elsewhere in Burma is a depressing story of forced displacement, exploitation, abuse, and seeking refuge over the borders, with no real solution in sight.

In Laos, a vigorous relocation program is gradually forcing scores of highland villagers into larger groupings within the Lao state's watch perimeter. Also, a deeply rooted mistrust between old royalist factions among certain highland groups (*sonphao*) and the socialist state has ensured that armed struggle has endured since the official revolutionary victory in 1975. The Xaysomboun Special Region has been established to isolate pockets of resistance, while other regions in which alleged

Hmong rebels are fighting the Laotian forces are sealed off from outside observers. Clearly, however, with nearly half its population belonging to one or another of many non-Lao ethnicities, Laos cannot afford to wage an all-out war on its minorities. A degree of negotiation must prevail.

In Thailand, communist "insurgency" brewing in the north and the northeast up to the late 1980s kept the state wary of certain groups connected to socialist Laos and Vietnam through ethnic networks. Resentment and defiance still creep into official rhetoric but have now been largely replaced by the environmental mantra of eliminating swiddening and erecting protected ecological zones from which long-resident minorities must relocate. With only 1 percent of its population belonging to the 11 *chao khao*, "hill tribes," registered in the official statistics, Thailand has arguably all the leverage it needs to end the negotiations at will.

Vietnam has officially made its peace with its minority nationalities, the *cac dan toc thieu so*, through official recognition since the 1970s. But in fact, the Vietnamese government still considers that dangerously high levels of political resistance are simmering in the Central Highlands and elsewhere, supported mainly by U.S.-based "right wing" diasporas. Christian missionary activism is a bone of contention, chiefly in the southern but increasingly in the northern highlands. Tourism, as in China, is seen as a tool for the state to preserve selected benign features of local highland cultures and present them to mass-tourists, thus emphasizing the positive impact of the state's minority culture preservation.

At present, perhaps only Cambodia does not have issues with its very small number of highland minorities, except when these are actually ethnic Vietnamese who settled in the eastern provinces during various waves of pioneering migration, the latest being during the decade-long occupation of the country by Vietnamese troops from 1979 to 1989. A mild concern is currently expressed about some other highland minorities presently filtering through from Vietnam's Central Highlands, looking for economic opportunities or taking refuge from their government's political exactions.

In all six countries there are serious problems and challenges; given the generally weaker position of the highland peoples and "minorities," these are usually more serious for them than for the lowland majorities and, by extension, national governments. How these challenges are resolved will have a great impact on this population of 80 million and determine in large part how they can adapt to change.

Four Hmong dignitaries in Xieng Khouang upland northern Laos, ca. 1920. Photographer: P. Kerbaol.

Caravan on the Imperial road heading for the Chinese customs, Mong-Tzeu, southern Yunnan province, China, ca. 1910.
Postcard by P. Dieulefils, Hanoi.

Three Yao (Kim Mien) women heading for the market and wearing silver breast plates and neckpieces, northern Vietnam, ca. 1930. Photographer: Unknown.

Hmong woman wearing a silver necklace chain, with her baby adorned with French silver coins (piastres) *on the hat, Lao Cai region, northern Vietnam, ca. 1930.* Photographer: Unknown.

Xo-Dang communal house in Kon Tum Province, Central High-lands, Vietnam, 1997.
Photograph by Nguyen Ngoc.

Clanic covered bridges are a feature of Dong villages; this is one of five in the Dong village of Zhaoxing in southeast Guizhou, 2005. Photograph by Candice Cornet.

Hamlet in the hills, with a drum tower characteristic of Dong culture, Zhaoxing valley in southeast Guizhou, 2005. Photograph by Candice Cornet.

Hmong rice terraces on steep slopes, San Sa Ho commune, Lao Cai Province, northern Vietnam, 2003. Photograph by Jean Michaud.

Palaung women attending the reading of Pathana at the Namhsan Buddhist monastery, northern Shan State, Burma, ca. 1995. Photograph by François Robinne.

Hmong female shaman with altar, bench, and accessories, Ta Phin commune, Lao Cai province, northern Vietnam, 1999.
Photograph by Jean Michaud.

Typical setting of a highland village in northern Laos. All dwellings and rice gran-aries (foreground right and background left) are made of material collected locally. Houses are built partly on the ground, partly on stilts, the overall layout of dwellings and footpaths not following any particular plan. Chakhampa village (Akha), Phongsaly district, 2005. Photograph by Steeve Daviau.

Hmong women selling souvenirs to national and foreign tourists in the "Ethnic Market," Sa Pa market, Lao Cai province, northern Vietnam, 1999. Photograph by Jean

Replanting wet rice in May. In the background, typical dispersed dwelling pattern of highlands agriculturalists. Ta Van village, Lao Cai province, northern Vietnam, 2003. Photo by Sarah Turner.

Hmong woman cutting and drying hemp. Hemp is still the chief fiber used to produce Hmong clothing in the Sa Pa district. Ban Ho commune, Lao Cai province, 2003. Photo by Sarah Turner.

Akha woman prepares to plant rice in a recently cleared swidden. Two metal-tipped digging spears lie in the foreground. Tree stumps are still smoldering after the recent burning of cut-down material. Phongsaly province, northern Laos, 2005.
Photograph by Steeve Daviau.

Bai couple mending their fishing nets on the shore of Erh Hai Lake, near Dali, western Yunnan, ca. 1990. Photo by Peter Foggin.

Akha women meeting at the office of a handicraft project. Their jewelry is a combination of silver, aluminum, and French colonial silver coins. Boun Neua district, northern Laos, 2005. Photograph by Jean Michaud.

The Dictionary

– A –

A HMAO. *See* MIAO.

ABADIE, MAURICE. French military officer posted in Tonkin (northern Vietnam) in the 1910s. Abadie published *Les races du Haut-Tonkin de Phong-Tho à Lang-Son* [*The Races of Upper Tonkin from Phong Tho to Lang Son*] in 1924, in which he drew a detailed picture of these highland cultures. The volume has recently been translated and published with the title *Minorities of the Sino-Vietnamese Borderland with Special Reference to Thai Tribes* (2001).

ABORIGINES. Strictly speaking, the term "aborigine" is meant to apply to the most ancient indigenous people known to have colonized a given country or region. Today, however, the term is often used to associate a particular people with a given territory, in a historical process involving the later arrival of migrants who came to take over that territory, or parts of it, and/or become the majority. An example is the **Han** Chinese on the islands of Taiwan and **Hainan**. In an even more restrictive sense, in the Western literature, the term "aboriginal" most often applies to relatively recent situations involving conquest and massive colonization by European powers. These situations include the British in Australia and New Zealand and, to a lesser degree, various European colonial states in the Americas.

In their most widely accepted sense, the political implications of the notion of "aboriginal peoples" are meshed with recent expressions of ethnonationalism by aborigines standing up to the dominant migrant group, and chiefly apply to the examples listed above. In the **mainland Southeast Asian massif**, the situation is markedly different. Far from all the ethnic groups can claim to have actually been associated over a long period of time with a particular territory that they might have been the first to populate. In fact, a large number of groups have actually been on the move for extended periods of time—for example, most highland groups in highland Thailand as well as many in northern Laos and Vietnam—and have only settled where they are today over the last couple of centuries. This explains why—in Thailand especially, where a majority of highland groups settled long after the **Thai** majority had come and conquered the land a millennium ago—applying the term aborigines to the "**hill tribes**" is not satisfactory. In China, at the other end of the spectrum, many groups, such as the **Tibeto-Burman**–speaking **Naxi**, **Bai**, and **Yi**, and the **Tai**-speaking **Dai**, are likely to be the oldest human groups living in **Yunnan** today. This might also be true of the **Miao** in **Guizhou**, and the **Zhuang** in Guangxi. In Vietnam, Laos, and Cambodia, **Austronesian** speakers still living in the **Annam Cordillera** are probably older than anyone else there today, while highland Burma harbors long-settled groups, such as the **Chin** and **Kachin**, who probably preceded the **Burmans**.

However, ignoring limitations inherent in modern borders, if the **mainland Southeast Asian massif** is to be regarded as a discrete social space regardless of which countries own which parts, then practically all ethnic groups living in these highlands to this day could be labeled aborigines, in the sense that they are the original inhabitants of the massif, and that they still inhabit it. It is very unlikely—at least **archeology** has not established it—that earlier, unknown groups may have elected these relatively inhospitable highlands as their permanent home. Most probably, if these peoples ever existed, they have since been absorbed by the groups known to us today.

ACHANG. According to official Chinese sources, the Achang (33,936 individuals in 2000) are a **Tibeto-Burman**–speaking group with a language that borrows significantly from **Shan**. They dwell mainly in **Jingpo** and **Dai** territory in western **Yunnan** around the Taiping River. Little is currently known outside China about them and their language. In neighboring Burma, some Achang have also been reported in the Shan State, where they work as seasonal laborers. The Burmese government does not specifically account for them.

ADOPTION. A widespread cultural strategy by means of which groups can maintain or increase their demographic weight beyond the natural limitations of reproduction or those imposed by the restrictive rules of marriage, or recover from wars, epidemics, and famines with a high cost in human lives. Most ethnic groups in the **mainland Southeast Asian massif** practice adoption. Candidates for adoption are generally young children and can originate from outside as well as from within the ethnic group of the adopters. The adopted children are in the vast majority of cases integrated completely within the **lineage** of their adoptive family, psychologically and economically, as well as ritually.

AHOM. The westernmost group belonging to the vast **Tai-Kadai language family**. The Ahom (numbers unknown) are directly related to the Hkamti of northern Burma and are located in the high reaches of the Brahmaputra River in the state of Assam in India. An Ahom kingdom has been reported to exist there since as far back as the 13th century A.D. The Ahom are thoroughly **Hinduized** today.

AIR AMERICA. A program of American military involvement in Southeast Asia. After World War II, U.S. involvement in Southeast Asia took many forms. Early on, it involved the provision of air support destined to convey logistical and military support to various Chinese Republican forces, which had taken refuge south of the Chinese border after the communists seized power in 1949. Air support operations from Southeast Asian bases were conducted wherever anticommunist resistance was rooted on the Chinese periphery, for example in Burma and Thailand, but also in Taiwan. This air support quickly spread to other anticommunist fighters in the **Peninsula** itself. French troops at Dien Bien Phu in 1954 received supplies in this way. In 1959, Central Intelligence Agency–sponsored air missions to northern Laos started in support of the royalist forces resisting the advance of the Pathet Lao, the latter assisted by communist Vietnam and the USSR. The airline providing this air support in Laos was eventually named Air America Inc. Using rear bases in friendly Thailand, Air America operations were instrumental in the maintenance of royalist armed opposition all over Laos, though not without going from official action to secrecy after the formation of the Second Coalition Government in 1962. It operated in this way until its final demise in 1975.

With as many as 200 aircraft in 1968, Air America was also a lifeline that made isolated guerrilla operations viable in remote areas of northern Laos. Of particular interest is the connection between Air America, the **opium** trade, and minority anticommunist fighters in that country. Based in Xiengkhuang province, **Hmong** resistance guerrillas, under the command of Hmong General **Vang Pao**, were able to count on the airline to bring them armaments and supplies. Aircraft also notoriously cargoed the local opium harvest, contributing importantly to a lucrative trade crucial to the maintenance of minority guerrilla operations.

AKHA. The generic name, possibly derived from the pejorative A-Kha, given by many specialists of the **Peninsula** to an extensive **Tibeto-Burman**–speaking group originating in southern **Yunnan**, otherwise called **Ikaw** in Thailand, **Kaw** in Burma, **Ko** in Laos, **Ha Nhi** in Vietnam, and **Hani** in China. The total number of Akha defined in this way is approximately 1,750,000, 80 percent of whom live in China.

ALAK. The Alak (16,594 in 1995) are **Mon-Khmer** speakers of the Bahnaric branch, dwelling in Sekong province in the south of Laos, with some located in adjacent portions of Saravane and Attapeu provinces. From colonial times, Alak and **Laven** leaders, such as Bak Mi and Ong Kommadam, involved in the **Phu Mi Bun revolt**, as well as the latter's son, **Sithon Kommadam**, left a lasting trace on Laotian history.

ALCOHOL. Produced locally in the form of fermented brews, or distilled, and chiefly made from **rice** and **maize**, alcohol is as widespread in the **mainland Southeast Asian massif**'s highlands as it is in the lowlands. Alcohol consumption by men, and sometimes by women, can occur both under secular and ritual circumstances and is part of all major cultural events, such as weddings, funerals, or healing ceremonies. It is also a source of substantial income on the market. Alcohol has been **traded** for a long time in the highlands, sometimes freely, at other times subject to government monopolies.

AMPHETAMINES. The "Amphetamine-Type Stimulants" (ATS) are undergoing a recent and disproportionate development, their production having exploded in the **Golden Triangle** since 1996 and the fall of **Shan** drug lord **Khun Sa**. ATS are synthetic drugs produced with ephedrine, the principal alkaloid of *Ephedra vulgaris*, a wild shrub growing in nearby Chinese **Yunnan**. The drug is widely available in the **Peninsula**'s highlands thanks to the illegal factories built in Shan State in Burma (between 200 and 300 million methamphetamine pills were produced in 1999), while laboratories have also been established in Thailand, the principal market for these substances—it is estimated that more than 100 million methamphetamine pills entered that country in 1998. Amphetamines have been gaining in popularity in the Burma–China–Laos–Thailand border area, often called the Golden Triangle. Their popularity grew as **opium** production was gradually repressed by national states. In a pattern similar to that of the past regarding the production of opiates, such as morphine and **heroin**, amphetamines are produced by factions waging armed opposition against their central government. In Burma, where most of the production laboratories are located, the **Wa**, with their United Wa State Army, and the Shan druglords-cum-warlords, use it as a means to finance their struggles. There are serious allegations that the Burmese military also derives significant profits from this **trade**.

The popularity of locally produced amphetamines among the **Peninsula**'s populations, including those in the highlands, has reached enormous proportions in the last few years. The drug is especially widespread among hard-working laborers, including highland peasants and rural and wage workers, who use it to enhance their capacity to cope with the physical demands of their occupations. In urban areas, recreational users are more and more numerous. Controlling and restraining the expansion of ATS in Southeast Asia presents a problem for the authorities that in some ways exceeds the past prominence of opium production and opiate consumption. It also adds to the negative image of highland **minorities** in the minds of lowland majorities, following directly from the earlier general condemnation of opium production by "**hill tribes**."

AMPHOE. In Thailand, an administrative subdivision of the *changwat* (province). *Amphoe* best translates as "district" and further subdivides into several *tambon*, or subdistricts.

ANGLICAN MISSIONS. *See* MISSIONARIES.

ANIMAL SACRIFICE. Among highland **animist** groups, offering the soul of an animal is perceived as an inescapable duty. Sacrificing a chicken, a pig, a cow, or even a **buffalo** must be done for various reasons, one being to feed the deceased on their journey to the otherworld, for instance at funerals and during subsequent commemorative rituals. It can also constitute a gift to powerful spirits in times of hardship, for instance with the intention of turning aside the interest of a malevolent spirit from a particular person or a family on whom it has inflicted illness and bad luck. Sacrifices normally involve the participation of a priest or a shaman, who takes charge of ensuring proper communication with the otherworld. The number, size, and value of the animals sacrificed are generally indicative of the seriousness of the problem or of the importance of the person being honored. Meat from sacrificed animals is immediately processed and eaten collectively by the participants at the ritual. Animal sacrifice is one of the practices deemed counterproductive by many modern Southeast Asian authorities, who actively discourage it.

ANIMISM. The oldest type of religious practice, sometimes referred to as "popular religion" or, in Christian **missionary** parlance, "paganism." Animism predates all great religious traditions of today, and many of its forms are still found in a large number of highland groups of mainland Southeast Asia. As a concept, animism is not a religion per se; it is above all a convenient umbrella notion encompassing various types of veneration of natural phenomena—hence the term "animism," that is, assigning a soul (*anima*) to inanimate objects and natural incidents. All over the **mainland Southeast Asian massif**, animistic populations have no choice but to negotiate with the world of benevolent and malevolent spirits, the realm of the ghosts of deceased ancestors, a whole invisible universe that constantly has to be actively dealt with as it influences everything in daily life, from a newborn's health to house location and shape, agricultural practices, food restrictions, migration patterns, to the final resting place of the dead. To appease these otherworldly spirits, cure illnesses, defeat bad luck, or simply plead for a better living, a range of intercessors are needed, both men and women, who are generally called "spirit doctors" in the vernacular or, more commonly in the West, priests and shamans. Even among lowland majority groups who have adopted **Buddhism**, **Islam**, or Christianity, residual animism is still present in the forms of superstitions and geomancy materialized in spirit houses, talismans, or divination.

An insufficient grasp of the local implications of animistic beliefs in the highlands by the authorities has caused—and still does create—misunderstandings between the local populations and national and international development agents sent to the highlands. Easily labeled "backward" or "unproductive," animistic practices are often shunned. **Animal sacrifice** in particular has been targeted for eradication. For their practitioners, however, animistic tradition is at the very core of social life.

ANNAM CORDILLERA (ANNAM RANGE). A major portion of the **mainland Southeast Asian massif** that extends far southeast into the **Peninsula** and contributes to separating Vietnam to the east from Laos and Cambodia to the west. Originally demarcated in **Yunnan** by the two valleys of the Mekong and the Black (Da) Rivers, this mountain range gradually slopes down as it proceeds southeast, until it widens and flattens into high plateaus, the edge of which reaches Vietnam's central and southern narrow coastal plain just north of the Mekong delta. The Annam Cordillera properly speaking is usually identified as reaching from the border between Xiengkhuang in Laos to Nghe An in Vietnam (summit at 2,700 meters). Its main ridge naturally marks an extended portion of the border between Vietnam and Laos. In Vietnam, the cordillera is known as the *Day Truong Son*, and its southern plateaus as the *Tay Nguyen*.

Historically, the Annam Cordillera has played a role as a natural barrier between Vietnam and the rest of the Peninsula. To highland groups, however, it has become a refuge. The range itself and its southern plateaus are home to more than 5 million highlanders from the **Mon-Khmer** and the **Austronesian** language families, most of them divided between eastern Laos and western Vietnam, with residual numbers in eastern Cambodia. Many among these highland groups have chosen the Cordillera's relative remoteness as a safe haven and a shield against the exactions of the lowland powers. Nevertheless, it was the location of fierce combat between pro- and anticommunist forces during the **Second Indochina War** (the Vietnam War, 1954–1975), in particular because of the intricate and fluid network of the Ho Chin Minh trails crisscrossing the Cordillera.

ARCHEOLOGY IN THE MASSIF. Scientific archeology has yielded little in the **mainland Southeast Asian massif**, for a variety of reasons. A crucial obstacle is that the cultures of a vast majority of inhabitants in the massif have long relied on biological resources for most of their material culture, from **clothes** to architecture. Such artifacts degrade rapidly in a subtropical climate, and standard archeologists know well that little is to be hoped for in field studies of an ancient highland residential site. Accordingly, national and international archeologists alike have shown little interest in the marginal populations of these remote highlands. Apart from a handful of **feudal** societies, such as the **Naxi**, Nan Chao, **Sip Song Phan Na** in **Yunnan**, and **Dong** in **Guizhou**, which have generated interest among Chinese archeologists and yielded some important findings, notably in the field of architecture, practically none of the highland societies in the massif has produced an important and original enough surviving material culture to match the expectations of today's archeologists, who remain more interested in prominent ancient cultural movements around the massif, such as the Dongsonian and Hoabinian cultures. Since these "high" cultures have only marginally penetrated the hinterland's highlands, the harvest of interesting artifacts there is expected to be meager.

Most likely the science of prehistorical archeology, of the sort practiced by anthropologists, may eventually become involved in seriously researching the highland's past through its physical remains. Experience has shown, in many locations around the world, in particular when digging to understand the past of aboriginal populations in the Americas, Africa, Australasia, and Oceania, that a rich history is encoded in minute fragments of stone, food remains, and refuse pits. Such cutting-edge prehistorical archeology, however, requires the assistance of expensive technology, currently available only in the wealthiest countries. As long as access to the field in nervous political regimes, such as socialist China, Vietnam, and Laos, or the Burmese dictatorship, is a major obstacle for outside scholars—especially when the object of their interest is not the dominant culture of the **Han**, **Kinh**, **Lao**, or **Burman**, but "unimportant **minorities**" on the politically sensitive outskirts of the country—that technology may elude local archeologists.

AUSTRO-ASIATIC LANGUAGE FAMILY. One of the five main language families found in the massif and the **Peninsula**, with about 150 **languages**. It comprises in particular the **Mon-Khmer** branch, which is widespread in mainland Southeast Asia. This branch includes key lowland languages, such as **Khmer** and Vietnamese (**Viet-Muong**), but also several ancient highland language clusters, such as Bahnaric, Pearic, and Katuic in the southern Annam Range, as well as Palaungic and Khmuic in northern Vietnam and Laos, **Yunnan**, and Burma. As a rule, the Austro-Asiatic language family is registral sesquisyllabic and nontonal, although linguists theorize that the influence of neighboring Chinese (Sinitic) might have introduced tones into the Vietic segment of the Viet-Muong branch. (*See* figure 1.)

Note: Active language branches and languages spoken in the Southeast Asian massif are marked with an asterisk.

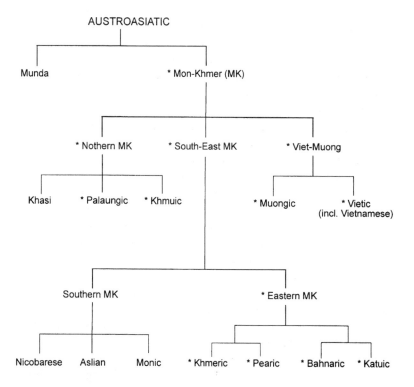

Source: Matisoff, James. "Genetic Versus Contact Relationship: Prosodic Diffusibility in South-East Asian Languages."*Areal diffusion and genetic inheritance: problems in comparative linguistics*, 291-347. In Aikhenvald, A., and R. M. W. Dixon (eds.) Oxford: OUP, 2001.

Figure 1. Austroasiatic Language Family

AUSTRONESIAN LANGUAGE FAMILY. Formerly called Malayo-Polynesian, a term still in use, Austronesian is one of the five main language families under study in this dictionary. Austronesian **languages** are polysyllabic and do not use tones. This language family includes parts of Asia and all of Oceania, with a staggering total of about a thousand languages. In Southeast Asia, current or ancient lowland majority languages of the Peninsula, such as Malay and **Cham** (Cam), belong to this family, plus virtually all of Insular Southeast Asian languages. In the **mainland Southeast Asian massif**, it is represented by only four groups of speakers dwelling in the southern **Annam Cordillera**, in Vietnam's **Central Highlands**, with extension into eastern Cambodia. These groups are the **Rhade (E-de)**, Raglai **(Ra-glai)**, **Jarai (Gia-rai)**, and Churu **(Chu-ru)**. These are considered to be residual Austronesian speakers from early times when Austronesian languages, through Proto-Malay and Deutero-Malay migrations from the north, were prevalent in the whole of the Peninsula. These early settlers were overtaken in the first millennium A.D. by new migrations of populations from the north that belonged to the **Mon-Khmer**, **Tibeto-Burman**, and **Tai-Kadai language families**. With the Cham, from whom it is theorized these four groups may have branched off, they are among the most ancient human societies known to live in the Peninsula today. Certainly, their few representatives are entitled to be called "indigenous" to the region, perhaps even "**aborigines**."

Over time these four long-sedentarized Austronesian groups have developed a strong attachment to the land and should not be lumped indiscriminately into the wider group of nomadic swiddeners. Their territoriality is underlined in their mythology and many of their **animistic** rituals, the latter involving in particular **animal sacrifices** in which the **buffalo** plays a key role. They are also a prime example of **lineage societies**, for whom primordial economic, political, and ritual links are based on **kinship** rather than political alliances. They provide a rare example of matrilineal descent groups: the **lineage** of all children is traced through the mother's side, and the people live in matrilineal longhouse groups, constituting the most important corporate kin group. They have

Note: Active language branches and languages spoken in the Southeast Asian massif are marked with an asterisk.

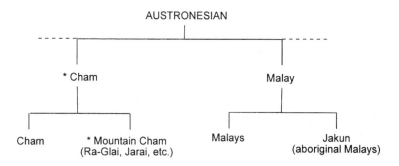

Source: Matisoff, James. "Genetic Versus Contact Relationship: Prosodic Diffusibility in South-East Asian Languages."*Areal diffusion and genetic inheritance: problems in comparative linguistics*, 291-347. In Aikhenvald, A., and R. M. W. Dixon (eds.) Oxford: OUP, 2001.

Figure 2. The Austronesian Language Family (Malayo-Polynesian)

been active and sustainable **swiddeners** over many centuries, their economy being centered on subsistence agriculture. Trade was usually a complementary means of acquiring elements of the diet and work implements that could not be produced locally. Since early colonial times, Christianity has made a significant number of converts among Austronesian groups in Vietnam. The active work of Western **missionaries** among the Vietnamese Austronesians to-day is a reason for the socialist state to keep a watchful eye on them. (*See* figure 2.)

AUSTRO-TAI LANGUAGE FAMILY. Some linguists consider this family to be the mother superstock of three of the five main language families found in the region: **Austronesian, Tai-Kadai**, and **Miao-Yao**. As a rule, **Austro-Tai languages** are nontonal and polysyllabic. However, the regional influence of Chinese is believed to have contributed to introducing tones into the Tai-Kadai and Miao-Yao families, where they constitute a fundamental feature today.

AUTONOMOUS COUNTIES. *See* ZIZHIXIAN. *See also* AUTONO-MOUS REGIONS; CHINA, ADMINISTRATIVE DIVISIONS IN THE PEOPLE'S REPUBLIC OF.

AUTONOMOUS PREFECTURES. *See* ZIZHIZHOU. *See also* AU-TONOMOUS REGIONS; CHINA, ADMINISTRATIVE DIVISIONS IN THE PEOPLE'S REPUBLIC OF.

AUTONOMOUS REGIONS. The practice of administrative distinction and isolation of mountainous areas in the **mainland Southeast Asian massif** can be traced back to French colonial times in **Indochina** with the Military Territories policy established in 1891, and to British Burma with the setting up of ethnic administrative enclaves, such as the **Kachin** and **Shan** States. These were all attempts to divide the local society along the upland-lowland fracture and for the colonial powers to ally with uplanders to defeat resistance within lowland majorities. Once victorious, most socialist regimes in the region took over this heritage and blended it with Soviet ideology to set up in their highlands what were named "autonomous regions." This practice of setting up autonomous regions in upland borderlands became policy for the first time shortly after the communist victory of 1949 in China, quickly followed elsewhere after the creation of the Democratic Republic of Vietnam (DRV; North Vietnam) in 1954 and the Lao People's Democratic Republic (LPDR) in 1975.

In China's southwest highlands, the philosophy underpinning this guiding principle has been enforced since the 1950s, with five province-size entities classified as Autonomous Regions (AR, *zizhiqu*), all located on the frontiers of China, two of which are in the southwest: the Guangxi Zhuang AR and the Xizang (Tibet) AR. Smaller ethnically named administrative divisions, such as the Autonomous Prefectures (*zizhizhou*) and Autonomous Counties (*zizhixian*), exist in these two AR as well as in neighboring provinces, such as **Yunnan** (which has 28), **Guizhou**, and **Sichuan**. In Vietnam, the concept of politically sovereign Autonomous Regions was initially promised by the fighting nationalist and communist forces to entice non-**Kinh** allies to enter the struggle for independence on their side. Watered down versions of these promises led to the creation in the north in 1955 of the Viet Bac AR and the Tay Bac (Tai Meo) AR. The AR policy, however, was made obsolete in Vietnam as soon as the war was won, and ARs were abolished in 1976. In Laos, where the Autonomous Regions strategy has never really taken off, due in large part to the highly diversified ethnic fabric of that country, it is solely the need to isolate internal resistance movements that triggered the setting up in 1994 of a much-distorted version of the Soviet AR, the Xaysomboun Special Region.

– B –

BA CHAY (PA CHAY) UPRISING (1918–1921). Also known as the Mad Man's Rebellion (*Révolte du Fou* in French colonial archives), this important **Hmong** armed uprising against the French colonial powers is the most widely documented of a series of Hmong revolts in **Indochina**. The uprising started in Lao Cai province in northern Vietnam in July 1918, in reaction to what was perceived locally as injustice and abuse. The Hmong resented the high level of taxation extorted by the **White Thai** of Lai Chau, who had been authorized to carry on this ancient practice by a complacent French administration. The initial unrest quickly spread among the Hmong in northwest Tonkin and penetrated into northern Laos, where most of the fighting was to take place. The colonial authorities, seeing the revolt getting out of hand, directed four companies of colonial troops to vigorously tame the rebels. By 1919, Ba Chay had proclaimed himself a messianic leader of the Hmong, raising the stakes by playing a powerful and highly sensitive card among his countrypeople, prone to accepting the episodic appearance of Hmong messiahs. The rebellion ended in March 1921 with the killing of Ba Chay by other minority foes in northeastern Laos, notably Lo Blia Yao, a pro-French Hmong leader and father of Laotian Hmong revolutionary hero **Faydang Lobliayao**.

Some Hmong today consider Ba Chay a hero and martyr. Ba Chay was a messianic leader who sought to free the Hmong from subordination to their Tai **feudal** lords and establish a Hmong Kingdom. The colonial authorities, however, despite some elements among the general staff being generally sympathetic to the grievances voiced, considered Ba Chay a dangerous radical, to be hunted down, producing in the process a reputation of the Hmong as an easily influenced group afflicted with a warlike nature. Nevertheless, the French learned a lesson and did redress some of the tax abuses by removing local Tai chiefs and putting Hmong officials in charge of local Hmong administration. *See also* MESSIANIC MOVEMENTS.

BA-NA. The Ba-na (174,456 in 1999) are the most numerous of **Mon-Khmer**–speaking groups in south-central Vietnam. All the Ba-na dwell in the provinces of Kon Tum, Binh Dinh, and Phu Yen. Called **Bahnar** by the French, the Ba-na's presence in coastal areas of what is today Binh Dinh province is attested to by ancient **Cham** inscriptions, in which they are known under the name Mada. Under the pressure of Cham expansion, the Ba-na eventually scattered to different altitudes in the hinterland, deep into **Gia-rai** territory. A Ba-na Romanized script similar to the one used to write Vietnamese was devised in the 1930s by French **missionaries**. The Bahnar were actively involved on both sides in the **Second Indochina War (1954–1975)**, along with the **E-de**, Gia-rai, etc.

BAHNAR. The common name used in Western literature to refer to a specific indigenous people of the **Central Highlands** in Vietnam, today called **Ba-na** by Vietnamese ethnologists. Within the **Mon-Khmer language family**, the ethnonym has been used to name the whole Bahnaric branch, which includes a dozen different **languages**. A number of Bahnar ethnic subgroups have been identified by early observers, including Alakong, Tolo, Bonom, Golar, To Sung, and Jo Long, though Vietnamese authorities do not officially recognize them.

BAI. An important **Tibeto-Burman**–speaking official minority nationality of China (1,858,063 in 2000) located in western **Yunnan**, around the town of Dali and the Erh (Eul) Hai Lake, where 80 percent of them live in concentrated communities in the Dali Bai Autonomous Prefecture. This area is likely to be the original home of the group, and they are recorded to have dwelled there since at least the **Han** dynasty (202 B.C.–A.D. 222). Archeological evidence positively linking today's Bai to Neolithic occupants is still scarce, however. Their linguistic affiliation is also a matter for debate among scholars. The Chinese have classified the Bai as a division of the **Yi** branch within the **Tibeto-Burman language family**, while Western linguists tend to see them as a distinct branch (i.e., Baic) within Tibeto-Burman.

In the second century B.C., the Western Han dynasty set up county administrations and moved a contingent of Han people to central Yunnan; this probably represents the beginning of more or less regular contact between the Bai of western Yunnan and Han representatives of the Chinese state. The Bai, then known to the Chinese as Minjia, Minchia, or Minkia—an ethnonym that endured until an official change of name was declared in 1956—were peasants adept at wet rice cultivation. They were formalized as early as the first millennium into a fiercely independent kingdom, whose success was based partly on **slavery**. The Bai are believed to have been instrumental in the success of the ancient kingdom of Nan Chao (eighth to 13th century A.D.), perhaps even ruling it. What is sure is that the Bai were running a **feudal** society centered on the Dali plateau when the Mongols, the new masters of the Middle Empire as the **Yuan** dynasty, invaded the Bai homeland in the 13th century A.D. and attached it firmly to the Han core through a tributary relationship. Since then, their constant exposure to Han culture has contributed to Sinicizing the Bai, particularly in their adoption of **Buddhism**, Confucianism, and Taoism, superimposed on an ancient **animistic** fabric.

Politically, however, they have remained relatively autonomous. In the mid-19th century, the Bai became involved in the **Panthay Rebellion**. During the revolt, a Muslim Sultanate was erected for a few years in otherwise non-Muslim Dali. The emperor's military might eventually prevailed, yet despite their insubordinate behavior, the Bai avoided significant military retaliation due to their ancient civilization, which meant that they were considered by the Chinese as more worthy than other **minorities**. Today, Dali has become a prime **tourist** destination for Chinese and international travelers alike, thanks to its unique landscape and what has been preserved of its ancient architecture, particularly the three pagodas at the Chongsheng Temple.

BAN. In Laos, the official name for the smallest territorial administrative unit, the village. Several *ban* together form a ***tasseng*** (subdistrict). In Thailand, the smallest administrative unit, the ***mooban***, is related to the *ban*. In highland Vietnam, *ban* (pronounced with a different tone than in Laos) is often used in the northern highlands with the meaning of "hamlet," an unofficial subdivision of the ***xa*** (commune).

BARTER. Barter, or the exchange of goods and labor without the use of **currency**, was until recently, and in many cases still is today, the main form of economic exchange between kin and neighbors in the uplands. For transactions beyond the restricted sphere of the village and the circle of relatives, various forms of currency have long been used with various intensity, depending on how firmly the local economy was attached to the regional market. The fact that barter is still important in a number of regions has an impact on national statistics and the assessment of poverty based on income in currency, making the official incomes of highland **minorities** who are adept at this form of exchange in kind appear lower than they are in reality. *See also* CURRENCY; TRADE.

BATIK. A cloth decoration technique based on wax and ink, practiced by a sizeable number of ethnic groups in the **mainland Southeast Asian massif**, among which subgroups of the **Miao** are prominent. Women's **hemp** or cotton skirts, as well as segments of jacket sleeves, are batiked, and then joined to the rest of the apparel. Natural **indigo** is used for dyeing, yielding a dark blue pattern on a light background. Abstract and geometrical patterns are dominant. *See also* CLOTHES.

BE VIET DANG (ca. 1930–1999). Be Viet Dang was a pioneer of the socialist ethnology of northern highland societies in Vietnam. Born among the **Tay** minority in Lang Son province, he started his career in the 1960s and was instrumental in the surveys leading to establishing the official list of national **minorities** in Vietnam in 1979. Director of the Institute of Ethnology in Hanoi until the late 1980s, he contributed from 1995 until his death to setting up the Vietnam Museum of Ethnology in Hanoi. In 1992, Be authored what is considered to be the first major ethnographic study of the large Tay and **Nung** minorities published in the Vietnamese language, *Cac dan toc Tay, Nung o Viet Nam* [*The Tay and the Nung in Vietnam*].

BERNATZIK, HUGO (1897–1953). An Austrian ethnologist, Bernatzik became a university professor in Graz in 1939 and is acknowledged as one of the founders of applied ethnology. In the area of minority studies in the **mainland Southeast Asian massif**, he published two famous books in German: *The Spirits of the Yellow Leaves* (1938), about the **Mlabri** of Thailand, and *Akha and Miao: Problems of Applied Ethnology in Farther India* (1947).

BIT. The Bit, derogatorily called Kha Bit in the past, only numbered 1,509 in 1995, all scattered among hamlets in the extreme north of Laos, in Phongsaly, Oudomxay, and Luangnamtha provinces. The Bit are **Mon-Khmer** speakers of the Palaungic branch.

BLACK FLAGS. *See* "FLAG" ARMIES.

BLACK THAI (TAI DAM, TAI DEN). *See* THAI.

BLACKSMITHING. Until recently, most iron or steel farming implements, knives, and **firearms** used in the highlands were produced in the village by local blacksmiths. Today, cheap market alternatives are attractive, but upland blacksmiths are still numerous. Most implements they need to perform their **trade** are produced locally, including the wooden bellows, the metal tools (but not the anvils and hammers), and the charcoal used to heat the steel. In general, highland blacksmiths are not specialists, but farmers also skilled in this art, to whom this ability was passed on by their forefathers. Renowned blacksmiths are solicited from a fair distance, in particular for the precise craft of piercing rods for musket barrels and assembling their delicate mechanisms. Others attend marketplaces once a week to shoe pack horses. Although sometimes blacksmiths can also double as jewelers, these two trades are most often in different hands.

BO Y. A very small number of Bo Y (1,864 in 1999), who are **Tai** speakers, can be found in the extreme north of Vietnam, dispersed in small pockets in northern Lao Cai and Ha Giang provinces. Also called Trung-cha (Chung-tra), they represent the southernmost extension of the **Buyi** (**Chung-chia**) minority of China, who are much more numerous there, with nearly 3 million individuals.

BONAN (BENGLONG). One of the smaller official **minorities** of China, these **Mon-Khmer** speakers (16,505 in 2000) live in the extreme southwest of **Yunnan** province close to linguistically related groups, such as the **Bulang** and **Wa**, who are, like them, part of the Palaungic branch. Because of a long proximity with **Hui** settlements, today most of the Bonan are Muslim, and Chinese has become the common written language among them.

BONIFACY, AUGUSTE (1856–1931). Arriving in Tonkin in 1894 as a young officer in the French colonial army, Auguste Louis Marie Bonifacy spent the next 37 years in Vietnam conducting ethnographic research while fulfilling his military duties. As early as 1903, he was made a correspondent of **Ecole Française d'Extrême-Orient**, and was highly influential in the production of the most important French ethnographic survey in highland Tonkin, the *Ethnographie des Territoires Militaires* [*Ethnography of the Military Territories*], published in 1904 under the supervision of Commander **Étienne Lunet de Lajonquière**. Among the colonial military officers, for whom serving in **Indochina** was also an opportunity to expand the usual scope of their assignment, Auguste Bonifacy held both a distinctive and a distinguished place. With more than 90 publications to his credit, including 14 in the *Bulletin de l'Ecole Française d'Extrême-Orient*, and more than a third of his writings being devoted to the highland non-**Kinh** populations in the massif, he personified the huge potential of colonial ethnography when military imperatives meet with an especially capable officer. Yet to this day none of Bonifacy's publications has been translated into English.

BORDERS IN THE MASSIF. By their modern definition, borders are geographical lines that circumscribe discrete political entities, the sovereign states. When such borders enclose one dominant ethnic group and isolate it from the next, a nation-state is born. When such enclosure also puts together with the one dominant ethnic group, other smaller or less powerful ones, the product is a multiethnic state in which a dominant ethnicity usually takes precedence over national **minorities**. In the process, borders can slice through the residential areas of some of these minorities, tearing kin and longtime neighbors apart and throwing them into two or more different, sometimes antagonistic political camps. In southwest China and mainland Southeast Asia, modern borders typically produce these three processes simultaneously. They confirm the dominance of major ethnic identities, such as the **Burman**, Siamese, **Lao**, **Khmer**, **Kinh** (Viet), and **Han**, by enclosing their customary domain and creating a national political entity centered on their definition of the nation. In addition, borders aggregate to these core nations a number of different ethnicities relegated to a role of minority, while in the process these borders slice through a number of ancient **feudal** states and cultural areas.

The borders dividing the **mainland Southeast Asian massif** today into discrete political entities were agreed to during colonial times by dominant lowland neighbors (sometimes represented by an occupying colonial power). These were set, wherever feasible, in the less contentious zones from the viewpoint of the lowlanders, preferably in little-populated highlands. These same highlands had been confined before by lowland kingdoms and empires to the role of marches acting as buffer zones with their neighbors. Modern borders thus turned what was until then margins into internal peripheries in need of being controlled, secured, colonized, and exploited. Their populations had to be submitted, secured, and preferably normalized through integration or assimilation into the nation. Ancient independent political domains therefore had to be defeated or abolished—the case of Tibet being a prime example.

Casting permanent modern borders has thus been a fundamental factor in fragmenting and segregating highland ethnic groups, turning them into "national minorities." Some groups have been totally enclosed within one country and have had to come to terms with the majority's definition of the national identity. This is the case for most **Zhuang**, the **Yi**, **Naxi**, **Bai**, and a number of others only found in China today. Likewise for the Rag-Lai, **Chu-ru**, **Ba-na**, **Ro-mam**, and **Muong** living in Vietnam. But more often than not, ethnic groups have been divided between adjacent countries. Very ancient **Austronesian** and **Mon-Khmer** speakers in the Central Highlands, such as the **Gia-rai**, **Xtieng**, **Chieng**, **Cho-ro**, and Bru, are now permanently split among Vietnam, Cambodia, and Laos. Farther north, the same fate applies to ancient Mon-Khmer, **Tibeto-Burman**, and **Miao-Yao** speakers, such as the **Khmu**, **Lolo**, **Akha**, **Lisu**, **Wa**, **Karen**, **Kachin**, **Hmong**, and **Yao**, all divided among two or more countries—Vietnam, Laos, Thailand, Burma, and southern China.

The adaptation of minorities to this complex political situation varies depending on factors, such as location, numbers, **languages**, religion, history, and cultural proximity to lowland majorities. A key distinction can be made between groups with a flexible **lineage-based**, nonterritorial social organization that can cope with geographical distance and separation, such as the Hmong, Yao, **Hani**, Lisu, and Lolo, groups for whom borders have a less fundamental impact; and other, deeply territorial groups for whom the integrity of the land is part of their core cultural identity, such as Austronesian and **Tai** speakers, for whom a division or the plain political disappearance of their customary domain has been and still is traumatic.

BRAU (BRAO). In southern Vietnam, the Brau form a small group of 313 **Mon-Khmer** speakers residing in Kon Tum province. Across the border, in Laos, where the majority of them live, they are called **Lave**. They have also been reported in eastern Cambodia, although the authorities there do not explicitly account for them, instead listing three groups considered by the Cambodians to be part of the Brao: the Kroeng (7,854 in 1995), the Kavet (3,585), and the Kraol (1,962).

BRIDEPRICE (BRIDE-WEALTH). Traditionally, in the **mainland Southeast Asian massif**, brideprice (also called bride-wealth) is paid in kind, labor, or money by the groom's family to the bride's parents in conclusion of an agreement for a matrimonial alliance. The vast majority of **lineage societies** in the massif negotiate the payment of a brideprice. For them, this is not seen as "buying" a spouse, but as a form of compensation from the groom's family for the loss of the bride's labor and her potential offspring. Paying the brideprice for his son(s) is often the most important expenditure in the life of a father, only compensated by the returns generated by his own daughters marrying out, or by the children his sons' wives will eventually contribute to his **lineage**. In case of divorce or repudiation, depending on whom customary law assigns the fault, the brideprice may be reimbursed against the return of the bride to her original family. The notion of brideprice is slightly different from the related notion of bride service, which in fact is a payment in labor by the groom to his wife's **household** when other arrangements could not be made.

BROU (BRU). There are three official national **minorities** in Laos (**Katang, Makong, Tri**) and one in Vietnam (**Bru-Van Kieu**) that could be classified as belonging to a larger Brou (Bru) stem. This latter ethnonym was commonly used in colonial times but is rarely employed today. All "Brou" **languages** belong to the **Mon-Khmer language family** and are part of the Katuic subfamily.

BRU-VAN KIEU. In Vietnam, the Bru-Van Kieu numbered 55,559 in 1999. They are considered to be within the Katuic branch of the **Mon-Khmer language family**. They dwell chiefly along the Laotian border in Quang Binh and Quang Tri provinces in central Vietnam, with residual numbers in Dak Lak province farther south. This group is the second smallest of four Katuic groups. Some argue that the Bru-Van Kieu could actually be grouped with the more numerous Brou Makong of Laos, who live just across the border in Khammouane province. *See also* BROU.

BUDDHISM IN THE MASSIF. Of the four world religions that have spread to the **mainland Southeast Asian massif** (Buddhism, Christianity, **Islam**, and **Hinduism**), Buddhism is the most important, in most cases mixing with or overtaking **animism**. Buddhism in the highlands came through diffusion from the lowland kingdoms that had adopted Mahayana Buddhism during the first millennium A.D. In the early part of the second millennium, Hinayana Buddhism became dominant in most states of the **Peninsula**. These made Theravada Buddhism—the form of Hinayana that became most popular—either the state religion, such as in Thailand and Cambodia, or the de facto dominant religious influence, which is the case in Burma and Laos. Mahayana Buddhism remained dominant in China and Vietnam (including in Tibet), the two complementary Sinitic philosophical traditions of Taoism and Confucianism creating an influential blend there.

Among the highland groups, those that are predominantly Buddhist have the closest historical, cultural, and geographical proximity to Tibetan, **Burman**, **Tai** (**Lao**), and **Khmer** influences, for instance the **Naxi** of **Yunnan**, the **Shan** and **Wa** in Burma, the **Lue** in China and Laos, practically all Tai speakers in Laos, and heavily assimilated groups, such as the **Kui** of Cambodia. **Han** and **Kinh** influence is also important in this regard but somewhat moderated by a strong atheist ideology. Syncretic forms of Buddhism vary enormously on the ground, with important blends involving ancient forms of local **animism**. Among such constant intrusion of pre-Buddhist beliefs into

Buddhist practice today are ancestor worship, the conciliation of evil spirits, and some shamanistic rituals.

BUFFALO. Central both as a draft and a ritual animal, the water buffalo is essential to performing the plowing associated with highland wet rice agriculture. It also provides milk, meat, and by-products, such as leather and horn. It is a prized possession for farmers and a major element of **trade** on the market. On the ritual side, it is the most significant animal that can possibly be involved in **animal sacrifices**, central to religious ceremonies and to the overall cultural reproduction among many groups, such as the **Mnong, Sre, Sedang,** and **Bahnar** of the southern **Annam Cordillera**, and among many others farther north in the massif.

BULANG (BLANG). In 2000, there were 91,882 Bulang belonging to the **Mon-Khmer language family** living in China in the southwest of **Yunnan**, on the Burma border. Although the Bulang are an official **minority nationality** of China, little valuable information on them has filtered outside that country.

BURIAL. The majority of ethnic groups in the **mainland Southeast Asian massif** dispose of their dead by burying them. These include **Islamic** groups, such as the **Hui**, all Christianized **minorities**, highland cultures influenced by Taoist and Confucian traditions from China and Vietnam, and most **animists**. One can find an enormous variation in burial rituals, shape of graves, or selection of burial sites, some clustering their dead in precise spots, others dispersing them around the landscape. Among the groups where ancestor worship plays a central role, the graves are maintained by descendants for several generations. Others simply allow this memory to fall into oblivion within a generation. In any case, burial site exploration is potentially an important yet little exploited element in the **archeology** of the highlands.

The only highland groups that do not bury their dead are among those converted to **Buddhism** (or, formerly, **Hinduism**) through long proximity with lowland Buddhist cultures, such as the **Burman**, Siamese, **Lao**, and **Khmer**. Their dead are cremated, and their ashes either kept in an urn or scattered. It should be noted that several highland Buddhist groups still bury their dead, an ancestral practice surviving from their animist past. Under Tibetan influence, highland groups following the

Buddhist Lamaist tradition and located in the extreme northwest of the massif, in Burma and **Yunnan** (China), display the corpses for animals to consume them.

BURMA, ADMINISTRATIVE DIVISIONS IN THE UNION OF. In Burma (Myanmar), as in China, administrative divisions take into account the location and demography of certain national **minorities**. The 1974 Constitution organized the country into seven lowland divisions (*taing*), populated primarily by **Burmans** (Irrawaddy, Magwe, Mandalay, Pegu, Rangoon, Sagaing, and Tenasserim), and seven ethnic minority states (*pyi ne*), located on the mountainous crown around the Irrawaddy and Salween deltas and plains: Arakan, Chin, Mon, **Kachin**, **Shan**, **Kayah**, and **Karen**.

BURMA, HIGHLAND MINORITIES IN THE UNION OF. The demography of non-Burman minority groups in the Union of Burma (estimated national population of 42,720,196 in 2004) is relatively unknown to the outside world, and perhaps even in Burma (Myanmar) itself. The last official national census was held in 1983, a sketchy exercise that many have dismissed as fraught with inaccuracies. That census included a chart titled "Table 11. Population by race, sex and religion," in which the highland groups listed were the **Kachin**, Kayah, **Karen**, **Chin**, and **Shan**, comprising a total highland population of 6.4 million, or 19 percent of the national population. In comparison, the 1931 national census listed 21 different mountain minority groups. Ethnic leaders of non-Burman groups in Burma themselves suggested in the early 1990s the approximate figures of 4 million Shan, 3.5 million Karen (including Kayah), 2.5 million Chin, 1.5 million Kachin, and 1.5 million **Palaung-Wa** (formerly clustered with the Shan), producing a possible total of 13 million. Clearly, both sources must be treated with some skepticism.

State policy toward the non-Burman minorities is equally confused and appears to be one of steady confrontation. Seen from Rangoon, half of Burma's territory is inhabited by highland groups and regarded as a backwater where mineral and timber resources are to be exploited without reserve, for the benefit of the political elite. If the number of opposition parties and armed groups stemming from the minorities challenging the central state, with its national troops, is an indication of the poor relationship between Rangoon and its minorities, Burma

Table 1. Minorities of Highland Burma, 2004
(Estimates based on 1931 official census figures, augmented proportionally to 2004 [factor 2.9].)

Language Groups Subgroups	N in 1931	N in 2004 (1931 x 2.9)	Percent of Minorities	Percent of Country
Karen:	1,341,066	**3,889,091**	42.1	9.1
Sgaw		1,413,138		
Pwo		1,373,788		
Taungthu		645,871		
Karenni		91,512		
Others		364,782		
Tai:	1,021,917	**2,963,559**	32.1	6.9
Shan		2,651,699		
Hkun		90,579		
Lu		87,090		
Others		134,192		
Kuki-Chin:	343,854	**997,177**	10.8	2.3
Chin		258,523		
Khami		89,557		
Lai		70,059		
Chinbok		58,566		
Kamhow		57,403		
Others		463,069		
Palaung-Wa:	176,024	**510,470**	5.5	1.2
Palaung/Pale		402,102		
Wa		108,367		
Kachin	153,897	**446,301**	4.8	1.0
Lolo-Muhso:	93,052	**269,851**	2.9	0.6
Kaw		117,180		
Lahu		77,906		
Lisaw		57,125		
Others		17,641		
Sak:	35,237	**102,187**	1.1	0.2
Kadu		58,885		
Others		43,303		
Mro	14,094	**40,873**	0.4	0.1
Naga	4,201	**12,183**	0.1	0.03
Man:	947	**2,746**	0.03	0.01
Miao		2,407		
Yao		339		
All Minorities	3,184,289	**9,234,438**	100	21.6
COUNTRY	14,667,000	**42,720,196**	—	100

Sources: J. J. Bennison, 1933, Census of India, 1931 Vol. 11, Burma (Rangoon) pp. 198–200; CIA Online.

wins the sorry award of most repressive administration in the region. The opposition includes the Kachin Independence Organization (established in 1961), the Arakan Independence Organization, the Karen National Union (1947), the New Mon State Party (1958), the Karenni National Progressive Party, the United **Wa** State Army, the Pao National Organization, the **Palaung** State Liberation Party, and the Shan Nationalities League for Democracy. Most have an armed branch and are fighting the central administration, which in turn responds with violent authoritarianism. As victims of this repression, it is estimated that over 300,000 Karens seeking refuge from the Burmese army have now crossed into Thailand, with an equal number of Kachin having crossed into China for the same reasons. The military junta heading the country since the 1989 coup—the self-appointed and ill-named State Law and Order Restoration Council (SLORC), equally poorly refashioned as the State Peace and Development Council in 1997—has to accept responsibility for this appalling situation.

Burma's highlands form a horseshoe open to the south, sloping inward into the Irrawaddy lower basin and delta. On the west the Chin and Arakan Hills border on Bangladesh and India. Because of this westward cultural, political, and historical attraction, these hills and their indigenous populations gravitating toward the Indian subcontinent will not be addressed in detail here. The north and east of this horseshoe border on China, Laos, and Thailand, three countries with whom Burma shares its highland groups. Of the seven minority states of Burma (the *pyi ne*), four stand adjacent to the northern and eastern borders. These are, from north to south, the Kachin, Shan, Kayah, and Karen States. The first is drained by the upper Irrawaddy River, the others by the Salween. But names can be misleading. Perhaps only just a quarter of the Karen population actually lives in the Karen state today, while important groups, such as the Wa, **Lahu**, and Pa-o, do not have a state of their own and live within the limits of the Shan State, a group with whom they are merged in government statistics.

One of the most irritating problems related to minorities in Burma is the lack of recent and reliable data on their basic demography, history, societies, and economy. Relatively few ethnic studies were completed in the 60 years of British rule, partly due to the colony being administered as a province of India until 1937, partly because Britain made a point of dealing with the highlands and their inhabitants only indirectly, turning to its advantage the benefits of this divisive policy and seeking, for strategic purposes, to aggravate the antagonism between the lowland **Buddhist Burmans** and the highland Christianized minorities. The effects of this colonial strategy are still strongly felt today. After independence in 1948, even fewer studies were conducted on highland societies during more than four decades of political instability and misgovernance, including the active promotion of the process of "Burmanization" of minorities and violations of basic human rights, constantly reported by Amnesty International since the late 1980s. In addition, due to the poor circulation of information, AIDS is on the rise in the mountains, thanks to both the availability of cheap intravenous drugs produced in the country and the rampant demand for sex workers for the Thailand market.

Facing this lack of support from the central government, antigovernment minority groups have set up and maintained not only their own armies, but also schools, hospitals, and elaborate administrative systems within the territories under their control. In more isolated areas, banditry is widespread in connection with considerable narcotics and gem production and trafficking, a cause of endless bouts of violence between drug barons. Simultaneously, excessive logging, authorized by the junta for its sole benefit, takes advantage of the civil confusion, taking a heavy toll on the forest. The timber is chiefly sent to China in return for arms used to further repress a recalcitrant population and fight the armed opposition in the mountains. In short, following decades of troubled politics, Burma today is in a state of chaos and lawlessness, which prevents outside observers from knowing what is really going on in the highland minority areas, and everyone is left to conjecture.

Since the 1931 census mentioned above, and quite deliberately according to critics, there has been no published attempt to take an accurate census of the country's population. For this dictionary, it has been decided to work on a projection based on the 1931 ethnic categories and figures, actualized to the year 2004. This exercise yields the figures of 3,889,091 Karen speakers representing 42 percent of the highland minority population and 9.1 percent of the country's population; 2,963,559 Tai speakers (respectively 32 percent and 7 percent); 997,177 Kuki-Chin speakers (10.8 percent and 2.3 percent); 510,470 Palaung-Wa (5.5 percent and 1.2 percent); 446,301 Kachin (4.8 percent and 1 percent); 269,851 Lolo-Muhso (2.9 percent and 0.6 percent); and small numbers of **Naga**, **Miao-Yao**, Sak, and Mro, making a grand total of a 9.2 million highland minority population, accounting for 21.6 percent of the country's population. These statistics, it must be repeated, are only estimates, with actual figures still unknown.

BURMAN. Used as a noun, this is the name most authors use for the inhabitants of Burma who belong to the Burman branch of the **Tibeto-Burman language family**. This definition thus bands together the majority in that country, namely 23,532,433 ethnic Burmans, accounting for 69 percent of the national population in the 1983 census. This useful semantic distinction allows the noun Burmese to be reserved for use as a national label applied to all inhabitants of Burma, regardless of their ethnicity and linguistic affiliation. Used as adjectives, Burman and Burmese follow the same rule.

BURMESE STATES. *See PYI NE.*

BUYI (BOUYEI, CHUNG-CHIA). The Buyi are the second largest **Tai**-speaking *shaoshu minzu* of China after the **Zhuang,** with 2,971,460 individuals officially registered in 2000. The Buyi were for a long time known in China as Chung-chia (Chong Kia), until the great renaming initiative of the new communist state in the mid-1950s. They are believed to be indigenous to the southern part of **Guizhou**, where they still reside today. Some authors believe that that region could perhaps also be the cradle of all Tai-speaking groups in Asia. Today, the Buyi are found in several Bouyei-Miao autonomous counties in Xingyi and Anshun prefectures, and in Qiannan Bouyei-Miao Autonomous Prefecture in Guizhou Province. Others are distributed among counties in the Qiandongnan Miao-Dong Autonomous Prefecture or near Guiyang, the capital of Guizhou.

The Buyi are a northern geographical and linguistic extension of the Zhuang in Guangxi, from whom they are frequently difficult to differentiate, and some Chinese linguists consider that the Buyi language could be categorized as a dialect of Northern Zhuang. Like the Zhuang, the Buyi have not been reached by Theravada **Buddhism**. Yet, while favoring ancestor worship, the group has definitely been influenced by Chinese Buddhism as well as Taoism, to such a degree that other non-Han groups often consider the Buyi to be **Han**. Through migration that could be as ancient as the 10th century A.D., some Buyi moved south and settled in pockets in **Yunnan**, while a small number are found today in extreme northern Vietnam, where they are called **Bo Y** or Trung-cha.

– C –

CAMBODIA, HIGHLAND MINORITIES IN THE KINGDOM OF. Cambodia is another country in the **mainland Southeast Asian massif**, where the situation of the highland **minorities** is difficult to appraise with precision. As a matter of fact, Cambodia is generally left out when authors address the highland minorities in mainland Southeast Asia. Reasons for this omission include the relatively small number of highland groups there, their uncertain identity and location, the poor state of national census information, and the embryonic state of the national ethnology of highland groups.

Statistics on minorities in Cambodia are unreliable partly because of a troubled history since independence in 1954, and partly for political reasons. The official numbers from the 1995 census indicate that of a national population of 11,240,367, 96 percent of nationals registered as ethnic **Khmer**, who thus form the overwhelming national majority. Of the remaining Cambodians of non-Khmer extraction (3.94 percent), nearly half belong to the **Cham** ethnicity (203,881) stemming from the ancient eastern Hindu kingdom of Champa, which at its peak covered most of today's south-central Vietnam. Then come the local representatives of neighboring majority groups, the **Viet** (95,597), the Chinese (47,180), the **Lao** (19,819), and the **Thai** (2,454), who settled in Cambodia at various times in its long history (numerous observers have denounced a governmental strategy of understating the numbers of Vietnamese and Chinese in the kingdom; to reflect reality, some have suggested that the official 1995 figures should be increased fivefold for these two groups). The number of highland minority peoples present in Cambodia can be estimated from the 1995 census by a simple subtraction, the total number boiling down to 70,024, or 0.62 percent of the national population. This modest figure makes Cambodia the

Table 2. Minorities of Cambodia, 1995
19 minorities, of which 14 live in the highlands
(Names of highland minorities are in all capital letters.)

Ethnic Groups	N	Percent of Minorities	Percent of Country
Cham	203,881	46.06	1.81
Vietnamese	95,597	21.60	0.85
Chinese	47,180	10.66	0.42
Lao	19,819	4.48	0.18
TUMPOUN	15,861	3.58	0.14
KUI	14,186	3.20	0.13
JARAI	11,549	2.61	0.10
KROENG	7,854	1.77	0.07
PHNONG	5,323	1.20	0.05
KAVET	3,585	0.81	0.03
STEANG	3,234	0.73	0.03
PROV	2,585	0.58	0.02
Thai	2,454	0.55	0.02
KRAOL	1,962	0.44	0.02
ROBEL	1,640	0.37	0.01
POR	1,440	0.33	0.01
THMAUN	453	0.10	0.004
LOEMOUN	280	0.06	0.002
SOACH	72	0.02	0.001
Other	3,714	0.84	0.03
All Minorities	**442,669**	**100**	**3.94**
Highland Minorities	**70,024**	**15.82**	**0.62**
COUNTRY	**11,240,367**	—	**100**

Source: Administration Department of Ministry of Interior, Cambodia, 1995.

massif country with both the smallest number of highland minorities and the smallest proportion of minorities within the national population.

Three-quarters of highland minorities of Cambodia inhabit the two easternmost provinces (**khett**), Ratana Kiri and Mondul Kiri, on the Vietnamese and Laotian borders, with small extensions into the northeast of Stung Traeng province and into the southeast of Kratie province. The area thus formed is adjacent to four provinces in the Vietnamese **Tay Nguyen**—Dak Lak, Kon Tum, Gia Lai, and

Song Be—as well as the Laotian southernmost province of Attapeu plus the southeast section of Champassack. In other words, within Cambodia, the area thus delineated covers that country's section of the southern **Annam Cordillera**. All minorities there belong to the **Austronesian** and **Mon-Khmer language groups** and include the **Tumpoun**, **Jarai**, Kroeng, **Phnong**, **Kavet**, Steang, **Prov**, **Robel**, **Por**, **Kraol**, and a few other very small groups. In a few pockets of forested hills elsewhere in the country, very small numbers of Mon-Khmer—yet non-Khmer—minorities have long dwelled, such as in Kampong Thom province in the center of the country, in the Dangrek mountains in the far north of Siem Reap province, and in the massif of the Cardamom and Elephant mountains in the southwest of the country. Groups found in these pockets include the **Kui**, Chong, **Por**, and **Saoch**. Virtually no anthropological research has been conducted on these latter four groups, and not much more on those in the eastern hills.

Reliable information on Cambodian highland minorities is so scarce that of the 14 groups explicitly mentioned in the 1995 official list produced by the Ministry of the Interior—see the demographic table—only 10 have had consistent information about them produced, in large part, it must be said, thanks to members from several of these groups having been studied across the borders in Laos and Vietnam. The four remaining groups are the Prov, Robel, **Thmaun**, and Loemun. In terms of political recognition by the government, the 1993 Constitution of Cambodia, amended in 1999, makes no mention of non-Khmer ethnicity or minorities, let alone the small proportion of these groups living in the highlands. Accordingly, there is no particular policy for addressing highland minority groups in the kingdom.

CARAVANS. As a necessary complement to river navigation, land caravans have been a major means of transportation for goods and travelers within and across the **mainland Southeast Asian massif** for centuries. Based in and around **Yunnan**, the Muslim **Hui** are known to have been particularly active in the caravan **trade**, though many other agents have also been involved, depending on the region and the period. Caravans were for a long time the main channel for supplying **salt**, metals, and various commodities to uplanders, ex-

changed for upland specialty items, such as medicinal plants, in demand for the lowland pharmacopoeia. This trade reached from China
to remote parts of Burma, Thailand, Laos, and Vietnam. In the 19th
century A.D., caravan trade in the massif came to include **opium**, a lucrative item that found an efficient way out of the production sites
and toward the mid- or lowland transformation centers and consumers. The local economic impacts of caravans as they moved
through the massif were generally limited to labor recruited on the
spot to accompany passing caravans, the sale of limited amounts of
food and fodder to caravan managers, and one form or another of taxation by some of the more powerful highland kingdoms, sometimes
on behalf of their own overlords.

The caravan trade, about which surprisingly little is known, connected ancient horse tracks and footpaths to more established roads
linking cities in the interior of southwest China, like Kunming, Dali,
Jinghong, and Chengdou, to maritime trading posts and capitals
south of the massif, like Moulmein, Ayutthaya, Bangkok, Vinh,
Hanoi, and Haiphong. As late as the 1950s, French anthropologist
Jacques Lemoine reported that there were still old **Hmong** in Laos
and Vietnam who remembered their travels with the Hui caravaneers
in the late 19th century, for whom they acted as guides and as grooms
for the horses and mules. In this way, highlanders, such as the
Hmong, **Yao**, **Lolo**, **Hani**, and others, could explore new, fertile, and
sparsely populated regions in the highlands of Yunnan, Laos, Vietnam, and Thailand. Back home, they could describe these opportunities to those willing or forced to migrate in the turmoil of the 1800s
in southwest China. Caravan trade was thus a crucial source of information, eventually allowing representatives from several highland
groups originally based in southern China to organize successful migrations into the **Peninsula**.

Modest caravans with mules and pack horses can still be seen in
the massif today moving between villages or marketplaces in areas
where the road infrastructure has not yet been developed. However,
their heyday is definitely over, due to the enforcement of border sovereignty by the six states sharing the massif, the rapid development
of transport infrastructure, and the growing popularity of modern
modes of transportation.

CARDAMOM. Medicinal cardamom (*Amomum villosum var. xanthoides*)—not to be confused with aromatic cardamom (*Elettaria cardamomum*)—is a nonligneous perennial plant growing wild in the **mainland Southeast Asian massif**'s tropical highland forests. It has been collected for centuries and **traded** with buyers on the plains as an ingredient in the traditional Chinese pharmacopoeia, in particular for the preparation of medicine for stomachaches. Historically, **tributes** to lowland powers could be paid in part with wild cardamom. Today, the active cultivation and trade of medicinal cardamom has become an appealing economic alternative among highlanders living on the Chinese periphery, due to a growing demand for it on the Chinese market.

CASH CROPPING. Cash cropping, or commercial agriculture, is the standard form of agriculture in the developed world as well as in most of Asia's fertile plains. It has—sometimes only recently and only partly—penetrated to the remote areas of the **mainland Southeast Asian massif**. It is a particular form of agriculture in which a large proportion of the harvest is sold on the market to generate income, which is then used to buy items necessary for daily life or luxuries, or is accumulated as capital for future use. Cash cropping is based on a strong bond with the market economy and thus constitutes a departure from self-sufficiency. On a temporal scale, cash cropping usually follows in the steps of its most common predecessor, subsistence agriculture, wherein agricultural production and consumption was determined solely by the reproductive needs of the **household**. Cash cropping, which implies producing surpluses and focusing on specialized crops, becomes structurally attached to market demand, which is used by the individual farmer to decide what should be grown in order to maximize his chances of economic success.

A relative rarity in the **Peninsula**'s highest lands for a long time, commercial agriculture first appeared thousands of years ago in fertile lowlands, among sedentarized groups where demography made it justified. It then spread to the neighboring midlands among semi-sedentarized groups dwelling immediately next to zones of denser habitation. This became the cradle of **feudal** states, whose existence depended on the production of agricultural surpluses. Most **Tai**-speaking groups, for instance, and **Tibeto-Burman** groups, such as the **Naxi**, **Yi**, and **Bai**, fall into this category. Apart from such relatively regular diffusion through centuries of commercial practice, historical circumstances have also triggered the sudden and somewhat eccentric appearance of cash crops among subsistence agriculturalists, most prominently the extremely successful **opium** poppy, which spread to virtually the whole massif from the mid-19th century onward, only to be abandoned in the late 20th century. Besides such peculiar cases, in recent decades the conversion to cash cropping of the remaining subsistence agriculturalists in the highest lands has been steady, subject to active, sometimes aggressive promotion by all the national governments in the region. This promotion is conceived of as an effective way to eliminate **swiddening**, considered unsustainable, and to fix the last mobile populations to the land for good. The scale of this conversion has been spectacular, and cash cropping is now widespread among upland farmers at all altitudes, though the degree to which local economies depend on it varies greatly from one country to the next, depending on levels of national embeddedness in the world economy, as well as between regions, and between ethnic groups within one given country.

A negative aspect of the spread of commercial agriculture to the highlands is undoubtedly the commensurate damage caused to the ecosystem by misinformed upland farmers new to the handling of the fertilizers and pesticides inevitably associated with cash cropping. Serious grievances are currently voiced across the massif by lowland farmers dwelling downstream from highland settlements that are now using chemicals for their agriculture, leading in many regions to deadlock about the use of the land, and sometimes to forced resettlement of populations.

CATHOLIC MISSIONS. *See* MISSIONARIES.

CENTRAL HIGHLANDS. English name for a portion of highlands in southern Vietnam *(Tay Nguyen* in Vietnamese), a part of the **Annam Cordillera** *(Truong Son* in Vietnamese) that spills over into eastern Cambodia and southeastern Laos.

CENTRAL INTELLIGENCE AGENCY (CIA). After World War II, containment of communist expansion in Asia was the driving force behind American involvement in intelligence gathering and covert operations in and around the **mainland Southeast Asian massif**. These operations were carried out chiefly by the Central Intelligence Agency and its affiliated agencies and companies, including the CIA's precursor in Asia, the Office of Strategic Services (OSS). Over the decades, OSS/CIA advisers and collaborators made contact with, organized, and supported many highland groups. This happened before 1949 in southwest China and Burma as well as in Vietnam and upland Laos and Thailand during the last years of the **First Indochina War (1946–1954)** and for the entire duration of the **Second Indochina War (1954–1975)**.

In the **Central Highlands** of southern Vietnam in the 1960s, a military branch called the "Special Forces," assisted by the CIA, was commissioned to contact, control, and train highlanders to resist communist assaults on their villages. Operations in less easy terrain also aimed at making sure that highland dwellers, or **Montagnards** as they were called by the Americans, would not provide support to the "Viet Cong" rebels or become their sympathizers. Military personnel and CIA-sponsored outside agents were embedded in highland villages to adopt their customs and influence their decisions from the inside. In Laos, the next country where the CIA was most active, a similar strategy was implemented. There, the CIA equipped, trained, and supplied the "**secret army**" of Hmong leader (General) **Vang Pao** operating in pockets behind Pathet Lao lines.

Many ethnographic investigations were conducted among highland groups over those years with the objective of learning how to better relate to the groups and convince their leaders to ally with anticommunist forces. These studies were performed under schemes more or less explicitly sponsored by the CIA, such as the Advanced Research Program Agency (ARPA) or branches of the U.S. Agency for International Development (USAID). Back in the United States, controversy among academics flared, most strikingly within the American Anthropological Association in the early 1970s, when it became clear that some anthropologists and higher education institutions had benefited from the CIA's financial support to conduct their field research among highlanders in Thailand.

The active role played by the CIA in the **Peninsula**'s highlands officially ended with the communist revolutionary takeovers of 1975.

However, some undercover operations are believed to have been prolonged ever since, such as support to some anticommunist **Hmong** resistance efforts in Laos, or the maintenance of exiled anticommunist Vietnamese in the United States, such as representatives of **FULRO**. It has also been suggested that the CIA may also have been involved in U.S.-based Christian **missionary** societies actively recruiting among highland groups in both northern and southern Vietnam.

CENTRAL UNIVERSITY FOR NATIONALITIES OF CHINA (CUN). In 1951, the Communist Party Central Committee approved the establishment in Beijing of the "Central Institute of Nationalities," supported by local branch institutes in minority provinces and **autonomous regions**. As the first minority higher education establishment in the People's Republic (PRC), its priority was to train minority cadres. In 1993, the State Education Commission approved the proposal to change the Institute's name to "The Central University for Nationalities." During its 50 years of existence, CUN has developed programs in the humanities, which is its main focus, with ethnology as its principal subfield. It also offers courses in the natural sciences, engineering, management, and the arts.

CHAM (CAM). The branch of the **Austronesian language family** to which belong all five Austronesian-speaking groups found in the southern **Annam Cordillera**, shared among Laos, Vietnam, and Cambodia. Cham is also the name of the most important groups of this branch, whose **Hinduized** kingdom, Champa, occupied a domain corresponding to today's south-central Vietnam, from the second century A.D. until its final demise, when the Vietnamese completed their southern expansion in the 18th century. The historical Cham are divided between southern Vietnam, where they still practice **Hinduism**, and Cambodia, where most are Muslim.

CHANGWAT. In highland Thailand, as in the rest of the country, the largest territorial administrative unit, translating as "province." *Changwat* are further subdivided into *amphoe* (districts), *tambon* (subdistricts), and *mooban* (villages).

CHAU. See ZHOU.

CHIENG (CHENG). The name used in Laos for representatives of a group also found over the border in Vietnam, where they are named **Gie-trieng**. The Chieng of Laos numbered 8,511 in 1995, all located in Attapeu province in the extreme south of the country. They are **Mon-Khmer** speakers of the Bahnaric branch.

CHIN. A **Tibeto-Burman**–speaking group in the lower western Burma border area, in the Chin Hills, part of the Arakan Range, often called Khyang in Burmese texts (pronounced "tching"). An estimate of Chin population in Burma for 2004 yields the significant figure of 258,523. Most Chin of Burma dwell in the *pyi ne* Chin State, which starts at the western limit of the Irrawaddy plain. Chin settlements are usually found at elevations above 1,000 meters. The Chin National Front (CNF) has been fighting the Burmese junta since 1988. International organizations have alerted the world to the plight of the Burmese Chin taking refuge in India to escape the Burmese military. A number of Chin and their close linguistic relatives, the Kuki, are believed to be native to the Indian states of Manipur and Mizoram and extreme eastern Bangladesh. In 1963, anthropologist Frank K. Lehman published his seminal *The Structure of Chin Society: A Tribal of Burma Adapted to a Non-Western Civilization.*

CHINA, ADMINISTRATIVE DIVISIONS IN THE PEOPLE'S REPUBLIC OF. Together with Burma, China is one of only two countries sharing the **mainland Southeast Asian massif** that make an official distinction in their administrative divisions between units with or without a concentration of minority people. The territorial classification in the mountainous southwest of the PRC today combines two systems side by side, one standard across China, and one adapted to regions inhabited by *shaoshu minzu*. At the top of the scale are the standard provinces (*sheng*) and, in five cases in the whole PRC, the equivalent for selected **minorities**, the **Autonomous Regions** (*zizhiqu*). The next level down is shared between the standard Prefectures (*diqu*) and, for minorities, the Autonomous Prefectures (*zizhizhou*). Another level down are the standard Counties (*xian*) and the Autonomous Counties (*zizhixian*). A product of the cultural politics of the 1950s in the PRC, minority territorial divisions do not always coincide wholly with the actual location of the majority population from the specific *shaoshu minzu* supposed to be represented. Nor do representatives of the majority *shaoshu minzu* in a given prefecture or county necessarily hold official levers of political power there. While these two parallel systems are merged within the same national-level administrative authority structure when it comes to economic development, infrastructure, or defense, the administrative divisions associated with minority nationalities also have direct access, at least on paper, to certain political bureaus regarding cultural matters.

CHINA, HIGHLAND MINORITIES IN THE PEOPLE'S REPUBLIC OF. Apart from the **Han**, with a population of 1.14 billion, the 2000 China census (total population of 1,242,612,226) officially identifies 55 ethnic **minority** groups, varying in size from just 3,000—the Lhoba—to more than 16 million—the **Zhuang**. Non-Han groups are officially referred to in the People's Republic of China as "minority nationalities" (*shaoshu minzu*) and constituted, in 2000, 8.5 percent of the national population, with a total of 105,225,073 people. Of direct interest here, 29 of these minorities are indigenous to the southwest of China, where they number 59,658,702, 56.7 percent of China's minority nationality population, or 4.8 percent of the PRC's total population.

Many non-Han minorities of China are certainly as ancient, if not older, than the Han majority. Not much is known, however, about their exact identities and demographic importance before the 20th century, when the first formal national censuses were conducted. Before that, Imperial China did not believe it needed to know much about the non-Han people dwelling on the fringes of its domain. All that was deemed necessary was to know what could contribute to preventing those peripheral groups from causing trouble for the core population and its economic performance or, for the more politically formalized, what would be useful to know in order to conduct profitable commercial transactions with them and make military alliances when needed. In the first half of the 20th century, with the toppling of the imperial regime and the advent of Republican China in 1911, the state's interest in its minorities took a political turn. By 1920, Sun Yat Sen, founder of the Republic, was concerned with the integration of the nation's frontiers. While remaining moderately interested in the indigenous inhabitants of

Table 3.   Minorities of Highland Southwest China, 2000
56 nationalities (*minzu*), 55 being minorities (*shaoshu minzu, s.m.*),
29 of which are found in the Southeast Asian massif, plus a proportion of Hui
(Names of southwest highland minorities are in all capital letters.)

Ethnic Groups	N	Percent of s.m.	Percent of Country
Han (Chinese)	1,137,386,112	—	91.53
ZHUANG	16,178,811	15.38	1.30
Manchu	10,682,262	10.15	0.86
Hui	9,816,805	9.33	0.79
MIAO	8,940,116	8.50	0.72
Uyghur	8,399,393	7.98	0.68
TUJIA	8,028,133	7.63	0.65
YI	7,762,272	7.38	0.62
Mongolian	5,813,947	5.53	0.47
Tibetan	5,416,021	5.15	0.44
BUYI	2,971,460	2.82	0.24
DONG	2,960,293	2.81	0.24
YAO	2,637,421	2.51	0.21
Korean	1,923,842	1.83	0.15
BAI	1,858,063	1.77	0.15
HANI	1,439,673	1.37	0.12
Kazakh	1,250,458	1.19	0.10
LI	1,247,814	1.19	0.10
DAI	1,158,989	1.10	0.09
SHE	709,592	0.70	0.06
LISU	634,912	0.67	0.05
GELAO	579,357	0.60	0.05
Santa	513,805	0.55	0.04
LAHU	453,705	0.49	0.04
SUI	406,902	0.43	0.03
WA	396,610	0.39	0.03
NAXI	308,839	0.38	0.02
QIANG	306,072	0.29	0.02
Tu	241,198	0.29	0.02
MULAM	207,352	0.23	0.02
Xibe	188,824	0.18	0.02
Kirghiz	160,823	0.15	0.01
Dagur	132,394	0.13	0.01
JINGPO	132,143	0.13	0.01
MAONAN	107,166	0.10	0.01
Salar	104,503	0.10	0.01
BULANG	91,882	0.09	0.01
Tajik	41,028	0.04	0.003
ACHANG	33,936	0.03	0.003
PUMI	33,600	0.03	0.003
Evenki	30,505	0.03	0.002

Ethnic Groups	N	Percent of s.m.	Percent of Country
NU	28,759	0.03	0.002
Gin	22,517	0.02	0.002
JINO	20,899	0.02	0.002
De'ang	17,935	0.02	0.001
BONAN	16,505	0.02	0.001
Russian	15,609	0.01	0.001
Yellow Uighur	13,719	0.01	0.001
Uzbek	12,370	0.01	0.001
Monpa	8,923	0.01	0.001
Oroqen	8,196	0.01	0.001
DERUNG	7,426	0.01	0.001
Tatar	4,890	0.00	0.0004
Hezhen	4,640	0.00	0.0004
Kaoshan	4,461	0.00	0.0004
Lhopa	2,965	0.00	0.0002
Other	734,438	0.01	0.06
Foreign	941	0.00	0.0001
All Minorities	105,225,173	100	8.47
Southwest Minorities	59,658,702	56.70	4.80
COUNTRY	1,242,612,226	—	100

Source: China Statistical Yearbook 2002.

the frontiers, he decided to acknowledge the existence of four non-Han minorities in the whole Republic, namely the Mongols, Manchus, Tibetans, and Tatars, that were believed to total 10 million or 2.5 percent of the national population. The Republic's flag was accordingly adorned with five stripes, one per official ethnic group—a symbol that survived in the five stars (four small ones circling a large one) on the current Chinese flag, adopted in 1949. Such ethnic and demographic inaccuracy was a reflection of a political will to ignore or negate the importance of multi-ethnicity in the Republic. The meager amount of early ethnographic research on non-Han minorities sponsored by the state was both a cause for this misguided view and the consequence of a lack of official interest. In reality, beyond political strategies, we know now that a number of Chinese ethnologists were interested at the time in highland minorities, such as Yan Fuli, **Ruey Yih-fu**, Tao Yun-kui, **Dai** Yixuan, or Fei Xiaotong.

The near constant state of combat over the next 20 years did nothing to alleviate this official indifference. During two decades of revolutionary civil war, the tactic on both sides was geared to securing political and military alliances with ethnic minorities in as many strategic areas as possible. Article 14 of the 1931 Jiangsi Soviet Constitution, drafted by the communists, gave minority areas a right of complete secession from China once the Revolution ended. On the republican side, a right of self-determination was guaranteed by the Kuomintang to Xingjian, Tibet, and Mongolia, should the communists be defeated. Such generous promises proved short-lived. After the Maoist victory in 1949, to steer clear of the possibility of multiple secessions, the Communist Party immediately promulgated a new policy toward minorities, one based on the notion of China being a multinational (i.e., multiethnic) unitary state, not a group of federated republics, such as the model set up earlier in the Union of Soviet Socialist Republics. Concurrently, it was also deemed strategically important to give a favorable impression of the new regime to the outside world. As a consequence, a new communist policy on national minorities was expressed in a few paragraphs of the 1949 Common Program for the Chinese People's Consultative Conference, and soon after, additional articles providing the revised definition of "minority nationalities" were prepared for the 1952 General Program for the Implementation of Regional Autonomy for Nationalities. Parts of this writing eventually found their way into the 1954 constitution (in particular articles 50–53 and 88). **Autonomous Regions** heralding minorities' rights to self-rule were set up throughout the 1950s. On the ground meanwhile, agricultural cooperatives were being implemented in the whole country from 1953 on.

To gain a better understanding of its poorly known non-Han minorities and speed up their integration into the nation, the PRC launched a massive ethnographic research program under the guidance and with the active supervision of state ethnologists from the USSR. No one at the time could agree on just how many minority groups there were and what their exact identity was. The explicit objectives of the ethnographic project were thus to list and classify the various non-Han groups living within the national borders. This classification project (*minzu shibie*) sponsored surveys that focused first on **languages**, with the explicit intention to design adapted writing systems (chiefly in a Roman script), develop an understanding of the non-Han languages, and ultimately train language cadres and install them as intermediaries and mediators devoted to the Party. Ten years later, by the end of the 1950s, it was touted by state representatives that 42 languages had thus been studied, and 14 new scripts devised for previously nonwritten languages. It was also in the 1950s that, in accordance with the Stalinist conception of "nationalities," a "minority nationality" was strictly defined as a group of people with a common origin, living on a common territory, using a common language, and sharing a sense of collective identity in economic and social organization and behavior.

The early embodiment of today's **Central University for Nationalities** (CUN), then called the Central Institute for Nationalities, was set up in 1951 to take charge of the formation of higher minority cadres that could be trusted by the Party. In a Central Government Directive of 1951, terminology was redressed so that exonyms once considered derogatory, such as **Lolo, Man**, or Yeren, were replaced by more palatable ones like **Yi, Yao**, and **Jingpo**. Pejorative ideograms using the dog, worm, or reptile symbols for names of minority peoples were purged from the Chinese writing system. Following the general pattern set up in the USSR, minorities were given notional autonomy embodied in the Autonomous Territory status, loosely based on the minimum of 30 percent minority population criteria. The five Autonomous Regions (*zizhiqu*) Xingjiang, Tibet, Mongolia, Guangxi, and Ningxia were set up along with what amounts today to 30 Autonomous Prefectures (*zizhizhou*) and 113 Autonomous Counties (*zizhixian*), nearly all located on the border belt of the country. In 1953, the first postrevolution national census announced that 6 percent of the population, that is, over 35 million people, belonged to non-Han ethnicities, which constituted clear progress compared to the 1920 exercise. By 1959, the *shaoshu minzu* were officially divided into 51 groups occupying 64 percent of the national territory. This number of minority groups grew to 53 in 1963, stabilizing at 55 in 1981 when the Gin and **Jino** were added to the list. Since then, the authorized list of 55 *shaoshu minzu*, plus the Han, has served as the basis for all official research and publications on minority nationalities in the PRC.

Research on the broader and more complex topic of social history only started in 1956. Ethnologists, such as Ma Changshu were asked to adhere to the Marxist principles of linear social development. The powerful State Nationalities Affairs Commission was established within the State Council, with a status equivalent to a ministry. Only a few years after its inception, however, the production of serious scholarship on minorities was brought to a standstill with the launch of the Great Leap Forward in 1958, a major lull that was to lasted until 1976 and the end of the Cultural Revolution. These difficult times in recent Chinese history were less than tolerant toward cultural distinction –the Tibet invasion of 1959 is a proof of that—and the global uniformity of all in the People's Republic became a top priority. Official nationality policies from earlier years that insisted on special treatment for minorities on the basis of their distinctiveness were put on hold. Massive Han migration from the overpopulated coastal regions and lowlands into the highlands was promoted and sustained by the national **collectivization** scheme. Radical economic changes to local economies were also pushed forward, often with disastrous results. The Cultural Revolution in particular launched forceful attacks on religious expression. The "Four Old Things" (old thinking, old culture, old customs, and old habits) were actively targeted for deletion, and assimilationism as a state policy was rampant.

With the death of Mao Zedong and advent of the new Deng Xiaoping administration, a certain liberalism toward cultural diversity could flourish again. The "Four Modernizations" were implemented in 1978, followed by the "Open Door" policy one year later. The right of minority nationalities to express and maintain their culture was recognized, or restated, in official texts like the 1982 Constitution (art. 3, 36, 112-120), including the right of self-government in Autonomous Regions and Prefectures—all minority cadres still having, however, to be vetted by the Party. In the 1980s, a revival of interest in minorities occurred through the activities of the Central Institute of National Minorities, particularly its Department of Minority Languages, both founded years earlier but silenced for two decades. A Center for Nationalities Research was established in 1977 at the Academy of Social Sciences, as well as a variety of concomitant official bodies, such as a Nationalities' Literature Committee (1979) within the Association of Chinese Writers and a Department of Nationalities and Education (1981) within the Ministry of Education. Politically speaking, a number of privileges, in the form of positive discrimination, were granted to the *shaoshu minzu*, such as the exemption from laws prohibiting sumptuary expenditures (at funerals for instance), preferential treatment in admission to universities, and the crucial exemption from the national rule of one child per family. The latter does indeed somewhat counter the demographic imbalance regarding the overwhelming majority of the Han. The United Nations estimates that by the year 2050, China's demographic increase to 1.477 billion will be largely created by minority natality.

Today, members of the *shaoshu minzu* can often attend primary school in their home region and listen to radio broadcasts in their own language. But there is still strict surveillance, and sometimes active intervention, regarding the information they receive in these ways. Lower education may be available with local cultural overtones, but the pan-China curriculum is still implemented. Whoever wishes to pursue studies at the next level is made well aware that higher education in China today, as well as career success, requires mastering the Chinese language and gaining an intimate understanding of Chinese society. Such necessities act as powerful incentives for cultural integration of the younger generations into Han society. Indeed, official tolerance only partly masks a national policy of cultural integration. This policy is also visible behind the public promotion of select elements of ethnic exoticism for the booming **tourist** trade.

Only China's minorities dwelling in the highlands of the southwest provinces are given specific attention here. Mountainous southwest China as defined here excludes Tibet (see the introduction) but explicitly comprises the entire provinces of **Yunnan** and **Guizhou**, the south and western highlands of **Sichuan**, and the western highlands of the **Guangxi Zhuang Autonomous Region**. To complement this area, some adjacent highlands are mentioned on occasion, but the provinces they belong to have not been covered extensively. Defined in this way, mountainous southwest China is the primary home to 29 of China's 55 *shaoshu minzu*, to which must be added a significant number of countrywide **Hui** Muslim who have for a long time elected the southwest as their home, as well as countless minority migrants from elsewhere in China. Consequently, indigenous ethnic minority population in the Chinese portion of the **mainland Southeast Asian massif** amounts to 59.7 million, to which an undetermined portion of the 9.8 million Hui became rooted in the south centuries ago must be added. At the end of the day, a grand total of 60 million appears a prudent estimate. A detailed ethnographic map of that southwestern region would show that Han representatives rule the valleys and a large portion of the fertile farmlands, while the non-Han dwell higher up in the valleys, and on the mountain slopes, high plateaus, and mountaintops, with an increased density toward the south and the west as one moves away from the coastal plains and the main areas of Han encroachment. Many of these highland groups straddle the borders with Vietnam, Laos, and Burma. Several can also be found as far south as Thailand, indicating how intimately connected China's southwest ethnic mosaic is to the **Peninsula**.

In addition to the Sinitic branch of the **Sino-Tibetan language family**, whose representatives are found in all urban areas and, for the Hui minority, in smaller and more isolated communities too, Chinese scholars currently recognize four linguistic families indigenous to the southwest: **Tai** (Zhuang-Dong), **Tibeto-Burman**, **Miao-Yao**, and **Mon-Khmer** (**Austro-Asiatic**). The southwest region actually forms a coherent linguistic assemblage with the Peninsula's highlands, one where, due to long exposure to the Chinese and each other's languages, while not necessarily being related genetically, languages share similarities on a significant scale, such as monosyllabism and/or tone-proneness.

CHINESE ACADEMY OF SOCIAL SCIENCES (CASS). Founded in 1977 at a time when economic liberalization began to be fully supported in the People's Republic of China, following the end of the Cultural Revolution (1966–1976), CASS branched off from the Philosophy and Sociology Department within the Chinese Academy of Sciences set up after the communist seizure of power in 1949. With a status equal to that of the Chinese Academy of Sciences, and thus directly under the State Council, CASS has been designed as a research center, with 32 fields and disciplines, including the ethnology of minority nationalities. Within CASS, the Center for Nationalities Research was set up along the lines of the Soviet Union's definition of ethnology, and this new field of inquiry was called *minzuxue*, "minority studies." CASS became one of the main institutional anchorages for foreign scholars wishing to conduct research on **minorities** in China. CASS publishes over 50 academic journals.

CHINESE IDEOGRAMS. Along with Chinese cultural and political influence in the southern highlands, Chinese forms of writing, in particular the Chinese ideogram system, have permeated into several non-Han cultures in the **massif**. All the groups dwelling in the China portion of the massif use these ideograms in one form or another, sometimes in conjunction with a vernacular script. South of China, in the **Peninsula**, some groups under greater Chinese cultural influence have also adopted ideograms. A good example is the **Yao**, whose priests use Chinese ideograms to record genealogies and encode ritual texts.

CHO-RO. A **Mon-Khmer**–speaking group of 14,978 in 1999, considered by some ethnologists to be a subgroup of the **Ma**. The Cho-ro dwell exclusively in Dong Nai province in southern Vietnam, closer to the Mekong Delta and Ho Chi Minh City than any other highland national minority group. This certainly helps explain why the Vietnamese language is widely used among them.

CHRISTIAN MISSIONS. *See* MISSIONARIES.

CHRISTIANITY IN THE MASSIF. *See* MISSIONARIES.

CHUNG-CHIA. *See* BUYI.

CHU-RU. The smallest of four highland **Austronesian**-speaking groups found in Vietnam, the Chu-ru numbered 14,978 at the time of the 1999 national census. Found exclusively in Vietnam's *Tay Nguyen*, where they are considered one of the oldest **aboriginal** peoples, they reside in Lam Dong province, with extensions into neighboring Binh Thuan. Like their Austronesian cousins in the region, the Chu-ru have a matrilineal descent group, which is otherwise rare in the **mainland Southeast Asian massif.**

CHUT. A small **Viet-Muong**–speaking group numbering 3,829 in 1999, the Chut are semisedentarized horticulturalists dwelling in Quang Binh province, in central Vietnam. The group was only formally identified in 1954 by Vietnamese ethnologists.

CLAN. A specific form of family grouping formed by the cluster of several related **lineages**, among which clanic relationship is expressed by a common name, and common ancestry is presumed but not necessarily proven. Clanic groups in the massif are most often patronymic— offspring and their spouses are attached to the male line and bear the male ancestor's surname. Clanic divisions serve in particular to assign religious rituals and to mark the boundaries of the preferred marriage group. One must marry outside his or her patronymic group (this is called clanic exogamy), while marrying within one's clan (clanic endogamy) is perceived very negatively as a violation of the incest taboo. A number of **lineage societies** in mainland Southeast Asia have this intermediary **kinship** feature, which stands between the smaller unit of the lineage and the ethnic group as a whole.

CLOTHES. One of the most distinctive, visible cultural features among highland groups in the massif is their clothing. There is a huge variety of colors, patterns, fabrics, decoration, and techniques that have interested countless observers throughout history. Individuality is so strongly associated with clothing that many groups have been named by outsiders using a clothing particularity: the White and Black Tai from the color of the women's blouses, the Red Karen for their skirts, the Embroided **Hmong** for their intricate needlework, the Long Board Yao after the plank of wood used in the women's headdresses, and many more. Some traits are constant, such as the male apparel being less adorned than the female, the general use of natural material grown locally, and the clothes being hand-made by female members of the group. Women are thus the main producers of clothes, from **hemp** and **indigo** cultivation to weaving, dying, and the final tailoring and decoration. In many groups, one complete set of new clothes per individual is produced each year, generally ready for the **New Year celebrations**, keeping women busy a considerable part of the time.

Beyond these recurrent traits, a huge variety exists. This variability in patterns and decoration in fact negates any serious attempt at classifying ethnic groups by their attire, as has been a rampant—and inadequate—habit for centuries. Moreover, within the same group, sometimes within the same village, and even in the same family, differences are constantly being developed by creative women, who take pride in displaying ever better dexterity and intricate work. Nowadays, however, cheap ready-made cloth and clothes available on the market tend to replace certain elements, sometimes even all of the customary apparel, adding even more to the taxonomic confusion.

The wearing of traditional clothing is often met with derision among more acculturated neighbors outside the village scene, in particular when highlanders attend mixed lowland market towns. To avoid this scornfulness, there is a clear tendency to switch into industrial T-shirts and trousers when venturing to outside locations, and dressing in the customary way has gradually become associated with the village scene. Paradoxically, under socialist regimes in China, Vietnam, and Laos, in which a policy of **selective cultural preservation** prevails, full displays of traditional garments are actually compulsory during annual Minority Festivals. Minority leaders attending Party meetings in towns are also expected to wear their finest apparel to express the support their particular culture receives from the central government. More recently, international demand linked to cultural **tourism** has encouraged many highland groups to sell their worn-out clothes to bulk buyers, or to produce their own variations of traditional pieces to fit the market's demand, thus contributing to altering patterns and styles, but also opening new economic prospects to highland women. *See also* BATIK; JEWELRY.

CO. The Co numbered 27,766 in 1999 and live in southern Vietnam, the only country where they are found. The Co are thus considered **aboriginal** to the area. They dwell mainly in western Quang Ngai province, with extensions into small adjacent segments of the three neighboring provinces Quang Nam, Kon Tum, and Binh Dinh. Like their direct neighbors and relatives the **Xo-dang**, the Co speak a Bahnaric language within the **Mon-Khmer language family**.

CO LAO. One of the smallest of Vietnam's 53 national **minorities,** with a population of 1,865 in 1999. The Co-lao are **Kadai** speakers within the **Tai-Kadai language family**. They can be found in the north of Ha Giang province along the Chinese border, where they were often called Kha-lao by the **Tay** (formerly known as the **Tho**). The bulk of their ethnic group actually lives in China, where they are officially known as the **Gelao**.

CO-HO (KOHO). In 1999, there were officially 128,723 Co-ho in Vietnam's **Central Highlands**. The Co-ho speak a dialect within the **Mon-Khmer** branch of the **Austro-Asiatic language family**. Often called Koho or Sre in colonial texts, they are mainly found in Lam Dong province but are also scattered in the adjacent provinces of Binh Thuan, Ninh Thuan, and Khan Hoa, in the vicinity of the **Ra-glai** and the **Mnong**. Their presence in this territory is ancient, and over the centuries they have exchanged many cultural characteristics with the Austronesian groups who had settled first on this land. The Co-ho are chiefly **animists**, but French Catholic **missionaries** designed a Romanized version of the Co-ho language in the early 20th century while trying to convert them.

COFFEE. One of the most recent and most aggressively promoted **cash crops** implanted in the **Peninsula**, particularly in the **Central Highlands** of southern Vietnam. Thanks to this industrial strategy, Vietnam has become in recent years one of the world's leaders in coffee production and exportation. The potential economic rewards of growing coffee have caused an important migration of lowland settlers into the Central Highlands, particularly from the **Kinh** majority. Non-Kinh indigenous groups have grown resentful of this undesired population movement and denounce the shortage of agricultural land and other resources it has caused. Coffee was an influential factor in the 2001 and 2003 uprisings in Dak Lac province, repressed in secret by the Vietnamese forces.

COFFIN WOOD. One of the most durable and sought-after forest products in the massif, this resinous wood is used to make long-lasting coffins by the groups who bury their dead and worship the ancestors at their graves, chiefly the lowland Chinese and Vietnamese. Coffin wood is sometimes found in a fossilized state, a quality that fetches the highest price in the lowlands for its near infinite durability. Dwellers at high altitudes have long been the chief providers of this resource, standing at the initial end of a long-haul **trade** network involving intermediaries in the mid-lands, eventually reaching the coastal populations. However, recent restrictions on tree felling in most countries of the massif have drastically curtailed this trade, causing a significant drop in earnings for all participants.

COLLECTIVIZATION. Socialist countries in Asia have set in motion major land or agricultural reforms aiming at curtailing or terminating the privileges of the landlord class and at collectivizing agriculture and produce ownership: China (1949–1978), Vietnam (1954 in the North, 1975 in the South, both until the 1990s), and Laos (after 1975), as well as Burma (1962–1980s) and Cambodia (1975–1979). In most cases, and prominently in China and Vietnam, land was appropriated by the socialist state, large landlords were dispossessed, and all former peasants were turned into rural workers in agricultural, labor, or industrial collectives. Such reforms, however, were most effectively implemented in populated lowlands among national majorities receptive to the cultural language used and connected to the mainstream channels of mass communication. On the periphery of the lowlands—and of the nation—its intensity faltered. In remote highlands populated by drastically distinct cultural **minorities**, collectivization only sporadically took root. Officials in Vietnam, for instance, acknowledge today that customary **land tenure** and traditional **barter** of goods and work among kin and neighbors survived undercover in the highlands during the socialist era and are today coming into the open with the dismembering of the collectivist economy and the reinstatement of forms of private land ownership.

COLQUHOUN, ARCHIBALD ROSS (1848–1914). British colonial administrator, traveler, and writer, correspondent in China for *The London Times*, and advocate of the British takeover of upper Burma. He headed an important British exploration mission across the Southeast Asian massif in 1881–1882 to scout the best route for a railway connecting Burma and southern China. His observations, which are also a valuable ethnographic report, are contained in the two volumes of *Across Chrysê: A Journey of Exploration through the South China Border Lands from Canton to Mandalay,* published in 1883.

COMMUNIST INSURGENCY. Considered by the Western powers, the United States in particular, as a threat to the political stability of the region, the rise of communist sympathizers among certain highland groups in south Vietnam, Laos, Thailand, and Cambodia during the **Second Indochina War (1954–1975)** was taken very seriously. This concern triggered the implementation, by the Central Intelligence Agency and the regional governments supporting the anticommunist struggle (the Republic of Vietnam, Cambodia before 1974, monarchist Laos, and Thailand), of "counterinsurgency" programs, undertaken in secret in Cambodia and Laos, these two countries being officially neutral following the 1962 Geneva Agreement. "Counterinsurgency" initiatives also materialized in lowland and highland Thailand, with an important series of measures designed to stop the progress of communist infiltration by isolating and eliminating sympathizers, including the Communist Party of Thailand. After the communist victories in Vietnam, Laos, and Cambodia, Thailand carried on the fight against communist influence on its territory, with U.S. support, for a few more years.

CONDOMINAS, GEORGES (1920–). Probably the most famous French anthropologist of mainland Southeast Asia alive. Georges Condominas has been professor and *directeur d'études* at the *Ecole* *des Hautes Etudes en Sciences Sociales* in Paris since 1960. Born in Vietnam at the time of French Indochina, he studied in France and started his career by studying Vietnam's **Central Highlands** groups. His most renowned book in English is his monograph on the **Mnong** of south Vietnam, first published in French in 1957, titled *Nous avons mangé la forêt de la Pierre-Genie Gôo* [*We Have Eaten the Forest: The Story of a Montagnard Village in the Central Highlands of Vietnam*]. He became interested in **Tai** cultures, which he studied in Laos and Thailand, and published in 1976 a groundbreaking study on the Tai *muang*, "Essai sur l'évolution des systèmes politiques thaïs" ["Essay on the Evolution of Tai Political Systems"].

CONG. A very small **Tibeto-Burman**–speaking group in northern Vietnam, the Cong, numbering 1,676 in 1999, all dwell in a few hamlets on the Chinese border in northern Lai Chau province.

CO-TU. A **Mon-Khmer**–speaking group of central Vietnam belonging to the Katuic branch, the Co-tu (50,458 in 1999) chiefly dwell in the hinterland to the west of Da Nang city, mostly in Quang Nam province, with a notable extension north into Thua Thien-Hue province. They inhabit the river valleys of the Song Giang, Song Cai, and Song Boun particularly. The group extends across the border into Laos, where approximately 17,000 of them live, and where they are known as the **Katu**. The Co-tu are **animists** and remained relatively isolated until the mid-20th century.

COUNTERINSURGENCY. *See* COMMUNIST INSURGENCY.

CUPET, PIERRE-PAUL (1859–1907). French colonial military officer posted in French Indochina starting in 1885. Between 1887 and 1891, Cupet was detached to join diplomat and explorer Auguste Pavie—the Pavie Mission—on a duty to map the southern borders of Laos. His topographic and cartographic contribution to the mission was of great importance. However, ethnographic observations made during his travels are also of value. They have been collected in the book *Voyages au Laos et chez les sauvages du sud-est de l'Indo-Chine* [*Travels in Laos and among Savages in the Southeast of Indo-China*] published in 1900, constituting volume 3 of the Pavie Mission publications.

CURRENCY. There is no common currency among the peoples sharing the **mainland Southeast Asian massif**; instead, the national currency within each of the six countries sharing these highlands is the legal tender. Over time and across space, however, an amazing number of objects, status symbols, produce, metal bars, coins, banknotes, and, in the collectivized economies, coupons, have been used by an array of groups in numerous political and economic circumstances. Attempting to list these currencies is a task far beyond the format of this dictionary. For instance, such a discussion would have to include considerations on **opium** used as money, or analyze mixed local economies using simultaneously and interchangeably silver bars, Chinese copper coins, Mexican silver dollars with Siamese punches, French piasters, Soviet rubles, and socialist coupons. Nevertheless, on a general level, it can be stated that except in rare cases of strong central government, such local or regional currencies have never been universal; that is, they were neither used in all transactions, nor valid across the whole range of possible goods, nor recognized everywhere in the massif. Equivalence always has to be calculated to mutual satisfaction in cash or in kind according to the desirability and quality of the goods on offer, their relative rarity, and the various currencies available or recognized at that moment. Residual use of some of these ancient currencies still exists, notably silver bars and silver coins, often preferred for ritual transactions, such as payment of the **brideprice**. *See also* BARTER.

– D –

DAI. A minority nationality of China composed of a cluster of **Tai**-speaking groups. The Dai, who numbered 839,797 in 2000, are primarily **Buddhist** and use a script akin to Siamese (or **Thai**). Dai is in fact a derivative and generic label (also written Pa-Y, **Pai-i**) for the Tai-speaking groups of south and southwestern **Yunnan**, who call themselves specific names, such as **Lue**—numerically the most important component of the Dai group—Nua, Baiyi, Tayok, or Chinese **Shan**, and whose **languages**, despite their proximity, are not always mutually intelligible. Little Sinicized, the Dai constellation of China has closer cultural, historical, religious, and linguistic bonds with the Tai-speaking groups of Burma, Thailand, and Laos than with those in the east, such as the **Zhuang** or **Dong**.

The Dai *muang* in Yunnan were certainly in contact with the **Nan Chao kingdom** (eighth to 13th centuries A.D.), probably more as vassal **feudal** states than as core components of it, the latter being an early hypothesis now largely discarded. Theravada **Buddhism** was, in the process, superimposed on an important **animistic** tradition. In terms of official residence today, the name of the Dai is most directly associated in China with two **Autonomous Prefectures** (*zizhizhou*): Dehong and Xishuangbanna, in west and south Yunnan, respectively. However, their largest numbers are found in Xishuangbanna, which lies at the heart of the longtime Lue domain formerly known in Tai as **Sip Song Phan Na**, a powerful federation of Tai *muang* analogous to the ancient federations of **Lan Na**, Lan Xang, or **Sip Song Chau Tai**. Xishuangbanna is also where national and international **tourists** have flocked in large numbers over the last decade, particularly Thai visitors from Thailand in search of a common historical past. A pleasant tropical ecosystem and the fine vernacular and religious architecture of the Lue also contribute to the region's popularity.

DAO. The official spelling in Vietnam for the group otherwise known as **Yao** or **Mien** in neighboring countries. Distributed in Vietnam above 300 meters all across the north of the country, the Dao numbered 620,538 in 1999, chiefly located in the province of Ha Giang (92,524), with remaining populations rather evenly spread among Lao Cai, Tuyen Quang, Yen Bai, Quang Ninh, Lai Chau, Bac Kan, Cao Bang, Lang Son, and Thai Nguyen. A majority of the Yao of Vietnam call themselves Kim Mun or Kim Mien, the "Red Mien." Before and during colonial times, the generic ethnonym used to refer to the Dao of Vietnam was Man, with a rich variety of subgroups, such as Man-ta-pan, Man Lanten, Man Coc, Man Sung, etc.

In Vietnamese, the spelling *Dao* contributes to a lasting confusion among Vietnamese and non-Vietnamese experts alike. This is due to discrepancies between the Roman alphabet and its 17th-century, Vietnamese adaptation devised by early French **missionaries**, known as *quoc ngu* (the "national language"). In *quoc ngu*, letters "D/d" are different from letters "Đ/đ," the latter representing the hard "d" as in English. "D/d" in Vietnamese is pronounced in two different ways depending on regional dialectical penchant. In the south of Vietnam, it is pronounced like "y" in English, thus rendering the official Vietnamese name *Dao* as "Yao," fitting the usual pronunciation of this ethnonym outside Vietnam. However, ethnologists working on the Yao are based chiefly in the north of Vietnam, where "D/d" reads like "z" in English. So there, the official ethnonym *Dao* is pronounced "Zao." This disparity, combined with the prominent position northern ethnologists occupy as producers of scientific knowledge on **minorities** in Vietnam, explains why in publications abroad that are based on Vietnamese ethnology, from anthropology books to development reports to international **tourist** guidebooks, the ethnonym is spelled variously as *Dao* (and thus mistakenly pronounced with a hard "d" by Western readership), *Zao*, or even *Dzao*, all equally incorrect. "Yao" would be preferable.

DE BEAUCLAIR, INEZ (1897–1981). German ethnologist associated with the Institute of Ethnology of Academia Sinica in Taiwan, who published several scholarly articles on the Kam, **Hmong**, and **Miao** in China, as well as *Tribal Cultures of Southwest China* (1970).

DEO VAN TRI (KAM-OUM, KHAMHUM) (ca. 1840–1909). Deo Van Tri was the Vietnamese name for Kam-Oum, a famous White Tai leader from the Deo family, which ruled the **Sip Song Chau Tai** in Tonkin at the time of the French conquest and until the 1950s. While his father Kam-Sen (Deo Van Seng) was still the leader of the Sip Song Chau Tai, Kam-Oum made a name for himself by associating with the **Black Flag** rebels of Liu Yin Fu (Liu Yongfu), based in the border trading post of Lao Cai on the Red River. Commissioned by the Vietnamese, both Kam-Oum and Liu Yin Fu led armed parties in fighting against the French conquerors. Arguably, Kam-Oum's most famous act at the time was to ambush and kill French lieutenant Francis Garnier, the explorer of the Mekong and short-lived conqueror of Tonkin during the siege of Hanoi in 1873. In the 1880s, Kam-Oum succeeded his father. Later in that decade, he seized an opportunity to associate again with the Black Flags and, under a joint command, sought personal revenge on the Siamese, who had just kidnapped three of his kin in an effort to snatch the Sip Song Chau Tai from the Vietnamese orbit and force it into paying **tribute** to Siam instead. A party of Tai and Yunnanese Black Flags pursued the Siamese party and went on to sack Luang Phrabang in 1887 but failed to recover the hostages. On their way back the Kam family used its new strength to win over several other White and Black Tai principalities (*muang*) and attach them to the Sip Song Chau Tai. The Kam family was thus at the head of a large highland territory lying between the upper Red River Valley and the Laotian border, drained by the Black (Da) and Ma Rivers, and revolving around the towns of Muang Lai (Lai Chau) and Muang Thanh (Dien Bien Phu).

Then Kam-Oum skillfully made a political volte-face and managed to earn respect and obtain privileges from the French conquerors. He achieved this through a personal relationship with French diplomat Auguste Pavie. Willing to win over this powerful foe to the French cause (Pavie was in Luang Phrabang during the sack of 1887 and had had to flee for his life), the diplomat negotiated with Siam for the liberation of the imprisoned Kam brothers. He personally escorted two of them back to Muang Thanh, where in 1889 he signed with Kam-Oum—thereafter officially known as Deo Van Tri—a protectorate treaty that ensured the Sip Song Chau Tai's quasi-total independence as long as it was faithful to France. Deo Van Tri became a staunch ally and immediately collaborated with **Pierre Lefèvre-Pontalis** in the exploration of northern Laos for the **Pavie Mission**. Deo Van Tri reigned over his domain until his death in 1909. His heirs carried on ruling their domain until the final son, Deo Van Long, was removed to Hanoi by the French on the eve of the battle of **Dien Bien Phu** in 1954.

DERUNG (DRUNG). According to Chinese linguists, the Derung of China (7,426 in 2000) are part of the **Jingpo** (Kachinic) branch within the **Tibeto-Burman language family**. This very small group dwells in the upper reaches of the Nu (Salween) River in extreme northwestern **Yunnan** close to their relatives the **Nu**, in the Gongshan Drung and Nu Autonomous County. The Derung have long been under the political and cultural influence of powerful **feudal** neighbors, such as the **Naxi** and the Tibetans. Chinese ethnologists consider the Derung one of the "most primitive tribal groups" in the country.

DIEN BIEN PHU, BATTLE OF. The battle of Dien Bien Phu was fought in the spring of 1954. It turned out to be the decisive communist victory that drove the French out of their colony of Indochina. The role played by highland **minorities** in that decisive clash, however, has received little attention.

The Dien Bien Phu plateau and town, in northwest Vietnam, were acknowledged by the French during the colonial period to be part of the Tai (**Thai**) Federation, centered on the town of Lai Chau, and therefore falling into the White Thai domain. The upland valleys that the plateau controlled were a strategic gateway to the valley of the Nam Ou River in Laos, the most direct route to Luang Phrabang and the Mekong River. The area was also the most agriculturally productive in the Federation, for both **rice** and **opium**. Nonetheless, traditional sovereignty over Dien Bien Phu and its riches was claimed by Black Thai leaders settled in its surroundings as well as in the Son La area, on whom the White Thai supremacy had been imposed thanks to the colonial power's complacency. White Thai leader Deo Van Long simply removed the local Black Thai leader, Lo Van Hac, and installed his own son in his place. French support for this White Thai hegemonic power over Dien Bien Phu proved ill-advised and contributed to alienating the Black Thai from the colonial cause. The latter's main leaders joined Lo Van Hac and retaliated by defecting to the communist Viet Minh in the early 1950s, paving the way for the coming military debacle.

After the French High Command in Hanoi had chosen the coveted Dien Bien Phu plateau for holding the battle and swiftly gained it back from the Viet Minh in late 1953, they then decided to abandon less well-defended Lai Chau and repatriate all its inhabitants to Dien Bien Phu to beef up the local defense. White Thai leader Deo Van Long had no choice but to agree to this evacuation; he himself was flown to Hanoi with his court and all the wealth he could carry. He was never again to see his domain, which thus came to an abrupt end.

This evacuation was a poor political decision that alienated most Federated Thai, who saw it as a humiliation and who consequently were to only half-heartedly support the French war effort—while nevertheless providing, along with a few representatives of other highland groups, nearly one-quarter of the French troops on location when the battle of Dien Bien Phu started. Nevertheless, many retreated to the mountains or simply defected to the Viet Minh. When the battle of Dien Bien Phu finally took place in spring 1954, numerous Black Thai from Son La and many White Thai, **Hmong, Yao**, and **Khmu** from **Sip Song Chau Tai**, not counting the **Tho (Tay)** and other **Montagnards** from east of the Red River, enrolled in the Viet Minh forces making themselves available to the communists. By the thousands, they helped to build and support a massive and totally unpredicted artillery pounding, encircling and undermining the French entrenched camp, and were a decisive factor in tipping the balance in favor of the communist forces.

DIGUET, ÉDOUARD (1861–1924). French colonial military officer posted in Tonkin (north Vietnam) from 1884 to 1902. He wrote several monographs on Indochinese linguistics and the ethnography of highland peoples, including *Étude de la langue Thaï, précédée d'une notice sur les races des hautes régions du Tonkin* [*A Study of Thai Language*] (1895) and *Les Montagnards du Tonkin* [*Montagnards of Tonkin*] (1908), both yet to be translated into English.

DIQU. In China, an administrative unit best translated as "prefecture." *Diqu* are a subdivision of the province (*sheng*), and further subdivide into "counties" (*xian*). There are two categories of prefectures. One is the Autonomous Prefecture (*zizhizhou*), found in remote areas and generally inhabited by minority nationalities. The number of *zizhizhou* is slowly decreasing in favor of the second category, the prefecture-level city (*dijishi*).

D'OLLONE, HENRI (1868– ?). Henri Marie Gustave D'Ollone, a French aristocrat with the title of viscount, headed a scientific mission bearing his name from 1906 to 1909, which endeavored to study the non-**Han** groups inside China. The expedition went from Hanoi in Vietnam to Mongolia, crossing the entire **mainland Southeast Asian massif**. The proceedings, which were of definite linguistic, historical, and ethnographic value, were made public in seven volumes, originally published in French in 1912, translated in English as *In Forbidden China: The D'Ollone Mission 1906–1909 China—Tibet—Mongolia*.

DONG (KAM, TUNG, TUNG-CHIA). Dong is the official Chinese name for this substantial and northeasternmost **Tai**-speaking highland minority group in China, who numbered a substantial 2,960,293 in 2000. The Dong call themselves Kam, and they are often referred to in the literature as Tung or Tung-chia. They are indigenous to a rugged territory at the junction of **Guizhou** (where half of them live), Hunan, and Guangxi. They have long practiced irrigated **rice** cultivation supplemented by cotton, their main **cash crop**. In cultural terms, the Dong have borrowed significantly from their neighbors the **Miao**. Due to a degree of isolation, their language drifted significantly from their other Tai-speaking neighbors, such as the **Zhuang** and the **Buyi**, with the exception of the **Sui**, with whom linguists cluster them in the Kam-Sui subgroup of **Tai-Kadai languages**. The

Kam language probably holds the world record for the number of tones: dialects of Kam are believed to have as many as 15. The central government designed a Romanized Dong written language in 1958. In the same decade, the Longsheng Autonomous County of the Dong, Zhuang, Miao, and **Yao** was founded, followed by the establishment of the Sanjiang Dong Autonomous County in Guangxi, the Tongdao Dong Autonomous County in Hunan, the Miao-Dong Autonomous Prefecture in southeastern Guizhou, and the Xinhuang Dong Autonomous County in Hunan.

In recent years, the Dong have become the object of growing **tourist** attention thanks to their spectacular vernacular architecture, notably the celebrated drum towers and covered bridges. A scholarly collection of articles on the Dong/Kam has recently been published, edited by Norman D. Geary et al.: *The Kam People of China: Turning Nineteen* (2003).

D'ORLÉANS, HENRI (1867–1901). French aristocrat Prince Henri Philippe Marie D'Orléans made several exploratory voyages in and around the **mainland Southeast Asian massif** between 1889 and 1901. His best-known publication, *Du Tonkin aux Indes, Janvier 1895–Janvier 1896. [From Tonkin to India by the Sources of the Irawadi]* (1898), details his 12 months of travels and reports on a number of highland groups he encountered during his trip.

DOUDART DE LAGRÉE AND GARNIER EXPEDITION (1866–1868). French officers Ernest Doudart de Lagrée (1823–1868) and Francis Garnier (1839–1873) were the two leaders of an exploratory voyage up the Mekong River made on behalf of the French colonial authorities, and aiming at assessing the river's navigability as a commercial and strategic waterway into **Yunnan**. The expedition helped disqualify the Mekong for such purposes. However, the expedition left written accounts and diaries, reporting on, among other things, encounters with highland peoples in the **mainland Southeast Asian massif**. The accounts were published in 1873 with a lavish collection of color sketches of such peoples (Francis Garnier, "*Album pittoresque*," 1873, first part of *Atlas du voyage d'exploration en Indo-Chine*), and this publication is one of the earliest of such documents produced by Europeans in upland **Indochina** and southwest China.

DOURNES, JACQUES (1922–1993). Young Jacques Dournes went to Saigon in 1946 as a missionary with the Paris Society of Foreign Missions (MEP, *Société des Missions Étrangères de Paris*). From 1947 to 1954 he was posted among the **Hre** (Sre), a **Mon-Khmer** group located in the **Central Highlands**. Using a pen name, Dam Bo, he published during this period his first texts on the Indochinese **Montagnards**, including his oft-quoted *Populations montagnardes du Sud-Indochinois* [*Mountain Peoples of South Indochina*] (1950). In 1954, he was sent back to Paris as a reproach for devoting more time to ethnographic research than to his missionary duties. In fact, Dournes had also started to antagonize powerful French planters who, according to him, abused the local minority labor. He was allowed back into the new Republic of Vietnam in 1955 and was sent to work among the **Austronesian Gia-rai** (whom he called Jörai). Over the next 14 years, neglecting any attempt to convert his hosts, he devoted all his time to collecting a formidable mass of information on Gia-rai culture and oral tradition, which he recorded, transcribed, and translated into French. In 1969, he was made redundant by the new missionary society assigned to that region in replacement of the MEP, the *Congrégation du Très Saint Rédempteur* (CSsR).

Realizing that he had actually been excluded because of his lack of enthusiasm for conversion, Dournes withdrew from his religious pledge in 1969 and returned to France. Upset by the war in Vietnam, he put his firsthand knowledge of the Gia-rai to work. He obtained a Ph.D. in ethnology in Paris in 1971 and was recruited by the French National Center for Scientific Research (CNRS) in 1973. He retired in 1987 and died in France in 1993. During his 25 years of residence in Vietnam's Central Highlands and his late scientific career, Jacques Dournes made a unique contribution to Gia-rai ethnohistory, ethno-botany, mythology, linguistics, and oral literature. His list of publications exceeds 250 entries, including major works, such as *Pötao, une théorie du pouvoir chez les Indochinois jörai* [*Potao: A Theory of Power among the Jorai Indochinese*] (1977) and *Forêt, femme, folie: une traversée de l'imaginaire jörai* [*Forest, Woman, Madness*] (1978).

DRY RICE. A type of **rice** mainly cultivated by groups residing at higher altitudes, where either terraces are difficult to carve out of steep slopes, or the lack of land ownership titles obstructs such conversion. Relying chiefly on rain water or, at best, occasional watering from mountain creeks or springs, dry rice yields considerably less per hectare than varieties of wet rice and is thus seen as the less attractive alternative for peasants. For nomads or seminomads, on the other hand, it has rightly been retained as the type of grain crop best adapted to mobility.

– E –

ECOLE FRANÇAISE D'EXTRÊME-ORIENT (EFEO). The EFEO is a scholarly body attached to the French Ministry of Education that specializes in philological, historical, archeological, and, residually, ethnological studies in several Asian countries, including the six countries covered in this dictionary. A product of colonial times, the EFEO was set up in Hanoi in 1899 with the mission to study Vietnamese and Cambodian high civilization. In the course of its existence, however, it was rapidly solicited by the Indochinese colonial authorities to conduct surveys of highland populations in French Indochina and southwest China, including **Hainan** Island. A number of early collaborators of the EFEO produced important ethnological reports, surveys, and publications on peoples of the highlands. These include military men—Lieutenant Emile Lunet de Lajonquière, Lieutenant-Colonel **Auguste Bonifacy**, Colonel **Henri Roux**—Father **François Savina**, and scholars André Georges Haudricourt, Henri Maspéro, **Guy Moréchand**, Charles Robequain, and Paul Mus. In its main publication series, *Bulletin de l'EFEO*, numerous works were published by these authors on the linguistics, history, and ethnology of highlanders in French Indochina, including the collective *Ethnographie indochinoise* [*Indochinese Ethnography*] (1921) and the excellent *Carte ethnolinguistique de l'Indochine* [*Ethnolinguistic Map of Indochina*] (1949). Forced to leave Laos, Cambodia, and Vietnam during the Indochina Wars, the EFEO had to wait until the 1990s before political conditions improved and small offices could be reopened in these countries. In Hanoi, its splendid former headquarter building now hosts the National Vietnam History Museum.

E-DE (RHADE). The second most numerous of only four highland **Austronesian**-speaking groups in the **mainland Southeast Asian massif**. In Vietnam, there were 270,348 E-de in 1999. Known to most outside observers as the **Rhade**, they live mainly in Dak Lak province (249,096) just south of the **Gia-rai**, with extensions into southwest Phu Yen and northwest Kanh Hoa provinces. An unknown number of E-de also dwell across the border in eastern Cambodia, though statistics there do not explicitly account for them. The E-de have a matrilineal **kinship** system. Like most other Austronesian and **Mon-Khmer** groups dwelling in the **Central Highlands**, they have long relied on **swiddening**, and they are **animists**.

During the **Second Indochina War (1954–1975)**, the E-de and other ethnic groups in the *Tay Nguyen* were implacably drawn into the fighting between north and south Vietnamese forces. Due to their strategic geographical location, much missionary, military, and intelligence attention was paid to them by the Americans. During the 1960s and 1970s, largely under the influence of the war agenda, and especially in reaction to the **Strategic Hamlets** initiative of President Diem, E-de leaders were active in setting up and running the "United Struggle Front for the Oppressed Races" (**FULRO**) ethno-nationalist movement. By the end of the war in 1975, many among these leaders had to flee the country and sought refuge in the West, chiefly in the United States. This is one of the reasons why today the Vietnamese authorities keep the E-de in constant check, especially in connection with the outside influence from U.S.-based Christian **missionaries** and former FULRO guerrillas still exerting, from exile, political influence on their former community.

ELEPHANTS. Domesticated elephants, ordinary or albino, are a fairly common sight in the lowlands of most countries in the Southeast Asian **Peninsula**. In the past, when capturing and taming them was still a flourishing activity, colonial observers reported that elephant **caravans** were often set up. For a long time elephants were, and some still are, used in the lumber industry. In the highlands of western Thailand and eastern Burma, a number of **Karen** have long specialized as caretakers, or *mahut*, for domesticated animals involved in logging. However, performing tricks and tours for **tourists** has now become the primary occupation for many of them. Nowadays, wild elephants are an ever less common sight in the massif, where they have retreated to the remaining forested highlands, their refuge. In southeast Laos and southwest Vietnam, where a few herds are regularly spotted causing occasional damage to local farming operations, elephants have been included in the ritual life of several **Mon-Khmer** and **Austronesian** groups. In northern Laos, where wild herds are now rare, the Khmu Rok and **Lamet** still include carved figures of elephants in the decoration of their **rice** granaries.

ELOPEMENT. *See* KIDNAPPING OF THE BRIDE.

EMBROIDERY. Decorating **clothes** with silk thread is a practice found in a large proportion of the groups in the massif. Patterns, colors, and stitches vary greatly between groups, from only a decorative touch for some groups to extreme intricacy among some others, such as several **Yao** subgroups. Embroidery adorns the clothes of the young and the old, both men and women, although female garments tend to be more ornamented. Stitching is performed by women who take great pride in this skill, passing it on to the next generation. Embroidery, along with clothes processing, can take up most of their time and is thus often seen by outside development agents as counterproductive. Under this modernizing influence, compounded with the fact that machine-made alternatives are now readily available on the market, the skill of high-land embroidery is disappearing, freeing women's time for other tasks. Nevertheless, against that trend, in recent years **tourist** demand for colorful highland garments in the entire massif has encouraged customary embroidery, often seen by international visitors as the most striking element of highland attire.

– F –

FAYDANG LOBLIAYAO (1910–1986). An official **Hmong** hero of the **Lao** Revolution. Born in Xiengkhuang province in the Lo clan, under the French his family had been given the position of *tasseng*, or district administrator, in the Nong Het region. His family having been dis-missed by colonial authorities in the late 1930s, Faydang and his brother Nyiavu joined the *Lao Issara* (Free Lao) resistance during World War II. They led **Hmong** guerrillas fighting against the French and their al-lies in Xiengkhuang province during all of the **First Indochina War** (1946–1954) and played a political role with the Pathet Lao during the **Second Indochina War (1954–1975)**. In 1950, Faydang participated in the first Congress of the Free Laos Front and was made minister in the Resistance Government under Prince Suphanuvong, as well as a member of its Central Committee in the capacity of representative of the *Lao Sung*, or Upland Lao. In 1961, Faydang moved his base from Xiengkhuang town to Nong Het, where he collaborated with his Hmong military commander, General Foung Tongsee Yang, otherwise known by his Lao name, Paseut. When the Lao People's Democratic Republic was promulgated in 1975, Faydang took office as vice president of the Lao Front for National Reconstruction and was given one of the four ceremonial positions of vice president of the Supreme People's Assembly alongside two other **minority** leaders, Sisomphone Lovansay (Tai Dam) and **Sithon Kommadam (Alak)**. Faydang's younger brother Nyiavu Lobliayao was appointed chairman of the Nationalities Committee. In the last few years of his life, Faydang returned to live as a farmer in his native Nong Het, where he died in 1986.

This is an interesting example of a family feud taking historic proportions. Faydang's father (known as Lo Blia Yao, from the Lo clan) had experienced some differences with his son-in-law and secretary, Ly Foung of the Ly clan (father of **Touby Lyfoung**). In 1938, differences turned to distrust when the eldest of the Lobliayao brothers was demoted as *tasseng* of Nong Het and replaced by the older Ly Foung, thanks to the latter's previous experience in the position. Ly Foung died the following year, and Touby Lyfoung got the job passed on to him, against the will of his cousin Faydang, also a contender for the post. When the Japanese came to **Indochina** in 1941, a bitter Faydang sent his Hmong supporters to assist the Japanese and build an armed opposition to the French, as well as to his cousin Touby and the Ly clan altogether. During all of the First Indochina War, the feud between the Lo and Ly clans was further fueled by the opposition between the Communist and Royalist parties, respectively supported by each of them, and for which they fought. Each Hmong leader was promoted on his side, commissioned to recruit more Hmong in Xiengkhuang and fight those taking the other side. Faydang was only moderately successful in rallying his countrymen to the revolutionary cause, while Touby had more success, thanks in large part to the major logistical and financial assistance he received from the American military and, at least for a while, from (General) **Vang Pao**, the highest ranking military leader of the royalist Hmong. Upon the communist victory of 1975, Faydang and the Lo clan were rewarded by the Pathet Lao for their indefatigable support, while Touby and his supporters, more numerous, had to quietly disband into the countryside or flee to Thailand. But the **clanic** feud did not end with the war and lives on through members of the Ly clan participating in a Lao Government in Exile (chiefly in the United States), while the Lo in Laos still actively support the socialist state.

FEI XIAOTONG (FEI HSIAO T'UNG) (1910–). A **Han** Chinese born in Wujiang County, Jiangsu Province, Fei Xiaotong is probably the most famous of China's anthropologists. Fei trained in sociology in Beijing before obtaining his Ph.D. at the University of London in 1938 under Bronislaw Malinowski's guidance. He then taught for several years at **Yunnan** University, then at Tsinghua University in Beijing, before cofounding there in 1951 the National Institute for **Minorities**, where he became professor. During the dark years of the Great Leap Forward and the Cultural Revolution (1958–1976), he was pushed to the sidelines and had to take on various jobs to ensure his livelihood. He came back into the public eye when the Open Door Policy was launched in 1977, and has been awarded many honors since. He has held a number of political positions, including vice minister of the Nationality Affairs Commission, deputy director of the Nationalities Research Institute, and director of the Sociological Research Institute, the latter two within the **Chinese Academy of Social Sciences**. He presided over the China Sociological Society and was a deputy to two of the China People's Congresses. Fei has published extensively on Chinese peasant life, countryside societies, rural economies, and ethnic minorities. His works have been instrumental in laying a foundation for the development of sociological and anthropological studies in China.

FEUDAL SOCIETIES IN THE MASSIF. Feudal societies were widespread in Asia's lowland prior to the implantation of European colonialism. Broadly speaking, in a feudal system, an elite controls the means of production, such as the land and the irrigation systems, and crucially, also the labor force: the peasant majority. Feudal lords ensure the maintenance of their domination over their peasant masses by setting up and controlling repressive forces, such as the military and the police, and enforcing widespread taxation on their vassals and feudatories, including rent on the land. Feudalism, which was widespread in medieval Europe, has also been the dominant social system in all coastal parts of mainland Southeast Asia for centuries, with monarchs and emperors ruling the lowland masses while vying with each other. Higher in altitude, in the **mainland Southeast Asian massif**, a number of societies also operated as feudal states. These included virtually all **Tai**-speaking groups via the particular feudal entity called the *muang*

(**Shan**, **Lao**, **Lue**, **Thai**, Siamese, **Nung**, **Dai**, **Bai**, **Dong**, **Zhuang**, and others) and a few **Tibeto-Burman** groups (**Naxi**, Bai, and **Yi** in particular). These societies were primarily found in the midaltitude regions of southwest China, northeastern Burma, northern Vietnam, and northern Laos. Feudalism in both the lowlands and highlands was nominally abolished at the time of European colonization, but not until the second half of the 20th century, with the socialist takeovers in China, Vietnam, Laos, and for a time Burma and Cambodia, combined with the end of absolute monarchy in Thailand in 1932, was it actively dismembered and the privileges of the feudal elite abolished.

FIREARMS. Firearms have been used by highland groups for a few centuries. In peacetime, firearms have been used principally for **hunting**, though they could also be employed to settle accounts between foes, or for banditry. However, several well-known **minority** resistance movements in Laos and Burma in particular, including highland groups, such as the **Wa**, **Karen**, **Shan**, and **Hmong**, make extensive use of traditional and modern firearms alike to oppose central governments and push their political agenda. This might also be the case in China and Vietnam, although incidents there do not reach the public ear. Conversely, government-armed minority militia set up as counterinsurgency forces in the highlands are also a cause for many more arms to circulate there, adding to the availability of ammunition and rifle parts in remote areas.

The firearm most common in the massif throughout history, and the one still preferred today by the average highland agriculturalist, is the homemade musket. This is a very simple rifle using gunpowder fed through the mouth of the barrel, firing bullets made of lead, stone, steel, or any other suitable material. The reason for the lasting attractiveness of the musket is that it is generally legal and much cheaper to obtain and operate than industrial rifles. Muskets have been and still are routinely made by highland **blacksmiths**. For such precision crafting, plates of discarded steel brought from the lowlands are used for the rifle mechanism, and five- to six-foot rods of either round or octagonal circumference are processed into barrels. These are painstakingly pierced, manually. The woodwork is carved out of local trees, and a cone of bear skin completes the apparatus, slipped over the well-greased mechanism to keep it dry and avoid firing a shot by mistake—muskets are routinely kept loaded in case of emergency. Short versions also exist in the shape of handguns and pistols, chiefly used in traps for large animals.

Despite industrial firearms having been available in the uplands for at least a century and a half, through legal **trade** or underground networks, national laws in most countries sharing the massif prohibit ownership or limit this right to a small number of highlanders. As a consequence, most of the time when modern weaponry is found in the hands of farmers in the mountains, it has been illicitly diverted from European, U.S., or local military supply and was intended either for official or insurgent fighters. The region has indeed been flooded with a variety of firearms during the rebellions of the 19th century in southwest China and subsequent independence and revolutionary wars of the 20th century in the whole massif. These conflicts have also contributed to spreading the knowledge and direct experience of such weapons among highlanders drafted by all factions.

FIRST INDOCHINA WAR (1946–1954). The name used in the international community of scholars to designate the war between Ho Chi Minh's Viet Minh nationalist and communist forces and the French colonial forces in Vietnam, Laos, and Cambodia. The war was won by the Viet Minh forces at the battle of **Dien Bien Phu** in April 1954. The conflict was officially ended in July 1954 by the Geneva Agreements, which divided Vietnam in two (north and south) and acknowledged independent Laos and Cambodia. The so-called Vietnam War that followed has accordingly been named the **Second Indochina War (1954–1975)**, while the Third Indochina War (1979–1989) refers to the Vietnamese invasion and occupation of Cambodia.

FISHING. Living away from the sea, uplanders in the **mainland Southeast Asian massif** only fish in fresh water. Small fish, shellfish, and turtles are caught in streams by hand, with fixed or handheld rattan traps, small nets, and sometimes fishing lines; shot at with spears, arrows, or crossbows; or, in more recent times, stunned with explosives, especially on larger watercourses or lakes. On lakes Erh Hai in **Yunnan** and Inle in Burma, and the Nam Ngum and the Hoa Binh reservoirs in Laos and Vietnam, such techniques as large nets and domesticated fishing birds—cormorants and hawks—are also used. Increasingly, fish ponds are being installed in remote highland communities thanks to national schemes supported by international aid agencies, such as UNICEF. Sadly, even if the strategy works well in the lowlands, the high altitude, combined with the lack of know-how on the part of the highland beneficiaries, often make these ill-adapted initiatives short-lived.

"FLAG" ARMIES. In the second half of the 19th century, during major rebellions flaring up in southern China, large numbers of defeated antiimperial troops from southern China entered the north of French Indochina—today's Laos and Vietnam—to seek refuge, loot, pillage, or continue the resistance from across the border. Although precise statistics on this flow of people are practically nonexistent, it is generally believed that these incursions have been a major vehicle of immigration for a number of highland ethnic groups found today in the **Peninsula**'s highlands.

Colonial observers interviewing highland elders report that from the 1860s onward, several thousand troops from the "Flag" armies were seen entering North Vietnam from **Yunnan**. Some witnesses in highland northern Vietnam remembered the violent clashes with those Chinese intruders, particularly in the upper Clear (Lo) River valley. In the **Sip Song Chau Tai** in Tonkin (northern Vietnam) and Xiengkhuang province in Laos, inhabitants witnessed hordes of troops from China belonging to the so-called Black, Yellow, White, and Red Flag armies, fighting their way through the mountain ranges while fleeing from Imperial troops in the north. These rebels were a composite of ethnicities, the most important probably being **Hui** Muslim Chinese, with the **Han** Chinese possibly coming second. These rebels were accompanied by members of a number of different other mountain ethnicities, many of whom fled China permanently to settle in more peaceful sections of the massif. The largest of these waves of migration appears to have taken place in 1868, after the Tai Ping rebellion was crushed in southern China. As an example, it has been reported that in this wave more than 10,000 **Hmong** from China migrated to Vietnam from Yunnan and Guangxi, to establish themselves in the provinces of Ha Giang, Lao Cai, Lai Chau, Son La, and Nghia Lo, some reaching as far as Thanh Hoa and Nghe An. In the 1890s, the bulk of the "Flag" armies were permanently expelled to China from northern French Indochina by colonial troops posted along the Chinese border.

FOREST PRODUCT COLLECTION. The oldest forms of **trade** between highlanders, and between them and the outside world, included forest products. The gathering and exchange of specific biological articles has long been a constitutive part of the highland economy. It has been a primary activity for collectors, such as the **Khmu**, **Hani**, **Lolo**, **Yao**, **Hmong**, **Lamet**, **Derung**, **Kachin**, and many others, or a secondary one via profits made as intermediaries, such as the **Shan**, White and Black Tai, **Hui**, **Lue**, **Muong**, **Bai**, and several other trading groups. The most important items in this exchange system are **coffin wood**; medicinal and edible plants; rare live animals, such as song birds for pets; and dead animals, such as snakes, bears, deer, and others, for either the flesh or body parts in demand as food, medicine, ritual implements, or ornaments. Growing restrictions on gathering forest products have been implemented by national governments concerned with wildlife protection and biodiversity conservation. These controls have severely curtailed this source of income for the forest dwellers and their trade intermediaries. Illegal trade networks do persist, however, as well as cross-border **smuggling**.

FULRO (FRONT UNIFIÉ POUR LA LIBÉRATION DES RACES OPPRIMÉES). Also known as *Front unifié de Lutte des Races opprimée,* the "United Struggle Front for the Oppressed Races" was created in 1964 in the ranks of the U.S. Army Special Forces in the Republic of Vietnam. Under American guidance, it became the most important "**Montagnard**" autonomist and anticommunist movement. Its founder was **Rhade (E-de)** leader Y Bham Enuol. Posing as the representative of the interests of the south Vietnamese mountain **minorities**, including **Khmer** and **Cham** lowland minorities in Vietnam, and opposed to communist propaganda as much as to south Vietnamese bullying, FULRO for 10 years played a key political role in the **Central Highlands** in the course of the **Second Indochina War (1954–1975)** and was used as a channel for the expression of Montagnard ethnonationalism. FULRO's political and military resistance to the communist state after the 1975 reunification was greatly diminished by the departure of its main leaders to the United States, and it slowly faded away, until the final armed group surrendered in Cambodia in 1992. The last refugee guerrilla contingent of FULRO arrived in the United States late that same year, where, it must be noted, it was welcomed with military honors by U.S. authorities. In the United States today, FULRO activists are lobbying vigorously from their North Carolina base to influence the American and Vietnamese governments and promote ethno-nationalism in Vietnam's Central Highlands. This is cause for the Vietnamese authorities to keep a vigilant eye on any expression of defiance in that region, in particular among the E-de of Dak Lak.

– G –

GELAO (KELAO). In China, mountainous northwest **Guizhou** was home in 2000 to a sizeable 579,357 speakers of the Gelao language, which some have related to the **Li** branch of the Tai family, others to the **Kadai** arm of the **Tai-Kadai language family**, while Chinese linguists are still debating the matter. The Gelao live in dispersed clusters of communities in about 20 counties in western Guizhou province, four counties of the Wenshan Zhuang-Miao Autonomous Prefecture in southeastern **Yunnan**, and the Longlin Multiethnic Autonomous County in **Guangxi Zhuang Autonomous Region**. A few smaller groups are found in northern Vietnam, where they are officially called **Co Lao**. In Guizhou alone, ethnologists have identified up to 10 subgroups of the Gelao, based on dress, economic, or habitat characteristics. German anthropologist **Inez de Beauclair** has suggested that the Gelao could be directly linked to the ancient **Lao** of **Sichuan** and, later, Guizhou, as described in Chinese historical records, in which these Lao were acknowledged to dwell in the region from the second century B.C. It is thus likely that the Gelao's ancestors were **aboriginal** to the region. Such long exposure to nearby **Han** culture has contributed significantly to their Sinization.

GENDER INEQUALITY. Most societies in the massif are patrilineal, a very small portion are matrilineal, and a few are bilateral (or cognatic). As a consequence, a gender imbalance in access to power exists, most of the time in favor of the male members of the domestic unit. Generally, access to education is easier for boys, while girls are retained in the **household** for domestic work and child care, an early sign of a fairly strict gender-based division of labor. Premarital sexual freedom is often equal for both sexes, though early pregnancy could cause serious embarrassment for a girl and her family if her momentary partner does not wish to acknowledge paternity and marry her. For most women, marriage means leaving their parents' home permanently and moving into their husband's kin and ritual group (virilocality), possibly a traumatic experience rendered even more difficult by the severance of all functional links with the original family. Polygyny (see **polygamy**) obviously contributes to further disempowering these uprooted wives by keeping them in permanent, stressful competition with each other. Sexual promiscuity by women outside of wedlock is generally disapproved of and is a cause for various forms of punishment, including death. Men, on the other hand, are rarely held accountable for promiscuity. Men's occasional purchase of sexual services outside wedlock introduces a major health hazard for wives, who can do little to avoid being infected by sexually transmitted diseases and HIV/AIDS. Divorce can only be obtained with substantial difficulty by a wife, and only if her husband's behavior is outright hazardous to her and her children. Should she prove to be infertile, however, or not working hard enough to satisfy the expectations of her in-laws, or should she simply fall out of favor with them, she can be repudiated fairly easily and expelled, most of the time losing custody of her offspring. Her original family may or may not agree to take her back. Finding a new husband after divorce or repudiation is almost impossible, and her fate will often be to play a role akin to a servant in her father's household for the remainder of her life. This cluster of prospective difficulties helps explain why among young married highland women, incapable of adapting to their new life and faced with no viable alternative, suicide is common. Finally, in her old age, the wife of a powerful man will benefit from her husband's status. When he passes away, however, her influence will greatly diminish in favor of her eldest son, who will claim authority of the household.

In **lineage societies**, which form a large proportion of the societies in the massif, collective decision-making processes involve the male elders of the **lineages** or **clans** coming together and trying to reach a consensus. Women can influence such processes by raising the husband's awareness about their viewpoint. But ultimately he is not obliged to take it into account. On occasion, wives can decide to join together to have their voices heard, but the outcome of such standoffs is always unsure, and the political price may prove dear.

An impressive number of nongovernmental organizations active in the massif, most often foreign-based, attempt to address the issue of women's unequal access to political and economic power. Initiatives take a variety of forms and, more often than not, yield only impermanent results. Although their proponents mean well, such projects often try to apply solutions considered viable from the developers' cultural viewpoint, with little grounding in local reality. Also, they fail to address the cultural causes of local gender inequality, and modest success is often linked to an incapacity to convince the whole community to partake in the empowerment scheme.

GIA-RAI. The largest and northernmost of the four **Austronesian**-speaking highland groups officially registered in Vietnam—the lowland **Cham** being the fifth. The Gia-rai (317,557 in 1999) live in one single territory located mainly in Gia Lai province (286,952) around the town of Pleiku, just north of their **E-de** neighbors and south of the **Ba-na**, with extensions into adjacent Kon Tum and Dak Lak provinces. The Gia-rai, one of the oldest societies in southern Vietnam, are believed to have migrated uphill from the adjacent coastal area over 2,000 years ago. Moving into the highlands, they displaced **Mon-Khmer** speakers who had already settled there. From these highlands, the Gia-rai then extended their dwelling territory into eastern Cambodia, where they are officially called the **Jarai**.

During and after the colonial period, several French ethnologists were interested in the Gia-rai, not the least because they are a rare case of a matrilineal descent group, as well as being practitioners of a complex form of **animism**. Their architecture, with longhouses similar to those of the E-de, have also attracted much attention. The historical Gia-rai "King of Fire" and "King of Water" have for long been a subject of scholarly scrutiny by this group. Ethnologist **Jacques Dournes** in particular published several books and articles on the group between the 1950s and the 1980s, including his 1977 *Pötao, une théorie du pouvoir chez les Indochinois Jörai* [*Potao: A Theory of Power among the Jorai Indochinese*].

GIAY (GIAI, NHANG). An officially recognized **Tai**-speaking group akin to the **Nung**. French colonial documents often labeled them as Nyang, the French phonetic transcription of *Nhang*. In Vietnam, the Giay are located in extreme northern areas, with extensions into China—among the **Buyi**—from where they migrated around two centuries ago, and into Laos, where they are called **Yang** (4,630 in 1995). The Giay of Vietnam numbered 49,098 in 1999. They farm pockets of the highlands in the provinces of Lao Cai, Ha Giang, and Lai Chau. Their habitat being too high and dispersed to have allowed the formation of a viable **feudal** society, the Giay have remained under the political rule of the **Thai** and the **Tay**. In the absence of an indigenous script, the Giay formerly used **Chinese ideograms** before adopting the Romanized alphabet.

GIE-TRIENG. The Vietnamese name *Trieng* should be pronounced "tchieng" in English, which helps explain the connection with the **Chieng** of Laos. There were 30,243 Gie-trieng in Vietnam when the 1999 national census was held. This **Mon-Khmer**–speaking group belongs to the Bahnaric branch and lives in an area located just south of the **Co-tu** along the Laotian border. They mainly dwell over the provincial border between Kon Tum and Quang Nam, just north of their direct neighbors, the **Xo-dang**. Their territory spills over the border into Laos, where a small group of them, called Chieng (Cheng), live. The Gie-trieng are customarily **animists** and rotational **swiddeners**.

GILHODES, CHARLES (1870–1945). A Catholic missionary from the *Société des Missions Étrangères de Paris* (MEP), Charles Gilhodes arrived in Burma in 1896. Soon he was dispatched among the **Kachin**, with whom he spent practically the rest of his life. Years of direct observation and linguistic familiarity enabled him to write an important book, *The Kachin: Religion and Customs* (1922), an English translation of several articles first published in French in the journal *Anthropos*.

GOLDEN TRIANGLE. A popular name in the West for an indefinite transborder mountainous area crossed by the Mekong River, where Laos (Bokeo and Luangnamtha provinces), Thailand (Chiang Rai), and Burma (the **Shan** State) meet and where illicit activities have been conducted by various groups in connection with **opium** poppy cultivation, its processing, and the trafficking of its derivatives, such as **heroin** and morphine. Recently, traffickers have also focused on gem **smuggling** and new varieties of drugs. While opiate production is a tributary of opium poppy growing and is affected by the spread of **replacement crops** among poppy growers, **amphetamine** production relies on *Ephedra vulgaris*, its main ingredient, which grows in the wild in **Yunnan**. It is thus estimated that 200 million methamphetamine pills are produced annually in the Shan State in Burma, with additional production centers in Thailand, Laos, and even Cambodia.

As a political or cultural space, the Golden Triangle has never had any particular historical reality. It has not even been the domain of one dominant ethnic group, apart perhaps from Shan druglords on the

Burmese side. International fame for the name Golden Triangle appears to have been the relatively recent result of Western **tourist** and journalist mythology more than of any real geopolitical quality. Indeed, in Thailand today its appeal is routinely used to lure tours to the **Thai** side of the tri-nation border zone, although there is absolutely nothing extraordinary to gaze at there other than the placid Mekong and a few peaceful villages.

GUANGXI ZHUANG AUTONOMOUS REGION (GZAR). One of only five official **Autonomous Regions** in China, this exceptional status equal to that of a province was granted to this administrative area in the 1950s. The name comes from Chinese *guang*, "vast," "flat," and *xi*, "West," with which has been associated the name of its foremost *shaoshu minzu*, the **Tai**-speaking **Zhuang**. Despite the geographical determinism embedded in its name, which is only valid from a coastal point of view, Guangxi is for our purposes the easternmost of the four mountainous provinces of Southwest China under study. To add to the confusion, Guangxi is also officially classified in China as part of the Central-South region. With a population of 44,980,000 in 2000, the GZAR stands on the eastern edge of the **mainland Southeast Asian massif**. It is mountainous in its western and northwestern portions, and it also shares an international border with Vietnam. The GZAR has a non-Han minority population of 39 percent of its total. The 16-plus million Zhuang alone, the most numerous minority group in China as well as in the whole massif, form 33 percent of GZAR's population. The other main **minorities** are, in decreasing demographic importance, the **Yao**, Miao, **Dong**, **Hui**, **Yi**, **Sui**, **Maonan**, **Gelao**, and **Mulao**, making a total of 2.7 million.

GUIZHOU. The "Flower Country" in Chinese. Guizhou's total population in 2000 was 35,250,000. It is one of four core mountainous provinces in southwest China. The 2000 census yields the figure of 34.7 percent of the province population, or about 12 million people being officially recognized as **minorities**, who, in turn, belong to more than 20 different *shaoshu minzu*. Among these, the **Miao**, the most numerous group, constitute 38 percent of the minority population in the province. The most numerous among the other groups include, in decreasing demographic importance, the **Buyi**, **Dong**, **Tujia**, **Yi**, **Gelao**, **Sui**, **Hui**, and Bai. Over half of the province's territory (55.5 percent) is administered either as Autonomous Counties or Autonomous Prefectures.

– H –

HA NHI. In Vietnam, Ha Nhi is the official name given to the **Tibeto-Burman** group otherwise called **Hani** in China, **Kaw** in Burma, **Ko** in Laos, and **Ikaw/Akha** and Thailand. The Ha Nhi of Vietnam (17,535 in 1999) are **animists** and dwell mainly in the extreme north of Lai Chau province in the northern highlands, where they practice a combination of horticulture and **swiddening**.

HAINAN. The "South Sea" in Chinese. The relatively small Chinese island province of Hainan (total population 7,870,000 in 2000) is geographically detached from mainland southwest China; however, its language heritage connects its upland population with the southwest's highland **minorities**. In 1984, the island, while remaining administratively attached to Guangdong province as it had been for a long time, became the Hainan Administrative Region. In 1988, it was made a province in its own right. Hainan's indigenous highland population belongs to the **Tai-Kadai** and the **Miao-Yao** language families, while the island's majority population is composed primarily of **Han** Chinese, all later migrants living in the coastal plains. Some 17 percent of the island's population belong to official *shaoshu minzu* and dwell chiefly in the forested hinterland, on the southern portion of the island. Of these 17 percent, 95 percent are Tai-speaking Li, the remaining 5 percent including some **Yao** (misclassified as **Miao** speakers), Be, and **Hui** representatives, the latter two groups living close to the lowlands. The first Western ethnologist to study Hainan's minorities was French missionary **François Savina**, who was jointly commissioned by the Chinese and the French colonial authorities to investigate **languages** there from 1925 to 1928.

HAN. The ethnic Chinese who, after the name of the influential Han dynasty (202 B.C.–A.D. 222), refer to themselves as *Han minzu*, the "Han nationality" (1,137,386,112 in 2001, or 91.5 percent of China's population). The Han all speak one or another of the **languages** of the Sinitic branch of the **Sino-Tibetan language family**, which subdivides into parent languages, such as Mandarin (commonly called Chinese), Cantonese, Hakka, Wu, Yue, Xiang, etc. The Han masses live primarily in the lowlands and fertile valleys of the People's Republic of China. Their traditional rural economy is based on wet rice agriculture, with rapid industrialization and urbanization now occurring practically everywhere they reside. Over centuries, due to demographic pressure and the attractiveness of the natural resources at the periphery, Han territorial expansionism has flourished, and Han migrants have steadily progressed from the coastal plains and fertile valleys of the hinterland into the country's forests, deserts, and mountain ranges. A significant percentage of Han speakers is now found in every urban area throughout the country, including the **mainland Southeast Asian massif**. From these urban cores, the Han become powerful vectors of linguistic and cultural standardization among non-Han **minority** groups. They are especially dynamic in marginal provinces, such as Tibet and Xinjiang, where the central state has a political interest in supporting their settlement. Many from the important **Hui** minority, who are not properly speaking Han but are heavily Sinicized, have also settled in the highlands of the **Peninsula** as farmers and **traders**.

HANI. The Hani of China, also called Woni, form an important **Tibeto-Burman** speaking minority. They officially numbered 1,439,673 in 2000. The Hani live in southeast **Yunnan** in the Honghe Hani-Yi Autonomous Prefecture, which includes Honghe, Yuanyang, Luchun, and Jinping counties, along the Mo (Red) River and its tributaries. This was probably their original homeland, though archeological evidence of this is still uncertain. The Hani also spill over the border into the **Peninsula**, where they are generally known as the **Akha**. The Hani are **animists** with a strong emphasis on ancestor worship. Some, sedentarized for a long time in China, have carved impressive wet **rice** terraces out of mountain slopes in a very rugged terrain. Their political situation is reminiscent of many non**feudal** highland groups originating from southwest China that became entangled in numerous revolts and rebellions, disrupting their ability to earn a livelihood. Over the last three centuries, in response to these problems, the Hani have migrated south into Vietnam, Laos, Burma, and eventually Thailand. In the late 19th and much of the 20th centuries, much like the **Miao-Yao** and several other Tibeto-Burman groups, the Hani became skilled growers of the **opium** poppy, a profitable **cash crop** that combined well with their **lineage** structure, their horticultural practices, and their migration. Today, replacement crops are promoted by the Chinese government to encourage highland farmers to abandon poppy growing. *See also* HA NHI; IKAW; KAW; KO.

HANKS, LUCIAN MASON (1910–1988) AND JANE RICHARDSON (1908–). Lucian and Jane Hanks, long associated with Cornell University, were among the earliest American ethnologists to work in Thailand. While their main focal point has been mainstream **Thai** society, notably in collaboration with Lauriston Sharp, they also undertook a significant number of studies of Thailand's "**hill tribes**" in the 1960s. Some of this material was recently put together in a monograph, *Tribes of the North Thailand Frontier*, published in 2001.

HAW (HO). In Thailand and Laos, Haw or Ho is the name given to Muslim Chinese from **Yunnan** who immigrated over the last 150 years. Their number in Thailand is unknown, as they are not officially accounted for. The same applies to Burma, where they are also called **Panthay**. In Laos, the Ho officially numbered 8,900 at the last census in 1995. The name Haw/Ho is likely derived from Hoa, a generic name for the **Han** Chinese throughout Southeast Asia (such as the Hoa national minority in Vietnam, who are mainly lowland non-Muslim Han). However, for the Chinese government, these Muslim Chinese are all officially called the **Hui**, a key minority nationality that numbers over 9.8 million there.

Many Chinese Muslim soldiers, mercenaries, **traders**, and farmers crossed the borders into the **Peninsula** during the major disturbances, uprisings, and subsequent military repressions of the 18th and 19th centuries in Yunnan, **Guizhou**, and Guangxi, in particular following the Imperial troops crushing the Taiping, **Panthay**, and **Miao Rebellions** in the second half of the 19th century. These Chinese Muslims are believed to have also formed a significant portion of the "**Flag**" **armies'** runaway troops, who roamed Tonkin and northern Laos in the last decades of that century. More entered the **Peninsula**'s highlands later as part of the Chinese Republican army when it was defeated by revolutionary forces in 1949. In Burma and Thailand, they set up what has been known locally as "Kuomintang villages," located a safe distance outside the Chinese border and tolerated by the host countries. From there, these anticommunist fighters contributed for years to harassing the Chinese regime in Yunnan while financing their activities through drug processing and trafficking, in particular narcotics processed from **opium**. But overall in Thailand and Laos today, most Haw/Ho, although remaining faithful to **Islam**, have fully integrated into local society, in which they play an important economic role.

HEALTH AND HEALING. Health has generally been precarious for inhabitants of the **mainland Southeast Asian massif**, life expectancy has been correspondingly low, and only the fittest survived. The harsh upland climate, combined with minimal comfort, has long been associated with quasi-chronic flu-like illnesses from the earliest age of infants. Remarkably tough work in agriculture has exhausted adults well before Western notions of old age. Malnutrition, in particular **salt** and protein deficiencies, has been a cause of high mortality rates at birth, in infancy, and even in adulthood. Other causes have included historical factors, such as regional wars, rebellions, repressions, **slavery**, drug abuse, and a lack of medical services and staff in remote areas, which not only directly affected mortality rates, but also favored conditions for further exacerbation: crop destruction, depletion of agricultural labor, famines, epidemics and epizootics spread by movement of people and animals, etc.

From most highlanders' viewpoint, health issues cannot be dissociated from religious beliefs. Health has been and still is chiefly conceived of as the result of the power imbalance between human and supernatural forces. Illness within a **household**, village epidemics, famines, mental illness, physical disabilities, and also natural disasters were, and for most still are, considered the expression of the discontentment of one or the other of a number of possible supernatural entities: spirits of deceased ancestors, spirits of various elements of the material world (forest, rivers, mountains, etc.), spirits of powerful animals, various ghosts, potentially malevolent creatures roaming the otherworld, etc. Healing of any sort traditionally requires a form of intercession with the supernatural world. To get rid of illness, spirits have to be implored for their forgiveness, and gifts have to be offered. In most highland groups, the household's male elder (but sometimes also the female) is automatically qualified to perform the necessary rituals. These can include food offerings, the burning of incense sticks, and sacrificing a small animal, such as a chicken, all of which are dedicated to the spirit believed to be responsible for the problem affecting one or several members of the household. If, in spite of this effort, an illness keeps progressing, it is a sure sign that the spirit is irritated to a degree that exceeds the household's capacities to appease it.

A more powerful intercessor is needed. Among **Buddhists** and certain Muslim groups with a vivid **animistic** fabric, this can be a healing monk or holy person. Among animists per se, still a majority in the massif, men or women of repute can be called in to perform additional rituals and pronounce powerful words—for a fee in cash or in kind. In certain animistic groups, such as the **Miao** and the **Hmong**, shamans become involved when household level mediation has failed, including communal ordeals, such as poor yields in the fields, famines, bad luck, and the like. They engage in chanting and fall into trances that allow their souls to leave their bodies and travel to the otherworld to confer directly with the spirits. In support of their plea on this diplomatic journey, gifts in the form of **animal sacrifices** play a major role. When a crisis affects an entire community, such bargaining with spirits may lead to the decision to punish individuals found to be responsible for the problem (often by exiling them), or to the community having to come together to conduct particular expiatory rituals or change certain habits, or even abandon the village altogether. These are all measures that, it is hoped, will end the crisis. Be it at an individual or collective level, it is usually only when customary healing rituals have all failed that modern medical help is sought, often too late to be effective.

In spite of this well-documented connection between health, illness, and religion, the response by national authorities in their attempts to address the problems linked to health and illness across the massif has been to insist on increasing agricultural productivity, on providing information and enforcing new hygiene measures, and on introducing dispensaries to highland villages, sometimes with nursing staff, often without. In the last decades, outside proponents of sexually transmitted disease prevention and lowland health officers have also been active in trying to alert highland populations of the dangers of relying only on customary knowledge to deal with major illnesses, such as HIV/AIDS and Hansen's disease (leprosy). In particular, the automatic association of an ill person with a transgression such person must have committed against supernatural bodies has been targeted for change. On the curative side, promoting a no-fault approach has considerably helped the highlanders to accept keeping very ill people within their communities and attending to them, rather than rejecting them irrevocably as liabilities to the whole community.

HEMP. *Cannabis sativa*, a tall domesticated plant whose stem provides the natural fiber customarily used in the highlands to manufacture canvas, cloth, rope, sandals, bags, etc. Until recently, virtually every highland rural **household** would have one or several plots of hemp growing around the house, planted in sufficient quantity to ensure the production of enough cloth for the whole family for one year. Growing and processing the hemp into **clothes** is a time-consuming responsibility bestowed on women, and modern alternatives, such as industrial cotton or synthetic cloth are now gaining in popularity, thanks in particular to better market links and the increasing monetization of the highland economies.

HEROIN. An opiate, more precisely a morphine derivative, used as a narcotic. Along with morphine, heroin is the most popular by-product of **opium** in the massif. Its illicit trafficking has dramatically increased since the 1960s, especially because of American troops stationed in mainland Southeast Asia. Since then, it has found an international market that justifies its relentless production, particularly in the **Shan** State of Burma, with extension into northern Laos and Thailand. Shan and **Wa** drug lords have used this profitable **trade** to finance armed resistance against their neighbors and the Burmese central government.

HICKEY, GERALD CANNON (1925–). American anthropologist whose study on the ethnohistory of the Vietnam **Central Highlands'** population, published in 1982 in two volumes—*Free in the Forest* and *Sons of the Mountains*—is still a landmark. Hickey went to the Republic of Vietnam (South Vietnam) in 1956 to conduct his doctoral study and stayed there for the next 18 years. Initially interested in rural **Kinh** in the Mekong delta, he was recruited in 1963 by the Rand Corporation, commissioned by the U.S. government, to study and report on the Central Highlands tribes. Playing at times the role of advocate, at times working to get them to side with the anticommunist forces in the south, Hickey gathered unique information on the **Mon-Khmer** and **Austronesian** groups in Vietnam's southern highlands. He was also one of the coeditors, with **Frank Lebar** and John Musgrave, of the compendium *Ethnic Groups of Mainland Southeast Asia,* published in 1964.

"HILL TRIBES." In Thailand, where they are known locally as *chao khao*, "mountain peoples," the term "hill tribes" has been used in English generically since the early 1960s for most of the non-**Tai**-speaking groups found in the country's northern and western highlands. The term is rarely used outside the **Thai** context, and is being gradually abandoned by Western scholars as outdated.

HINDUISM IN THE MASSIF. Once a major religion in continental Southeast Asia that had taken roots through the Funan, Champa, Pyu, Mon, Chenla, and **Khmer** kingdoms (first through 13th centuries A.D.), Hinduism was virtually wiped out of the region following the penetration of **Buddhism** a thousand years ago, which absorbed its predecessor. Only a part of the **Cham** ethnic group living in lowland Cambodia and southern Vietnam still practices a form of Hindu Brahmanism. Other **Austronesian** speakers found in the **Central Highlands** today who are linguistic relatives of the Cham had never converted to Hinduism in the first place, retaining instead their **animistic** heritage.

HKAMTI SHAN. *See* SHAN.

HMONG. Pronounced "mong" in English. With an estimated 4 million plus individuals, the Hmong are one of the major mountain **minority** groups of the **mainland Southeast Asian massif**. Moreover, along with the much larger family of **Tai** speakers, the Hmong are the only highland minority group found today in all six countries sharing the massif. Due to their tendency to occupy the highest lands, their dwelling pattern has been highly fragmented over this "archipelago" formed by mountaintops over 1,000 meters high. Linguistic data shows that the Hmong of the **Peninsula** (1.26 million) stem from the **Miao** of southwest China (8.9 million in 2000), being one among a collection of ethnic groups belonging to the **Miao-Yao language family**. In large part due to their active participation in the **Second**

Indochina War (1954–1975), especially in Laos, which triggered their diasporic migrations to the West, but also because they had already caught the attention of colonial observers, many of whom saw in them a proud, fierce, and independent people, the Hmong are among the most thoroughly studied ethnic groups in the massif.

A few centuries ago the lowland Chinese started moving into the mountain ranges of China's southwest. This migration, combined with major social unrest in southern China in the 18th and 19th centuries, caused minorities of **Guizhou**, **Sichuan**, and **Yunnan**, where the majority of the Hmong in China (believed to number around 2.5 million) still live today, to migrate south. A number of Hmong thus settled in the ranges of the **Indochina** Peninsula to practice subsistence agriculture and **opium** poppy cultivation.

In Vietnam, where they are known as H'mông, their presence is known to have existed from the late 18th century. Vietnam is probably the first Indochinese country into which the Hmong migrated. During the colonial period in Tonkin (1883–1954), a number of Hmong opted for joining the Vietnamese nationalists and communists, while many Christian Hmong sided with the French. In particular, numerous Hmong took part on both sides in the battle of **Dien Bien Phu** in 1954. After the Viet Minh victory, pro-French Hmong had to migrate to Laos and South Vietnam. Those remaining in the Democratic Republic of Vietnam (North Vietnam) had to accept living under communist rule. Traditional **trade** in **coffin wood** with China and the opium cultivation—both legal until 1992–1993—long guaranteed a regular cash income. Today, conversion to **cash cropping** is the main economic agenda. In Vietnam, as is the case in Laos, there is a degree of Hmong participation in local and regional administration. At the time of the 1999 national census, there were 787,604 Hmong living in mountainous Vietnam north of Ha Tinh province, with a concentration in Ha Giang (183,994), Lai Chau (170,460), Lao Cai (123,778), and Son La (114,578). In the late 1990s, in search of new economic opportunities and, in many cases, at the government's invitation, several thousand Hmong also moved into Vietnam's **Central Highlands**, particularly into Dak Lak province, where the 1995 census registered 10,891 of them.

In Laos, Hmong settlements are nearly as ancient as in Vietnam. After decades of distant relations with the **Lao** kingdoms, closer associations between the French military and some Hmong on the

Xiengkhuang plateau were established. There, a particular rivalry between members of the Lo **clan** of leader **Faydang Lobliayao** and the Ly clan of **Touby Lyfoung** degenerated into open enmity, dragging in those connected by **kinship**. Clan leaders took opposite sides in the war and, as a consequence, several thousand Hmong fought alongside the Pathet Lao communists, while perhaps just as many were enrolled in the Royal Lao Army. As had been the case in Vietnam, numerous Hmong in Laos also genuinely tried to avoid being dragged into the conflict in spite of the extremely difficult material conditions under which they had to live during wartime. After the 1975 communist victory, thousands of anticommunist Hmong from Laos had to seek refuge abroad. Some estimate that 30 percent of the Hmong in that country crossed its borders, although the only concrete figure available is that of 116,000 Hmong from Laos and Vietnam together seeking refuge in Thailand up to 1990. In 1995, the Hmong in Laos officially numbered 315,000, present in all provinces north of Borikhamxay, with a concentration in the Xaysomboun Special Region, Xiengkhuang, and Huaphanh.

In Thailand, the presence of Hmong settlements is documented from the end of the 19th century. Initially, the Siamese paid little attention to them. But in the early 1950s, the state suddenly took a number of initiatives aimed at establishing links. Decolonization and nationalism were gaining momentum in the Peninsula, and wars of independence were raging. In northern Thailand, armed opposition to the state triggered by outside influences started in 1967, although once again, most Hmong refused to take sides in the conflict. Communist guerrilla warfare in Thailand had stopped by 1982 as a result of an international concurrence of events that rendered it pointless. Priority has since been given to sedentarizing the Hmong, implementing **replacement crops** for opium poppy and commercially viable agricultural techniques, and introducing national education, with the aim of integrating these non-Tai **animists** into the nation. In 2002, the Hmong in Thailand officially numbered 153,955, which makes them the second largest highland national minority, after the **Karen**. In official documents, Thailand mentions the subgroups of Blue Hmong (Hmong Njua), White Hmong (Hmong Daw), and Hmong Gua M'ba. They are found in 13 provinces, the most important concentrations being in Phetchabun, Tak, Chiang Rai, Chiang Mai, and Nan.

Burma probably includes a modest number of Hmong (estimated at around 2,400 in 2001), but no precise census has been conducted there recently. As for Cambodia, the presence of Hmong within its borders is probably less than 10 years old, connected to their movement within Vietnam from the north to the Central Highlands. Over 12,000 Hmong now officially dwell in southern Vietnam, and a number of them have been seen crossing the border into Cambodia over the last few years in search of new land to farm, constituting the first certified presence of Hmong settlers in that country. *See also* MEO; MIAO.

HMONG DIASPORA. As a result of refugee movements in the wake of the **First** and **Second Indochina War**s (1946–1975), an important Hmong diaspora has formed in the West. The largest **Hmong** contingent to settle outside Asia went to the United States, where approximately 100,000 individuals had already arrived by 1990. California became home to half this group, while the remainder went to Minnesota, Wisconsin, Washington, Pennsylvania, and North Carolina. At the time of the 2000 national census in the United States, there was an official total of 186,310 Hmong in that country. By 1990, 10,000 Hmong had migrated to France, including 1,400 who settled in French Guyana. Canada admitted 900 individuals, while another 360 went to Australia, 260 to China, and 250 to Argentina. Over the following years, and until the final closure of the last refugee camps in Thailand, additional numbers of Hmong left Asia, including a block of 15,000 arriving in the United States in 2005. Nevertheless, definitive figures on the international Hmong diaspora are yet to be produced.

HMU. *See* MIAO.

HO. *See* HAW.

HOA. *See* HAW.

HOUSEHOLD. The household is the functional building block of most **minority** groups in the **mainland Southeast Asian massif**. It is the smallest residential, economic, and ritual unit in highland societies with a **kinship**-based (or **lineage**) social structure, often called "tribes." A series of households linked together through kinship form the base of the lineage, whether these households are located in the same vicinity or not. Household ties ensure immediate help among members in times of need, and the household is also a defensive unit. It provides the primary labor for agriculture and any other production, and it is the milieu for food and biological reproductive security. The household can encompass three or four generations of kin living under the same roof, and reciprocity among them is generalized. In terms of politics, it is most often the oldest man who holds responsibility for the well-being of his relatives. He is the most respected member and also the person who, in **animist** groups, is entrusted with conducting ritual offerings to the lineage's ancestors. The household has also remained a fundamental residential element in nonlineage, nonanimist groups, as kinship ties permeate social, economic, and religious life everywhere in the massif.

HRE (DAVAK). A **Mon-Khmer**–speaking group of the Bahnaric branch of Vietnam, where 113,111 Hre were recorded at the time of the 1999 census. They dwell in Quang Ngai and Binh Dinh provinces in the **Central Highlands**, immediately east of **Xo-dang** territory. **Animists**, they are presumed to be indigenous to this region. The Hre were especially targeted by the opposing sides during the **First Indochina War** (1946–1954) as their territory was key to a large portion of the Central Highlands.

H'TIN (T'IN, THIN). A **Mon-Khmer**–speaking group of the Palaungic branch, of ancient migration, found in both countries along the northern Thailand–Laos border. Autonyms they apply to themselves include Mal and Prai. In Thailand, the H'tin (42,657 in 2002; also called T'in, Tin, Thin, or, derogatively, Kha T'in) dwell in northern Nan province, with a handful in Phetchabun. In Laos, where 23,193 were recorded in 1995, they are called Thin, Phai, or Kha Phai, and practically all of them live in the uplands of Xayabury province. It is believed that the H'tin of Thailand migrated from Laos around 100 years ago.

HUI. A particularly important **minority nationality** dispersed throughout China (9,816,805 in 2000) who have permanently adopted Sinitic **languages**. The name Hui (originally Hui-Hui) has been used in the past in China as a convenient label for various groups of Muslims of Middle Eastern origins. Today, however, most of these Muslim groups have become acculturated with each other and have blended culturally into this Hui minority nationality, itself under a strong cultural influence from the **Han**.

Contacts and migrations between China and the Middle East predate the birth of **Islam** (seventh century A.D.). However, the group today called Hui in China was recruited during the Mongol invasions of the 13th century and taken back to the north of China either as slaves, soldiers, craftspeople, or scholars and artists. Later, the Ming dynasty (1368–1644 A.D.) favored the further immigration of Middle Eastern **traders**, who boosted the number of Hui in China. Over a 29-year period during the Ming dynasty, pioneer Hui navigator Zheng He led massive Chinese fleets making visits to dozens of Asian and African countries. A number of Hui poets, scholars, painters, and playwrights also became famous in Han society, including Sadul, Gao Kegong, Ding Henian, Ma Jin, Ding Peng, and Gai Qi. A very mobile and dynamic workforce, over time the Hui spread to most other regions of the Middle Empire and are found today in significant concentrations in the Ningxia Hui Autonomous Region and the provinces of Gansu, Qinghai, Henan, Hebei, Shandong, and **Yunnan**, and in the Xinjiang Uygur Autonomous Region. They are also present in virtually every urban area in the country, around 180,000 of them living in Beijing alone.

Soon after first entering China, some Hui came to Yunnan as settlers when the **Yuan** (1280–1368 A.D.) conquered the land "south of the clouds" in the 1290s A.D. From there, many Hui settled as farmers, while others became active as tradespeople and **caravaneers** throughout the massif. Thus they penetrated into the uplands of the **Peninsula**, initiating commercial networks, or following established routes of such commodities as, from the 19th century, **opium**, which came to be associated with their name south of the Chinese border. Not only did Hui traders and caravaneers venture long distances south of the borders; a number also settled permanently in Burma, Thailand, and Laos, where they became known as **Haw**, Ho, or **Panthay**. They also settled in many locations in Vietnam along the Chinese border, where they acted as local middlepeople for their long-haul trading networks. They are categorized there as part of the Hoa national minority.

The fact that the Hui have been granted the status of **shaoshu minzu** by the Chinese communist state despite their involvement in anti-Han activism in the 19th century, and above all despite not fitting the official Stalinist definition of a "nationality"—for lack of a common territory and for their permanent switch to Chinese languages—is probably indicative of the importance of this composite group in China's **trade** and economy. *See also* HAW.

HUNTERS-GATHERERS. There is only a very limited number of highlanders in the **Peninsula** still living in nomadic bands and making a living chiefly from hunting game and gathering fruit and forest products. Hunters-gatherers typically have no agricultural activity. In the massif, apart perhaps from the rapidly vanishing **Mlabri** in the forested area shared by Thailand, Laos, and Burma, all other highland groups that were once hunters-gatherers have sedentarized, acculturated to more powerful neighbors, and adopted one form of agriculture or another, and hence they no longer fit this category. *See also* HUNTING.

HUNTING. Hunting in the uplands has been performed from time immemorial by all highland groups, and is still performed by a large number of them. Before **firearms** became available, highland hunters used spears, bows, crossbows, snares, and traps, all of which are still used by many today. Hunting has been the work either of individuals alone or of groups using techniques, such as battues and baiting with live animals. A crucial contribution of protein to the diet, hunting for food normally targeted large wild game, such as the **elephant**, tiger, bear, leopard, deer, boar, and monkey, and a range of smaller creatures, such as the porcupine, pangolin, and snakes. With the shrinking of the forest combined with increases in human populations, large game has become rare or protected, and smaller prey formerly neglected, such as the bird, frog, squirrel, rat, and an assortment of small mammals, have found their way onto the menu. Hunts have also long been conducted in connection with **trade**, in the sense that the choice of prey could be determined by market demand in the lowlands for food, medicine, decoration, entertainment, etc. Such catches were made live, in particular snakes, turtles, and songbirds, while other animals were chiefly wanted for specific parts and organs, such as bear gall bladders and tiger bones. Hunting is now one of the traditional activities in the highlands subject to government curtailment in connection with the protection of biodiversity.

Today, hunting is more actively performed in times when there is less need for agricultural labor. It is chiefly a male activity. Individuals hunt at any time of the day or night and for any length of time, from a short nocturnal trip to set an ambush in a promising location known to the hunter alone to a week-long venture into the wilderness. The bounty brought home by hunters is shared among kin. Group hunting with neighbors or relatives, often using dogs, concentrates on larger, faster, or dangerous prey, mainly when collective agricultural work is in a lull. The catch from such expeditions is always divided among all participants along the customary ritual hierarchical line.

While hunting equipment today still includes the old crossbow and arrows, the preferred weaponry is definitely the firearm, either gunpowder muskets or modern rifles. Apart from modern rifles, all other weapons, including muskets, are home-made and thus cost relatively little.

HUYEN. In Vietnam, the territorial administrative unit generally translated as "district." The *huyen* (*huyên* in Vietnamese) further subdivides into a number of *xa* (communes), while several *huyen* together form a *tinh* (province).

– I –

IKAW. In Thailand, the Ikaw (**Akha**, **Kaw**, E-Kaw), a **Tibeto-Burman** group forming the southernmost extension of the much more numerous **Hani** of China, numbered 68,653 in 2002 spread over five provinces, with 90 percent living in Chiang Rai province. Due to the relatively high altitude of these settlements, the Ikaw, like the **Hmong, Yao**, and **Lisu**, were very active in **opium** poppy cultivation. **Replacement crops** implemented by the **Thai** government have only partially made up for the loss in income since growing the poppy has been banned. *See also* HA NHI; KO.

INDIGENOUS PEOPLES. Although widely used in the literature when referring to the populations in the **mainland Southeast Asian**

massif, this notion is not wholly appropriate to discussing their situation there. In its narrowest application, the category "indigenous peoples" refers to people who were born on the land where they live. Recently, however, in particular under the impetus of the struggle for Amerindian First Nations' land rights in North America, which paved the way for the declaration of the International Decade of the World's Indigenous People by the United Nations (1995–2004), this notion has become entangled with that of **aborigines** and aboriginal peoples, that is, peoples believed to be the first human inhabitants on a given territory. Adding to the confusion, in the massif one must consider that many among the highland societies are actually not ancient dwellers at all, but have been on the move for long periods before settling relatively late where they are now officially registered.

More broadly speaking, however, the notion of indigenous peoples applied to the massif's populations can offer a useful tool for conducting political analyses. For lack of a better or clearer term, it serves to highlight the uneven distribution of the land and its resources. It also emphasizes the discrepancies in the sharing of political power within the borders of a sovereign state between dominant lowland majorities and subjugated highland **minorities**. This latter point can be seen as an explanation of why no organizations from Burma, China, Vietnam, and Laos are found on the list of members of the UN World's Indigenous People. This absence points to a reluctance by heavily centralized states to label their minorities in this way. In the socialist states especially, the old Stalinist definition of "nationalities" is still seen as the most appropriate label, and accordingly, the existence of **Autonomous Regions**, prefectures, and counties, in China in particular, is said by the governments to answer best all the needs of "minority nationalities," by the same token cutting short potential surges of unwarranted ethnonationalist demands.

INDIGO. A product of *indigofera*, a small green bush cultivated in the highlands in similar social conditions as **hemp**. Soaked in water, mixed with ashes and lime juice, the fresh indigo leaves produce the dye of the same name used to give a dark blue color to cloth across the region. The dark color resulting from this process has prompted a number of exonyms, such as Blue Miao or Black Hmong.

INDOCHINA (INDO-CHINA). In a geopolitical sense, the Indochina **Peninsula**, that is mainland Southeast Asia, the geographical and political space comprising the five countries of Burma, Thailand, Laos, Cambodia, and Vietnam, plus continental Malaysia. The term originates from European scholarly considerations of the two main historical influences on the populations of the Peninsula, those of India and China. This understanding of the term Indochina is widely accepted in the world, despite the Indochinese themselves not using it. "French Indochina," however, is now only used as a historical designation. It refers to the French colonial occupation of a space that included one formal colony, Cochinchina, and four protectorates: Annam, Tonkin, Cambodia, and Laos; in other words, today's Vietnam, Laos, and Cambodia.

INSTITUTE OF ETHNOLOGY OF VIETNAM. From its self-proclaimed foundation in 1946, postcolonial Vietnam has endeavored to systematize its knowledge of ethnic **minorities** living on its territory, largely for strategic reasons. Ethnographic information gathered during the French colonial period was still used, but a new socialist dimension and ideology had to be brought to this scientific pursuit. During the **First Indochina War**, which lasted from 1946 to 1954, studies of highland **minorities** were conducted only in the north in very difficult conditions by the communist Bureau for Highland Citizens and the Committee for the Highlands. After 1954 and the international acknowledgment of the Democratic Republic of Vietnam (DRV, North Vietnam), research on minorities devolved to the new Committee for Literary, Historical, and Geographic Research. In 1958 an ethnology division was set up for the first time within the history faculty at the University of Hanoi, with the chief aim of working toward a rational, scientific classification of ethnic groups in Vietnam. Also at that time the first of a cohort of Vietnamese ethnologists was dispatched to the Soviet Union and its satellites to obtain degrees in the discipline. This led to the establishment in 1968 of the Institute of Ethnology of Vietnam (*Vien Dan Toc Hoc*), with ethnology defined as the study of national minorities. Research on lowland **Kinh** society was assigned to the Institute of Sociology.

Research in the 1970s focused on investigating the origins of all ethnic groups, or "**nationalities**" (*cac dan toc*), in both North and South Vietnam, with emphasis on the history of the "minority nationalities" (*cac dan toc thieu so*). This strategy was in harmony with the Soviet definitions of "nationality" and "minority," heavily tainted by the Marxist and Stalinist ideology of social evolution, and subjected to the priority given to cultural integration, socialist transformation, and modernization through industrialization and **collectivization** as part of the national agenda. Throughout the 1960s and the 1970s, the classification exercise conducted by the Institute of Ethnology was intended to provide the state with a detailed and accurate map of the ethnolinguistic and geopolitical landscape of Vietnam. Once the official figure of 54 *dan toc* was finally reached and promulgated in 1979, the Institute could focus on the political objectives of national unity, development of "backward" groups, and documentation of material culture for future generations.

After the Economic Renovation (*Doi Moi*) was launched in 1986, gradual political liberalization led to Vietnam opening its doors to foreign researchers interested in studying the national minorities of Vietnam. In the 1990s, the main focus of activities at the Institute shifted from amassing information and making policy suggestions to the state to being a host and anchorage for foreign anthropologists and development organizations, ranging from modest NGOs to the World Bank. In 1995, in an institutional shift a portion of the staff attached to the Institute moved to set up the Vietnam Museum of Ethnology.

INTELLECTUAL ELITES AMONG HIGHLAND MINORITIES. Within **minority** groups in certain countries of the **massif** has emerged a select group of men and women educated in national, sometimes international, institutions, who now form the core of a nascent educated, intellectual minority elite. The first to actively encourage this phenomenon were the European colonial powers, eager to profitably run their colonies and put in place indigenous social elements who would show sympathy to, and like-mindedness with, the colonial regimes. From the uplands of Burma, Laos, and Vietnam, British and French colonial authorities brought to provincial towns and lowland urban centers chosen members of minority groups to be schooled in the metropolitan language, these members in turn becoming spearheads of European political and cultural influence in isolated minority areas. In British Burma, **Karen Dr. San C. Po** exemplifies this strategy, although in his case opposition to the central state was a by-product of his formal education. In colonial Laos, the **Hmong** Lyfoung family is also a good example, as well as the White Tai Deo family ruling the **Sip Song Chau Tai** in colonial Tonkin. Christian **missionaries** in the field also saw to the building of a social stratum of local converts schooled in the missionaries' **languages** and impregnated with the love of God—and metropolitan culture. Crucially, teaching those converts to read and write a Romanized version of their own **language** ensured a lasting influence.

However, it was with the advent of socialist regimes in China, Vietnam, and Laos that the formation of a local educated elite became a systematic policy. The socialist program of "protecting and modernizing" minorities within the national borders made it necessary to recruit, form, and supervise local beachheads of the Party. Authorities brought hand-picked candidates to hubs of state administration and appropriately instructed them in the socialist ideology, which they could in turn introduce and promote back home. The socialist state thus felt entitled to claim that the ranks of national minorities were ensured fair representation at local, provincial, and national levels of the people's government. National minority study institutions also promoted from among their staff selected minority representatives targeted for higher education in the capitals, who in time could be entrusted with teaching, research, and managerial positions. In a number of cases, these intellectual elites, persistently subjected to the dominant state discourse on modernity and gradually imbued with the virtues of socialism, ended up more or less willingly becoming distant from their ethnic origins and embedding themselves permanently in national institutions and ideology. Others opted for veiled intellectual resistance behind a pretense of conformity, quietly promoting an ethno-nationalist agenda while avoiding taking on the institutions that they knew could crush them at will. In this regard, Burma is perhaps the most polarized case, with the minority intellectual elite often siding with armed opponents to the current military regime. Thailand is a notable exception in the region, with minority intellectuals now feeling able to openly challenge the **Thai** administration about its mismanagement of "**hill tribe**" issues.

ISLAM IN THE MASSIF. One of four major world religions that penetrated the **mainland Southeast Asian massif**. However, different from **Hinduism**, **Buddhism**, and Christianity, Islam blended only slightly with local **animism**, because apart from the case of the lowland **Cham**

now found in central Cambodia, it mainly arrived as an attribute of particular groups originating from the Middle East and migrating to China after the 13th century A.D. From the Chinese portion of the massif they later migrated to the **Peninsula**'s highlands. Of all official highland national **minorities** found in the massif, the **Hui**, the Ho, the **Haw**, and the **Panthay**, all related, form the bulk of local Muslims.

IZIKOWITZ, KARL GUSTAV (1903–1985). A Swedish anthropologist, professor at Lund University, Izikowitz conducted part of his research in northern Laos during the French colonial era. Between 1948 and 1954, he was also a correspondent of the *Ecole Francaise d'Extrême-Orient*. Izikowitz's best-known work in the field of highland minority studies is his monograph, *Lamet: Hill Peasants in French Indochina* (1951).

– J –

JARAI. One of the **aboriginal** peoples of the region. Approximately 330,000 Jarai are unevenly divided between Cambodia and Vietnam, all living in the **Central Highlands** of the southern **Annam Cordillera** in the vicinity of the only three other highland **Austronesian** groups remaining in the **mainland Southeast Asian massif**: the **Chu-ru**, **E-de** (**Rhade**), and **Ra-glai**. The group are called Jarai in Cambodia, with 11,549 officially registered in the 1995 national census, all living in the eastern provinces of Ratana Kiri and Mondul Kiri. The same group is named **Gia-Rai** in Vietnam, where, in French colonial archives and publications, it was most often referred to as Djaraï, Jörai, or Joraï. Jarai became their most widely used ethnonym among Anglo-Saxon authors during the **Second Indochina War (1954–1975)**.

JEH (YE, DIE). Part of the Bahnaric branch of the **Mon-Khmer language family**. In 1995, there were 8,013 Jeh reported to inhabit eastern Sekong province in southern Laos. A number of Jeh have also been seen just over the border in Kontum province in Vietnam, although that country does not officially account for them today; a 1960 estimate suggested the figure of 7,000. **Swidden** cultivators, they are **animists** and are a good example of a **lineage society**.

JEWELRY. The use of jewelry is widespread in the **mainland Southeast Asian massif**: earrings, headpieces, neckpieces and chains, breastplates, wrist and ankle bracelets, and rings come in a wide variety of sizes and shapes. Silver, more than any of the other metals used at various times, such as brass or copper, has been, and still is, the preferred material for jewelers in the highlands. Gems are rare, and so is gold, monopolized by the lowland market. Jewelry is worn ostentatiously on market days, at important rituals, during festive days, in fact at any communal event. The aim is to expose publicly to distant kin and neighbors the wealth of one's **household** and **lineage**, as jewelry constitutes the main reserve of wealth for most highlanders. It is shown especially by unmarried youths of both sexes to attract suitable candidates into wedlock. Silver ornaments are fashioned locally from silver bars from the lowlands imported through **trade** networks. There is a great variety of patterns, which can often be directly associated with one specific ethnic group. Aluminum and tin jewelry imitations have been used more and more in recent decades by less fortunate families to keep up appearances, and are also used on a daily basis by wealthier families to keep the real wealth secure at home.

JINGPO (JINGHPAW). In China, the name by which members of the minor portion of the **Kachinic** branch within the **Tibeto-Burman** family are officially known. In 2000, 132,143 Jingpo were registered as dwelling in **Yunnan**, in the western portion of the province along the Burma border, with a concentration in the Dehong Dai-Jingpo Autonomous Prefecture plus a few in the Nujiang Lisu Autonomous Prefecture. *See also* KACHIN.

JINO. A small **Tibeto-Burman** group in China, part of the **Yi** (Loloish) branch, the Jino numbered 20,899 in 2000. Their villages are all interspersed with the **Hani** in southern **Yunnan**.

– K –

KACHIN. The name used in Burma for the group called **Jingpo** (Jinghpaw) in adjacent Chinese territory, where they constitute a **minority** nationality registered under that name. The Burmese Kachin, with an estimate of 446,301 individuals in 2004, are, however, over three times more numerous than the Jingpo in China. Part of the **Tibeto-Burman language family**, the Kachin language gave its name to the Kachinic language branch. Kachinic **languages** stand at a linguistic crossroads of the Tibeto-Burman language family, mirroring its strategic geographical location: it ties together Tibetan to the north, Burmese to the south, and **Yi** to the east. The Kachin ethnic category has been used for a long time in Burma; it appeared both in the British census of 1931 and in the last national census held in that country, in 1983.

A large number of Kachin, though not all, live in the Kachin State in Burma in the extreme north of the country. The Kachin State borders on a long stretch of China, a short segment of India, and the northern limit of the **Shan** State (also in Burma), all adjacent places where some Kachin people can also be found in small numbers. The chief towns in the Kachin State are Myitkyina, the capital, and Bhamo, both located on the upper Irrawaddy River. About half of the territory of the Kachin State is hills or mountains up to nearly 6,000 meters in altitude.

The history of the Kachin before the 19th century is speculative. Their exact origin remains unclear. It is suspected that they may have migrated from farther north, perhaps from Tibet. Before British colonization, the territory they now occupy was largely independent from the **Burman** central power. Like most of the rest of the **mainland Southeast Asian massif**, this territory played the role of buffer between lowland Burma, Tibet, and the Chinese Empire. Early on, the influence of the **Tai**-speaking neighbors of the Kachin, in particular the Shan, appears to have been important, as analyzed by British anthropologist **Edmund Leach** in his *Political Systems of Highland Burma: A Study of Kachin Social Structure* (1954). During British rule, the Kachin highlands were governed independently from the lowlands, following a well-known strategy of divide-and-rule applied by the British to most highland groups in their Burmese colony. A railway link to Myitkyina was completed in 1899 but failed to connect **Yunnan** to the Bay of Bengal, the initial purpose of this initiative. Among other consequences of this direct link established with the Burmese lowlands, Kachin highlanders were increasingly exposed to Christian **missionizing**, which brought formal education to them along with economic benefits (*see* Father Gilhodes' *The Kachin: Religion and Customs*, 1922). The number of Christian Kachin remaining in Burma today is small, and in direct competition with state-sponsored **Buddhist** proselytism, while deeply rooted **animistic** practices are still widespread. Combined with the political changes linked to national independence, a Kachin state was set up in 1947 by the new rulers of independent Burma in an attempt to federate the numerous Kachin chiefdoms in the hills.

The Kachin State's territory is rich in natural resources, such as jade, teak, and gold, and thus attracts the "attention" of the central government. Today, much as is the case in other highland states in Burma, antigovernment resistance is vigorous. In this case, it is led by the Kachin Independence Organization, established in 1961, which has its own military forces. *See also* JINGPO.

KADAI. The minor arm of the **Tai-Kadai** linguistic family, with approximately 1.8 million speakers, thought to originate from a common South China Neolithic substratum. The assembly of Kadai speakers, according to some linguists, includes the **Li** of **Hainan** Island and the **Gelao** (Kelao) of **Guizhou**, both in China, as well as small pockets of **Co Lao**, **La Ha**, **La Chi** (Lati), and **Pu Peo** (Laqua) in northern Vietnam.

KAM. *See* DONG.

KAREN. A major **Tibeto-Burman**–speaking group of over 4.3 million, found chiefly in Burma (an estimate 3,889,091 in 2004), with a significant presence in Thailand (438,131 in 2002, twice that number if **refugees** from Burma are counted). As a measure of their weight, the Karen and their various subgroups actually form the most numerous highland minority ethnicity in each of these two countries. They are part of the Karenic branch of the **Tibeto-Burman language family**.

Although their origin is unclear, it is believed the Karen have been in Burma since the 13th century A.D. The majority are **Buddhist** with a persistent **animistic** background. They have come to occupy the Burma–Thailand border highlands, from the **Shan** State to the north to the southern tip of the Bilauktaung Range, where the Isthmus of Kra begins. They are mainly found in two official upland administrative subdivisions, or *pyi ne*, the **Kayah** State and the Karen State. The 1931 National Census of Burma, the last reasonably accurate source on ethnic minority demography in Burma, identified four Karen subgroups: Sgaw (White, 1,423,238 in 2004), Pwo (White also, sometimes confused with Red Karen, 1,373,788), Taungthu (Burmese for **Pa-O**, Black, 645,871), and **Karenni** (or Kayah, Red Karen, 91,512). In the 1983 census, the last officially taken in Burma, the Karenni category had disappeared, replaced by the Kayah (141,028).

In Thailand, where they are called Kariang or **Yang** (not to be confused with the **Tai**-speaking **Yang** of the northern Laos–Vietnam border area) and chiefly practice Buddhism, the Karen are believed to have migrated from Burma over the last three centuries. Present in 15 provinces, they are mainly located in the mountainous zone along the western border with Burma, from north to south, in Chiang Mai, Mae Hong Son, Tak, Kanchanaburi, and Phrachuap Khiri Khan provinces. The Tribal Research Institute of Thailand has acknowledged four subdivisions of the Kariang in the national territory (population numbers unknown): Skaw (the main group, White, same as Sgaw in Burma), Pwo, Pa-o (Black), and Kayah (Karen-ni, Red Karen). Recently, an additional subgroup of the Kayah called the **Padaung** has gained a degree of fame thanks to the "long neck" women, who have become a **tourist** attraction in a few settlements set up in western Mae Hong Son province. Notwithstanding the refugee issue complicating the picture, long-resident Kariang in Thailand have markedly acculturated to **Thai** society, which in return recognizes them today as the most "advanced" of all "**hill tribes**" and cites them as an example of those with appropriate **land tenure** and sustainable agricultural practices.

The political issues facing the Karen are daunting. The Karen in Burma have long opposed the central Burmese state. Somewhat favored by the British as part of their divide-and-rule policy aimed at antagonizing important factions of Burmese society, the Karen received preferential treatment in a number of ways, including from the 1820s monetary and educational benefits attached to the Christian **missionary** presence, which turned a large number of Burmese Karen into Christian converts (possibly as much as one-third of the Karen in that country) as well as contributing significantly to raising their level of education above that of neighboring groups, thanks in particular to the designing of a Romanized script for their previously unwritten language. A new elite of Karen doctors, teachers, clergy, and provincial officials was thus gradually shaped. **Dr. San C. Po,** an intellectual leader of the Karen in the 1920s, embodied this combination of the Karen educated, politically savvy, and resolutely autonomist elite. At the end of World War II, the Karen, facing the imminent departure of the British and in fear of becoming a mere minority in a **Burman**-dominated country, demanded to be granted a state independent from Burma, a request the British refused.

After independence in 1947, the situation was ripe for steady clashes with the Burman and Buddhist central government. In response to Karen demands, but also in part to undermine growing Karen ethno-nationalism, a Karen state within the Union of Burma was officially created in 1952. Subsequent attempts by Rangoon to force the Karen and all other highland groups into submission quickly resulted in the organization, among most of them, of armed resistance forces. Active fighting has continued ever since under different but generally insensitive, and sometimes brutal, Burmese regimes. The Karen National Union, founded in 1947, has exercised major political leadership in this antigovernment struggle. The price paid has been high. Amid repeated accusations by international organizations of blatant human rights abuses, an estimated 300,000 Karen have crossed the border into Thailand to seek refuge from the Burmese troops' brutality, with an acceleration in the mid-1990s when government forces stepped up their attacks in an all-out effort to exert total control over the "**Myanmar**"–Thailand border. The political status and living conditions of these **refugees** in Thailand are at best fragile.

KARENNI. A branch of the **Karen**, the Karenni numbered an estimated 91,512 in Burma in 2004, although their ethnonym was absent from the last Burmese national census held in 1983. The name Karenni derives from Burmese Kayan-ni (Red Kayan), turned into Karen-ni (Red Karen) by British writers. In Burma and Thailand, this group is officially known today as the **Kayah**.

KARIANG. *See* KAREN.

KATANG. Also called the Brou Katang, this minority of Laos numbered 95,440 in 1995. It is the largest of four officially recognized

minority groups belonging to the **Brou** cluster within the Katuic language subfamily of the **Mon-Khmer language family**, two others dwelling in Laos (**Makong** and **Tri**) and one in Vietnam (**Bru-Van Kieu**). The Katang inhabit a single highland area split evenly across the border between the provinces of Savannakhet and Saravane.

KATU. The Katu are an early **Mon-Khmer**–speaking group of the northern portion of the **Central Highlands,** totaling 67,482 individuals. In Vietnam, where the majority live, they are called **Co-Tu.** In southern Laos, 17,024 Katu were officially reported in 1995, living in Sekong province, with some in adjacent Saravane province. Linguists also gave this name to a branch of the **Mon-Khmer language family**, Katuic, to which belong other nearby groups, such as the **Makong**, **Katang**, and **Ta-Oi**.

KAVET. *See* BRAU.

KAW. The name given by British officials to a **Tibeto-Burman**–speaking highland group of Burma whom linguists and ethnologists have matched with the larger **Akha** ethnicity, and whose representatives are found in most countries in the **mainland Southeast Asian massif**. The Kaw of Burma were estimated to number over 117,000 in 2004, being chiefly located in the highlands along the southern Chinese, northwest Laotian, and northern **Thai** borders. *See also* HANI; HA NHI; IKAW; KO.

KAYAH. This **Tibeto-Burman**–speaking group, also known as **Karenni**, dwells in Burma and, residually, in Thailand. In Burma, the group nominally heads the Kayah State—the name having been changed from Karenni State in 1952—traversed by the Salween River, with Loikaw as its capital. *See also* KAREN.

"KHA" ("XA," "TSA"). A pejorative generic term considered to mean "slave" and long used in Laos to designate non-**Tai** minority groups in the country, especially in the north, where the term has long been explicitly connected to particular ethnonyms, such as Kha Bit, Kha Mu, Kha Ko, Kha Phai, Xa Kha, and A-Kha. The Vietnamese **Thai** version of *Kha* is *Xa* or *Tsa*, and is in turn found in names, such as Xa Cau,

Xa Pho, Xa Xip, Xa Khao, and Tsa Khmu. These three terms were used abundantly in colonial times, including in scholarly literature. In contemporary Vietnam, residual use of the term *kha* can still be found, sometimes in the form *kho,* such as in the ethnonym Kho-mu.

KHA REVOLT (1875–1901). A revolt that erupted in the Laotian province of Huaphanh, chiefly among **Mon-Khmer**–speaking groups tired of being exploited by the lowland **Lao**, their **feudal** lords, and pushed around by the newly arrived **Hmong** attempting to find a niche for themselves. The Lao monarch in Luang Phrabang could not control the rebels and had to ask for the military assistance of Siam (Thailand), Lan Xang's overlord at the time. With this assistance, the leader of the revolt, Thao Nhi, was killed in 1886, but resistance in remote sections of Huaphanh continued until 1901.

KHAMU. *See* KHMU.

KHANG. Mon-Khmer speakers—possibly of the Khmuic branch— dwelling in the **Thai** area in the western portion of Lai Chau province, as well as in pockets between Lai Chau and Son La. Some 10,272 Khang have been listed in the 1999 national census of Vietnam.

KHETT. In Cambodia, the largest territorial administrative unit, which can be likened to the notion of province.

KHEU. A small **Tibeto-Burman** group of only 1,639 (1995) located in the northern tip of Laos in Phongsaly province, possibly related to the **Lolo**.

KHMER. The ethnic Cambodians proper, making up over 90 percent of that country's population. They form the bulk of the Khmer branch within the **Mon-Khmer** linguistic family. Khmer or Khamen are also the names officially attributed to the Khmer-speaking **minorities** in Vietnam, Laos, and Thailand.

KHMU. A **Mon-Khmer**–speaking group, part of the Khmuic branch named after them, 568,000 of whom inhabit the **mainland Southeast Asian massif**. The Khmu dwell chiefly in Laos (88 percent of the group), with a presence in Vietnam (10 percent) and Thailand (2 percent). A noteworthy number of alternative spellings for this name have been used through time, including **Khamu**, Khmu, Kho-mu, Kmhmu, Khmou, Khomu, Kamu, and Khamuk, and there seems to be no agreement as to which would be preferable to use today, Khmu simply being the most common version in Anglo-Saxon literature. The Khmu subdivide into numerous groups, such as Rok, Ksak, Mee, and Luu. There is no agreement either on the precise moment of their migration to their current locations, but it does predate the arrival of **Tai** and **Lao** speakers. Until recently, the Khmu were **swiddeners**, but national policies of relocation and sedentarization have permanently settled the vast majority of them, now turned into farmers. They customarily practice **animism**. A typical **lineage society**, they have no central political organization beyond the level of the village.

In Laos, where they have long been derogatively called Kha Khmu ("slave" Khmu), they constitute the largest national **minority** group, with 500,957 members (1995), or 11 percent of the country's population. Accordingly, they are present in every province of the northern half of the country except Bokeo, in the extreme northwest. In Vietnam, where they are officially called Kho-mu, there were 56,542 registered under this ethnicity at the 1999 national census, with a concentration in Nghe An province and pockets scattered along the Laotian border in Lai Chau and Son La provinces. In Thailand, there were 10,573 Khmu in 2002, primarily located in Nan province and dispersed over three adjacent provinces along the Laotian border.

KHO XIONG. *See* MIAO.

KHO-MU. *See* KHMU.

KHOUENG. In the Lao People's Democratic Republic, the largest territorial administrative unit, best translated as "province." *Khoueng* further subdivide into *muang*, *tasseng*, and *ban*.

KHUN SA (ca. 1934–2000). The nickname of a famous Chinese **Shan opium** and **heroin** baron, born in northeastern Burma under the name Chang Chi Fu. In Burma in the 1960s, under the Ne Win government, Khun Sa first came to public attention as a Shan militia chief. Soon, however, he managed to redirect the forces under his command toward protecting his own interest in opium dealing. But many competing parties in the Shan highlands, all attracted to the lucrative opium growing and transformation business, had interests in curtailing his growing power, and he was betrayed to the Burmese military, who arrested him. After spending five years in jail between 1969 and 1974, Khun Sa quickly got back on his feet. With his Shan United Army (later renamed Mong Tai Army, MTA), he soon regained a 150,000-square-kilometer chunk of the Shan State in Burma and went on to control the opium production and processing into morphine and heroin in that entire territory. Khun Sa consistently declared that he was not a drug baron but merely taxed drug runners moving through his territory to help fund the cause of Shan liberation. Yet at the height of his power in the late 1980s, he was believed to be at the head of 15,000 troops, with his army **smuggling** hundreds of tons of heroin into Thailand and on to the international market. Eager to diversify his operations, Khun Sa also became involved in gem trading and the construction business.

Khun Sa's MTA was a dominant force in Southeast Asia's narcotics **trade** and the world's largest producer of heroin in the early 1990s. However, with the networks of his drug industry reaching as far as the United States, he was indicted in a U.S. court in December 1989 on various charges of heroin trafficking, and the U.S. government wanted him handed over to stand trial in the United States. This marked the start of Khun Sa's downfall. In 1990, the Burmese junta—in a deal struck with the United **Wa** State Army, with which Khun Sa's MTA was in constant competition—provided direct military support to the Wa, thanks in large part to U.S. backing. Gradually weakened by this growing opposition, in January 1996, Khun Sa and part of his MTA were besieged by government troops in his mountain stronghold of Ho Mong. Unable to defeat a government junta–Wa coalition, Khun Sa chose to negotiate his surrender. The terms of the capitulation stipulated that in return for ending his insurgency and handing over his weaponry, Khun Sa would be allowed to live in a military intelligence compound—reputedly on the same street as Ne Win himself—in Rangoon under close government surveillance, from where he would be allowed to engage indirectly in legitimate business, and would not be prosecuted for his trafficking activities or extradited to the United States.

Khun Sa's long-awaited arrest was hailed by Rangoon as a major counter-narcotics success, though it hardly dented drug trafficking in the **"Golden Triangle**." An unknown number of his former soldiers in Shan State remained loyal to Khun Sa and set up **amphetamine** factories along the borders with Thailand and Laos. Opium has become less important, due to much of its main production zone having moved meanwhile to Afghanistan. In the meantime, the emergence of the methamphetamine market has meant that there has been no noticeable reduction of overall trafficking from Burma, as other groups, particularly the Wa, filled the void left by the dissolution of MTA's monopoly. Khun Sa, once the most-wanted man on the U.S. list of international drug dealers (a $2 million reward had been offered as part of the counter-narcotics rewards program established by Congress to help the U.S. government identify and bring to justice major drug traffickers), lived in relative comfort in Rangoon until his death in 2000.

KIDNAPPING OF THE BRIDE. More correctly called elopement, abducting the chosen bride has long been, and still is, an acceptable practice for the prospective groom among several highland groups when a boy and a girl attracted to each other have reasons to believe that the parents of one or both side(s) will oppose their union. In general, elopement is eventually accepted by all parties and marriage ensues. Genuine kidnapping of a girl against her will by a boy wanting her as his wife is very rare, as it would mean that no **brideprice** would be paid to the bride's **household** in exchange, undermining the moral and social position of the boy's family in front of its peers. Elopement to avoid paying the brideprice nevertheless exists in the case of very poor families, but it is generally frowned upon.

KINH. ("Capital," and by extension, "people of the capital"; also Viet). The official ethnonym of the most numerous "nationality" (*dan toc*) in the Socialist Republic of Vietnam (SRV) (65,795,718 in 1999, or 87 percent of the country's population). Kinh is the name most ethnic Vietnamese prefer to call themselves, and to make a distinction from other dominant lowland identities in the region, such as the **Han** in China, the **Thai** in Thailand, the **Lao** in Laos, etc. Among these other groups, however, Viet is commonly preferred to Kinh to name the Kinh **minorities** in neighboring countries sharing the massif.

Within Vietnam, Kinh is used to establish a distinction from the non-Kinh national minorities (*cac dan toc thieu so*) dwelling within the borders of Vietnam and forming the remaining 13 percent of the national population.

KINSHIP. Relations between people based on a blood tie, alliance (marriage), or **adoption** that bind individuals together in specific social arrangements: family, **household**, **lineage**, **clan**, etc. In most of the **mainland Southeast Asian massif** today, kinship ties are still the dominant factor in cultural, political, and economic activities. Even among groups fast acculturating to national majorities or joining in the market economy, as is the case, for instance, for a number of the minority groups living closest to the lowland population concentrations or dwelling in peri-urban areas, the modern productivist social logic has not yet wiped out the prevalence of kinship ties in political, entrepreneurial, and even industrial activity—involving in this case what has been called social capital. Kinship can be further analyzed through its components, mentioned above, and through its rituals: birth, adoption, marriage, divorce, funerals, and ancestor worship, to name a few.

KO. In Laos, Ko and Iko are two of the numerous different names given elsewhere to a group generically called the **Akha**, the most widespread ethnonym for this group due to the popularity of studies that ethnologists produced on the group thus named in Thailand (*see* IKAW). The Ko of Laos were officially reported to number 88,108 in 1995 and were located close to the Chinese border in Phongsaly and Luangnamtha provinces. *See also* HA NHI; HANI; KAW.

KOMMADAM (ca. 1880–1936). A prominent resistance fighter against French colonial authority in Laos. Born into the **Laven** ethnic group, he is often called by the honorific title Ong Kommadam, this partly to avoid confusion with his son, **Sithon Kommadam**, also an anti-French activist and hero of the revolution in Laos.

Kommadam joined the armed resistance in the early 1900s in the wake of the **Phu Mi Bun Revolt**, which broke out on the Bolaven Plateau under the impetus of Bak Mi, a minority leader of **Alak** ethnicity. Bak Mi was captured in 1907 and died in French custody. In 1910, Kommadam was wounded by the French but escaped. He was able to evade French police for another 15 years, during which he kept a low profile. He resurfaced actively in 1925 when, helped by his sons and a number of followers, he circulated anti-French calls-to-arms among highland **minorities** on the Boloven Plateau. This eventually led to a two-year armed outbreak in 1934. Kommadam was killed by French troops on September 23, 1936, an event that effectively ended this resistance movement. His sons, including Sithon Kommadam, then 26, were imprisoned.

KRAOL. *See* BRAU.

KRI. **Mon-Khmer** speakers of the Vietic branch living in eastern Khammouane province. A small contingent of 739 Kri were reported in the 1995 national census of Laos.

KROENG. *See* BRAU.

KUI (KUY, KUOY). A **Mon-Khmer**–speaking (or **Tibeto-Burman**, according to some authors) highland **minority** straddling the borders of Cambodia, Thailand, and Laos. In Cambodia, the Kui (14,186 in 1995) dwell in the hills of the extreme northwest, along the border with Thailand. Their number is believed to have reached a much higher figure (perhaps 100,000 individuals) in and around the Thailand portion of the Phanom Dongrak range. The Kui do not appear in the official censuses of highland minorities in Thailand. They are locally called Suei or **Suay**, and have been steadily absorbed into the surrounding mass of **Tai** (**Lao**) speakers and, as a consequence, they are difficult to trace today. In Laos, where they have also acculturated to the lowland majority, the Kuy, also known as Suay, numbered 6,268 in 1995, and were located in Saravane province in the south of the country.

KUNSTADTER, PETER (1931–). An American anthropologist specializing in population and **health** issues among highland groups in Thailand. In 1967, Kunstadter edited the two volumes of the seminal *Southeast Asian Tribes, Minorities and Nations*, the first comprehensive analytical review of ethnic groups in each country sharing the highlands of mainland Southeast Asia.

KUY. *See* KUI.

– L –

LA CHI (LATI). In Vietnam, a group of **Kadai** speakers within the **Tai-Kadai language family**, who numbered 10,765 in that country in 1999. They all live today in the Sin Man district in the upper Clear (Lo) River in Ha Giang province, on the Chinese border, next to their linguistic cousins the **Pu Peo**. The La Chi are quickly assimilating into the larger **Tay** group, their most influential neighbor. Their number across the Chinese border, in **Yunnan**, is unknown due to their official amalgamation there, along with other Tai-Kadai speakers, into the larger **Dai** minority nationality.

LA HA. According to Vietnamese ethnologists, the La Ha national **minority** is a small group of **Kadai** speakers indigenous to northern Vietnam, where 5,686 (1999) of them live in dispersed dwellings in Son La province.

LAHU. A member of the **Tibeto-Burman language family**, originating from southern China, from where some have migrated into the **Peninsula** over the last two to three centuries. Today, the Lahu are found in five countries in the **mainland Southeast Asian massif** and total approximately 650,000 individuals. Since the mid-19th century, the Lahu in the massif were active in the growing of the **opium** poppy, which contributed to shaping their relationships with their trading partners and with the central governments. **Animists**, the Lahu have customarily been a **lineage society** without a political structure beyond the smallest residential unit, the village.

In China, where over 70 percent of them live (453,705 individuals in 2000), the Lahu dwell in southern **Yunnan** between the **Nu** (Salween) and Lancang (Mekong) Rivers, in the Lancang Lahu Autonomous County in Simao Prefecture, in Southern Lincang Prefecture, and in Menghai County in western Xishuangbanna, Yunnan. Situated in the highest inhabited parts of the **feudal** domains of the **Yi** and the **Dai**, the Lahu of China used to base their livelihoods on **swiddening** agriculture. To this day they have only been partially sedentarized. Like the **Hani**, their linguistic relatives, the Lahu language spoken in China is close to Yi (**Lolo**) and has received much attention (*see* **James Matisoff**'s *The Dictionary of Lahu*, 1989). In

Burma, there were in 2004 an estimated 77,906 Lahu, living chiefly dispersed in the **Shan** state. The Shan used to call them Muhso ("hunters"). In Thailand, where the Lahu are also known by their Shan name (Musuh, Mousseu), six subcategories are recorded: Lahu Nyi (Red), Lahu Na (Black), Lahu Sheleh, Lahu Laba, Lahu Phu, and Lahu Shi, numbering together 102,876 in 2002, spread over nine provinces, though very thinly in four of these, with concentrations in Chiang Rai and Chiang Mai. In Laos, 8,782 individuals dwelling in Bokeo province were registered as Mousseu at the 1995 national census. In Vietnam, where ethnologists prefer to write their name La Hu, they numbered officially 6,874 in 1999, all located in Lai Chau province.

LAK KIA. *See* YAO.

LAMET. Mon-Khmer speakers belonging to the Palaungic branch, the Lamet were reported to number 16,740 in Laos in 1995, evenly spread between the provinces of Luangnamtha and Bokeo in the northwest of the country. This group, also called Kha Lamet in the past, and Rmeet today, is known to Western social scientists thanks in particular to the classic monograph *Lamet: Hill Peasants in French Indochina*, published in 1951 by Swedish anthropologist **Karl Gustav Izikowitz**. The Lamet are close relatives of the **Khmu**, with whom they share numerous cultural features in addition to their **animistic** religious beliefs, a **lineage** system, and the absence of a formal political organization. Both groups could be considered aboriginal to this region.

LAN NA (13TH–18TH CENTURIES A.D.). "The Million Rice Fields." An important and early **Tai** kingdom centered on the town of Chiang Mai at the heart of the domain of the Tai Yuan, and covering most of what constitutes northern Thailand today. In the highlands of the kingdom of Lan Na resided many highland groups politically and economically dependent on this Tai *muang*.

LAN XANG HOM KHAO (14TH–18TH CENTURIES A.D.). "The Million Elephants and White Parasol." A **Tai** kingdom which, for over three centuries, federated most of the independent *muang* of today's Laos, but also those over the borders in northeastern Thailand. In the early 1700s, Lan Xang divided into two independent entities, the kingdom of Luang Phrabang in the north and that of Champassack in the south.

LAND TENURE. Land tenure in most of the highlands of the **mainland Southeast Asian massif** has followed over time a number of different but related models. Being the oldest inhabitants of the **Peninsula**'s highlands, **Austronesian** groups, while sharing many characteristics with other **lineage societies**, have established a long, collective, and primordial link to the land, which translated, for instance, into rituals addressing the spirits of the soil. But among other, perhaps less ancient societies, such as most **Mon-Khmer** and Miao-Yao speakers, as well as many within the **Tibeto-Burman** family, either in China or in the Peninsula, land itself was not subject to ownership properly speaking; there were instead rights for growers to use the land they and their family had cleared, which gave them the privilege of disposing privately of its produce. In these societies, land rights were managed collectively within one **lineage** or **household**. In general, the religious links with the soil were much less specific than for the more ancient groups, although deities associated with the soil could exist in certain cases. When and where **feudal** systems came to prosper, however, such as among most Tai speakers as well as some among the Tibeto-Burman family in southern China, land tenure became a crucial political, economic, and political lever of power. Typically, land belonged to an elite, an aristocracy, who allowed landless peasants to exploit it for rent, the exact form of which has varied considerably over time.

With the establishment of European colonial powers in the region, feudal privileges were severely curtailed, and private ownership of the land was promoted until it permeated highland land tenure systems. This novelty caused a syncretic reaction by which a local community would still abide by the ancient rules—religious, communal, feudal, or other—but would deal with the colonial state under the new rules. When socialism and the subsequent **collectivization** of all land took place in the second half of the 20th century in China, Vietnam, Laos, and Cambodia, large and small landowners were dispossessed and the land was appropriated by the state—the people. In the countries that turned to capitalism instead, like Thailand and, to a degree, Burma, private ownership was guaranteed to whomever could show recognized land titles or afford to buy some. Today, modern land tenure in the massif is regulated by national laws and is under a strong capitalist influence, even in socialist regimes. Open ownership of the land and its commoditization is the rule in Thailand, Cambodia, and, again to a degree, Burma, whereas in Laos, Vietnam, and China, land is still nominally owned by the socialist state, but liberalization and decollectivization have over the last 25 years or so allowed for local communities to take back, if not individual ownership, at least local responsibility for the management of communal land.

In most cases, however, scrutiny of local practices shows that—especially when state officials are looking the other way—the old customary land rights still effectively pervade the management of the soil by villagers and agriculturalists. **Kinship**, for instance, as well as inheritance rules, debt settlement, or simply claiming an ancient customary right on a given plot, will all play a role in the decision-making process at the local level.

LANGUAGES. According to veteran Southeast Asian linguist **James Matisoff**, 500 to 600 languages can be pinpointed in mainland Southeast Asia. For scientific purposes, these languages can be clustered into five linguistic families: **Austro-Asiatic** (comprising 11 branches of the **Mon-Khmer**, plus the Munda branch), **Sino-Tibetan** (Chinese languages, plus around 300 languages in the **Tibeto-Burman** family), **Tai-Kadai** (about 20 **Tai languages** plus a few smaller **Kadai** languages), Miao-Yao (or Hmong-Mien, around 40 languages shared between **Miao** and **Yao**, plus several intermediate languages), and **Austronesian** (or Malayo-Polynesian, i.e., the Malay and **Cham** branches in the **Peninsula**, and around 1,000 other languages in Oceania). This clustering has been adopted in this dictionary. However, different assemblages of these basic macro-groupings have been proposed, one in particular clustering together the last three families into one superstock, the **Austro-Tai**. As a consequence, in the absence of consensus among linguists, caution must be exercised in classifying languages.

A number of linguistic areal features characterize the region in the fields of grammar, lexicosemantics, and phonology, in particular regarding syllabism (mono- and pluri-) and a large incidence of tone-proneness (up to 15 tones in some languages). *See also* LANGUAGES OF TRADE.

LANGUAGES OF TRADE. With its staggering linguistic diversity, it was unavoidable that **trade** in the **mainland Southeast Asian massif** would require a number of vehicular **languages**, or lingua francas, to be used to bridge the linguistic gaps between regions and trading partners. As a rule, for any given subregion in the massif, the local politically dominant ethnic group was able to impose its language on weaker **trade** partners. **Feudal** powers like the Tibetan, **Naxi**, **Bai**, **Yi**, **Lue**, **Shan**, Vietnamese **Thai**, **Tay**, **Nung**, **Zhuang**, and **Buyi**, all dominant at various times in their history, thus enforced their idioms on trade in and around their domains. On a very local scale, less prevalent highland languages could reign in areas of ethnic concentration, such as the **Khmu** and **Lamet** in northern Laos, the **Katu** and **Bahnar** in the **Central Highlands**, and the **Lahu** in northern Thailand. For long haul trade, as well as trade on the lower fringes of the massif, lowland languages would become automatically prevalent, including forms of Chinese, Vietnamese, Tai, **Khmer**, **Cham**, and **Burman**. Today, national languages are dislodging the remnants of these prior lingua francas to become the most convenient medium of communication within national borders, especially with the increasing availability of media in the national language and the ever-growing number of highland youth educated in the national tongue.

LAO. As an ethnic label, Lao applies to all speakers of the Lao (southwest) branch of the **Tai-Kadai language family**, spread over several countries. With approximately 25 million of them clustered under the northeastern Isan umbrella identity, Thailand accounts for the vast majority of 28 million or so Lao speakers in Asia. Laos, a Lao historical kingdom, accounts for only 2.4 million Lao speakers, which is, however, just enough to claim a demographic majority, 53 percent of that country's population. There are also Lao **minorities** officially registered in neighboring northwestern Vietnam (11,611 in 1999) and northern Cambodia (19,819 in 1995). In this light, it is advisable to only apply the term Lao to a linguistic category—thus, to a language—instead of a nationality, and use the term Laotian to name the inhabitants of Laos, regardless of their ethnic and linguistic affiliations.

LAO LOUM, LAO THEUNG, LAO SOUNG. An official division of all ethnic groups in the Lao People's Democratic Republic that prevailed for a few decades before it was abandoned. In the late 1970s, at the time of the first census held by the communist regime, in place since 1975, based on an idea dating back to the 1950s—allegedly from Hmong monarchist leader **Toulia Lyfoung**—the new national leaders adopted a politically convenient division among three major "nationalities" (*sonsaat*) based on the altitude of habitation: the *Lao Loum* dwelling in the plains, chiefly **Lao-Tai** speakers; the *Lao Theung* living on the slopes, grouping in theory all the **Austro-Asiatics**; and the *Lao Sung* in the mountains, composed of the **Tibeto-Burman** and the Hmong-Yao (**Miao-Yao**) groups. These somewhat impractical categories were nevertheless swiftly raised to the status of national symbols in the shape of the "three Lao sisters," depicted on the country's banknotes. It has been argued that this system corresponded to a political logic more than a cultural one, not the least because it emphasized that all ethnic groups in Laos were Laotian above any other possible identity. Over the last five decades, important and incessant population movements have rendered this rigid classification vastly irrelevant. It was eventually quietly abolished in 2001, so quietly in fact that it is still widely used by the Laotians.

LAOS, ADMINISTRATIVE DIVISIONS IN THE LAO PEOPLE'S DEMOCRATIC REPUBLIC. Current administrative divisions in highland Laos follow the national system for rural areas, with, in decreasing order of size, the *khoueng* (province), *muang* (district), *tasseng* (subdistrict), and *ban* (village). At *ban* level, as is the case in Thailand too, further subdivisions into village fragments or hamlets, sometimes inhabited by different ethnic groups, is rarely accounted for in provincial and national statistics.

LAOS, HIGHLAND MINORITIES IN THE LAO PEOPLE'S DEMOCRATIC REPUBLIC. Out of a total population of 4,574,848 in 1995 (an estimated 5.4 million in 2002), Laos includes 2,170,957 million individuals of non-Lao extraction, that is, 47 percent of the population (including several **Tai**-speaking, yet non-Lao groups), most of whom are mid- and upland dwellers. This makes Laos by far the most balanced multiethnic country of those sharing

Table 4. "Ethnicities" of Laos, 1995
47 "ethnicities" (*sonphao*) including the Lao, the 46 non-Lao being considered minorities

Ethnic Group	N	Percent of Minorities	Percent of Country
Lao	2,403,891	—	52.55
Khmu	500,957	23.08	10.95
Phoutai	472,458	21.76	10.33
Hmong	315,465	14.53	6.90
Lue	119,191	5.49	2.61
Katang	95,440	4.40	2.09
Makong	92,321	4.25	2.02
Ko	88,108	4.06	1.93
Suay	45,498	2.10	0.99
Laven	40,519	1.87	0.89
Phounoy	35,835	1.65	0.78
Ta Oy	30,876	1.42	0.67
Nyouan	26,239	1.21	0.57
Thin	23,193	1.07	0.51
Talieng	23,091	1.06	0.50
Yao	22,695	1.05	0.50
Phong	21,395	0.99	0.47
Tri	20,906	0.96	0.46
Lave	17,544	0.81	0.38
Katu	17,024	0.78	0.37
Lamet	16,740	0.77	0.37
Alak	16,594	0.76	0.36
Pacoh	13,224	0.61	0.29
Nge	12,189	0.56	0.27
Ho	8,900	0.41	0.19
Mousseu	8,782	0.40	0.19
Chieng	8,511	0.39	0.19
Jeh	8,013	0.37	0.18
Kuy	6,268	0.29	0.14
Xingmoun	5,834	0.27	0.13
Nyaheun	5,152	0.24	0.11
Yang	4,630	0.21	0.10
Khmer	3,902	0.18	0.09
Sek	2,745	0.13	0.06
Toum	2,510	0.12	0.05
Samtao	2,213	0.10	0.05
Sila	1,772	0.08	0.04
Kheu	1,639	0.08	0.04
Bit	1,509	0.07	0.03
Lolo	1,407	0.06	0.03

Ethnic Group	N	Percent of Minorities	Percent of Country
Ngouan	1,344	0.06	0.03
Hani	1,122	0.05	0.02
Sehdang	786	0.04	0.02
Kri	739	0.03	0.02
Lavi	538	0.02	0.01
Mone	217	0.01	0.00
Minorities	**2,170,957**	**100**	**47.45**
COUNTRY	**4,574,848**	—	**100**

Source: *Lao PDR Census 1995.*

the **mainland Southeast Asian massif**. Following a list first established in the late 1970s, then redesigned in 1992 for use in the 1995 census, Laos officially counts 47 ethnic groups (*sonphao*), including the ethnic **Lao** majority. Today, ethnic groups are officially clustered by the Laotian government into five ethnolinguistic families: the Lao-Tai (66.2 percent, 3.3 million), which, as well as Lao properly speaking (2.4 million), includes five other groups (0.9 million), half of whom are Phoutai (0.47 million); the **Mon-Khmer** (22.7 percent, 1.2 million) with 30 groups, dominated by the **Khmu** (0.5 million); the Hmong-Yao (7.4 percent, 0.34 million), where the **Hmong** are predominant (0.32 million); the **Tibeto-Burman** (2.9 percent, 0.14 million), with nine groups, the **Hani** (0.09 million) being the largest; and finally the small **Ho** Chinese group, with only 8,900 speakers. Due to difficult historical circumstances, no complete national census was carried out in Laos between 1943 and 1985, which forestalls an analysis of long-term trends in population growth.

Prior to French colonization starting in the 1890s, local lowland monarchs paid little attention to highland **minorities** at the periphery of their kingdoms, which all belonged to the Tai tradition of the *muang*. Under French rule, a policy of strict control of national territory within secured borders was implemented. Logically, minorities were thus approached and accounted for, and alliances were made by the colonial powers with a number of them. Following World War II, civil disorder raged for three decades in the region. The political situation was first aggravated by France's determination to regain power over its domain of **Indochina** after the war, until it became obvious, following its military downfall in Vietnam and the Geneva Agreements of 1954, that it had no choice but to withdraw. Civil unrest was further compounded by the royalist struggle against the communist revolutionaries of the Pathet Lao during the **Second Indochina War (1954–1975)**, during which the development of a sound state policy on minority issues in Laos was not really practicable. Or more pragmatically, minority issues were a matter of ad hoc military alliances following the fluctuations of the frontlines and the priorities of military objectives. Both the Pathet Lao forces on one side, and the Royal/Neutralist Lao Government on the other—vigorously supported by a coalition of U.S.-led forces—tried to draw local mountain peoples to their cause, as such strategic alliances proved crucial for occupying the highland terrain that formed most of Laos's territory. Thus, until the communist victory of 1975, minorities in mid- and upland Laos were not subject to clear national policies but, instead, faced more immediate dangers. They could not realistically "opt out" of the war effort, taking sides being not so much a matter of choice but a necessity just to survive.

The war over, promises of political autonomy made to certain minority allies in the heat of the action were drastically toned down, much as had been the case under similar circumstances in China and Vietnam. Meanwhile, the Soviet and Chinese models advocated the setting up of semiautonomous regions for minorities just after victory. But the secretary general of the Communist Party of Laos at the time, Kaysone Phomvihane, espoused the Vietnamese example instead. He made it clear early in his long tenure that the indissoluble unity of the Laotian people was the foremost priority. Thus, the territory would remain a Laotian territory for all the people, and all belonged to the Lao nation. Local customs could still be practiced, but egalitarianism would be ensured by the communist state, and any thought of ethno-nationalism or regional autonomy was deemed undesirable. In fact, however, the Lao-Tai identity was actively promoted as the national cultural norm and presented as the cement that would join together the multiple ethnicities in communist Laos for eternity. More strongly than in any of its brother socialist states, Laos enforces the usage of Lao as the national language and makes no effort to devise scripts for its illiterate minorities.

Under the influence and guidance of Vietnamese ethnologists, who had been called in for help, a near obsessional priority was given to the establishment of a definitive classification of ethnic groups. Soon after 1975, a Committee of Nationalities was set up within the new Lao Front for National Reconstruction, with the specific mandate of taking a scientific inventory of minorities in the People's Republic. Under this impetus, the first census held by the new regime used the figure of 68 "ethnicities" (*sonphao*). The three-tiered division of the population (**Lao Loum, Lao Theung, Lao Soung**) also dates from this time. In the 1985 national census, a new, open question on the self-ascribed ethnicity of respondents generated hundreds of autonyms in excess of the 68 official ethnonyms the state had already recognized. This confusing situation triggered the invitation to numerous foreign experts to come to Laos and help, leading to the creation in 1988 of a national Institute of Ethnography. A somewhat artificial consensus was eventually reached in 1992 around the figure of 47 official ethnicities in Laos, just in time for the 1995 census, in which these *sonphao* were used. At last, the state could formally associate with a given minority group an architectural tradition, costumes, rituals, and beliefs, all operations needed to be able to make public the "good keeping" in which the Lao authorities held its minority peoples.

Of importance in the Laotian case, a dominant feature of the Lao government's policy toward its national minorities has been a focus on their resettlement via what has been called the relocation policy. Back in the 1960s, the Royal and Neutralist Lao governments had initiated an early form of relocation policy in an effort to enhance the living conditions of the non-Lao groups. That decision could barely hide a political strategy that actually aimed to pull the rug out from under the communist insurgents' feet by emptying rebel regions of their civilian populations, a strategy also applied by Diem's regime in the Republic of Vietnam (South Vietnam) in the early 1960s. In Laos at the same time, and until 1975, during years of war and civil unrest, the communist revolutionary strategy was also officially to bring economic development to the highlands by providing uplanders receptive to the revolutionary project with goods essential for their survival, maintenance in the highlands, and active support of insurgent actions. Concurrently, however, in zones seized by communist forces prior to 1975, minorities that had supported the Pathet Lao were often rewarded with pieces of land located in the lowlands, thus initiating a de facto relocation movement. The victorious communists only amplified this movement after 1975 and brought many isolated populations closer to the country's road infrastructure, particularly in areas prone to persistent armed resistance to the regime. Further complicating the picture, from 1977 to 1985, some Tai-Lao groups from the mountain slopes—officially the Lao Theung domain—who had fled their homes during the war, returned and demanded that their former land, which had often been reallocated to deserving relocated highlanders, be given back to them. The state frequently answered their demands favorably, setting in motion further population movements. By supporting this return of Tai-speaking populations to the mid- and sometimes even the highlands, the Lao state saw an opportunity to spread its collectivized ideology to the upland areas and populations at low cost. After the launch of the New Economic Mechanisms liberalizing Laos's economy in 1986, this relocation policy gained momentum.

In parallel, thanks to the growing impact of the international environmental lobby, moving highlanders around can be officially legitimized by arguing that forest and watershed protection can put an end to the widespread and allegedly unsustainable practice of both pioneering and rotational **swiddening**. Highland populations in Laos have thus been brought down to new "focal zones" set up as development centers, emphasizing the two themes that dominate the history of policies directed toward ethnic minorities in Laos since 1975: economic modernization and the establishment of a Lao nation-state. By the year 2000, it was estimated that as many as 1 million peasants in Laos had been so relocated, about one-fifth of the total Laotian population. Much as in Vietnam and China, local protests against this policy are quickly gagged, and news of them rarely reaches the outside world.

LAVE. In 1995, in Laos, there were 17,544 officially registered **Mon-Khmer** of the Bahnaric branch who spoke Lave. There, they live in the southeasternmost province of Attapeu on the heights of the Boloven Plateau, and are spread over the borders into Cambodia and, residually, Vietnam, where they are officially known as the **Brau**.

LAVEN. This **Mon-Khmer**–speaking group of southern Laos belongs to the Bahnaric branch, as do their close relatives, the **Lave** and **Lavi**. The Laven were reported to have a population of 40,519 in the 1995 national census. They inhabit the Boloven Plateau area in Champassack, Attapeu, Sekong, and Saravane provinces—*bo loven* meaning "country of the Loven," an alternative name for that group. It is from among the Laven that Ong **Kommadam** originated and, later, his son **Sithon Kommadam**, heroes of anticolonial and procommunist struggle in Laos.

LAVI. Only 538 Lavi were officially accounted for in Laos in 1995. They live on the Boloven Plateau in southern Laos, close to their neighbors and linguistic relatives, the **Laven** and the **Lave**.

LAWA (LUA). In Thailand, where they are also called **Lua** (Lua'), the Lawa constitute an official highland minority, with a population of 22,260 (2002) distributed over five provinces, the majority living in Chiang Mai, Mae Hong Son, and Chiang Rai. The Lua' were the pre-**Tai** indigenous population of Chiang Mai, and according to legend, they were clearly differentiated from a pre-Tai Khmeric population of nearby Lamphun. Linguists and ethnologists have suggested that the Lawa are to be grouped with the **Mon-Khmer**–speaking **Wa** of China and Burma, within the **Palaung-Wa** linguistic subfamily, with whom they share similarities. American anthropologist **Peter Kunstadter** wrote a substantial monograph on this group, *The Lua' (Lawa) of Northern Thailand; Aspects of Social Structure, Agriculture, and Religion* (1965). Some confusion exists due to the fact that another ethnic group in Thailand is officially referred to as Lawa; they are the Chaobon on the Khorat Plateau, a Tai–speaking subgroup.

LEACH, EDMUND (1910–1989). A British anthropologist, professor at the London School of Economics, who specialized in Sri Lanka and the Burmese highlands, where he became an authority on the **Kachin** minority. Leach is arguably the most famous Western anthropologist of mainland Southeast Asia. His Burma fieldwork was carried out before and during World War II, and yielded his celebrated monograph *Political Systems of Highland Burma* (1954), now a classic.

LEBAR, FRANK (1920–). An American anthropologist commissioned by the American government in the early 1960s, along with several colleagues, such as **Charles Hickey**, John Musgrave, **Lucian** and **Jane Hanks**, and William Smalley, to establish a compendium of all ethnic groups in mainland and maritime Southeast Asia. Of particular interest to this dictionary is Lebar's *Ethnic Groups of Mainland Southeast Asia* (1964), published by the Human Relations Area Files, which contains one of the best ethnolinguistic maps of the **mainland Southeast Asian massif** ever published.

LEFÈVRE-PONTALIS, PIERRE (1864–?). A French diplomat, member of the **Pavie Mission**. Lefèvre-Pontalis explored Upper-Tonkin, Upper-Laos, and Southern **Yunnan** during two trips. The first, from April to June 1891, was made in the company and under the guidance of **Deo Van Tri**, the White Tai leader of the **Sip Song Chau Tai**, newly aligned with France. The diplomat thus visited most of the main valleys of upper northern Laos, parts of the **Sip Song Phan Na** in southern Yunnan, a section of eastern Burma just west of the Mekong River, and nearly all of the Sip Song Chau Tai in northwestern Tonkin. He also navigated the Black (Da) River to Hanoi several times. During his second trip in 1894–1895, Lefèvre-Pontalis joined both the commission in charge of formalizing a section of the border separating China from French Indochina between the Mekong and the Red Rivers, and the Anglo–French border commission in western Laos, set up to draw a mutually acceptable limit to separate the two colonial domains. He thus had the opportunity to explore the Nam Ou and Nam Ta valleys, the mid-Mekong River, and its surroundings on the Laos–Burma frontier. These voyages are described, with abundant references to the peoples met on the way, elements of their ethnography, and their economic and political associations, in his *Voyage dans le Haut-Laos et sur les frontières de Chine et de Birmanie* [*Travels in Upper Laos and on the Borders of Yunnan and Burma*] (1902), the fifth volume of the work published by the Pavie Mission.

LI. An important cluster of **aboriginal** groups on **Hainan** Island believed by Chinese archeologists to have colonized the island at least 3,000 years ago. The Li officially numbered 1,247,814 at the time of the 2000 national census. Some Chinese linguists argue that the Li could be **Tai** speakers long separated from the continental Zhuang-Dai (**Tai-Kadai**) branch, while others suggest that they are actually **Kadai** speakers. In any case, they constitute the furthest extension east of the **Tai-Kadai language family**. The Li live at the foot and on the slopes of the Wushi Mountains, in and around Tongze, capital of the Hainan Li-Miao Autonomous Prefecture established in 1952, as well as in Baoting, Ledong, Dongfang, and a few more counties in that same prefecture. Mentioned in Chinese texts in the ninth century A.D. when the first elements of Chinese administration were introduced on the island, the Li gradually retreated into the mountains at a distance from the coastal **Han**, with whom they nevertheless violently clashed in the course of dozens of rebellions. They eventually sided with the revolutionary guerrillas and helped them drive Kuomintang troops out of Hainan in the mid-1940s. Communist historiographers have since actively romanticized the Li procommunist insurrection and made it an example for other minority nationalities in the country.

LINEAGE. The lineage is a fundamental **kinship** building block linking individuals through the closest possible blood relations, marriage, and **adoption**. An operational definition of lineage includes the group of relatives, both men and women, who have a common ancestor they all recognize and remember, who in turn connects together all descendants over a few generations. A given lineage is materialized by closely related **households** that constitute its smallest units, while several adjacent lineages can cluster into a broader form of organization called the **clan**. All highland societies in the **massif** show important social, cultural, religious, political, and economic reliance on kinship ties based on lineage.

LINEAGE SOCIETIES. A social form common in the **mainland Southeast Asian massif** in which all decisions are made among kin at the **lineage** level. Also called segmentary, acephalous, or stateless societies, lineage societies have no formal political existence beyond the lineage (or in certain cases, the **clan**), not even with neighbors in the same village who might belong to a different lineage. Within the autonomous lineage, the decision-making process relies primarily on the congregation of men, with elder males having the most influence. No one, however, can claim formal authority, consensus always being sought through negotiation and persuasion instead. The notion of lineage societies has most often been used to distinguish the political organization of "tribal" groups from the more complex and more stratified peasant groups that are part of **feudal** systems, where power is in the hands of an elite controlling the means of production and the state. Lineage societies are normally associated with an economy focused more on subsistence agriculture than on market exchange, with labor-intensive work often in the particular form of shifting cultivation. In religious terms, lineage societies are mainly **animistic**. In the massif, examples of lineage societies are exceptionally common. They include all Miao-Yao and **Austronesian** groups, the vast majority of **Mon-Khmer** and several **Tibeto-Burman** groups, and some among the more isolated groups within the **Tai-Kadai language family**. They can be found in all six countries in the massif.

LISAW. *See* LISU.

LISU (LISAW). A minority belonging to the **Tibeto-Burman language family**, the Lisu are found in China, where they originate from and where nearly 83 percent of them live today, with smaller numbers in Burma (10 percent) and Thailand (7 percent). In these three countries, the Lisu are customarily **animistic**, and practiced **swiddening** agriculture until their move to **cash cropping** in recent years.

In China, the Lisu constitute 480,960 individuals (2000) and live mainly in the mountain ranges of **Yunnan**, with a concentration along the Burma border. They are concentrated in Bijiang, Fugong, Gongshan, and Lushui counties within the Nujiang Lisu Autonomous Prefecture in northwestern Yunnan. Elsewhere in that province, many are scattered in Lijiang, Baoshan, Diqing, Dehong, Dali, and Chuxiong prefectures or counties. Some Lisu can also be found in Xichang and Yanbian counties in **Sichuan**. That broad area, it is believed, constitutes their original dwelling location, and Chinese documents attest to their presence there in the fourth century B.C. A **lineage society**, the Lisu usually congregate in small communities dispersed in higher locations among the **Han**, **Bai**, **Yi**, **Naxi**, and farther south, the **Shan** and **Thai** domains. Throughout history, the Lisu were subordinated either to Tibetan and Yi overlords who shared the rule of the upper **Nu** (Salween) and upper Lancang (Mekong) valleys, or to Han **feudal** lords inhabiting central Yunnan. In the early 20th century, a few scripts for the Lisu language were designed by Western Protestant **missionaries** and converted Lisu under the influence of preexisting neighboring syllabic scripts. Outside China, the Lisu are generally called Lisaw. In Burma, an estimate of their population is 57,125 for the year 2004. In Thailand, the group numbered 38,299 in 2002, spread thinly over 10 provinces, with the largest numbers in Chiang Mai, Chiang Rai, and Mae Hong Son. William Dessaint and Avounado Ngwama's *South of the Clouds: Myths and Tales Collected Orally among the Lissou Highlanders* [*Au sud des nuages: Mythes et contes recueillis oralement chez les montagnards lissou (tibeto-birmans)*], published in 1994, is an excellent introduction to this group.

LIVESTOCK. Livestock is of limited economic importance in the massif. No highland group specializes in breeding and raising animals because, for one thing, the rugged landscape does not allow the development of sizeable pastures beyond plateaus and narrow plains. At the **household** level, however, livestock is of great importance. The diet of most rural families is dependant on a few domesticated animals they maintain for their own consumption. Each family will customarily own, breed, and raise a few chickens, ducks, or pigs, as well as cats and dogs; if the family is wealthy enough, a few additional animals will also be kept, such as goats, horses, cows, oxen, or **buffalo**. Most of the time, any given highland house will have a combination of these, the exact balance depending on culture, environment, climate, size of the household, and financial capabilities of the moment.

Livestock, such as fowls, ducks, pigs, or goats, are destined for family consumption; maintaining and guarding the house, which is the chief role of pest hunting cats and dogs, roosters also making a notable contribution; and agricultural and pack functions, the job of horses, cows oxen, and buffalo. By-products, such as eggs, milk, meat, hide, and organs are always carefully collected and put to some use. Of all the regular livestock, fowl, pigs, oxen, and buffalo are prime candidates for ritual **animal sacrifice**. Finally, all can be **traded** in the marketplace.

LOEMOUN. A **minority** of 280 individuals, officially listed in Cambodia in 1995, one of four in that country about which no information is available.

LOLO. The generic name given in the **Peninsula**, and formerly in China also, to a massive **Tibeto-Burman**–speaking group whose name was officially replaced in China with the ethnonym **Yi** during the linguistic rectification campaign of the 1950s. Relatively modest numbers of Lolo dwell in the Peninsula—an undetermined number in Burma, 3,307 in Vietnam (Lo Lo), and 1,407 in Laos—where they have been subdivided by colonial and subsequent observers into related subgroups, such as Penti Lolo, Xa Cau, Xa Kha, and Xa Pho. But the Lolo's main residence remains China, with a staggering 7,762,272 of them recorded as Yi in 2000.

LUA. *See* LAWA.

LUE (LU, LÜ, LEU, PAI-I). A **Tai**-speaking group, and one of the few highland **minorities** found in five countries of the **Southeast Asian massif**. Linguists believe that the Lue language is spoken in southern China by about 260,000 people, also known locally as **Pai-i** (Dai), with another estimated 87,090 speakers in Burma, and approximately 70,000 in Thailand. There are 119,191 (1995) Lue registered in Laos, and 4,964 (1999) in Vietnam, both countries recognizing them as official minority groups. A very rough estimate of the total Lue population of Asia could be in the vicinity of 540,000.

The Lue of China are not explicitly accounted for and are officially clustered within the larger **Dai** minority nationality in southern **Yunnan**, of which it is estimated they represent about one-quarter. They live in or around the **Xishuangbanna Dai autonomous prefecture**, formerly at the heart of the **feudal** state of **Sip Song Phan Na**, the traditional Lue stronghold. In Burma, they are located in the Kengtung region in the eastern portion of the **Shan** State. In Laos, the Lue dwell chiefly in the northern border provinces of Phongsaly and Luangnamtha. In Thailand, where they are not officially distinguished from the northern **Thai**, the Lue generally live in Chiang Rai, Nan, Phayao, and Chiang Mai provinces. In Vietnam, where they are formally called Lụ·, their very small population is located in the extreme north of Lai Chau province.

The Lue are culturally akin to the Shan, **Yuan**, and **Lao**, with whom they share language proximity and a predilection for Theravada **Buddhism**. A new Tai Lue script was developed in China during the 1950s, which was based on and replaced the ancient **Lan Na** script. This new script is gaining in popularity among all the Lue in the massif. The problems linked to tackling Lue identity have been addressed by several authors, including a seminal article published in 1965 in *American Anthropologist* by Micheal Moerman, "Ethnic Indentification in a Complex Civilization: Who Are the Lu?"

LUE REVOLTS. Two revolts against colonial authority conducted by the **Tai**-speaking **Lue** living in French Indochina. First in Phongsaly province in 1908, followed in 1914 by Muang Sing district in Luangnamtha province, local Lue leaders rebelled, partly in reaction to what the elite in both *muang* perceived as an attempts by the French to curtail their traditional **feudal** prerogatives to exploit at will the weaker highland societies around them. In reality, a concurrent contention was also the fact that these two *muang* were formerly part of the greater Lue domain of **Sip Song Phan Na** and had recently had to sever that historical link to be attached to the French-supervised **Lao** kingdom instead. In both uprisings, the insurgents were demanding to be removed from the French/Lao domain and reunited with Sip Song Phan Na. Each of these revolts lasted two years before the colonial military restored its full authority, without granting the rebels their wishes.

LUNET DE LAJONQUIÈRE, ÉTIENNE E. (1861–?). French colonial infantry officer posted to Tonkin in the 1880s. Lunet de Lajonquière was partially detached from his duties in 1899 to begin a longterm attachment to *Ecole Française d'Extrême-Orient* (EFEO) in Hanoi. Over the following years, his contribution to the **archeology** of ancient **Indochina** was substantial. He was also instrumental in enriching scientific knowledge on highland **minorities** in upper Tonkin, thanks especially to his work as chief editor of the *Ethnographie des Territoires Militaires* [*Ethnography of the Military Territories*], published in 1904, the most complete field study of highland groups of Indochina produced during colonial times. Field research was conducted between 1898 and 1903 by numerous officers all over northern Tonkin, notably involving the prolific **Auguste Bonifacy**. Lunet de Lajonquière's 1904 publication was slightly edited and republished in 1906 for a larger audience under the title *Ethnographie du Tonkin septentrional* [*Ethnography of Northern Tonkin*].

– M –

MA (MAA). Mon-Khmer speakers belonging to the Bahnaric branch, along with their direct neighbor and relative, the **Mnong**. Living exclusively in western Lam Dong province in Vietnam's **Central Highlands**, the Ma (or Cau Ma) were registered as an official national **minority**, numbering 33,338 at the time of the 1999 national census. French ethnologists have stated that the Cho-to, Cho-sop, and **Cho-ro** are the three main subgroups of the Ma; of these, only the Cho-ro have been officially acknowledged as a full-fledged national minority by Vietnamese ethnologists and, thus, distinguished from the Ma. The Ma have been thoroughly studied by the French agronomist and ethnologist Jean Boulbet, who published such works as *Pays des Maa', domaine des génies* [*Country of the Maa', Domain of the Spirits*] published in 1967 by *Ecole Française d'Extrême-Orient* (EFEO).

MA TOUAN LIN (13TH CENTURY A.D.). A Chinese scholar and officer with encyclopedic knowledge, in the early 13th century Ma Touan Lin collected studies on southern and eastern non-**Han** "barbarians" that had been written by predecessors, such as Fang T'cho (ninth century). He combined this material with his own observations, made during trips in the southern marches of the Middle Empire, to produce his *Wen hsien t'ong k'ao* [*Comprehensive Study of Civilization*], translated from Chinese into French in 1883 by Sinologist Marquis D'Hervey de Saint-Denys (1823–1892) under the title *Ethnographie des peuples étrangers à la Chine* [*Ethnography of the Peoples Foreign to China*], of which volume 2, on the southern country, is of particular interest. However, due to the centuries separating the original work from today's readership, it becomes extremely difficult to assess precisely who the peoples were that Ma Touan Lin actually described. Translator D'Hervey de Saint-Denys has usefully included scholarly footnotes in his translation.

MAD MAN'S REBELLION. *See* BA CHAY UPRISING.

MAINLAND SOUTHEAST ASIA. *See* PENINSULA, SOUTHEAST ASIAN.

MAINLAND SOUTHEAST ASIAN MASSIF. Scholars' term for the network of mountain ranges and high valleys extending southeast from the higher portion of the Himalayas and the Tibetan Plateau. This designation is above all geomorphological and does not take people, cultural areas, or countries into consideration. Over time, political borders have artificially disjointed the Chinese portion of these highlands from their geographical continuity in Burma, Laos, Thailand, Cambodia, and Vietnam, these countries further subdividing ownership of the massif among themselves. As a response to this political fragmentation, it is argued that all these different segments could be reconnected to form a meaningful, though far from uniform, physical, historical, social, and cultural space. Thus defined, the mainland Southeast Asian massif would include approximately all land higher than a few hundred meters south of the Yangtze River in China, east of the **Chin** and **Naga** hills on the India–Burma border, with a southern limit at the Isthmus of Kra in southern Thailand. This definition delineates a space of approximately 2.5 million square kilometers, nearly four times the size of Texas. The notion of the mainland Southeast Asian massif thereby becomes a most appropriate way to address a social space inclusive of a multitude of highland societies, some spreading over several of the countries concerned, a space that was neglected until recently because its political fragmentation had also entailed a legal breakup of its population. *See also* PENINSULA, SOUTHEAST ASIAN.

MAIZE. Maize (*zea mays* L.) was unknown in China before it started being imported from America via the Philippines by the Spanish in the 16th century. Maize quickly became a popular crop in China, especially in its southern mountainous periphery. It required neither rich soils nor irrigation, it could be planted on slopes, and it was perfectly suited for the temperate climate of the highlands. Maize helped the **Han** masses in the lowlands deal with demographic pressures by facilitating their moving into the less fertile mountain ranges and plateaus of the massif, and settling where previously only mountain groups had been dwelling. Together with excessive state infringement, such as heavy taxation, this invasion was an important cause of conflict between the Han administration and highland **minorities** trying to preserve their integrity vis-à-vis the imperial centralized government and the regional rulers and warlords.

As a crop, maize has also proven extremely attractive to highlanders. Easy to grow, harvest, and stock, it does not deplete the thin highland soil of too much of its nutrients. Its root system helps consolidate soil on slopes, and it can profitably be grown concurrently with beans, peas, or the **opium** poppy on the same plot, the tall stem of the maize plant both protecting the smaller growth from direct rain or wind and also conveniently hiding the coveted poppy from onlookers. Ground to a fine flour with a air of portable milling stones that practically every **household** owns, in many groups maize has become a main element of the pigs' diet. Maize also doubles as a type of food suitable for human consumption, although many groups prefer **rice** and only resort to eating maize in times of rice shortage. Last but not least, maize has also become a favorite raw material to produce home-made distilled **alcohol**, consumed in large quantities in the massif and subject to a thriving **trade**.

MAKONG (MANKONG, MAKOI). The Makong of Laos, of whom there were 92,321 in 1995, belong to the **Mon-Khmer language family** and live in the highlands of the province of Khammouane, with extensions in neighboring Savannakhet and Borikhamxay. They are the second largest group out of four registered in Laos and Vietnam as belonging to the **Brou** (Bru) branch within the Katuic language subfamily. The Makong form the geographical continuation of one of these groups, the less numerous **Bru-Van Kieu** of Quang Binh and Quang Tri provinces in central Vietnam.

MALAYO-POLYNESIAN LANGUAGE FAMILY. The name formerly given to the **Austronesian language family**, still officially in use in Vietnam due to French tradition. It is applied there to a few ethnic groups of the **Central Highlands**.

"MAN." A negative generic term, possibly bearing the meaning of "slave," long used in colonial French Indochina to designate non-Kinh minority groups in the north. It is believed that the word was picked up from vernacular use by colonial officials, and that it was probably imported from China, where "*Man*" was also often used generically, much like "Miao" or "Lolo," by the **Han** Chinese when lumping together the highland "barbarians" on the southern fringes of the Empire. In **Indochina**, the name was later specifically attached to various subgroups of the **Yao**, globally referred to as Man, in ethnonyms, such as Man-tien, Man-quan-trang, Man-lan-ten, and many others abundant in French colonial literature on the northern highlands. Today, the term Man is obsolete.

MANG. Speakers of a dialect of the **Mon-Khmer language family**. Only 2,663 members of the Mang ethnic group were registered in Vietnam in 1999, all living in two main clusters in the northern province of Lai Chau.

MAONAN. The Maonan, a **Tai**-speaking group of the Kam-Sui branch of China, number 107,166 individuals (2000) living in a small area within the **Zhuang** domain in the northern **Guangxi Zhuang Autonomous Region**, in the vicinity of their linguistic cousins, the **Mulao**. The Maonan are now plains dwellers converted to wet **rice** cultivation and have been undergoing steady Sinization.

MAPPING MINORITIES IN THE MASSIF. A comprehensive map of the distribution of all highland peoples inhabiting the **mainland Southeast Asian massif** does not exist, and perhaps never will. Major obstacles to such an endeavor include the lack of coordination between countries to identify highland groups, their misrepresentation in national censuses, a lack of scientific foundations sufficient to produce a formal and final list of groups, and some linguistic disagreements about the division of the great language families found in the highlands, not to mention a lack of political will in most of the six countries concerned to reopen the question of their official listing of national **minorities**. However, should some or all of these obstacles be overcome some day, other technical problems could then prove very hard to solve. These problems are often found with existing maps produced at the scale of one given country, an endeavor that each country in the region has attempted at one time or another. Problems include concerns with representing groups existing across borders, difficulties linked to the two-dimensional mode of representation of social reality, and limitations in printing a final product that could fit a manageable format.

In terms of concrete representation, nearly all maps produced so far in the region give no clear indication on orography, thus leaving out crucial elements of topography, such as elevation and slope. The only indirect indications of elevation are rivers, which give an initial idea of the lower terrain in a specific region, and borders, which often suggest higher terrain, often being range crests. No sure correlation between people and specific landscapes can therefore be suggested by examining such maps, which fail to communicate to the reader the fact that specific groups or subgroups may live at certain altitudes, occupy different ecological niches, and, accordingly, undertake specific types of lumbering, gathering, and agriculture. Also, using color codes, a widespread practice, can prove tricky. Apart from the rare double-feature over a given area, such as two zones distinguished by two colors overlapping in a bicolor stripe fashion, the notion of ethnic heterogeneity on the terrain is lost in one-color (or one-pattern) zones concealing the possibility of several groups dwelling in close contact in one area. Such standardized color- or pattern-codes also fail to detail the unavoidably uneven demographic density. Finally, the very large scale of even the most detailed of these maps precludes drawing conclusions about anything meaningful at lower administrative levels, such as the communes/villages and hamlets, which in the massif are often pluri-ethnic.

Notwithstanding these severe reservations, two of the most promising solutions to bring ethnic map readers closer to accurately comprehending the reality on the ground are using color-coded dots instead of zone colors or patterns, for instance one dot per village for a given group, which was attempted for Thailand by the Tribal Research Institute, leading to an interesting, very colorful mosaic; or using the latest Geographical Information System technology to build computerized three-dimensional images, over which are electronically draped color-coded zones representing ethnic groups, a potentially fruitful initiative that is still limited by color but has the advantage of at last associating in one picture cultural variety and geomorphology.

MARCO POLO (1254–1323). Venetian merchant and explorer, the first known European visitor to the **mainland Southeast Asian Massif**. With his father and uncle, he arrived in China in 1275 and stayed for 17 years. This was the time of the great Mongol (**Yuan**) expansion. Marco Polo reported participating in military expeditions to the southern marches of the Middle Empire. The lands he visited are believed to include what are now **Guizhou** and **Yunnan**. In his memoirs, Polo mentions non-**Han** "barbarians" he met there, although without enough detail to confirm beyond any doubt whom he actually met among the highland **minorities** of southwest China.

MARKETPLACES IN THE HIGHLANDS. Essential sites for individuals from scattered communities to meet at and **trade**. In the frequent absence in isolated rural settings of technologies of communication, such as the telephone, the conduct of normal social life demands that individuals be in the physical presence of one another for the purposes of, for example, communicating, negotiating, or finding a suitable spouse. Trade in highland marketplaces also bears a specific signature. At such sites, produce cultivated or gathered by highlanders isolated in more or less distant hamlets is sold to, or exchanged with, other highlanders as well as with outsiders in exchange for cash, commodities, or consumer goods of various types. The fundamental social side of a marketplace in the highlands is, however, often underestimated by national economists and developers, who tend to see marketplaces purely as economic phenomena.

Over the last few decades, the story has become increasingly complex, as even in socialist countries, a fast-growing influx of goods and persons from the lowlands has contributed to boosting trade and modifying the architecture, size, and functions of marketplaces, while the range of goods on display has been both increased and altered to fit modern demands. Despite this modernizing push, for most highlanders the marketplace is still used for the same social purposes as before. For others, however, new opportunities make it an increasingly desirable place to be on a permanent basis. But the numbers of lowland newcomers to the highlands in each of the six countries sharing the massif have soared to the point that these migrants are now taking over the marketplaces, both in a physical and a legal sense. Little space is left for the often less profit-minded highlanders. Social and political tensions are on the increase, leading to the suggestion that the highland societies that created these marketplaces, and whose traditions sustained them for hundreds of years, are being made increasingly redundant.

One of the many implications of the modernization of highland marketplaces has been to change the calendar of market activities. In most areas in the massif outside the urban centers, markets were customarily held once every five, six, or seven days. With the increased involvement of central governments and the growing urbanization in many formerly modest rural settlements in the mountains, demand in these new towns has reached a level where markets need to start following the lowland model of permanent operation. Who traders are has also been affected by the level of urbanization of market towns. While many of the traders and most of the customers on weekly market days in the countryside belong to one or another of the many ethnicities indigenous to the highlands, the extended trading period in urban settings attracts people for whom trading is the main activity, sometimes their only source of income. These are most often outsiders who elect to migrate to the mountains for this specific economic purpose.

The main reason for the colorfulness of markets on days highlanders is present. Because of their exotic appearance, highland market towns are becoming a prime object of **tourist** consumption, a must see destination where the "authentic and untouched" is believed to be on display for all to see. This phenomenon is particularly vigorous in locations where there are few other cultural elements (original domestic or religious architecture, for instance) considered worthy of **tourists'** attention. Exotic peoples thus are the primary tourist attraction, the more so if they dress in colorful and traditional apparel, and behave accordingly. On a model well studied in older exotic tourist market towns, like Otavalo in Ecuador or Chichicastenango in Guatemala, several formerly isolated towns in the massif, such as Mae Hong Son in Thailand, Muang Sing in Laos, Sa Pa in Vietnam, and several locations in **Guizhou**, are good examples of such trends. *See also* BARTER.

MARSHALL, HARRY I. (1878–1950?). With his wife Emma, Reverend Harry Ignatius Marshall lived on a mission in Burma with the American Baptist Foreign Mission Society. In 1922, he published *The Karen People of Burma: A Study in Anthropology and Ethnology* in which, meshed with ethnographic description, he took a strong stance in favor of setting up a pan-**Karen** movement against **Burman** influence. Based in part on his own observations, made chiefly among lowland acculturated Karen, the book also used many earlier missionary sources from highland Burma, especially what Francis Mason had written.

MASSIF. *See* MAINLAND SOUTHEAST ASIAN MASSIF.

MATISOFF, JAMES (1937–). American scholar and leading linguist of mainland Southeast Asia, including the highlands of the massif. His proposed division of language families in the region has been authoritative, though specifics are still open to debate. This division is the one used in this dictionary.

MEO. Hmong migrants to the **Southeast Asian Peninsula** have long been named Meo (Méo, Mèo, Meauw) by outside observers in Vietnam, Laos, and Thailand. In China, from where the Hmong migrated and where the majority of them still live today, they officially belong to the minority nationality called **Miao**. In that word lies the origin of the term "Meo." As an ethnic label, the autonym Hmong is now preferable, although Meo can still be heard or found in official documents.

MESSIANIC MOVEMENTS. Several messianic risings have been recorded in the **mainland Southeast Asian massif** over the last century-and-a-half, causing much debate regarding the origin of the messianic dimension behind such political actions.

Messianism blends with the parent notion of millenarism, which is the expectation of the coming of paradise on Earth when Jesus (or an equivalent in non-Christian religions) returns to rule in person for a thousand years. Millenarism overlaps with messianism when this return is to occur under the guidance of a charismatic leader, a messiah. In its broad definition, messianism essentially involves the coming of a savior who will put an end to the current order of things and set up a new state of perfect justice and happiness. Clearly, messianism is intrinsic to Semitic religious traditions, such as Judaism, **Islam**, and Christianity. But it is incorrect to infer from this, as many Western observers since colonial times have done, that it is merely due to the early contact with Christian **missions**, from the 16th century A.D. onward, that messianic beliefs have spread in Asia and were eventually adopted by local groups in the mainland Southeast Asian massif. While some cases of such diffusion have undoubtedly happened in particular circumstances, the source of messianic religious ideas in Southeast Asia appears to be Chinese, conveyed in particular by Taoism. For example, the founder of the Tang dynasty (618–907 A.D.) notoriously tried to use the messianic fervor among his Taoist subjects for his own political benefit. Later, when messianism and the revolutionary spirit combined in modern China's secret societies, such as the White Lotus resistance to the Ming and Qing dynasties (14th to 20th centuries), or in opposition to foreign influence, such as the Boxer Uprising (1898–1900), Western observers concluded that these ideologies must have been borrowed from the Christian heritage.

In the massif properly speaking, scores of messianic uprisings have occurred, although only a few have been observed and properly documented. The Taiping Revolt of 1851–1864, for instance, under the appearance of a political movement, is believed to have harbored several messianic movements unfolding concurrently, though little is actually known about these. One reason for this ignorance is that when they occur among small minority highland groups, such messianic movements would most of the time be confused in the outsider's mind with a more straightforward rebellion against injustice or excessive taxation. Among the movements that have been recognized as properly messianic is the **Phu Mi Bun revolt** of 1901–1907 during which **Mon-Khmer** speakers in the Boloven Plateau in southern Laos rebelled under the guidance of **Alak** leader Bak Mi, who had proclaimed himself a messianic king. The **Ba Chay uprising** (1918–1921), or "Mad Man's revolt," which greatly impressed the French colonial observers, spread among the **Hmong** from northern Vietnam, then into northeast Laos, while their leader Ba Chay, after prophetic dreams, proclaimed himself a messianic leader. In this latter case, during their fight against the French military sent to crush the revolt, messianic propaganda inspired among the rebels dramatic forms of reckless behavior supported by faith in the magical powers of their messiah. Provided that they had received the proper blessings from him, Hmong fighters were happy to advance toward the enemy in the open, strengthened by the conviction that bullets could never touch their bodies, let alone cause any harm. The results, needless to say, were devastating, and the uprisings, short-lived.

MIAO. One of the largest official **minority** groups in China, with a massive 8,940,116 members in 2000, all part of the **Miao-Yao language family.** Nearly half of the Miao are located in **Guizhou,** where they form the most important minority nationality. They also make up significant proportions of minority populations in **Yunnan,** Hunan, Guangxi, **Sichuan,** and Hubei. The Miao language group subdivides into four sublanguages, not mutually intelligible: **Hmong,** Hmu, Kho Xiong, and A Hmao. Dozens of local names also exist, often given by outside observers, many of them apocryphal and confusing. Nevertheless, this huge number of nearly 9 million is above all a political construct by **Han** officials concerned with the integration of all nationalities into the nation, and would certainly gain in definition as well as relevance if it were broken down into smaller components.

Ancient Chinese documents often used the term Miao generically, designating in this way any non-**Han** groups in the southwest mountains, creating great confusion and raising skepticism as to whether Chinese annals can actually be of use in tracing back the history of the Miao per se. With the massive Han expansion in the Guizhou highlands in the 17th century A.D., those then known as the Miao clashed with Han troops and settlers, and began disbanding. Over the next two centuries, violent unrest, including a major uprising called the "Miao rebellion," was cause for large numbers of Miao to migrate farther south and west to escape annihilation or assimilation, triggering waves of migration into Yunnan, their second most important homeland today, and from there, farther into northern Vietnam, Laos, Burma, and Thailand. After 1951, a number of Miao autonomous divisions were established in Guizhou, Yunnan, Guangxi, Guangdong, and Hunan, most of them multiethnic, mixing with the **Tujia,** Bouyei, **Dong, Zhuang,** Li, and Han. In the first decade of the 20th century, Western Christian **missionaries** had introduced to the A Hmao of northwest Guizhou and northeast Yunnan a syllabic script—the **Pollard script**—inspired by a transposition of shorthand symbols designed for Amerindians in Canada by other missionaries, a script still used in both locations today. Later, a subsequent script—the **Romanized Popular Alphabet** (RPA)—was designed and implemented by the American missionaries Barney and Smalley while working with the Hmong in Thailand; it has become dominant today among the **Hmong diaspora**. In the 1950s, a Chinese initiative contemporary with the RPA also produced a Romanized script, found today only in China, which conforms to the Pinyin system used for Mandarin. International scholars who have studied the Miao subgroups in China include **Samuel Pollard**, David Graham, **Inez De Beauclair**, **Ruey Yih-fu**, Claudine Lombard-Salmon, Joakim Enwall, Thomas Lyman, Cheung Siu-Woo, Norma Diamond, Louisa Schein, and Nicholas Tapp.

In the **Peninsula**, the term Miao has been widely used by early Western scholars, practically always to designate one specific subgroup, the Hmong, members of the other three linguistic subgroups of the China Miao having not entered the Peninsula in significant numbers. These early scholars' publications, notably based on observations in Thailand and Laos, influenced local authorities to officially use the Miao ethnonym, most of the time, however, in the distorted form "**Meo**." Today, the proper endonym Hmong prevails in the Peninsula.

MIAO REBELLION. *See* PANTHAY AND MIAO REBELLIONS.

MIAO-YAO LANGUAGE FAMILY. One of the five main **language** families found in Asia with about 30 to 40 **languages** divided between two main branches, the **Miao** (Hmongic) and the **Yao** (Mienic)—each in turn subdividing into a number of languages—plus a third branch counting only one language, **She**, which some scholars prefer to locate within the Miao branch. Found in an immense territory spreading from the Yangtze River to central Thailand, and from Burma to Vietnam, Miao-Yao languages and dialects are originally from China, some having penetrated into the **Peninsula** since the 17th century A.D. From there, they have now reached the United States, France, Australia, and a few other non-Asian countries via diasporic movements caused by the Indochina Wars of the second half of the 20th century.

A number of predominantly American linguists have lately preferred to call this whole language family *Hmong-Mien* after the name of the demographically dominant group within each of the two main branches; this proposal is still being debated. The Miao, Yao, and She languages, though related, are distinct enough to suggest that their branches separated from the common protolanguage very early. Linguistic evidence suggests that the original Miao groups were based in **Guizhou**, where most of them can still be found today, while the Yao groups were originally located farther east in Hunan. All Miao-Yao languages have intricate tone systems.

With the **Austronesian** dwellers of the southern **Annam Cordillera**, the Miao-Yao–speaking groups have long epitomized what colonial observers liked to term "tribal groups." Their social organization was **lineage** based, with no political formalization above the **household** head or the lineage council of elders, making them a highly fluid society very difficult to control. They lived in the highest and most remote locations in the simplest of material conditions, in a highly fragmented residential pattern, farthest away from the groups with more complex social systems. Thanks to the imagery popularized by the colonial and postcolonial military in **Indochina**, these groups inherited a reputation for toughness, fierceness, independence, and uncompromising pride, with an inclination to revolt. Most of the Miao-Yao groups dwelling in China have been sedentarized for a long time. Those who migrated into the Peninsula were seminomads practicing pioneering shifting cultivation. From the mid-19th century onward, the **opium** poppy had become a major cash crop for them. Most were **animists**, including shamanistic practices, some also blending in a fair amount of Taoism. A number were also Christianized during colonial times as well as during the **First** and **Second Indochina Wars** (1946–1975). In this language family, only some Yao have produced texts, using a writing system borrowed from **Han** ideograms, to record their genealogies and rituals. (*See* figure 3.)

MIEN. The autonym used in several areas of the **mainland Southeast Asian massif** to designate subgroups of **Yao** speakers. In Thailand and Laos, for example, most Yao refer to themselves as Iu Mien (Yu Mien), while in Vietnam they use Kim Mien (Kim Mun). American linguists have suggested that since the Mien subgroup is the most

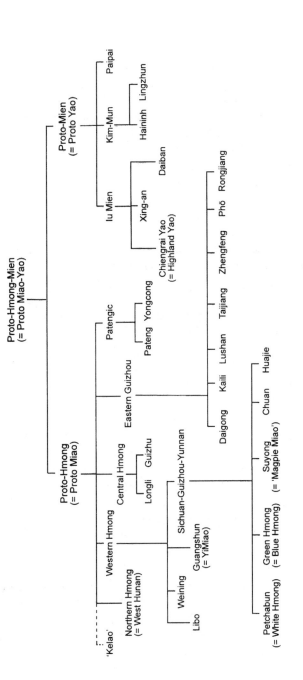

Source: Matisoff, James. "Genetic Versus Contact Relationship: Prosodic Diffusibility in South-East Asian Languages." *Areal diffusion and genetic inheritance: problems in comparative linguistics*, 291-347. In Aikhenvald, A., and R. M. W. Dixon (eds.) Oxford: OUP, 2001.

Figure 3. The Miao-Yao (Hmong-Mien) Language Family

important of all Yao groups numerically, it should replace the term Yao in the linguistic category "**Miao-Yao language family**."

MIGRATIONS OF HIGHLANDERS INTO INDOCHINA. A majority of highland peoples found in the **mainland Southeast Asian massif** today originate from China, with some coming from the Indian and Himalayan highlands farther west. Many of these people are believed to have moved from some lowlands into the highlands under growing demographic, political, and military pressure. A number of groups, it is believed, are also indigenous to the massif, though archeological evidence is still scarce to assess the validity of such a claim. In the current state of knowledge, the ethnolinguistic evidence is often the most reliable source of information to trace the various and successive migrations of highlanders, in particular for those from southwest China who migrated into the **Indochina** portion of the massif, which is arguably the longest of migratory journeys from China. In the near future, research scrutinizing the DNA heritage of highland peoples today should also provide a major scientific boost to this inquiry into the history of migrations.

Based on what history has officially recorded, some broad statements can be made. In China over the centuries, **Han**, Mongol, and Manchu rulers sent many war parties to the southern frontier of the Middle Empire. These expeditions were generally sent to subordinate, extort, tax, or simply suppress recalcitrant populations. Local resistance was frequent and revolts numerous, and were mercilessly repressed. These clashes were a major catalyst to the migration south.

The 18th, 19th, and early 20th centuries were an era of disturbances in China and Southeast Asia. This turmoil affected the whole of Southern China. Famines and epidemics in the region during most of the 19th century, particularly during the **Panthay and Miao Rebellions**, contributed significantly to pushing a number of highlanders from various origins to look for better opportunities farther south in the more sparsely populated highlands of the Indochina **Peninsula**. The migrants were predominantly members of the **lineage societies**, such as the **Mien, Lolo, Lahu, Lisu, Akha, Hui**, and a large number of the **Hmong** subgroup of the **Miao**.

Among the sets of factors contributing to catalyzing the confrontation between the Han State and the **minorities** of the **massif** in the late 19th century was the presence of European colonial powers south of the border. From the early 1860s, the French and the British were competing to secure a way into south China and its lucrative resources and market potential. Since the exclusion decree of 1723 and up to 1844, all that had remained of Christian activities in China was clandestine. After 1844, in part as a repercussion of the first Opium War, new treaties allowed Christian missions to penetrate inner China again while guaranteeing the safety of the **missionaries** and converts. However, the Manchu (Qing) dynasty barely tolerated this religious and commercial infiltration by foreign powers through its southern border and was seriously annoyed that tributary rulers and **minorities** in its own domain could be involved in such a movement. Strategically speaking, there was no choice for Peking but to increase its administrative and military presence on the southern frontier, and a clash became inevitable. After a few decades of fighting, the loss of human lives was in the millions.

However, it is important to keep in mind that pull factors were also a major element at play. In this regard, the case of the Hmong in Thailand is particularly enlightening. At the turn of the 20th century, this group came chiefly from Laos, where it was believed that no specific danger was threatening them, at least not great enough to explain them moving far into Siamese territory. The general causes for this particular migration to promising and barely inhabited land are to be found in the search for new **swiddens**.

Recent ethnographic and historical studies have highlighted the fact that a significant factor in the decision to migrate and the choice of the territory to pioneer was the particular relationship between highlanders and Muslim Chinese caravaneers, the **Haw**. Based chiefly in **Yunnan**, these Haw were for a long time instrumental in providing lowland produce and goods, such as **salt** and metals to the highlanders. This traditional relationship came to include the most lucrative item, **opium**, which could thus find an easy way out of isolated valleys and remote villages, a crucial factor encouraging the small-scale highland producers to confidently enter the poppy cultivation circle. The caravan **trade**, about which little is known today, followed classical routes that for centuries had linked hinterland cities of China like Kunming, Dali, Jinghong, and Chengdu to maritime trading posts and capitals like Moulmein, Ayutthaya, Bangkok, and Vinh and Hanoi in northern Vietnam. In the 1970s in Laos and Vietnam, elderly highlanders still remembered their travels in the late 19th century with Haw caravaneers, quite often as caretakers for the horses and mules loaded with cloth, salt, or opium. Some say that they explored new fertile and vacant regions like the Tran Ninh plateau in Laos and the mountains north of Nan in Thailand. These areas offered new possibilities for those who wanted to move, and the Hmong migration to the southwest was not embarked upon blindly. A blend of fertile and available forest land with proximity to a Haw caravan route was perfectly suited both to escape the Han wrath and to simply try one's luck farther away.

For more than a century, since the adoption of European geopolitical thinking, which led to the establishment of modern and secured national borders in the Peninsula fragmenting the massif, only tiny, mostly disjointed migrations from southern China as well as between countries sharing the massif have occurred. There have, however, been two notable exceptions to this rule. The first involves significant **refugee** movements triggered by political reshuffling and wars linked to the establishment of, or fighting against, socialist regimes in China, Vietnam, Laos, and for a time at least, Cambodia and Burma. The second links with a long-term process scholars have named "the agrarian transition" and concerns economic migrations within—but sometimes also across—national borders, one flow taking jobless lowlanders from the overpopulated coasts and deltas into the roomier highlands, the other flowing in the opposite direction, taking uprooted highland peasants to the lowland urban metropolis to look for wage work, higher education, or commercial opportunities.

MILITARY TERRITORIES IN FRENCH INDOCHINA. *See TERRITOIRES MILITAIRES.*

MILLENARISM. *See* MESSIANISM.

MINCHIA. *See* BAI.

MINORITIES. All official ethnic groups of the **mainland Southeast Asian massif,** in each of the six countries where they currently live, are explicitly listed as minorities. This categorization is a consequence of their location inside specific national borders of countries where the dominant majority is of a different ethnicity. However, some comparative demographics can help challenge this political minorization. For instance, nine "minorities" of China are more numerous than the entire population of Laos. One alone, the **Zhuang**, with 16 million, even matches the combined populations of Laos and Cambodia. With Asia's sheer demography, this kind of comparative arithmetics can also be played on a larger scale: the **Hui** are roughly as numerous as the Greek, the **Yi** match the population of Switzerland, the **Miao** and **Tujia** together are four times the population of Norway, and there would be enough **Karen** to swap with the population of New Zealand. The transnationality of many groups also poses a challenge to their status as minorities, such as when the **Hmong**, a minority in Laos, are considered a cultural entity regardless of the country where they currently live. Their total number, approximately 4 million, is practically twice the number of the **Lao** "majority" in Laos. The concept of ethnic minority thus appears in a new light, not so much a demographic, positive reality, but instead a political construct serving political, economic, and strategic purposes. In the massif, most of these purposes concur to minimize the importance of "minorities" and to emphasize the cultural and historical preponderance of each of the national majorities over their "national minorities."

MINZU. *See* SHAOSHU MINZU.

MISSIONARIES. Linked to European expansion and colonization, Christian missionaries have often accompanied colonial troops in their takeover operations, sometimes even playing the role of the spearhead in isolated uplands. This function was supported by the colonial governments with a political vision of securing mountainous border areas and their populations, culturally distinct from lowland majorities.

Christian missionaries prioritized learning vernacular **languages**, first to be able to communicate with prospective converts, and then to translate the Bible into their hosts' tongues. They frequently devised new scripts for that purpose and often became the first linguists and lexicologists in the **mainland Southeast Asian massif**. A lasting political consequence of this missionary interest was its contribution to firmly linking a number of highland **minorities** to the Christian colonial state, an alliance that could initially prove profitable to the converts but which later translated into lasting resentment, still visible today, by majorities toward minorities in countries where independence was paid for dearly. In this way, in Vietnam and Laos, because of their long-standing links with Western churches, Christianized highlanders are treated today with some suspicion by the governments, who see in this connection a continuation of the reprehensible collusion between highland minorities and the former colonial rulers. In Burma, a lasting hostility between the **Buddhist** majority and highland Christians was deliberately triggered and nurtured by the British when there was a need to control the highland frontiers while at the same time undermining Burmese resistance. The **Shan** and **Karen** resistance movements of Burma, among others, are still fueled in large part by this dynamic.

American and British Protestant and Anglican missionaries of many denominations came to the massif in the wake of the British takeover of Burma and Malaya from the late 18th century onward. For a century, they limited their work to the lowlands. Then the mid-19th century Opium Wars and the ensuing negotiations with China ensured missionary penetration into the northern and central portions of the massif from European emporiums on the Chinese coast. In China, a country that was to remain beyond the grip of actual colonization, Protestant and Anglican missionaries came to play an important role as intermediaries, and sometimes advocates, between southwest minorities and British colonial agents. In **Guizhou** and **Yunnan** in particular, from the 1850s onward, numerous Methodist missionaries soon federated within the China Inland Mission, founded in 1866. Presbyterians and a contingent of Anglicans connected with the London Missionary Society also entered the field. Although learning the vernacular languages was a priority in order to translate the scriptures, as most highland languages had no indigenous script, some enterprising missionaries, such as **Samuel Pollard**, had to devise entirely new ones. Bold men and women criss-crossed the massif on their mission and could observe and catalog non-**Han** ethnic groups. Many, including, in addition to Pollard himself, Samuel Clarke, E. C. Bridgman, C. Broumton, J. Edkins, W. H. Hudspeth, and David C. Graham, have left significant linguistic works as well as descriptions of highland groups. The French were also active in the Chinese portion of the massif through Catholic priests belonging to the *Société des Missions Étrangères de Paris* (MEP), which had been commissioned by the Pope to set up Catholic vicariates in Guangxi (1840), Yunnan (1843), and Guizhou (1849). French missionaries, such as **Vial**, Schotter, Lietard, Goré, and Desgodins, produced meaningful texts on highland societies.

Meanwhile, highland Burma was also invested by Anglican and Protestant, as well as Catholic missionaries, such as the Frenchman **Charles Gilhodes** and his MEP and Italian colleagues, who had been active among lowland **Burmans** there since the early 18th century. The first highland group targeted in the 1820s was the nearest one, the Karen. Missionaries who became valuable contributors to the general ethnography of these and other groups in upper Burma include, in addition to Gilhodes, Adoniram Judson, D. M. Smeaton, L. P. Brockett, M. Mason, W. C. B Purser, **Harry I. Marshall**, M. Milne, and W. W. Cochrane.

On the eastern side of the **Peninsula**, the propagation of the Catholic faith was mainly in the hands of France and Spain, focusing on French Indochina, with complementary work in Siam. A Jesuit presence began in Vietnam in the early 17th century, but missionizing only really expanded with the military takeovers of the mid-1800s. For France, the MEP became the main provider of missionaries to **Indochina**. For the Spanish missions, with a rear base in the Philippines, the Dominicans took charge of the northeast of Tonkin. Official proselytizing among uplanders in that portion of the massif started with the relatively late establishment of highland vicariates in Cambodia (1853), Upper-Tonkin (1895), Laos (1899), and the Kontum in the **Central Highlands** (1920). Notable MEP Catholic missionaries who wrote on mountain populations there include **François-Marie Savina**, Pierre Dourisboure, Léopold Cadière, and **Jacques Dournes**. Undoubtedly the dominant Christian faith in French Indochina during colonial times, Catholicism lost significant ground during the **Second Indochina War** (1954–1975), being repressed in the Democratic Republic of Vietnam (North Vietnam), while it found itself competing with a variety of American Protestant denominations in the south. Even the added help of smaller Catholic orders, such as the *Congrégation du Très Saint Rédempteur* (CSsR) in Dak Lak province, from the late 1960s, was not sufficient for Catholicism to regain its former glory. With the communist victories in Vietnam and Laos in 1975, an age of isolation came to local Catholics and Protestants alike, which has only recently receded slightly thanks to the national liberalizations of the 1990s. In the Vietnamese and **Lao** states, though, the Christian faiths are still strongly associated with colonialism and resistance to socialism, and Christian populations in the highlands, being also culturally distinct, remain under constant security watch.

MLABRI. Possibly the last **hunting-gathering** society in the whole **massif**, the Mlabri officially account for 282 individuals, moving between Nan and Phrae provinces in Thailand and Xayabury in Laos. The Mlabri appear to be **Mon-Khmer** speakers, but their exact dialectical affiliation is uncertain. One hypothesis is that the Mlabri could in fact be a composite of members from several regional groups who opted to adopt hunting-gathering as their main activity. In Thailand and Laos, the Mlabri are also called Mrabri, Yumbri (allegedly their autonym), and *Phi Tong Luang*, or Spirits of the Yellow Leaves in Tai.

MNONG. A **Mon-Khmer**–speaking group located in Vietnam's **Central Highlands**, neighbor to the **Co-Ho**, **Xtieng**, Rag-lai, and Ma. The Mnong reside chiefly in Lam Dong and Dak Lak provinces, where they numbered 92,451 individuals in 1999. It is also possible that some Mnong live just across the border in Cambodia, where they are supposedly known as **Phnong** (Pnong). The Mnong are **animists**, with an emphasis on **buffalo** as an important sacrificial animal. For their livelihoods, they have customarily relied on **swiddening**, which they practiced in a sustainable way for hundreds of years before being pushed toward fixed agriculture by the Vietnamese state. The Mnong of Vietnam have gained a degree of celebrity thanks to the published work of French ethnologist **Georges Condominas**, in particular his monograph *We Have Eaten the Forest,* first published in 1957 under the title *Nous avons mangé la forêt de la Pierre-Génie Gôo.*

"MOI" ("MOÏ"). A pejorative generic expression meaning "savage," used in Vietnam long before, during, and in some cases even after the colonial period (1858–1954) to designate non-**Kinh** upland minority groups in the country, especially in the **Central Highlands (*Tay Nguyen*)**. The term has been used there for a long time in ethnonyms, such as Moi Da Vach, Moi Luy, etc.

MONE (MON). The smallest official **minority** in Laos, a Vietic-speaking group within the **Austro-Asiatic** family, who were a mere 217 in number in 1995 and live in eastern Xiengkhuang province. They are believed to be related to the **Muong** in Vietnam, hence their name. This small group should not be confused with the more numerous lowland Mon of Burma and Thailand, who form the Monic branch of the southern **Mon-Khmer** family.

MON-KHMER LANGUAGE FAMILY. A major branch of the **Austro-Asiatic language family**, Mon-Khmer subdivides into 11 branches comprising lowland populations, such as the **Khmer** in Cambodia and the **Mon** in Burma and Thailand, but also many dispersed highland groups, such as the Palaungic-speaking **Wa**, **Bulang** and **Bonan** minority nationalities in southwestern **Yunnan**, the Khmuic-speaking **Khmu** and **Lamet** in northern Laos, with extensions into Vietnam and Thailand, as well as the Katuic and Bahnaric speakers in southern Laos and the Vietnamese **Central Highlands**. In terms of identity, Mon-Khmer speakers from one or another of the few dozen highland groups within this language family found in the massif live in social organizations that were often labeled "tribal" in the past, a conception replaced today with the more appropriate and less controversial notion of **lineage societies**. These groups generally practice subsistence-oriented forms of agriculture and horticulture combining **swiddening**, gardening, and sometimes, when they are permanently sedentarized, wet **rice** cultivation. Only a portion of their production is exchanged on the market for various necessities or consumer goods that cannot be produced locally. Politically speaking, these groups are customarily very loosely centralized, although historically, most of the time they were attached to a **feudal** state controlled by the **Tai**-speaking elite, to whom they had to contribute **tributes**, rent, labor, or the provision of certain forest products linked to a demand in the lowlands. Most Mon-Khmer speakers in the highlands are **animists,** unless they have been influenced by the proximity of one or another of the major religions that penetrated the massif, in the first instance **Buddhism**, followed by Christianity wherever European **missionaries** have been active—notably in Vietnam's Central Highlands. (*See* figure 2.)

MONTAGNARDS. In the **Indochina** Peninsula, the label Montagnard refers specifically to approximately 20 highland minority societies belonging to the **Mon-Khmer** and **Austronesian language families**, dwelling in moderately elevated valleys and plateaus in the south of Vietnam—the *Tay Nguyen*. They are also found in adjacent portions of southeastern Laos and northeastern Cambodia. In each country, they are a small minority. The word *montagnard* is a legacy from French colonial times, meaning merely "mountain people" in French. The colonists applied it generically to all mountain dwellers in Indochina and beyond. Its restricted use in English dates from the American involvement in Vietnam, and despite its popularity with English speakers, this use is subject to debate.

It is widely accepted that the Austronesian Montagnards inhabited the region since at least the proto-Malay peopling of the **Peninsula**, while Mon-Khmer–speaking Montagnards migrated there later. All were pushed into the highlands over several centuries by the expansion of the successive and more powerful lowland kingdoms, particularly Champa. These otherwise culturally and linguistically heterogeneous ethnic groups eventually came to dwell in this same ecosystem in the southern **Annam Cordillera**, stretching north-south between coastal Vietnam and the Mekong watershed. In the second half of the 19th century, social systems among dwellers there were mainly **lineage**-based and nonliterate, and the economy was centered on permanently sedentarized rotational **swidden** agriculture. In times of peace, settlement patterns would be stable and the relationship to the natural environment balanced. **Trade** among neighbors consisted of necessities, such as metals and **salt**, exchanged for forest products, basketry, and silver. **Tributes** were paid to lowland monarchs. Customary law consisted of a system of negotiation between **households** and **lineages**, and **animistic** beliefs implied constant arbitration between the temporal world—the human domain—and the supernatural world inhabited by spirits.

During colonial times, occasional co-optation became a politically and militarily useful device for French colonial rule. Outside these specific needs, age-old prejudice was prevalent. The Montagnards were considered by outside observers to be savages (*moi* in Vietnamese), superstitious, and backward. Later, Vietnamese, American, and various pro-American troops stationed in the Republic of Vietnam (South Vietnam) needed to ally with the inhabitants of the highlands as their habitat bordered eastern Cambodia and southeastern Laos, where the intricate network of the Ho Chi Minh trails was used by the communists to convey military support south from the Democratic Republic of Vietnam (North Vietnam). In the process, the South Vietnamese regime tried to curtail customary law and created the **strategic hamlets** resettlement scheme, forcing the highland populations to abandon their usual dwellings to regroup in guarded villages, thus inspiring among many Montagnards armed resistance and a degree of nostalgia for "benevolent" colonial rule. With their traditional religious practices outlawed, many Montagnards turned to communism as an act of protest. Against this, Christian **missionary** work met with some success among the **E-de**, **Gia-rai**, **Chu-ru**, **Co-ho**, and Lat in particular. At the end of the **Second Indochina War** (1954–1975), the number of Montagnard casualties was estimated at 200,000 in Vietnam alone, while more than 85 percent of the **Central Highlands** population was forced to flee or resettle at one time or another, often across the borders. In the midst of this ordeal, **FULRO** (*Front unifié pour la Libération des Races opprimées*) was created in 1964 in the ranks of the U.S. Army Special Forces in Vietnam and became the most important Montagnard autonomy and anticommunist movement. FULRO's political and military resistance to the communist state after 1975 slowly faded until the surrender of the last FULRO armed group in 1992 in Cambodia.

The highland peoples of Vietnam, Laos, and Cambodia are—most of the time erroneously—blamed for the deforestation occurring in their upland environment. In the Vietnamese Central Highlands in particular, the massive migration of **Kinh** from the plains, which was officially launched by the state in 1975 under the **New Economic Zones (NEZ) scheme**, put intense pressure on the natural resources of that ecosystem. Economic immigration further developed at the end of the 1980s due to the Economic Renovation (*Doi Moi*), and was encouraged by crop substitution schemes aimed at installing ever more farmers. This strategy still goes on today in the form of economic migration from other parts of the country, notably lowland **coffee** growers and other minority peoples from the north, such as the **Tay**, the **Nung**, and the **Hmong**. This excessive stress on resources causes social tensions—triggering severe social unrest as was the case in 2001 and 2003—and a deterioration of the environment, most dramatically visible in the rapid deforestation and the lowering of the groundwater tables.

In search of a sustainable solution, Vietnamese scholars and their **Lao** counterparts are conducting research on issues, such as customary law in relation to natural resource management, indigenous knowledge and indigenous strategies for improved fallow management, and community-based forest management institutions. But in the process, preserving cultural identity is low on the list of priorities. In Laos and Vietnam in particular, following the Chinese example, selective preservation of minority cultures is practiced, in which the state decides unilaterally which aspects of a culture are sufficiently valuable—and politically tolerable—to be retained, and which should be actively discouraged.

MOOBAN. In Thailand, the smallest territorial administrative unit normally translated as "village." Several *mooban* form together a *tambon* (subdistrict).

MORÉCHAND, GUY (1923–2002). An anthropologist and member of *Ecole Française d'Extrême-Orient* (EFEO) and a specialist on the **Hmong** of Laos and northwest Vietnam, where he conducted extended fieldwork in the early 1950s and the late 1960s. He published, in French, an important monograph: *Le chamanisme hmong* [*Hmong-Shamanism*] (1968).

MUANG. A traditional **Tai** feudal political entity that can be translated as "kingdom" or "principality." Within Tai-speaking groups, **feudalism** crystallized in a system called the *muang* in the vernacular language, a form of small monarchy centered on a town from where the elite ruled the commoners around their stronghold. The whole of the **mainland Southeast Asian massif**'s midregion, from Chinese Guangxi in the East to Indian Assam to the West, was dotted with principalities applying such systems, notably in the **Lue** domain of **Sip Song Phan Na** and the White **Thai** realm of **Sip Song Chau Tai**.

Over a huge geographical area can still be found hundreds of toponyms derived from the word *muang*, from Mong Hpayak in Burma, to Muang Nan in Thailand, Muang Sing in Laos, Menglang and Mengla in Yunnan, and, in Vietnam, Muong Lai (Lai Chau), Muong So (Phong Tho), and Muong Khuong.

The Tai-language prefix *chiang*, "fortified city," is also frequent, as seen in the names Chiang Tung (Keng Tung) in Burma, Chiang Rai and Chiang Kham in Thailand, Xiang Khouang in Laos, Jiangcheng in Yunnan, and Giang Mung Pho in Vietnam. The word *ban*, meaning "village," also exemplifies this influence, as it is an extremely frequent toponym in highland Burma, Thailand, Laos, Yunnan, and Vietnam, even as far south as in Buon Ma Thuot, the head town of Dac Lac province in the Central Highlands of South Vietnam, where Buon is derived from *ban*. A seminal analysis of the *muang* has been written by the French anthropologist **Georges Condominas**, *Essai sur l'évolution des systèmes politiques thaïs* [*Some Remarks on Thai Political Systems*] (1976).

In Laos, the term *muang* is also used to designate the official administrative and territorial unit best translated as "district," a territorial subdivision of the larger *khoueng* (province), and, until recently, comprising several *tasseng* (subdistricts).

MULAO (MULAM). Tai-speaking group of China (207,352 in 2000) dwelling in **Zhuang** territory in northern Guangxi. The Mulao belong to the Kam-Sui branch and are intimately related to the **Kam (Dong)** and the **Maonan**, with whom they share most of their cultural characteristics.

MUN. The Mun constitute the second largest subgroup of the **Yao** after the **Mien**. Subgroups of the Mun include the Kim Mun and the Kim Meun.

MUONG. The Muong of Vietnam form the Muongic branch of the **Viet-Muong** subfamily within the **Austro-Asiatic language family**. The Muong numbered 1,137,515 in the 1999 national census, making them the third largest national minority of Vietnam after the **Tay** and the **Thai**. The Muong are grouped on a relatively well-delineated territory located close to the **Kinh** lowlands on the western fringes of the Red River delta, for the most part in Hoa Binh (479,197), Thanh Hoa (328,744), and Phu Tho (165,748) provinces, with additional communities in adjacent territory. The Muong have produced no archives of their own, but it is believed that this group arrived in northern Vietnam at roughly the same time as their close relatives the Kinh, that is, the ethnic Vietnamese. Yet it is suggested that due to the direct influence of **Han** culture during a millennium of Chinese occupation of north Vietnam (111 B.C.–938 A.D.), the Kinh moved toward a higher degree of Sinization, while the Muong were largely left to themselves. Meanwhile, they developed a **feudal** political organization and paid **tribute** to the Vietnamese monarch while retaining a religious system based on **animistic** practices, much as their most important neighbor after the Kinh, the Thai, the longtime masters of the upper Black (Da) River valley, had done. During colonial times, as French anthropologist Jeanne Cuisinier showed in her 1946 monograph *Les M'uong: Géographie Humaine et Sociologie* [*The Muong: Human Geography and Sociology*], the Muong were even believed to be part of the **Tai** language family. This confusion was due in part to the fact that early observers thought the ethnonym Muong and the fundamental Tai political and geographical entity, the *muang*, were one and the same. What was true, however, was that the long proximity of these two groups had allowed for the mutual borrowing of many social traits and agricultural techniques. Today, the Muong have again turned to the lowlands and have become the most Vietnamized of all national **minorities** in that country.

MYANMAR. Myanmar is the name the military junta, in power since the 1989 coup, has elected to replace the name **Burma**. It is now considered the official name of the country by many formal international institutions that had decided that the disputed legitimacy of brutal regimes should not preclude accepting the decisions these regimes make about the countries they have power over—consider for instance the renaming of **Cambodia** to Democratic Kampuchea under the Khmer Rouge. This name change in Burma, however, is seen by a number of independent observers as a crude maneuver to help legitimize the military junta. The name Myanmar has thus been rejected by a large number of authors, including the author of this dictionary, preferring the former name, Burma.

– N –

NAGA. An estimated 12,183 **Tibeto-Burman**–speaking Naga lived in Burma in 2004, all located on the western edge of the country, in the uplands of northwestern Sagaing province (*taing*). However, the Naga of Burma are a very small portion of the larger Naga identity, most representatives of which live across the border in eastern India. There, an estimated 2 million Naga dwell in Nagaland, with extension into the adjacent states of Manipur, Assam, and Arunachal Pradesh.

NAN CHAO (CHAU) KINGDOM. The "Southern Prince" or "Southern Kingdom." Between the eighth and 13th centuries A.D., a **feudal** highland kingdom that thrived in the region of the adjacent headwaters of the Yangtze, Red (Yuan), Mekong (Lancang), Salween (Nu), and Irrawaddy Rivers, a territory that is today split between western **Yunnan** and northeastern Burma. Its capital was located in the town of Dali, on Erh Hai Lake in western Yunnan, the heart of **Bai** country today. From a **Han** point of view, an independent and strong Nan Chao kingdom—renamed Tali (Dali) Kingdom in 937 A.D.—served, through a **tributary** relationship, as a buffer to contain Tibetan expansion on the southwest margins.

It had for a long time been thought that Nan Chao was a **Tai** kingdom, or more precisely, a federation of Tai principalities (*muang*) more or less firmly associated while retaining a large degree of individual autonomy. French scholar Paul Pelliot proposed as early as 1904, and recent scholarhsip agrees, that the rulers of Nan Chao were of **Tibeto-Burman** origin, perhaps Bai, and that their kingdom was multiethnic, with a majority of Tibeto-Burman groups. In 1253, the Mongol Yuan troops of Kublai Khan invaded Nan Chao, causing a revival of political autonomy for some Tai principalities in the upper region that became emancipated from Nan Chao/Tali rule. The heirs of several of these are believed to be today located in Assam in India, in **Shan** and **Kachin** States in Burma, and in southern Yunnan, particularly the Xishuangbanna-Dai Autonomous Prefecture, formerly the Tai Lue domain of **Sip Song Phan Na.**

NANZHAO. *See* NAN CHAO KINGDOM.

NATIONAL MINORITY CULTURAL DAYS. Socialist China and Vietnam have made a point of holding national days for **minority** nationalities. These typically involve neatly choreographed events held in the capitals and main towns under the gaze of the political elite, while in the uplands, rural local authorities set up singing and dancing contests in traditional attire. These days are aimed at showing publicly and to the world that protecting and promoting multiculturalism is a definite socialist state policy. However, such days have been severely criticized by outside observers as contrived events, promoting only the benign aesthetic elements of minority cultures that are allowed to survive under pervasive policies of "**selective cultural preservation**." Any contentious issues in the fields of economics, politics, or cultural resistance to integration into the nation are carefully kept out of the spotlight. Such national minority cultural days, which can take many formats and be held at different times of the year depending on the national, provincial, and local agendas, have become important **tourist** attractions and probably are for most tourists, foreign and national alike, the only glimpse they will ever have of highland minority life.

NATIONALITIES COMMISSION OF LAOS. The ministerial-level body in Laos responsible for ethnic **minority** affairs.

NATIONALITY. A specific notion regarding highland minorities, largely confined to the communist rhetoric on minorities, and officially used in Laos, Vietnam, and China as a building block of the policies on ethnicity. The Chinese term *minzu* translates as "nationalities," while *dan toc* in Vietnamese and *sonsaat* in Lao translate as "nation." This concept owes much to the Soviet influence on Asian socialist regimes.

In a long article published in 1913 titled "Marxism and the National Question," young Joseph Stalin made an attempt at summarizing—and distorting—the thinking of Otto Bauer and Karl Kautsky and declared that "The nation is a stable human community, historically constituted, born on the basis of common language, territory, and economic life, with a psychological formation that translates into a common culture." In Stalin's view, the absence of only one of these characteristics meant that this was not yet a nation (*natsiya* in Russian), but an earlier, cruder form, the "nationality" (*narodnost*). For instance, in the absence of a common block of territory—which paradoxically is the case for most societies in the **mainland Southeast Asian massif**—a group could not possibly be considered a nation.

Clearly, during the revolutionary struggle, when allies were needed, peripheral ethnic groups had been promised by militant leaders that, in the event of victory, the new socialist regime would grant them forms of political autonomy. Stalin and the heads of the Communist Party of the Soviet Union at the time also had in mind the ideological organization of the administration of the many non-Russian, non-European groups living in the huge territory falling under their control. After victory, however, promises were forgotten, and the centralized state instead tightened its grip on those peripheral ethnicities while, under intense international scrutiny, also sending objective signs of respect for the principle of multiculturalism as embodied in constitutional texts.

This restrictive, strategic concept of "nations" and, not quite as Stalin had originally conceived it, "nationalities," the two notions becoming synonymous, was then passed on to "brother" fighters in their struggles against colonial or reactionary powers. The fighting Marxist leaders in China, Vietnam, and Laos used the Soviet rhetoric and tactics, and in this way gained the support of many highland ethnic minorities during the revolutionary wars and, once victorious, also ended up backtracking on their early promises of political autonomy.

In these three countries, the administration of ethnic minorities, and particularly highland minorities in the massif, is still based on the principle that all "nations" in the country, including the majority **Han**, **Kinh**, and **Lao**, are equal in political terms. Some highland minority groups have even been granted **Autonomous Regions** (or counties or prefectures) to administer. In reality, however, their political autonomy is negligible, and the central government remains in control of all major sectors of the decision-making process.

NAXI (NAKHI, MOSO). The Naxi, members of the **Tibeto-Burman language family** close to **Yi (Lolo)** and indigenous to **Yunnan**, numbered 308,839 in 2000. They dwell in very high areas on both sides of the upper Yangtze River loop in northwestern Yunnan, close to the **Sichuan** border. The Naxi are confirmed to have resided in this location since at least 1000 A.D. It is believed that they were pushed out of Sichuan into western Yunnan by **Han** expansion. In Yunnan, they have become the **feudal** rulers of a domain centered on the town of Lijiang, an area today called the Lijiang Naxi Autonomous Prefecture, in which most Naxi live. The rest are scattered among Weixi, Zhongdian, Ninglang, Deqin, Yongsheng, Heqing, Jianchuan, and Lanping counties in Yunnan, as well as in a few counties in Sichuan, and Mangkang county in Tibet.

The Naxi practice Bon shamanism, a form of **animism** linked to Tibetan **Buddhism**, the latter having been a lasting influence. Ancient and strong historical, cultural, religious, and political ties with Tibet have translated into shared agricultural practices, rituals, and food habits. This proximity was also a cause for the Naxi to side with their Tibetan neighbors in an attempt to resist the communist takeover in the late 1940s. Since the 1980s, the main transformations of Naxi culture and economy are linked to the **tourist** boom that occurred as a consequence of the ancient town of Lijiang, an architectural jewel, and its stunning mountain landscape being made a "Chinese National Treasure" in 1986. Its reputation was then further boosted in 1997 by the granting of the status of United Nations Educational, Scientific, and Cultural Organization (UNESCO) World Heritage site. Ever since, both national and international tourists have been flocking to the town, with important consequences in terms of economic development and modernization, environmental degradation, and Han in-migration.

The Naxi **language** shows significant similarities to Yi. Two Naxi scripts exist. The older, intriguing one, is pictographic and probably indigenous, from a time when ritual texts were encoded as well as literary works; it depicts animals and objects in a straightforward way and is used primarily by priests as for its mnemonics. Producing an indigenous script is a rare occurrence among the highland **minorities** in the **mainland Southeast Asian massif**. The second script is syllabic and brings together elements borrowed chiefly from the Tibetan script.

NEW ECONOMIC ZONES SCHEME (NEZ). After its official recognition on the international scene in 1954, the Democratic Republic of Vietnam (DRVN, North Vietnam) launched a series of programs to put in place the socialist system in the north. One such scheme was designed to alleviate demographic pressure in the Red River (Song Hong) delta by sending back **refugees** who had flocked to urban areas during the **First Indochina War** (1946–1954). The government relocated massive numbers of lowlanders into more sparsely populated regions, essentially the highlands surrounding the delta, ensuring by the same token that border peripheries would become more resolutely attached to the socialist cause and the nation. This was called the New Economic Zones scheme. Recruits were provided with seeds, farming implements, building materials, and food for several months in order to assist their establishment in their new homes. After that, it was expected that they could make a living on their own. By 1975, approximately a million peasants had thus been relocated in the north. After reunification in 1975, a similar program was applied to the former Republic of Vietnam (South Vietnam), the **Central Highlands** being this time targeted for the collective relocation. By 1980, 1 million people in the south had thus been repositioned.

Both in the north and the south, the New Economic Zones scheme left little space for more ancient highland dwellers to voice disagreement with this sudden in-migration of lowlanders ill-prepared for their new life in the mountains. The drain on local resources, such as fuel wood, water, and land, was significant, the damage to the forest due to clearings was massive, but all this was perceived by the state as a small price to pay for the national cause and triumph of socialism. The NEZ scheme was officially ended in the early 1980s. Nevertheless, "spontaneous migrations" to the highlands have continued since, helped by state-sponsored new economic opportunities initiated in the form of industrial plants, the building of dams, or, in the southern highlands, plantations, **coffee** in particular. Today, friction with ancient highlanders worsen and clashes flare up episodically, quickly repressed by the armed forces.

NEW YEAR CELEBRATIONS. All societies in the **mainland Southeast Asian massif**, as well as all those surrounding them, attribute particular significance to the passage from one year to the next. Thus, they all conduct ritual and festive activities to mark this transit. A common feature is the use of the lunar calendar to determine the date of the celebrations. Among Sinicized and Vietnamized groups, it is most commonly held in the first or second lunar month after the winter solstice. For **Tai** speakers—in Thailand, Laos, northeastern Burma, southern **Yunnan**, north Vietnam—the New Year falls in mid-April and doubles as a water festival celebrating the approaching new agricultural season. As the most important collective gathering of the year for many ethnic groups, New Year festivities in the massif typically extend over a few days and provide many social opportunities, such as visiting kin and looking for spouses, as well as allowing political dealings to take place, such as agreeing to various types of cooperation regarding the important matters of the moment. New Year festivals are usually lively, very colorful events, with highlanders wearing their newest and finest attire, displaying as much of their **jewelry** as feasible, and behaving in a playful and relaxed manner.

NGE. Katuic speakers within the **Mon-Khmer language family**. In 1995, 12,189 members of the Nge (Ngeh, Nghe) **minority** were recorded living in eastern Saravane province in southern Laos. They practice a mixed agriculture combining wet **rice** cultivation and **swiddening**, and are **animists**.

NGOUAN. A small group of 1,344 of these Vietic speakers are listed as an official minority in Laos, dwelling in eastern Borikhamxay province. They constitute an overspill from Vietnam.

NHANG (NYANG). An ancient generic name used during colonial times to label a **Tai**-speaking cluster of groups called **Giay** in Vietnam and **Yang** in Laos. Their Tai dialect is close to the **Nung**'s.

NOMADISM. Forms of nomadism have been practiced in the **mainland Southeast Asian massif** since the earliest human presence there and are still undertaken today by a few groups. Nomadism was normally adopted by groups that had not been economically incorporated into a **feudal** state as peasants. This includes, for instance, many groups living in the higher reaches of the massif, such as a majority of **Tibeto-Burman**, **Mon-Khmer**, and Miao-Yao groups. Alternatively, nomadism could also be used as an escape or a survival strategy adopted temporarily by populations needing to move, such as the **Hmong** and **Lolo** from China. These once sedentarized groups were set in motion by adversity, wars, climatic change, or untenable demographic pressure in their homelands. Before the enforcement of tight borders in the 20th century, vast numbers of highland populations could in this way move across the mountains and high valleys without much hindrance. Since the formalization of modern, enclosed states across Asia, nomadism in the massif has been severely curtailed, not least because the modern governments do not look upon populations within national borders that cannot be accounted for, nor taxed, with a benevolent eye.

Nomadism and seminomadism in the massif have also been strongly associated with **swiddening**, a form of itinerant agriculture most adapted to populations willing, or required, to keep on the move. This, combined with security motives, is why most Southeast Asian governments wish to put an end to swiddening, considered by those in control to be unsustainable and environmentally damaging. Nomadic populations have been consistently earmarked for complete and final sedentarization.

NONG DUC MANH (1940–). General secretary of the Executive Committee of the Communist Party of Vietnam (CPV)—in other words, president—since 2001, Nong is the first highland minority representative to hold the highest office in any country in the **mainland Southeast Asian massif**. Born to a **Tay** farming family in present-day Bac Kan province in the northeast, he joined the Communist Party in 1963 and was sent to study forestry in Leningrad. He returned to (then) Bac Thai province in 1972 to become a civil servant and eventually was promoted to political leadership. In 1989, he became a member of the Central Committee of the CPV and its head Ethnic Group member. He joined the Politburo in 1991, and presided over the National Assembly of 1997. His final selection for the highest political position came at the meeting of the Ninth National Assembly in April 2001. A persistent rumor in Vietnam suggests that Mr. Nong could be an illegitimate son of former president Ho Chi Minh.

NOSU. *See* YI.

NU (LUTZU, NUTZU). Members of the **Tibeto-Burman language family**. There are 28,759 (2000) Nu in China. They inhabit the upper Nu (Salween) River in northwestern **Yunnan** and Bijiang, Fugong, Gongshan, and Lanping counties, including the Nujiang Lisu Autonomous Prefecture. Others are found in Weixi county in the Diqing Tibetan Autonomous Prefecture. Throughout history, the Nu were in a state of subordination to Nan Chao, the **Naxi**, the Tibetan, and the **Bai** feudal rulers. The British colonial administration pushed into the upper Nujiang valley, followed by Christian **missionaries**, until the Red Army reclaimed the region. The Nu are customarily **swiddeners** and practice a combination of Tibetan Lamaism and **animism**. The Nu have no indigenous script but use the Tibetan alphabet.

NUA (TAI NUA). *See* SHAN.

NUNG. A **Tai**-speaking group of the Central Tai branch, found on both sides of the border between China and Vietnam, whose overall numbers may well be in excess of 2.5 million. In China, the Nung are found in western Guangxi. They are not specifically accounted for there, as the Chinese authorities amalgamate them with the huge, 16-million strong **Zhuang** minority nationality. Outside observers in the mid-20th century estimated that the Nung were roughly twice as numerous in China as in Vietnam, which could put their number in Guangxi today as high as 1.7 million.

In Vietnam, the Nung are the third largest Tai-speaking group and sixth overall among national minority groups. They numbered 856,412 in 1999, dwelling in the highlands east of the Red River delta, in the north of the country. In terms of residential patterns as well as in linguistic, religious, and cultural terms, they continuously mingle with their cousins, the **Tay**, with whom they share these midaltitude lands along the Chinese border from Lao Cai in the north to the Gulf of Tonkin in the east. The Nung of Vietnam are chiefly found in the provinces of Lang Son (302,415) and Cao Bang (161,134), with substantial numbers also in Bac Giang, Ha Giang, Thai Nguyen, Lao Cai, and Tuyen Quang. Over 100,000 Nung have also moved south within

Vietnam to settle in the provinces of Lam Dong, Dak Lak, and Dong Nai in the **Central Highlands**, attracted by the agricultural opportunities opened up there by the Vietnamese government.

Nung economy is agriculture based, with **maize** and wet **rice** as the staple crops. **Trade** has been important too, as the geographical position of the Nung places them right between important Chinese and Vietnamese populations. For some time, the Nung have ceased being a **lineage society**, though they have never set up their own **feudal** domains, probably stopped by their immediate proximity to the **Kinh** and **Han** heartlands. Much like their neighbors the Zhuang, they have been steadily Sinicized/Vietnamized. They have grafted onto an active **animistic** substratum forms of Confucianism, Taoism, and **Buddhism** with original syncretic practices. The Nung use the **Chinese ideograms** in China, and Vietnamese Romanized script in Vietnam.

NYAHEUN (NHA HEUN). A **Mon-Khmer**–speaking group of the Bahnaric branch with a modest population of 5,152 located in the eastern Boloven Plateau in Southern Laos. The Nyaheun are a **lineage society** that practices **swidden** agriculture.

NYIAVU LOBLIAYAO (1921–1999). A prominent **Hmong** leader of the **Lao** Revolution and, after its establishment in 1975, of the administration of the Lao People's Democratic Republic (LPDR). A younger brother to another prominent Hmong leader, **Faydang Lobliayao**, Nyiavu followed a similar route to political power and national fame. He was elected to the Central Committee of the Lao Issara Front in 1950 and joined the Lao People's Party when it was established in 1955. He was elected to the Central Committee of the Lao Patriotic Front in 1956 and presided over its provincial committee in Xiengkhuang until 1972, when he was appointed to the Central Committee of the Lao People's Revolutionary Party. At the formation of the LPDR, he was made chairman of the Nationalities Commission, in charge of minority affairs for the country. He retired in 1990 and died in 1999.

NYOUAN. A **Tai**-speaking group, the 26,239 Nyouan found in lowland Xayabury province in northwestern Laos are an extension of the

Yuan of Thailand, the majority lowland Tai-speaking group in northern Thailand. The Nyouan share all the major cultural characteristics of the Yuan.

– O –

O-DU. With only 301 members residing in Nghe An province in 1999, the O-du are the smallest official national minority in Vietnam. They also appear in some accounts of minority population in Laos under the name Oe Du, but their location and numbers there are unknown. They are **Mon-Khmer** speakers.

OPIUM AND THE HIGHLANDS. One of the most persistent associations in the minds of outside observers regarding highland economies is the one linking higher-dwelling groups, such as the **Hmong, Yao, Hani, Lolo, Lisu**, and others to the cultivation of the infamous opium poppy (*papaver somniferum* L.). While this association is largely justified, the historical, political, and economic logic behind it deserves more scrutiny.

Due to the marketing of large quantities of opium in China, first by the Portuguese in the 18th century and then by the British and the French, who wished to generate profits locally to support their colonial efforts, a high level of opium consumption emerged in China in the 19th century (15 million Chinese opium addicts in 1870, according to McCoy). This trend was significantly stimulated and skillfully maintained by the British, who could have the poppy grown in Bengal and its products distributed through the network that the East India Company developed throughout Asia in the 18th and 19th centuries. As early as the 18th century, China's leaders were worried by this growing **trade** and the huge loss in revenue the net importation of thousands of tons of opium involved. Gradually, as a result of such high stakes, the main protagonists clashed in what were called the Opium Wars (1838–1842 and 1856–1858), both lost by China. Following the treaty of Nanking (Nanjing) in 1842, China was forced to allow the Europeans and the Americans to set up commercial posts at a number of locations on the Chinese coast and to trade almost freely with the huge Chinese market. The only option left to the Chinese to compete with the intruders was to promote and support the national production of opium, which the central authorities quickly did. The populations dwelling in the areas suitable for this production, essentially the limestone mountains and plateaus of the southwest, were then pushed into growing the poppy and producing raw opium to be sold to government agents. The state in turn processed the raw substance and sold it on the interior market.

Concurrently, however, many of these same producers in the southwest highlands were also courted by the British and the French, who were able to reach the central parts of the massif through the valleys leading north from their Burma and **Indochina** colonial domains. Brought to Moulmein, Rangoon, Haiphong, and Saigon, the processed opium was shipped to the European trading posts on the Chinese cost and to other colonies elsewhere around the world where Chinese consumers had settled. So profitable was this trade and so substantial the sums it entailed that to help appreciate the size of the business, Descours-Gatin has recently shown that between 1898 and 1922, the contribution from the industry of opium to the total gross income of the colonial budget in French Indochina fluctuated between 25 and 42 percent, figures that compare with the income the same trade helped channel toward British India thanks to its Bengal operations. To translate this contribution into practical terms, it has been estimated that at the time of the **First Indochina War** (1946–1954), if all the opium produced or transported in one year through Tonkin's highlands alone had fallen into the Viet Minh's hands, it would have been sufficient to equip its entire regular army forces of 1952 (six divisions) with arms supplied through **barter** with southern China arms dealers.

Highland **minorities** in southern China were becoming actors in a fierce international competition, the stakes of which largely exceeded their usual political understanding and their military capabilities. Locally, having understood the lucrative potential of this new trade and noticed the competition between China and the European powers, highlanders tried to make the most of the opportunity. This path at times led to economic confrontation with the Chinese administration. The violent revolts and rebellions that shook the southern part of the country during the second half of the 19th century, such as the **Panthay and Miao Rebellions**, and the subsequent waves of migration into the highlands of the **Peninsula**, can be linked, at least in part, to the strong urge to control the production and sale of opium.

Throughout the second half of the 20th century, being in control of opium production and trade remained crucial for various belligerent groups, for whom it provided a means of financing their armed struggles. Even American forces during the **Second Indochina War** (1954–1975) were instrumental in the transportation, storage, distribution, and, above all, consumption of opium and its most popular derivative—**heroin**—among the U.S. forces stationed in Southeast Asia. But when wars in the region began subsiding, national governments saw more harm than good in this peculiar trade and started putting an end to it. They were financially assisted in this by the United States and some West European countries, which now had to contain the drug addiction problem that had been brought home by returning troops. Thailand was the earliest Southeast Asian country to legislate against poppy cultivation, in 1959, and all countries sharing the massif were to eventually join in signing the 1988 UN Drug-Convention. This includes Burma, which has nonetheless remained the major regional producer of the poppy due to political turmoil and armed opposition within its national borders, rebels using opium to make money. Laos is a distant second, where the opium production and trade help alleviate a weak economy in remote rural areas.

Over the past three decades, most local governments and outside observers have been oblivious to the historical factors that led to the regional explosion of the opium business, with the economic dependence on opium cultivation it entailed for many highland groups. The label "poppy cultivators" was used by national governments and many international development agencies to stigmatize highland groups in the massif, many of which have come to be considered pariahs. This, it seems, is enough to authorize national governments to cause major disruptions in the minorities' lives. The new logic put forward is that in addition to contributing to a reprehensible trade, intensive poppy cultivation imposes a particularly aggressive tax on the capacity of the land to regenerate. It causes quick top-soil depletion and, as a consequence, is a prime cause of erosion in the highlands. Trying to put an end to this downward spiral that ultimately affects large populations in the lowlands, **replacement crop** schemes have become the order of the day everywhere in the massif. Income from agriculture centered on the poppy has thus fallen drastically, while the real benefits of replacement cash-crops for the highland peasants are uncertain.

ORANG ASLI. "Original" or "First" Peoples in the Malay language. A generic construct used in Malaysia to identify all minority **Austro-Asiatic** (Aslian, Semang-Senoi branch) and **Austronesian** (Malay branch) groups considered **aboriginal** to the Malaysian peninsula (former Malaya), who together number approximately 100,000 people. The Semang include the Lanoh, Semnan, Sabum, and northern Aslian speakers except the Chewong; the Senoi include the Temiar and Semai; and aboriginal Malays include the Temuan, Jakun, Orang Kanaq, and Orang Selitar. All these groups live mainly on the heights of the hinterland and keep a separate cultural identity from the lowland components of Malaysian society, the Malays, Indians, and Chinese. In political terms, Malaysia's government has included the *Orang Asli* in its nationalistic category of *Bumiputra*, the "Sons of the Soil," originally designed to give historical precedence to the Malay speakers in the country as opposed to more recent Chinese and Indian migrants. A detailed review of particular subgroups of the *Orang Asli* is outside the scope of this dictionary because they are more closely associated with Maritime Southeast Asian highland **minorities**, in particular those in Sumatra and Borneo, rather than with those found in the **mainland Southeast Asian massif** proper.

OY. The Oy of Laos numbered 14,947 in 1995 and are **Mon-Khmer** speakers of the Bahnaric branch. They live on the slopes of the Boloven Plateau in Attapeu province in the extreme south of the country. The Oy were subject to slave-hunting by the **feudal** Siamese on such a scale that, combined with migration and epidemics, it is believed to have significantly curtailed their demography until the early 20th century. *See also* SLAVERY.

– P –

PA THEN. A small fraction of the **Miao-Yao language family** that migrated from China into Vietnam starting in the 18th century A.D. In northern Vietnam, the Pa Then numbered 5,569 in 1999, all located in Ha Giang and Tuyen Quang provinces.

PACOH. A **Mon-Khmer**–speaking group belonging to the Katuic branch and living in Central Vietnam and southeastern Laos. In Laos, the Pacoh (13,224 in 1995) dwell in the east of Saravane province. In Vietnam, where they are not officially accounted for and their exact number is unknown, reports from colonial times on the "Kha Pacoh" indicate that they could be found in the western portion of Hue province in Vietnam. This location, where the Bru-van-kieu also live, suggests that there could be a link between the Pacoh and the **Brou** (Bru)-speaking groups in that region.

PADAUNG. A Karenic-speaking **Tibeto-Burman** subgroup, part of the Burmese **Kayah** (Red **Karen, Karenni**), not to be confused with the **Mon-Khmer Palaung**. Although the Padaung ethnic category is not officially recognized or accounted for in Burma, it is believed that Burma is where a vast majority of them currently live. In Thailand, the tentative figure of 30,000 Padaung has been suggested, all dwelling in Mae Hong Son province, where they are subject to avid **tourist** demand thanks to the striking feature of the "long necks," an anatomical oddity, among some of the women as a consequence of wearing accumulated brass necklaces from an early age. *See also* KAREN.

PAI-I. An ethnonym of unclear origin, which cannot safely be assigned to any particular ethnic group due to multiple associations made in the past. "Pai-i" has been associated with alternative names or subgroups of **minorities** belonging to different language families among the **Tibeto-Burman** Bai and **Yi**, and the **Tai**-speaking **Shan** and **Lue**. The fact is that Pai-i (Pa-y, Pai) could well be the original form of the name for two unrelated official minority nationality groups of China, the **Bai** and the **Dai**.

PALAUNG (TA-ANG). A **Mon-Khmer**–speaking group found in Burma (an estimated 402,102 in 2004) in two separate clusters at the extreme north of the **Shan** State, in regions of high altitude. The Palaung call themselves Ta-ang. The northwestern group, the majority, overlaps with the old Palaung state of Taungbaing (Tawngpeng). Although evidence is scarce, historians believe that the Palaung precede Shan and **Kachin** settlement in that region, making them possible **aborigines** there. The Palaung **feudal** state of Taungbaing paid **tribute** to the **Burman** court, but its main cultural influence seems to have come from the Shan, including the use of Shan language as lingua franca for **trade** with their neighbors, inclusive of the Shan script used to write Palaung chronicles. The ethnonym Palaung appeared in the colonial census of 1931 but was missing in the 1983 Burma national census, the last one taken in that country. An unknown number of Palaung have also been reported in adjacent Chinese regions of **Yunnan**, though statistics are nonexistent there since the group is not officially recognized as a *shaoshu minzu* in China. Consequently, it is conceivable that they may have been clustered with the **Wa**. The Palaung are mainly sedentarized agriculturalists, who have developed a feudal political organization on the Shan model, and they practice a syncretic form of Theravada **Buddhism** and **animism**.

PALAUNG-WA. A linguistic category used only in Burma, comprising the **Palaung** and the **Wa**, two northern **Mon-Khmer languages** that are otherwise considered distinct by specialists, some of whom suggest placing the Wa language inside a larger Palaungic cluster.

PANTHAY. The name sometimes given to Chinese Muslims in upland Burma. These Panthay of Burma are in fact part of the **Hui** Muslim minority of China, who were thus named when they revolted against **Han** power in the mid-19th century in what has been known since as the Panthay Rebellion. *See also* HAW.

PANTHAY AND MIAO REBELLIONS. By 1850 A.D., the Qing dynasty (1644–1911) in China was encountering various internal and international problems. It was experiencing a dynastic fight and had just lost authority at home in the disastrous setback of the First Opium War (1839–1842), won by European colonial powers. Seizing this opportunity to shake off **Han** dominance on the outskirts of the Empire, the Taiping Rebellion erupted and spilled over Guangxi's borders between 1850 and 1864, coexistent with the Nian Rebellion in northern China, which raged from 1851 to 1868. Appearing further weakened by the initial success of the Taiping and Nian rebels, Qing dominance soon had to deal with other rebellious outbreaks in China. Two of the most central ones involved scores of southern minority insurgents: the **Panthay** Rebellion (1855–1872), chiefly involving the **Hui** minority in southwest China, and the so-called **Miao** Rebellion (1854–1873) in **Guizhou**, which also involved, in addition to the Miao, considerable numbers from other **minorities**.

In the mid-1850s, the opportunity to rise and oppose the faltering Han hegemony and contest crippling poverty, misadministration, and discrimination was seized by disgruntled Muslim and Han mine workers in **Yunnan**. At much the same time, a variety of Miao, Hui, **Buyi**, and Han local insurrections succeeded each other in neighboring Guizhou. These quickly got out of hand. Social disorder became endemic in Guizhou due, among many factors, to adverse ecological conditions, millenarian vernacular religion, and severe difficulties for the people in securing the most basic livelihood under relentless and abusive taxation and extortion. Initially, Panthay and "Miao" rebels captured cities in quick succession and set up their own administrations, in some regions for as long as 10 years. For instance, the Hui rebel leader Tu Wensiu installed an independent sultanate in Dali in western Yunnan, which held out until the Imperial forces defeated the Panthay rebellion in 1872. Before that time, imperial troops were unable to regain control of the situation because disturbances had also spread to other Hui Muslim groups in the north and west of China, in Shaanxi in 1860, Gansu in 1862, and Turkestan (Xinjiang) two years later, where a series of victories had led in 1873 to the erection of an independent Turk state. By 1860, 18 Chinese provinces were escaping in part or completely the control of the imperial state.

Disagreements began to divide the insurgents who, beyond a common desire to put an end to their exploitation, did not have much in common in terms of cultures and values. The cultural discrepancy was particularly striking between minority peoples on the one hand, and Han sympathizers on the other. In 1876, Governor Zuo Zongtang and his imperial army could take advantage of these internal divisions and, with the active help of European powers interested in restoring civil order in order to develop business in China, contained the insurgents in the north. That done, Zuo led the reconquest elsewhere, which he completed in 1884. Imperial hegemony over the minorities was thus reasserted, stronger than ever. Attitudes of condescension and contempt harbored by the Han elite toward ethnic minorities, which had been instrumental in the rebellions, returned in force, and the rampant extortion practiced by mandarins was fully reinstated.

The number of casualties in the Panthay and Miao rebellions is uncertain. Authors have suggested that in Guizhou alone, out of a total population of approximately 7 million at the time, nearly 5 million died, victims of combat, famine, and infectious diseases that flourished in the chaos of civil war.

PA-O. *See* KAREN.

PAVIE MISSION OF 1879–1895. French explorer and diplomat Auguste Pavie (1847–1925) was appointed head of a major scientific and diplomatic mission across the **Indochina Peninsula** launched in 1879, which was active to various degrees for over 16 years. Several missions were in fact launched, sometimes simultaneously, in different areas of Thailand, Laos, Cambodia, and Vietnam, with various tasks ranging from diplomatic relations and searching for **trade routes** and partners to joining commissions for the establishment of international land borders, but also gathering knowledge on the Peninsula's cultures, arts, and ethnography. This long endeavor came to be known as the Pavie Mission. It involved a range of scientists, diplomats, and military officers, a number of whom authored independent papers that were published in the 10-volume collection *Mission Pavie Indo-Chine 1879–1895: Géographie et voyages,* which appeared between 1898 and 1903 (volume 3 by **Lefèvre-Pontalis** and volume 5 by **Cupet**). In addition to the geographical and historical information covering both lowlands and highlands, specific volumes in this collection provide informative evidence on highland societies dwelling in upper Tonkin and Laos.

PENINSULA, SOUTHEAST ASIAN. A part physical, part political entity most commonly defined as the land located east of India and Bangladesh and south of China. The countries included are Burma, Thailand, Laos, Vietnam, Cambodia, and mainland Malaysia. This is the broad definition adopted in this dictionary whenever the term "Peninsula" is used.

However, when the region is called instead mainland Southeast Asia, a notion inherited from World War II strategic geopolitical thinking, it can also be interpreted less strictly and expanded into a somewhat larger transnational historical and cultural area. In this way, the southern limit of mainland Southeast Asia is pulled northward, roughly to the Isthmus of Kra close to the Thailand–Malaysia border, excluding mainland Malaysia on grounds of its predominantly Malay heritage, shared with maritime Southeast Asia but not with the rest of the Peninsula. At the northern limit, the perimeter can be pushed farther up into China. The reason for this northern expansion, it is argued, is that a large proportion of the highland populations present in the mountains of the Peninsula are closely related to their even more numerous highland counterparts in southwest China. Therefore, included in this expanded "greater Peninsula" are all of the southwest mountainous Chinese provinces of **Yunnan** and **Guizhou**, as well as significant portions of the Autonomous Region of Guangxi and the provinces of **Sichuan**, Hunan, and **Hainan**, where non-**Han** ethnicities form very significant portions of the population.

PHI TONG LUANG. *See* MLABRI.

PHNONG (PNONG). A small, listed highland minority of Cambodia (5,323 in 1995), the **Mon-Khmer**–speaking Phnong live in Mondul Kiri province, just over the border from an area in the Vietnamese **Central Highlands**, where, it has been suggested, they could be related to the **Mnong**. However, the exact association of a particular ethnic group with the name Phnong is unsure. The reason is that in Cambodia, the **Khmer** word *phnong* (mountain people) has long been used as a generic term for all the highland non-Khmer groups of the country. As is the case with the derogatory labels **kha**, *man*, and **moi** used in Burma, Thailand, Laos, China, and Vietnam, the term *phnong* culturally and politically marginalizes the peoples it is used to refer to.

PHONG. In Laos, part of the Khmuic branch of the **Mon-Khmer** family. They numbered 21,395 in 1995 and were dwelling in the eastern portion of Huaphanh province on the Vietnam border. There are suggestions that the Phong, or a group called by that same name, belong to a larger linguistic cluster called So, whose members, in the early 1950s, were located at a much lower altitude, on the Mekong River.

PHU LA (FU LA). A group linguistically related to their La Hu, Lo Lo, and **Ha Nhi** neighbors, and like them **animistic** agriculturalists who migrated from China in relatively recent times. The 1999 Vietnam census reported 9,046 **Tibeto-Burman**–speaking Phu La living in scattered hamlets in Lao Cai province in the north of the country, with pockets in adjacent Ha Giang and Lai Chau provinces. One should note that in Vietnam, Phu La is pronounced *"fu la,"* and this group has to be distinguished from the **Kadai**-speaking Phu La, pronounced *"pu la"* — the "La" people—an alternate name for the **La Chi**.

PHU MI BUN REVOLT (1901–1907). On the Boloven plateau in southern Laos, a local **Alak** minority leader named Bak Mi decided to represent himself to his countrypeople as a prophet. He was soon renamed "Phu Mi Bun" (pronounced *"pu mee boun"*), literally "the Man with Merits," or Holy Man of the **Buddhist** faith. The cult that quickly developed around him alarmed the French authorities, who misjudged the reactions their intrusion to curtail it would cause. Unsuccessful police action caused a rapid degeneration of the situation, to the point that a revolt erupted on the entire Boloven Plateau and in the lowlands surrounding it. By 1902, Bak Mi had proclaimed himself a messianic king and was using local resentment against French administrative abuses to galvanize the insurgents and link up with lowland peasants across the Mekong River, who had similar feelings toward the Siamese administration. Siam (Thailand) was quick to stamp out the revolt on its soil, but France was not so swift in its Laotian protectorate. A major clash with French troops in Savannakhet in April 1902 left 150 rebels dead and forced the rest to retreat to the mountains. For a few years, troops pursued the insurgents in remote locations, but it was only in October 1907 that Bak Mi surrendered and was killed by the French while in detention. In the wake of the conclusion of the Phu Mi Bun revolt, one of his lieutenants, **Kommadam**, went on to continue the armed resistance until his own death in 1936.

PHU NOI (PHOUNOY, P'U NOI). A **Tibeto-Burman**–speaking group in Laos whose name is pronounced *"pu noy"* in **Tai**. The exact meaning of the name remains unsure, some suggesting "Small/Minor People," others favoring "Small Mountains," though everyone agrees it is an exonym assigned to them by their powerful **Lue** and **Lao** neighbors. There were 35,835 Phu Noi officially living in northern Laos in 1995, all in Phongsaly province. They practice rotational **swiddening**. **Animism** has gradually been replaced by Theravada **Buddhism**, probably introduced by the Lue. The Phu Noi of Phongsaly are believed to be from the Muang Sing area in nearby Luangnamtha province, and their oral history suggests Burma as their possible site of origin. The Phu Noi say they moved to Phongsaly about two centuries ago in search of a location more secluded from the feuds between lowland powers, in which they became entangled on numerous occasions. In both locations, they remained within the political, economic, and cultural orbit of the Tai Lue and Lan Xang **feudal** organizations.

PHU TAI (PHOU THAI). Pronounced *"pu tai,"* the "Tai people" in **Tai**, this is the most important Tai-speaking group in Laos distinct from the **Lao** majority. At the time of the 1995 national census, there were 472,458 Phu Tai in central Laos, distributed from Khammouane to Champassack provinces. Although considered a minority group in Laos, the Phu Tai all live in the lowlands, and their major cultural characteristics are those of the Lao majority.

PMSI. An acronym for the French *Pays Montagnard du Sud-Indochinois*, the Mountain People Country in Southern Indochina. Established in 1946 when the **First Indochina War** (1946–1954) broke out between the French and the Viet Minh, this was a late French initiative to ethnicize and territorialize the Central Highlands' minorities in a new political entity where they would enjoy special status (*Statut Particulier*). A tactical move against Vietnamese nationalism, the strategy aimed to permanently detach the non-**Kinh** southern highlanders from the Kinh, who had traditionally been seen by highlanders as a foreign group; thus the French hoped to turn the PMSI population into strong allies for the French cause. The same strategy was to be used two years later in the establishment of a **Tai Federation** in western Tonkin, called by some *Pays Montagnard du Nord*. To make the PMSI economically viable as well as to occupy the territory, land was granted to and plantations were developed by French colonists. In 1949, new political imperatives made the French return the political responsibility and ownership of the PMSI to Vietnamese emperor Bao Dai. The acronym PMSI led to the French neologism *pemsiens* ("pemsians"), briefly used in the 1950s and 1960s, notably by **Jacques Dournes** in his *Les populations montagnardes du sud-indochinois* (1950). It was seen as a convenient term to artificially label all highland populations of the Central Highlands, regardless of their linguistic affiliations, into one group that could then be dealt with as a single political entity.

PO, DR. SAN CROMBIE (1885–1946). Educated Skaw **Karen** Christian leader in Burma, who, in the 1920s, based on his conviction that Karen and Burman interests would never converge, advocated self-determination for his countrypeople and asked for Tenasserim to be handed over to a Karen administration that would remain federated with Burma. In 1928, he published his famous ethnonationalist manifesto, *Burma and the Karens*.

POLLARD, SAMUEL (1864–1915). A British Protestant from Cornwall who arrived in **Yunnan** in 1888. He was part of the Bible Christians Society under the umbrella of the China Inland Mission. Posted to Zhaotong in northeast Yunnan, he spent the rest of his life there. Initially expected to missionize among the **Han** Chinese, Pollard quickly turned his attention to the A Hmao **Miao** minority instead. In close collaboration with his colleague Samuel Clarke, Pollard gathered enough valuable information to write *The Story of the Miao*, published posthumously in 1919. Pollard is also remembered for devising an original script for the A Hmao language, the **Pollard script**.

POLLARD SCRIPT. A syllabic script used for a century in **Yunnan** and western **Guizhou** among Christianized **A Hmao** (Hua Miao), with versions also used among the Gopu, **Yi**, **Lisu**, and Laka, all in Yunnan. **Samuel Pollard** (1864–1915) was a British Methodist Protestant missionary from Cornwall affiliated with the Bible Christians Society. Posted in northern Yunnan in 1888, he met highlanders of the A Hmao Miao group, with whom he developed an affinity. By 1904, helped by A Hmao collaborators, he had devised an original script for their previously non-written **tonal language**. The Pollard script, as it came to be called, is syllabic and is based on a similar script devised in the 1840s for the Ojibwa, Cree, and Inuit Amerindians of Canada by another British Methodist missionary, James Evans, who himself had been inspired by the Taylor shorthand.

POLYGAMY. The practice of taking more than one spouse. Polygamy has existed for a long time in the massif, and is still found among a number of groups, in particular **animist** ones. In a majority of cases, it involves men electing a second, a third, sometimes even a fourth or a fifth wife unrelated to each other; this practice is more accurately called polygyny. Until it became frowned upon by outside observers and lowland lawmakers, and actively discouraged, polygyny was popular among men of many ethnicities who, to publicly express their economic standing, elected to pay the hefty **brideprice** more than once and, consequently, take on the task of feeding a much larger family. Rewards, besides the accrued prestige such a man would invariably enjoy, were in the form of more offspring to work the land and bring economic success to the **household** and, eventually, ensure the parents a comfortable old age.

The reverse of polygyny, that is, when a woman has more than one husband, is polyandry. It is much rarer and generally limited to populations under the direct influence of Tibetan culture, where polyandry has been common. In this case, the practice generally involves the woman taking several brothers as her rightful husbands, a strategy some have surmised was aimed at avoiding the division of family land among male siblings, each founding an independent household and taking away part of the family's patrimony.

Strictly speaking, the official and socially accepted practice of polygamy in the highlands differs in principle from the widespread custom in the lowlands throughout the massif for a wealthy man to establish a second family through a relationship with an unofficial partner, most of the time called in the vernacular a "minor wife." Though frequent among the lowland **Thai**, **Lao**, **Kinh**, and **Han**, this custom is generally deemed morally objectionable.

POR (PEAR). A very small **Mon-Khmer**–speaking group in Cambodia (1,140 in 1995), also called Pear, part of the Pearic branch of the Eastern Mon-Khmer cluster, and living in Siem Reap province in or around the Dangrek range. A long association with the lowland **Khmer** has largely eroded their cultural distinctiveness, with the exception of their **animistic** religious system.

PROSTITUTION. In Southeast Asia and China, though sometimes formally illegal, the practice of buying sexual services for pleasure has been, and still is, widespread in all strata of society. This is particularly true among men buying the services of female sex workers. In the mountains, however, among highlanders, the habit has always been much less prevalent, in part due to the fact that pre- and extramarital sex is often seen in a more permissive light. When prostitution enters the picture, it chiefly concerns upland men traveling to midland or lowland towns for economic reasons, who, exposed to the availability of sex services, seize the opportunity to "play with women," as vernacular **languages** describe this act. The other main impact of prostitution on highlanders is the ever-increasing demand, encouraged by the **tourist** industry, for young prostitutes in the lowlands to cater to national and international consumers. Recruiters now visit highland villages to scout for potential newcomers, which for many highland peasant families struggling to make a living is a terrible yet alluring economic opportunity. Both practices, highland men consuming outside, and local women and men going to work in lowland brothels, have created a major vector by which sexually transmitted diseases and HIV/AIDS are penetrating highland societies. *See also* HEALTH AND HEALING.

PROTESTANT MISSIONS. *See* MISSIONARIES.

PROV. A minority of 2,585, officially listed in Cambodia in 1995, living on the Sesan River in Ratana Kiri province. The Prov are one of four groups in Cambodia about whom no information is available as to their linguistic classification.

PU NU. *See* YAO.

PU PEO (LAQUA). A very small group of 705 **Kadai** speakers from the **Tai-Kadai** family, living in Dong Van district, Ha Giang province, in the north of Vietnam. Also called Laqua, this group, and the nearby **La Chi** (Lati), are believed to be indigenous to this region.

PUMI (PRIMI). Members of the **Tibeto-Burman language family**, considered close relatives of the **Qiang**. In 2000 in China, 33,600 individuals were accounted for as part of the Pumi minority nationality, all living on the border separating southwest **Sichuan** from northwest **Yunnan**. In Yunnan, they are found in the counties of Lanping, Lijiang, Weixi, and Yongsheng, as well as in the **Yi** autonomous county of Ninglang, while some live in the autonomous county of Muli and in Yanyuan county, both in Sichuan. Formerly herders on the Tibetan Plateau, the Pumi are believed to have settled down in their current location in the 13th century A.D. Over the centuries, they have come under the political, cultural, and economic influence of the Tibetans and the **Naxi**.

PWO. *See* KAREN.

PYI NE. An "ethnic state" in Burma, that is, a highland administrative unit on the same level as the lowland "divisions" (*taing*), but specifically designed in 1974 for upland peripheries where ethnic **minorities** were dominant. There are seven *pyi ne* in Burma: Mon State, Rakhine State, Chin State, **Shan** State, **Kachin** State, **Karen** State, and **Kayah** State. Only the last five are part of the **mainland Southeast Asian massif** as defined in this dictionary.

– Q –

QIANG. Dwelling in China, the Qiang, with 306,072 representatives registered in the 2000 national census, belong to the Qiangic branch of the **Tibeto-Burman language family**. Most are located in western **Sichuan**, on the fringes of the Sichuan "rice bowl," where they constitute only 0.4 percent of the province's population. They dwell in the Maowen Qiang Autonomous Prefecture; a small number live with Tibetan, **Han**, and **Hui** in nearby towns, such as Wenchuan, Dali, Heishui, and Songpan. There is written evidence suggesting that the Qiang have been known to the Han since the second millennium B.C., although for a long time the name was used to refer generically to a number of nomadic herders dwelling in western China. It is not known how the generic "Qiang" came to be associated exclusively with today's Qiang *shaoshu minzu*. The Qiang **language** is divided between southern Qiang, with six tones, and northern Qiang, with no tones at all, one major factor making these two languages mutually unintelligible and forcing the Qiang to rely on Chinese as their lingua franca. Most Qiang have retained their **animist** practices, while those closer to the Tibetan domain have been influenced by Tibetan Lamaism.

– R –

RA-GLAI. One of four **Austronesian**-speaking highland groups of southern Vietnam, the Ra-glai numbered 96,931 in 1999. They are dispersed in several residential areas in three provinces of the **Central Highlands (*Tay Nguyen*)**. Their most important dwelling sites are in Ninh Thua and Khanh Hoa provinces, with extensions into Binh Thuan and Lam Dong. Like the other Austronesian groups there, the Ra-glai have a matrilineal **kinship** system. They are agriculturalists, mixing **swiddening** with **cash crops**, and they practice **animism**. They were also targeted by Christian proselytism during French colonial times as well as during the short existence of the Republic of Vietnam (South Vietnam, 1954–1975).

RED THAI (TAI DENG, TAI DO). *See* THAI.

REFUGEES. Despite its relatively low demographic density compared to the surrounding lowlands, the **mainland Southeast Asian massif**'s history is rich in political turmoil. Throughout history, people have been set in motion in vast numbers, displaced by wars, famines, political offensives, and the like. Giving them all due consideration, even merely listing them, is a task well beyond the capabilities of this dictionary. Instead, this survey is restricted to a short selection combining both the most important and most recent known occurrences of population displacement in and around the massif.

It is probably fair to state that the highland populations who migrated from China to the **Peninsula**'s highlands over the last five centuries were, at least in part, pushed from their homelands by aggression from more powerful neighbors, including **Han** expansion. In this sense, they fit a category that can be called proto-refugees. During the 18th and 19th centuries, scores of recorded peasant revolts, upheavals, and rebellions took place in various locations in southwest China. Each was met with fierce military repression and retaliation by dominant groups, chiefly the Han. Large numbers of people who survived the turmoil could no longer elect to stay in their homelands. Instead, they moved farther south in spontaneous flows of population that gradually came to fill the little-inhabited highlands in the southern portion of the massif. While exact figures are unavailable due to the lack of reliable statistics produced in those times and places, estimates—in the millions of people—can testify to the gravity of the refugee situation at that period. The combined **Panthay and Miao Rebellions** alone (1854–1873) are believed to have been responsible for the forced migration into the Peninsula of a majority of **Hmong**, **Yao**, **Hani**, and **Lolo** groups, found there in large numbers today.

As a rule, the major refugee movements in the 20th century involved mainly lowland majority populations. However, in most cases they also affected significant numbers of highlanders. While colonial wars and occupations in the region appear to have had only a modest impact in terms of setting refugees in motion, independence movements and wars, to which must be added the communist commotion—especially the clash between communist and republican forces in China—have in turn been considerably more effective in dislocating social groups and settlement patterns. Refugees had to abandon their homes and flee either elsewhere within the country or across borders.

In the Peninsula, the official accession to independence of the Democratic Republic of Vietnam (DRV), or North Vietnam, in 1954 triggered a 2-million strong refugee movement out of the new country into the Republic of Vietnam (RV, or South Vietnam) and Laos. In Burma, conditions there had more to do with internal political disorders unfolding over the five decades after independence, whose chief manifestation to the outside world took the form of **Karen, Karenni, Kachin, Chin,** and Rohingya populations, some being rebel troops fighting the Burmese government, some being simply civilians indiscriminately repressed by the Burmese troops, looking for a refuge beyond the borders. It is estimated that over 300,000 such refugees from Burma crossed into Thailand during that period, while a further 32,000 fled into China, India, and Bangladesh.

However, to the majority of outsiders, the two most publicized refugee movements to ever affect Southeast Asia have been linked to the defeat of anticommunist forces in Vietnam, Laos, and Cambodia. In 1975, the year of the triple communist takeovers, a flow of refugees, most of them having actively fought the communists' advance, reached Thailand, where temporary refugee camps were established. These camps' goal was to filter candidates to be sent to resettlement in a third country (mainly the United States, Canada, Australia, and France) under the supervision of international bodies, predominantly the United Nations High Commissioner for Refugees (UNHCR). To shelter and process this massive influx of several hundred thousand, Thailand had to set up six camps for highlanders from Laos, three for the **Lao** proper, and seven for the Cambodians, supplemented by four processing centers clustered in the Bangkok area.

The second refugee movement during the 1980s and 1990s involved the so-called Boat People. This second wave of asylum seekers included people from Vietnam set in motion chiefly for economic reasons, who came to be grouped in refugee camps in Hong Kong, the Philippines, Malaysia, and residually, Thailand. Considered of a less urgent nature by the international community, the "Boat People" phenomenon entailed a much larger proportion of repatriations than the post–Indochina Wars one. Between 1975 and 1997, these two movements combined produced a total of 839,228 refugees from Vietnam, 359,930 from Laos, and 239,562 from Cambodia. Of these, a total of 1,287,399 were eventually resettled in the United States,

202,178 in Canada, 185,700 in Australia, and 119,182 in France, the rest either being received in one of the remaining dozen countries who agreed to host them or being returned to their country of origin. Among these refugees, a large portion belonged to various highland groups, the most numerous being returned the Hmong from Laos, approximately 120,000 of whom were accepted for permanent third-country relocation, over 100,000 in the United States alone.

Refugees can also be within the borders of a single country. China, with the successive upheavals of the Republican (1911) and Communist (1949) Revolutions, combined with a merciless Japanese occupation (1937–1945), the Great Leap Forward, and the Cultural Revolution (1958–1976), has experienced the most substantial internal refugee movements of the 20th century, along with that triggered by the India–Pakistan partition of 1947—possibly in both cases the largest population movements in human history. Little is known of how many highlanders in the Chinese southwest might have been involved in population transfers over those 70 years. Next to the Chinese case, probably the most populous and most tragic case was the fanatic **Khmer** Rouge regime in Cambodia (1975–1979), during which there was a massive forced relocation of the urban population into the countryside; here again, the number of highland minority groups caught up in this storm remains unknown. Various troubled regimes in Burma have pushed an estimated 2 million people into internal displacement; the same lack of details regarding **minorities** is found here. War sent tens of thousands of highlanders in Laos to take refuge elsewhere in the country, depending on where the frontlines were most active at any given time. Governmental schemes of forced population redeployment, such as the **New Economic Zones** initiative in the DRV (late 1950s and early 1960s) and the **Strategic Hamlets** scheme in the RV's **Central Highlands** (1961–1963), which together displaced 8 million people, can also qualify as internal refugee situations. The long-lasting Relocation Policy of highlanders in Laos, active now for over two decades, could perhaps also be added to the list. *See also* RELOCATION POLICIES IN LAOS.

RELOCATION POLICIES IN LAOS. All over the **mainland Southeast Asian massif**, relocation of highland populations has been a government strategy at one time or another, sometimes only temporarily, occasionally in times of national security crises, or, often in the past two decades, to enforce protection of the highland environment. Each time, however, these policies have also been linked to the management of highland groups and to their integration into the nation. In the Lao People's Democratic Republic, this type of political strategy has assumed a unique importance, explicitly aiming at "rehabilitating and sedentarizing ethnic minorities" as well as totally eradicating **swiddening**.

In the early 1960s, the Royal Lao government had made the relocation of isolated highland minorities to lower settings an explicit objective to modernize non-**Lao** groups. Clearly, imperatives linked to the **Second Indochina War** (1954–1975) also necessitated draining from the forested highlands all possible supporters of communist guerrillas. On the communist side, to oppose this drain, material support was provided to highland villagers wishing to remain on location against orders from Vientiane. After 1975 and the communist victory, the issue was put aside for a while, then returned to the forefront from 1985 onward with the promotion of "development nervous centers," or focal zones. Officially presented as a strategy to fight poverty, massive relocation of isolated hamlets into larger clusters along the expanding road infrastructure helped bring modernity to highlanders in the remotest parts of the country, while also allowing the government to keep a better watch over its highly dispersed and little integrated non-Lao population.

The major economic and cultural impacts on highland societies were far-reaching, including reshaping of traditional village layouts, standardization of house architecture along the Lao model, and even standardizing building materials and the interior plan of such houses. These relocated villages became subject to an active modernization strategy involving village militia drills, compulsory schooling for children, generalization of **cash cropping** in fixed plots, and full connection to the market. The government could thus concentrate its human, managerial, and financial resources to pursue the objectives laid down in its national plan for rural development.

In the early 1990s, the Lao government set the goal of "rehabilitating and sedentarizing" 1.5 million people: 180,000 households, 60 percent of which were targeted for relocation before the year 2000. Since highland relocation is a sensitive topic in Laos, it is difficult to assess today whether the government has been able to attain its objectives. *See also* REFUGEES.

REPLACEMENT CROPS. Also called substitution crops, replacement schemes involving new **cash crops** have been steadily implemented by national governments in the whole of the massif. On paper, these were meant to assist highland farmers in converting from so-called damageable **swiddening** practices or, in many cases, from **opium** poppy growing, to standard **cash cropping**. Also conveniently suiting the national and international governments' modernist agendas, replacement crops have been actively promoted over the last 30 years in each country where swiddening and the poppy cultivation have both finally been banned, that is, all countries sharing the massif. In the case of opium, this amounts to no less than a 180 degree turn after decades of encouragement and support for poppy growing by the colonial and, later, national governments, which derived large profits from the opium **trade**. The replacement crops that were promoted, and for which a number of highlanders initially received subsidized seeds, pesticide, fertilizers, and free expert advice, have included anything from ginger to cabbages, **coffee**, and plums, provided that there was—or may some day be—a demand on the regional market for a given product. Catching the wave of growing international discontent linked to new global concerns about environmental degradation, governments in the massif have also secured major technical and financial aid from international agencies, and countless NGOs have come to propose, finance, implement, and assess conversion programs. This windfall of international capital and technology made it possible to substantially subsidize farmers turning to new crops.

To this day, however, the results have not been particularly encouraging. "Learning the ropes" of commercial agricultural production and competition in a capitalist market has proven difficult. Many new crops promoted to the farmers for their conversion have not been as successful on the market as was initially theorized, either because of lack of demand or the use of dangerously high levels of chemicals by ill-informed farmers, or even worldwide price crashes (e.g., coffee in the early 2000s). Conversion farmers who, for the most part, own little land if any and are faced with no viable alternatives, are thus at the mercy of poor programming, with little support to live through a bad year. Upland farmers throughout the massif nearly uniformly declare that their economic situation was significantly better when they were still authorized to grow the opium poppy or use the customary techniques of swiddening. In the end, a failure in conversion often forces them onto the unskilled labor market.

RHADE. The name formerly given to the group today called **E-de** in the south of Vietnam. A majority of French and Vietnamese ethnologists of the colonial period have used "Rhade" in their publications, and the term was picked up by most Anglo-Saxon writers of the 1960s, who based their research on colonial publications.

RICE. Rice (*oryza sativa*) is the most important cereal cultivated and consumed in the **mainland Southeast Asian massif**, much as in the rest of Asia. It is the staple food ingredient in everyday meals, the main source of carbohydrates. The only competitor to rice in the massif is **maize**, which comes in a distant second. A growing number of varieties of rice are grown in the highlands in one of two fundamental ways. As in the lowlands, "wet rice" is cultivated in flooded terraces wherever an appropriate combination of forms of **land tenure**, workable flatlands or mild slopes, and sedentarized labor, makes the carving of permanent terraces both feasible and suitable. This combination has occurred chiefly in highland valleys and on high plateaus, where a form of social organization akin to **feudalism** has prevailed historically. Highland kingdoms and federations, such as Nan Chao, **Sip Song Phan Na**, and Lan Xang, were all based on wet rice cultivation by masses of sedentarized peasants.

Elsewhere, however, where populations were still on the move, slopes were too sharp or the terrain too rugged, and land ownership was not secure, the "**dry rice**" option prevailed. This type of cultivation applies the usual techniques of agriculture but rarely chemical additives, and relies on rain water only. Year in, year out, its productivity is less predictable because weather conditions dictate the outcome, and the soil eventually becomes depleted, forcing the rotation of fields in a cycle of fallows—rotational **swiddening**. This is the dominant form of rice production among **lineage societies** in the massif, among seminomadic groups also, and is best adapted for groups for whom terracing slopes is not an option either because they have land titles or have reasons to want to remain mobile. When the right conditions are met, though, most dry rice cultivators are willing to switch to terraced wet rice production, considered more productive and less hazardous.

Processing rice from its harvest to the final product requires appropriate technologies. Storage away from rodents is in family rice granaries. De-husking, an unavoidable burden, is performed using a variety of human-powered or hydraulic wooden pistons, with engine-propelled de-husking machines becoming more and more common. Rice is boiled in water or steamed, and this chore on a daily basis in every **household** requires the constant provision of firewood or charcoal, which dramatically taxes the capacity of **forests** to regenerate in balance with the demographic density increase. When natural fuel is permanently exhausted in a large area, governments have to find a low-cost alternative, which often turns out to be coal. Solid fuel is also needed to transform rice into **alcohol**, its most important secondary use. For this, rice is distilled in home-made stills, and the alcohol is stored in containers of various sizes, being used in a number of ways, from home consumption on ritual and festive occasions, to gifts to the authorities, to **trade** in the **marketplace**.

In feudal societies, rice has long been used as one possible form of payment for renting land. Rice can also be used as a reserve of value and be put forward to secure loans, pay debts, pay the **brideprice**, or be **bartered** on the marketplace. Rice also has a number of ritual uses.

ROBEL. A minority of 1,640 individuals officially listed in Cambodia in 1995, one of four in this country about which no information is available regarding linguistic affiliation.

ROCHER, ÉMILE (ca. 1840–ca. 1910). A French customs administrator posted in China. Around the time when the Doudart de Lagrée and Garnier Mekong expedition was coming to an end, Emile Rocher traveled to **Yunnan** as a member of a diplomatic mission launched in the wake of a recent agreement to provide Yunnanese rulers with Western weaponry to fight the **Panthay** Rebellion raging in the region. Rocher published his account of those years in a two-volume publication, *La Province chinoise du Yün-Nan* [*The Chinese Province of Yunnan*] (1879 and 1880). This appears to be the first French-language published account on the high region that included a section devoted specifically to ethnography of highland societies.

RO-MAM. The Ro-mam (352 in 1999) are **Mon-Khmer** speakers and constitute one of the smallest ethnic minority groups officially registered in Vietnam. They live in Kontum province in the **Central Highlands**.

ROMANIZED POPULAR ALPHABET (RPA). Linwood Barney and William Smalley, both American Catholic **missionaries** and linguists, were the most important contributors to the development of the **Hmong** script called the Romanized Popular Alphabet. The RPA is a version of the Latin alphabet developed to communicate in writing with the Hmong of Thailand, the missionaries' underlying intention being, at least initially, to make the Bible accessible to their potential converts. One of its most original features is to take tones into account by using the final consonant as a key to tone pronunciation. With time, it became an important element in communication among royalist Hmong forces in neighboring Laos during the **Second Indochina War** (1954–1975).

Barney and Smalley came from the United States, the country where the majority of the Hmong fleeing **Indochina**, Laos in particular, took refuge in 1975. For this reason, but also because many of those **refugees** were already in close contact with the U.S. forces in Laos, the RPA became extremely popular among American Hmong, becoming their favorite script to communicate with one another in the vernacular language and to connect with other diasporic Hmong overseas. In addition, today the American Hmong contribute to spreading it among Asian Hmong through publications in RPA Hmong, correspondence, and the Internet. However, as widespread as RPA appears to be from a Western point of view, it is far from being used universally by all Hmong, reaching in fact perhaps as little as 20 percent of the total Hmong population. Over the years, each country in Southeast Asia has devised its own Hmong alphabet, some in Romanized forms (China, Vietnam), some in the vernacular national script.

ROUX, HENRI (ca. 1885–ca. 1955). French colonial military officer posted in northern French Indochina from the early 1910s until the early 1950s. Roux participated in numerous expeditions in Upper Tonkin and Laos and collected enough information to write, once back in France, despite partial blindness, his much cited *Quelques* *minorités ethniques du nord-Indochine* [*A Few Ethnic Minorities in Northern Indochina*] (1954). Most of the information in this work comes from the specific locations of his main postings, that is, as head of, successively, the 4th and 5th colonial Military Territories on the Chinese border, today's provinces of Lai Chau in Vietnam and Phongsaly in Laos.

RUEY YIH-FU (JOUE YI FOU) (1898–1991). An important Chinese ethnologist who left China during the final stages of the Communist Revolution and joined the National Taiwan University. His work focused on the classification of China's ethnic groups, the ethnography of minority peoples, and the ethnohistory of non-**Han** ethnicities in southwest China. With little reliance on actual fieldwork due to difficulties in access, Ruey used numerous modern and ancient texts produced by **Han** Chinese writers. One of his most important papers was his joint publication with colleague Ling Shun-sheng, *A Report on an Investigation of the Miao of Western Hunan* [which originally appeared in 1947 in Shanghai as *Xiangxi Miaozu Diaocha Baogao*], translated and published in 1963 by the Human Relations Area Files.

– S –

SALT. Salt is one of the products most necessary to life. Salt deficiency is the cause of major physical dysfunctions, such as goiter, still a frequent occurrence in the **mainland Southeast Asian massif**. There, since demand for salt as a dietary supplement has always exceeded supply from local extraction, salt has constantly been a prime item for **trade**. Coming chiefly from the coast all around the **Peninsula**, salt has routinely been brought up to the highlands via waterways and **caravan** trails. There, it was generally **bartered** against highland forest goods and produce that were in demand in lower settings. Over the years, various states have considered salt a primary target for taxation, trade restrictions, and monopoly. China, for instance, started taxing salt as early as 685 B.C. In French Indochina, the colonial administration imposed a state monopoly on salt as well as **alcohol** and **opium**. Salt has also been used as **currency** and as payment for salaries (from Latin *salarium*, *sal*, salt). Salt substitute in many highland marketplaces is now also found in the cheap, low-quality, synthetic form of monosodium glutamate industrially produced in China.

SAMTAO. In 1995, a small contingent of 2,213 Samtao were registered in Laos, living in Oudomxay province in the northwest of the country. They speak a Palaungic dialect within the **Mon-Khmer language family** and are related to the **Lamet**. However, it is believed that the Samtao are of **Wa** extraction and are related to their Wa cousins in the **Shan** State in Burma and in the former **Sip Song Phan Na** kingdom.

SAN CHAY. A **Tai**-speaking group of northern Vietnam, the San Chay (147,315 in 1999) dwell in pockets in **Tay** and **Nung** territory in northeastern Vietnam, namely in the provinces of Tuyen Quang (54,095) and Thai Nguyen, with some dispersion in adjacent provinces. The San Chay have traditionally been political and economic satellites of the more numerically significant Tay and Nung groups, with a marked **Kinh** influence as well. A Chinese cultural heritage is also visible among them in the form of San Chi language (a Cantonese dialect) used for songs and prayers. This suggests that there could be San Chay representatives over the border in the **Guangxi Zhuang Autonomous Region**, but Chinese official census data do not specifically account for them.

SAN DIU. A **Sino-Tibetan**-speaking group of the Sinitic branch in northern Vietnam, the San Diu numbered 126,237 in 1999. They are found in the midlands of seven provinces in the eastern Red River delta, and are believed to have migrated from western Guangdong (today's Guangxi) in the 17th century. They are one of the few cases of Sinitic speakers outside China who are found living in the highlands among non-**Kinh** and non-**Han** minority groups, in this case among **Nung** and **Tay** speakers. Like these neighbors, they practice a mixed agriculture and worship ancestors and spirits.

SAOCH. The 72 remaining members of the **Mon-Khmer**-speaking Saoch registered in 1995, who live in the Cardamom massif in southwest Cambodia, are believed to be the last representatives of a larger group once called Chong, which has now entirely assimilated with the **Khmer**.

SAVINA, FRANÇOIS MARIE (1876–1941). Arguably the most prolific Catholic missionary in the **mainland Southeast Asian massif** when it comes to linguistic and ethnographic publications. François-Marie Savina was born on March, 20, 1876, in Brittany, France. He joined the *Société des Missions Étrangères de Paris* (MEP), and arrived in Tonkin in 1901. He spent the remaining 40 years of his life in various postings of the Upper-Tonkin Vicariate, as well as on official assignments in Laos (1918–1921) in connection with the **Ba Chay Uprising**, and on **Hainan** Island (1925–1928) as a representative of *Ecole Française d'Extrême-Orient* (**EFEO**) on official ethnographic field research, including several stays at the MEP printing house in Hong Kong. Over 28 years, from 1911 to 1939, Savina published four lexicons and eight language dictionaries totaling over 5,000 pages covering highland and lowland **languages** (Vietnamese, Chinese, **Tay, Nung, Miao**, Man, Be, Hoklo, Hiai, Ao, and Day). In 1939, Savina returned to missionary work for good in Upper-Tonkin, this time to Ha Giang, back to the same region where he had started his missionary career four decades earlier. In March 1941, ill with pneumonia, he was hospitalized in Hanoi, where he died on July 23, 1941 at age 65.

Each of Savina's dictionaries was, for the most part, based on original data collected by himself. Facing such a wealth of firsthand data from many remote areas, linguists who have come after him have found large portions of this work useful. They have also discarded segments as unusable by today's more rigorous standards. But Savina's work was such a massive contribution to the understanding of several obscure Asian minority languages that one must stand in awe of his painstaking work. His dictionaries, as a source of ethnographic information in the form of contextualized vocabulary, comparative lexicons, and short but dense introductions about specific groups, still wait to be systematically explored. Savina also published two specifically ethnographic works: *Histoire des Miao* [*History of the Miao*] (1924), his most famous and most often cited publication today, which was a highly original yet controversial work of applied ethnography and largely conjectural history; and his much shorter *Monographie de Hainan* [*Monograph of Hainan Island*] (1929).

SECOND INDOCHINA WAR (1954–1975). The name given by historians to the war alternatively known as the Vietnam War, the American

War in Vietnam, the Civil War in Vietnam, the Reunification War, and a few other names. That war, which was never officially declared, initially pitted the Vietnamese communist forces from the Democratic Republic of Vietnam (DRV, otherwise known as North Vietnam) against the anticommunist forces of the Republic of Vietnam (RVN, or South Vietnam). But the conflict grew much larger when the United States (and allies) became involved on the side of the RVN, opposed by a coalition of communist allies, including the USSR and China, supporting the DRV. The conflict quickly expanded into neighboring Laos and Cambodia, although both these countries had been declared neutral by the 1962 Geneva Agreements. The end of the Second Indochina War is generally accepted to be the fall of Saigon in 1975, two years after the departure of the bulk of American troops. The starting year, however, is contentious. The most frequent choices are (as used in this dictionary) 1954, when North and South Vietnam were separated and immediately started their armed struggle, and 1965, when the first official contingent of U.S. troops was sent to Vietnam. *See also* FIRST INDOCHINA WAR.

"SECRET ARMY." In Laos during the **Second Indochina War (1954–1975)**, the American **Central Intelligence Agency** (CIA) organized, funded, and maintained what has been called a "secret war" against Laotian communist sympathizers backed by North Vietnamese forces. This war was deemed secret for the reason that by actively engaging in it, the United States contravened the Geneva Agreement of 1962, which had guaranteed the neutrality of Laos. Drafted from among supporters of **Hmong** leader **Touby Lyfoung** and put under the command of Hmong military leader **Vang Pao**, highland troops were recruited in northern Laos from 1961 onward to fight behind communist lines. Although the bulk of that "secret army" was initially of Hmong extraction, several other ethnic highlanders also became involved, notably from **Yao** and **Khmu** background, but also large numbers of **Lao** mercenaries. With the arrival of battalions of **Thai** troops, the less and less "secret" army had by 1970 grown to 30,000 troops, fighting as a well-equipped regular force. The "secret army" was dispersed in 1973 and officially integrated into the Royal Lao Army. After the communist victory in 1975, it is from these ranks that most highland **refugees** came, in particular the Hmong. This helps to explain the strong anticommunist and promonarchist stance a number of Hmong now living in the West have maintained and are still vigorously promoting.

SEDANG (SEHDANG). *See* XO-DANG.

SEK. There were 2,745 members in the Sek minority of Laos in 1995. Formerly **Mon-Khmer** speakers, the Sek have now totally adopted **Lao-Tai** language and culture. They live in the lowlands on both sides of the Mekong River in northeastern Thailand and central Laos.

SELECTIVE CULTURAL PRESERVATION. Socialist Vietnam, having made national unity a priority at the time of reunification in 1975, needed a specific strategy to overcome the problem of integrating the **minorities** into the Vietnamese nation. This strategy came to be called "selective cultural preservation," as explained in 1978 by Vietnamese ethnologist Nong Quoc Chan in an article titled "Selective Preservation of Ethnic Minorities Cultural Tradition." As stated in the Constitution, national minorities have a right to maintain their traditions, but only as long as they do not pose a threat to the socialist progress of the country. As a consequence, "counterproductive" and "superstitious" practices, such as shamanism (branded "sorcery"), **animal sacrifice**, lavish funerals, **brideprice**, and even **swiddening**, were deemed "backward" and targeted for "eradication." Politically reprehensible "bad habits," such as crossing borders unchecked or owning **firearms**, were also banned. On the other hand, other cultural activities, chiefly the benign and aesthetic ones, were encouraged, including wearing colorful attire, singing, dancing, and playing traditional music. Doing so on **National Minority Cultural Days** in particular was considered patriotic.

As a reward for their cooperation in this cultural realignment, highland "little brothers" have been helped to "catch up" with the lowland economic standards and have been invited to approach, like the rest of the country, "socialist bliss." The selective cultural preservation policy has never been revoked, and quite conveniently, it has allowed the survival of precisely what is needed to ensure that minorities will still be attractive to the growing national and international **tourist** crowd.

SHAN. A major **Tai**-speaking group of the southwest branch living in upper Burma, where their number was estimated in 2004 to be 2,651,699. The Shan in Burma are associated with the Shan State, which has Taunggyi as its capital. Lashio and Kengtung are other important towns. However, it is estimated that the Shan themselves only form half the population of their namesake state. The bulk of the Shan in Burma call themselves Tai Yai ("Great Tai"). Their nearest parent **languages** are **Yuan**, **Lue**, and **Lao**. Their script is derived from Siamese with a strong **Lan Na** and **Burman** influence. As a statistical category, the Shan have been explicitly mentioned in both the 1931 and 1983 national censuses of Burma. In China, where some Shan also live, the group is known locally as **Tayok** (Tai Hok), and the group locally called **Tai Nua** ("Northern Tai") can perhaps also be assimilated with the Tayok/Shan. Their exact number is unknown, as they are not one of the official **minorities** recognized in China; instead, they are clustered with the Tai-speaking Dai *minzu*. They dwell in the region of the Dehong Dai-Jingpo Autonomous Prefecture in western **Yunnan**. Understandably, Tayok nobility is more Sinicized than the Burmese Shan one. Finally, some **Hkamti Shan** dwell in extreme northern Burma in the **Kachin** state, in the highest reaches of the Irrawaddy valley, where they are politically associated with the **Tibeto-Burman**–speaking Kachin, some spilling over into Indian Assam. The Hkamti are believed by some authors to be the remnant of an ancient Shan *muang* that stayed behind when the southern Shan core was established.

All Shan settlements in Burma and its periphery are remnants from the 13th to 16th centuries A.D.—possibly older—Tai **feudal** kingdoms or *muang*, which quickly spread from China across most of the mid-altitude lands in the massif, where they established feudal domains based on wet **rice** economy. Stimulated by the defeat of Nan Chao and the Burman king in Pagan by the Mongols in the late 13th century A.D., which combined with the growing success of the Tai in Lan Na, Sukothai, and Lan Xang, the Shan in Burma absorbed many smaller groups in their vicinity and actually grew bold enough to fill the vacuum in power and take control of a large proportion of today's central Burmese territory, also pushing into present-day Thailand to take control of Chiang Mai and Lan Na. To hold together such an expanded domain, they established a loose federation of semi-independent *muang,* each ruled by a semi-independent monarch. However, the resurgence of Burman power in the 16th century eventually forced the Shan to retreat back to the high plateaus and valleys, bringing with them Theravada **Buddhism**, the new faith they had converted to during this period of intense contact with their neighbors.

Despite being a federation, in the 19th century the Shan domain was still fragmented among dozens of petty rulers skirmishing with each other, and fighting the Kachin incursions from the north and the Burmans and the Siamese to the south. These Shan *muang* were by then paying **tribute** to the Burman king. Then, under British rule (1886–1942), what came to be known as the "Shan States" became tributary of the British crown. Interested in the natural resources of the area, the British actively engaged in political alliances with Shan representatives and established outposts and Christian **missions,** whose role it was to tie these allies to British interests while skillfully nurturing anti-Burman sentiment. Education was promoted, and many Shan local leaders were sent outside the country for higher studies. In 1922, most of the Shan states were clustered in the Federated Shan States under a British commissioner, who also administered the **Wa** states.

In 1947, a single Shan state, absorbing the former Wa states and comprising also significant numbers of Kachin, **Lahu**, **Akha**, and **Palaung**, among others, was established by the new independent Burmese constitution along with most of the other *pyi ne*, or highland ethnic states, that still exist today. Shan political autonomy to run the Shan State was eroded by increased intrusiveness from the central Burmese government during the 1970s and 1980s. When the Burmese junta seized power in 1989, open political opposition flared up, in large part in the hands of the Shan Nationalities League for Democracy, founded in 1988. The central government's appetite today is chiefly focused on the presence in the Shan and Kachin states of valuable timber, particularly teak, as well as precious metals and gems, which have for centuries attracted Chinese, Indian, British, and Burmese adventurers, entrepreneurs, and **traders**. Yet to most outsiders today, the Shan State is above all the heart of the "**Golden Triangle**," where a considerable proportion of the world's **opium** and its derivatives (**heroin**, morphine) and many **amphetamines** have been illegally produced. The growing, processing, and distribution of these drugs is controlled by local warlords (such as Shan big man **Khun Sa**, arrested in late 1996), who control private armies of thousands of soldiers and run a large number of laboratories and processing facilities in the southern part of the Shan State, close to the **Thai** and Lao borders.

SHAOSHU MINZU. In China, the concept of *shaoshu minzu*, often simply referred to as *minzu*, embodies the communist position on **minorities**. The term best translates as "minority nationalities," *minzu* standing for the Stalinist definition of the concept of "**nationality**" designed, in the young Soviet Union, to address the issue of the inclusion of non-Russian ethnic groups into the new USSR. The concept was adopted in communist China in the early 1950s under Soviet guidance.

SHE. There were 709,592 She registered as an official *shaoshu minzu* in southeastern China in 2000, chiefly located in Zhejiang, Jiangxi, and Guangdong provinces. However, the **She** are not genuinely a highland minority, or at least not anymore. While it is widely accepted that some of the She in Guangdong speak a language of the Miao-Yao family, the Chinese assume that the majority of She elsewhere spoke a Sinitic language close to Hakka before acculturating to the **Han** and adopting Mandarin permanently. A majority of She today have Chinese **languages** as their native tongues, and despite living in hilly areas, they are heavily Sinicized and therefore share few cultural characteristics, if any, with the non-Han *minzu*.

SHENG. In the People's Republic of China, an administrative level best translated as "province," a rank that five other "**Autonomous Regions**" (*zizhiqu*) also have. The Chinese *sheng* further subdivides into "counties" (*xian*) and "prefectures" (*zizhizhou*).

SHIFTING CULTIVATION. *See* SWIDDENING.

SHUI. *See* SUI.

SI LA (SILA). In 1995, a small group of 1,772 **Tibeto-Burman**–speaking Sila dwelled in the extreme north of Laos in northern Phongsaly province. Across the border in northwest Vietnam, 840 Si La were officially reported in 1999.

SICHUAN. The northernmost of the four provinces of mountainous southwestern China. With a population of 83,290,000 in 2000, Sichuan—"Four Rivers"—also known as the Rice Bowl of China, includes a highland minority population of only 5 percent on its southern and western mountainous periphery. Sichuan's heavy demographic weight means that practically all of China's **minorities** indigenous to other provinces have, through migration, representatives living within its borders. Groups indigenous to Sichuan's highlands, however—though not exclusively to Sichuan—include the **Qiang, Yi, Miao**, and **Pumi**.

SIEDENFADEN, ERIK (1881–1958). A Danish military officer who spent 40 years in Siam (Thailand) between the 1910s and the 1950s. Siedenfaden became a correspondent of the *École Française d'Extrême-Orient* (EFEO) on several occasions between 1939 and 1954. In 1958, his main work, *The Thai Peoples: The Origins and Habitats of the Thai Peoples with a Sketch of their Material and Spiritual Culture*, was published posthumously. It is a rare monograph, addressing all of the **Tai**-speaking societies throughout the massif.

SINO-TIBETAN LANGUAGE FAMILY. One of the five main language families found in East and Southeast Asia, the **Sino-Tibetan** family includes all Chinese **languages** (Sinitic), and 250 to 300 other languages belonging to the **Tibeto-Burman** subfamily. Some authors prefer to include under the Sino-Tibetan label the **Miao-Yao language family** instead of seeing it as a distinct branch within the **Austro-Tai** superstock. (*See* figure 4.)

SIP SONG CHAU TAI (SIP SONG CHAU THAI) (SSCT). Literally, the "Twelve Tai (Thai) Districts," although the figure 12 should not be taken literally since it is above all used as an auspicious number. As a political entity, Sip Song Chau Tai does not exist anymore. Until its final demise around 1950, it straddled the northern Laos–Vietnam border, roughly comprising today's Lai Chau and Son La provinces, and parts of northeastern Laos in the border areas of Phongsaly, Luang Phrabang, and Huaphanh provinces. The **Tai** populations who inhabited and controlled it, namely the White, Black, and Red Tai (spelled Thai in Vietnam) still live in the same locations.

Note: Active language branches and languages spoken in the Southeast Asian massif are marked with an asterisk.

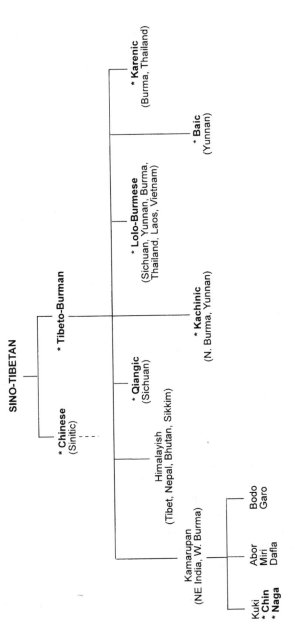

Source: Matisoff, James. "Genetic Versus Contact Relationship: Prosodic Diffusibility in South-East Asian Languages." *Areal diffusion and genetic inheritance: problems in comparative linguistics*, 291-347. In Aikhenvald, A., and R. M. W. Dixon (eds.) Oxford: OUP, 2001.

Figure 4. The Sino-Tibetan Language Family

In the upper valley of the Black River (Song Da), Muang Lai, present-day Lai Chau, is known to have existed as a Tai principality since at least the Mongol invasions in the late 13th century A.D. The loose federation of the SSCT was formalized around Muang Lai and Muang Thanh (Dien Bien Phu) at least as far back as the 17th century. Paying **tribute** to Lan Xang or Siam (Thailand) at certain times, to Burma or China at others, it came into the Vietnamese orbit in the 19th century. Its history is better known from the moment the first French observers started visiting it in the 1870s. French Diplomat Auguste Pavie, accompanied by the troops of Colonel Pennequin, considered it essential to sign a treaty with the SSCT and the Deo family heading it that would create an alliance of the French with the Deo dynasty, whose members were from then on referred to in French official documents as the Lords of Lai Chau. This was a strategic move that paid lasting dividends for both sides, at least until 1948, when the French, then concerned with winning the war against the nationalist Vietnamese, created a new entity called the **Tai Federation** (*Fédération Taï*), replacing the old **feudal** body. This new Federation only survived five years, until the French downfall following the Dien Bien Phu defeat in 1954. In the hands of the new communist masters of the Democratic Republic of Vietnam, the old Sip Song Chau Tai domain was reshaped into the **Tay Bac Autonomous Region**, itself abolished in 1976 to make place for the establishment of regular provinces.

SIP SONG PHAN NA (SSPN). Literally, the "Twelve Thousand Rice Fields" in Tai, 12 being an auspicious number, not necessarily reflecting the actual number of fields. As a political entity, all that remains of Sip Song Phan Na's former glory is the name **Xishuangbanna Dai Autonomous Prefecture**, an administrative district at the southern tip of **Yunnan** province in China. The district, called after the former kingdom, is inhabited for the most part by **Tai** speakers of the **Dai** minority nationality, of which the dominant group is the Lue, former rulers of the domain themselves.

The Tai settled in the southern Yunnan region at least a millennium ago, first clustering into independent villages, and later becoming federated in a **feudal** system under the political control of an indigenous elite. This domain was carved out of those of other powerful neighbors, such as the **Yi**, but even with this influence and the growing **Han** presence in Yunnan, the SSPN remained a discrete political and cultural entity, paying **tribute** in turn to various lowland kingdoms, such as Burma or Siam (Thailand), and of course China. Along with its cousins and Tai neighbor the former **Sip Song Chau Tai** in northwestern Vietnam, the **Lue** of SSPN were more closely related, in terms of language, script, culture, and religion, to the southern and western Tai, such as the **Shan**, the Siamese, the **Yuan**, and the **Lao**, than to the eastern groups, such as the **Zhuang**, **Buyi**, **Sui**, or **Dong**.

It has been estimated that in the 19th and early 20th centuries, roughly one-third of the population of the SSPN were non-Tai groups dwelling in the higher lands, on whom the Tai Lue maintained a tight economic grip in an uneven and highly profitable **trade** system—at least for the masters. Under Republican China, following the toppling of the imperial regime in 1911, Sip Song Phan Na remained a fairly independent "tribal" state on the margins of the Republic. With the permanent establishment of international borders separating communist China (1949), Vietnam, Laos, and Burma, the historical territory of the SSPN became permanently fragmented, the largest section remaining in China. Feudalism did not survive socialism and modernization, and the SSPN, as a political entity, was forever dissolved in the mid-20th century.

SITHON KOMMADAM (1910–1977). A famous minority revolutionary leader from the Boloven Plateau in southern Laos, Sithon Kommadam was the son of anti-French resistance fighter **Kommadam**, born among the **Laven** highland minority. Sithon was educated as a teacher in the French colonial education system. However, in 1936 he and his brothers were sent to jail in Phongsaly by the colonial authorities following the killing of their father at the end of his 1934–1936 armed revolt against the French. It was only in 1945 that Sithon was freed by the Japanese in the course of their short rule following their takeover of French Indochina. Sithon made his way back to his homeland in the south and joined the local guerrillas fighting the French, who had returned after World War II. He became for several years a key player in anticolonial resistance in southern Laos. In the mid-1950s, when the French departed and the royalist and communist factions were each trying to fill the void, Sithon joined the

Central Committee of the Pathet Lao Resistance Government under Prince Suphanuvong. In 1956, he was elected vice president representative of the **Lao Theung** to the Central Committee of the Lao Patriotic Front, and then to the National Assembly in 1958. At the final communist victory in 1975, he was made one of the four vice presidents of the Supreme People's Assembly along with another minority vice president, **Faydang Lobliayao**, a **Hmong** representing the Lao Sung. Sithon Kommadam was considered an official hero of the **Lao** Revolution. He died on March 1, 1977.

SKAW. *See* KAREN.

SLASH AND BURN AGRICULTURE. *See* SWIDDENING.

SLAVERY. Throughout history, highland populations in the **mainland Southeast Asian massif** have had a range of experiences with slavery, reflecting values at different times in East and Southeast Asia. Slavery, in one form or another, was often the bleak prospect of people defeated in times of political weakness or economic decay. It was the plight of victims of banditry and the vanquished in wars. It was an integral part of the booty in regional hostilities. There are innumerable records, from a variety of sources, of one kingdom invading the next and returning home with scores of defeated soldiers and peasants as slaves, such as during the numerous clashes between the Siamese, the **Burman**, and the **Khmer** kingdoms. Starting in the 17th century A.D. slavery was gradually checked by European colonialism. In the British colony of Burma, slavery became morally reprehensible from the moment it was actually made illegal in England in the mid 19th-century. The French, who had abolished slavery in their overseas domain in 1848, did not encourage it in **Indochina**. In China, the 1949 Revolution officially put an end to that "**feudal** bad habit" which was still tolerated, although discouraged since the end of imperial rule in 1911.

In the massif, the ancient practice of taking uplanders into slavery crystallized into the most common and pejorative nicknames for upland peoples generically. In Laos, the term *kha*, used throughout precolonial times, conveyed the combined meanings of "slave," "uncivilized," and "barbarian." So did the terms *moi* in southern Vietnam, *phnong* in Cambodia, and several additional markers used in various regions of China, such as *man* and *miao*, all written in prerevolutionary times with derogative radicals. Certain highland feudal societies used slavery as a demographic prop, for example the Nan Chao leaders, who would raid **Sichuan** to replenish their population. Other feudal states encouraged a permanent social stratification within one group that could entail slavery, for instance in **Yunnan** among the **Bai** and, above all, the **Yi**, where the Black Yi aristocracy (also called **Nosu**), could hold large proportions of the White Yi, their serfs, in a miserable state.

Across groups, colonial authors in the highlands often noted the state of virtual slavery imposed on many weaker highland groups by some of their powerful feudal highland neighbors. French Catholic **missionary** Paul Girod, who was attached to upland Tonkin in colonial north Vietnam, wrote in 1900 that in his vicariate, the **Tai** affiliated with the **Sip Song Chau Tai** domain had turned the Man (**Yao**) and Méo (**Hmong**) **minorities** living in the highlands of the Tai domain into "veritable slaves." In many cases, especially after slavery was made illegal, enslavement became more a matter of usury and economic exploitation, using the leverage of debt to enslave defaulters. When a debtor could not repay what he had borrowed, the creditor used him as free labor for varying periods of time, sometimes years, even for the rest of his life.

In the massif today, criminally using captured persons as free labor persists in certain forms: forced labor under military rule in Burma, forced **prostitution** of highland girls and boys kept locked in lowland brothels throughout the region, and indefinite debt payment to unlawful creditors, with the liability carrying on from one generation to the next. All these forms are officially banned by the states concerned. *See also* OY.

SMUGGLING. By definition, smuggling occurs when goods and people crossing a legal border are unchecked by the authorities. In this sense, smuggling in the massif has been the rule more than the exception ever since early kingdoms tried to impose their right to levy taxes on the circulation of goods and persons. Such a task has been daunting from the start, and still is. The massif is an extremely rugged environment, crossed by thousands of kilometers of borders and inhabited by an array of local groups knowing better than the central authorities how to negotiate all the local footpaths, trails, and waterways. Even when the most strongly centralized states, such as socialist China and Vietnam, have put in place a very strict watch on their upland borders, finding law enforcement officers willing to be posted in these border towns, villages, and outposts has always been difficult. The greater the distance from the lowland cultural hubs, the more border officers have to be drafted from among the local population, and the more they are likely to be convinced to turn a blind eye to local customary practices. In effect, perhaps the most important obstacle to fulfilling the state's desire to secure its borders and derive income from the cross-border traffic in the uplands is the fact that from the highlanders' point of view, these cross-border circulations and exchanges do not constitute smuggling. The rationale of this position is that since a very large proportion of ethnic groups in the massif dwell on the other side of one or more of the modern borders, all put in place relatively late, exchanging goods with their relatives is not only legitimate, it is an obvious right. This aspect of the "smuggling" problem in the highlands therefore has a lot to do with a misinterpretation of the concepts of border, state, and taxation.

Beyond such misunderstandings based on cultural differences, the highlands are also plagued by illegal cross-border activities associated in particular with drug trafficking on a large scale (opiates and **amphetamines**); arms trafficking to war and guerrilla zones; the circulation of goods criminally obtained, such as rare timber or endangered species; the forced displacement of persons taking refuge across borders; and economic migrants seeking better livelihoods and being smuggled outside their country by professionals. Loss of income for the governments concerned is thus only one dimension of the problem, the others being corruption, political instability, and economic uncertainty. How many highlanders are actually involved in this activity beyond acting as local hands, labor, or scouts is impossible to assess. Members of two groups in northeastern Burma, the **Wa** and the **Shan**, are known drug producers and traffickers, with gems another of their prized commodities. Otherwise, it is generally believed that large-scale trafficking across upland borders is in the hands of organized crime with roots outside the massif, often protected or supported by elements embedded in some of the governments in the region, especially among the military.

SOCIÉTÉ DES MISSIONS ÉTRANGÈRES DE PARIS **(MEP, THE PARIS SOCIETY OF FOREIGN MISSIONS).** A French missionary society founded in the 17th century in Paris, which later became the main provider of Roman Catholic **missionaries** to French Indochina, Burma, and southwest China. Along with British, German, and American Protestant and Anglican missions, it took root in **Yunnan**, Tibet, **Sichuan**, and **Guizhou**. Many MEP missionaries have actively contributed to the linguistics of the **mainland Southeast Asian massif**, often being the first Westerners to learn vernacular **languages**, decipher their grammar, and produce multilingual lexicons. In their postings, often for decades and without a family to keep them company, a number of these single men also produced ethnography of impressive quality. Among such contributors are **Paul Vial** and Alfred Liétard in Yunnan, Aloys Schotter and Joseph-Marie Esquirol in Guizhou, Francis Goré and Auguste Desgodins in western Yunnan and Tibet, Léon Girod and **François Savina** in Tonkin, Léopold Cadière and **Jacques Dournes** in Vietnam's **Central Highlands**, Antoine Bourlet in Laos, and **Charles Gilhodes** in northern Burma. National independence and communist revolutions in Asia forced the MEP out of these countries. Amid bouts of socialist antireligious irritation, local converts took over proselytizing, and recent religious liberalization in the region has allowed cautious renewed contacts between metropolitan religious congregations and the local church.

SRE. *See* CO-HO.

STIENG (STEANG). *See* XTIENG.

STRATEGIC HAMLETS. In order to deprive the procommunist People's Liberation Army forces of South Vietnam (derogatively dubbed the *Viet Cong* by the Diem regime) of their rural support in the **Central Highlands** and the Mekong Delta, where they had found recruits and received supplies, in 1961 troops of the Republic of Vietnam (RV) launched, with American assistance, the Strategic Hamlets scheme. Highland and lowland peasants were forcibly moved and concentrated into nearly 7,000 such hamlets, having an impact on 8 million inhabitants. The strategy behind these concentrations of population, also experimented with by French troops in Algeria in the late 1950s, was to make sure the communist guerrillas could not, in Chairman Mao's terms, move in the countryside "like fish in water." These hamlets were fenced and heavily guarded, and identities were regularly checked. Inhabitants of the hamlets could leave to attend their fields during the day but had to return every night. Troops put in charge of every hamlet would patrol a security perimeter around it and create a danger zone for *Viet Cong* guerrillas. This highly controversial scheme was abandoned at the end of 1963 in the confusion following President Ngo Dinh Diem's assassination.

SUAY (SOUEI). The last national census of Laos, taken in 1995, recorded 45,498 Suay dwelling in Muong Lao Ngam and Thateng in Saravane province, in the south of the country. Although a **Mon-Khmer** group of the Katuic branch, the Suay are now heavily Laoized. They are also often amalgamated with the **Kui**, their close relatives.

SUBSISTENCE ECONOMY. An old form of organization of production prevalent around the world among societies little involved in commercial exchange, and found in the **mainland Southeast Asian massif** among groups living in relative isolation from the market. Subsistence economy refers more precisely to the balance between agricultural production and consumption and their social context. Subsistence agriculturalists place decisive emphasis, in determining the desired level of production, on the **household**'s needs in terms of food for a yearly cycle, also taking into account the surpluses needed to obtain through trade necessary items to supplement their diet. A highland subsistence household, for example, will produce **rice** and a few vegetables, and keep a small number of chickens and pigs, all in quantities that would normally suffice to get through a year. Planned surpluses in any of these items, or circumstantial ones, such as a larger number of piglets than foreseen or an overproduction of rice due to better weather conditions in a given year, would be considered dispensable and would be redistributed within the **kinship** network, or brought to the marketplace to be exchanged for **salt**, gunpowder, medicine, fertilizers, cloth, medicine, and the like. Beyond the satisfaction of these basic reproductive needs, additional production is generally seen as unnecessary, and even dangerous, as it could attract the attention of bandits, tax collectors, or hungry neighbors.

"Pure" subsistence economy is now rare because policies for market exchange and **cash crops** are actively implemented all over the highlands. It is thus mainly poorer households and isolated villages, with no access to the market, that still scale their economy in accordance with their subsistence needs. Occasionally, this could also be a sign of resistance to modernization.

SUI (SHUI). The Sui of China, who numbered 406,902 individuals in 2000, form a part of the Kam-Sui section in the **Tai-Kadai language family**. They are chiefly located in **Guizhou** to the southwest of the **Dong (Kam)** homeland. They dwell along the upper Longjiang and Duliu Rivers in southern Guizhou and in compact communities in the Sandu Shui Autonomous County (established in 1957), plus Libo, Dushan, and a few other counties. Some Shuis are also found in the northwestern part of the **Guangxi Zhuang Autonomous Region**. The Sui homeland has been attached to the Chinese administration since at least the **Yuan** dynasty (1271–1368), and Sinization has progressed steadily ever since. The Sui also share historical, social, and cultural characteristics with their Tai-Kadai–speaking neighbors, the much more numerous Dong, **Buyi**, and **Zhuang**. Like them they are **animists**, with an influence from Chinese **Buddhism**. The Sui have an indigenous, basic script made of symbols and pictograms, used for divination and geomancy, that is too limited, however, to write their language.

SWIDDENING. Known in the past as slash-and-burn, nowadays often referred to as shifting cultivation, this very ancient agricultural technique has been used and still is today, either as the main form of agriculture for isolated groups, or as a supplement to sedentary agriculture on the fringes of the populated plains, plateaus, and valleys. Throughout history it has proved to be best suited for mobile and semi-mobile populations, and for life in mountainous areas with insufficient conditions to develop wet **rice** agriculture. Swiddening as practiced in the **mainland Southeast Asian massif** involves cutting down small portions of forest; removing the valuable wood; letting the remaining biological material dry, then setting fire to it; using the cleared plots to grow plants for a few years; and finally returning the plots to wilderness either for good before moving on to start all over again elsewhere (pioneering swiddening), or for a period of regenerative fallow allowing the maintenance of village sites for very long periods (rotational swiddening). The length of fallow varies between one and more than 15 years depending on the location, the type of soil, the nature of the previous and next crops, the availability of other swiddens in the vicinity, the local demographic balance, and the strategies of the agriculturalists involved.

To maintain fertility, fallows were a necessity because the only fertilizer used was the ashes produced at the time of burning the dried-out, cut-down forest cover or regrowth. Swiddening was long used to grow tubercles, to which were later added a more varied selection, including **dry rice**, **maize**, beans, and eventually, in the highest lands, the **opium** poppy. More recent **cash crops** like cabbage, potatoes, carrots, ginger, and the like, part of the globalization of the highland economy, are now commonly grown on old swiddens turned into permanent plots. Often now, the fallow cycle has been halted, and chemicals are permanently needed to keep productivity at a reasonable level.

Generally, however, in most highlands of the massif, swiddening in its rotational form persists, usually on a small scale, most of the time performed by sedentarized groups to supplement permanent agriculture. This strategy provides an opportunity to grow a few additional crops that the prevalence of wet rice terraces in the flat lands does not allow for lack of available land. Swiddening is also a convenient way to circumvent the predicament of the lack of land titles, a small swidden being easily carved out of a nearby state forest and abandoned a few years later before authorities notice it.

After millennia of being appropriate, in the past decades swiddening has come to have a bad press among governments in the region. This is due to swiddening now being seen as a destructive use of forest cover responsible for irreversible soil **erosion** at the head of watersheds. Swiddening has been perceived, and more and more publicly presented, in a negative light, and it has been targeted by most governments for phasing out as quickly as possible. Rather questionably, under governmental guidance it has generally been replaced by sedentary agriculture that makes abundant use of chemicals whose impacts on the environment are becoming worse and worse. Nonetheless, and even more radically, large highland populations have been removed from forested areas by their national governments and relocated among lowland peasants, adding pressure where a demographic problem already exists.

Against such an accusatory discourse and the authoritarian policies it entails, recent studies have emphasized that given the right balance between demographic pressure and the availability of forested land, comprehensive rotational swiddening performed competently can actually offer an adapted and sustainable way of using the land as well as favoring a low-cost form of management of the remaining highlands forests. Unfortunately, and unrelated to this partial rehabilitation, the environmental problem has been further aggravated by several countries in Southeast Asia—Vietnam in particular—having recently pushed lowland surplus population to settle in the less-populated highlands. The ecological consequences are severe, these migrants often having little knowledge of the specifics of highland ecosystems. The delicate balance between human population and nature there is thus stretched to the limit, and the erosion of higher lands often becomes significantly worse, thus reinforcing the position of those who would like to see the practice of swiddening banned forever.

– T –

T'AI. *See* THAI.

TAI LANGUAGES. The Tai language subfamily, a branch of the **Tai-Kadai language family**, is the most important collection of **languages** found among highland **minorities** in the **mainland Southeast Asian massif**. A majority of the non-Han peoples of south China are Tai speakers, and this is also true of the highland groups in northern Vietnam and northern Laos.

In English, *Tai* is the accepted spelling to name this subfamily comprising dozens of related languages spoken by the large **Lao**, Isan, **Yuan**, and Siamese majorities in Laos and Thailand, but also among many official highland minorities: the **Zhuang**, the **Buyi**, the **Dai**, the **Kam**, the **Sui**, the **Mulao**, the **Maonan**, and the **Li** in China; the **Shan**, Hkamti, and Lu in Burma; the **Tay**, **Thai**, **Nung**, **San Chay**, **Giay**, Lu, and **Bo Y** in Vietnam; and the Phuthai, Lu, **Nyouan**, **Yang**, and **Sek** in Laos. Not counting the 70 million or so inhabitants of Thailand and Laos, the total number of minority speakers of some Tai language in mainland Southeast Asia is 33 million. Tai languages are generally monosyllabic and **tonal**. The number of tones across Tai languages is generally around five or six, with a peak of 15 for the **Dong** (Kam) in China. The dominant **Tai scripts** are phonetic and adapted from Indian Pali, with Romanizations also found in Vietnam and China.

Most Tai-speaking groups in the massif have been historically attached to the land and to a **feudal** political system through their original political organization, the *muang*. Until the regional takeovers by European colonial powers and the imposition of a strong central state of a capitalist type, Tai speakers were divided in a manner typical of feudal states with, on the one hand, an elite in charge of the political affairs of each *muang* and owning the land, and on the other, a mass of peasants working that land without owning it and paying rent in kind and labor to the landlords. Widespread wet **rice** agriculture in terraces has long been the dominant agricultural practice, though some isolated groups have also relied on **swiddening**.

For Tai-speakers living in a *muang*, **trade** was also an essential part of daily life. At one end of the spectrum, isolated Tai peasants would perhaps only trade at sporadic **marketplaces** when in need of some essential goods that they could not produce themselves, such as iron or steel. But on the rest of the spectrum, Tai groups living closer to concentrations of population included a strata of active and enterprising traders, who could take advantage of their strategic geographical location, between the lowlands and the highlands and along all major waterways, to become the indispensable intermediaries in all kinds of exchanges between these two domains. The Tai elite actually developed extensive commercial networks well beyond their particular political territory, electing their Tai cousins living all over the massif as preferential partners.

Western and central Tai speakers are for the most part Theravada **Buddhists** and have been influenced by the prevalence of this religion among the largest demographic masses of Tai speakers in and around the massif, namely the Siamese and the Lao. But a number of Tai groups in the eastern portion of the massif have been too distant physically to be reached by that influence and have remained **animists**; this includes all the Tai speakers in northern Vietnam and many among those living in western Guangxi. However, the mass of Zhuang in central Guangxi and their Sui, Kam, Molam, or Maonan neighbors have gradually abandoned animism to drift toward the Chinese model, and have adopted either Taoism, Confucianism, Chinese Buddhism, or a combination of these. (*See also* map 2; figure 5.)

TAI FEDERATION. A short-lived political entity in northern Vietnam (then Tonkin) during the last six years of the French presence there. In reaction to the proclamation of independence of the Democratic Republic of Vietnam by Ho Chi Minh in September 1945, followed by his takeover of a large chunk of the mountainous part of eastern Tonkin, a temporary arrangement was worked out between the embattled French and their long allies in Tonkin's northwest, the **Thai** of the **Sip Song Chau Tai** and their hereditary rulers, the Deo family. In an attempt to cling to the highlands against the communist push, and using the same logic that had led to the establishment of the *Pays Montagnard du Sud Indochinois* (**PMSI**) two years earlier in the south, an agreement was promulgated by the French in July 1948 creating an independent **Tai** (Thai) Federation inside the French Indochina Union, a Federation grouping the present-day provinces of Lai Chau, Phong Tho, and Son La under the presidency of White Thai leader Deo Van Long. As a result, while the White, Black, and Red Thai in the northwest of Tonkin were supporting the French Colonial Army during the **First Indochina War** (1946–1954), other Tai-speaking **Tay** (Tho) and **Nung** guerrilla units in the northeast were siding with the Viet Minh.

The legal status of the so-called subminorities inside the Tai Federation, essentially **lineage societies**, such as the **Hmong**, **Yao**, **Khmu**, and **Lolo**, was claimed to be one of de facto inclusion managed by the Thai rulers alone. In a dominant position in their domain since before the French had arrived, the Thai took advantage of the French support to exploit even more these subminorities landlocked in the upper reaches of their territory, particularly by taking control of the highly profitable **opium trade**. In return for their support of the colonial cause, unusual benefits were bestowed on the Federation by the French: modern European arms flowed in, local military recruits were drafted and regularly paid, the Federation's capital Lai Chau was made a small fortress, and local education in the Thai language and script was swiftly organized from Hanoi with the help of the *École française d'Extrême-Orient* (EFEO). No other minority in that region enjoyed such privileges, and bitterness soared accordingly among neighbors. The rapid deployment of Viet Minh activities in upper Tonkin during the conflict reinforced this political division: the Federated Thai drew ever closer to the French while, understandably, subminorities exploited by them tended to side with the communist guerrillas to challenge the might of the Thai rulers from within their own domain. After the battle of **Dien Bien Phu** and the Geneva accords signed in 1954, the communist victors made the Tai Federation obsolete as a political body, replacing it with a new entity called the **Tay Bac Autonomous Region** under direct control from Hanoi.

TAI MEO AUTONOMOUS REGION. *See* TAY BAC AUTONO-MOUS REGION.

TAI NUA. *See* SHAN.

TAI SCRIPTS. A **Tai** script whose invention has been attributed to Siamese King Ramkamhaeng (13th century A.D.) was inspired by Pali imported from Ceylon, connecting this Tai script to the general Sanskrit stem. Owing in particular to its rapid spread among Theravada **Buddhist** monks, it has gradually been adopted by a majority of Tai speakers dwelling in and immediately around historical Siam (Thailand). Forms of this script have followed the spreading of Tai political and religious influence in the **Peninsula**, often through Siamese military and **feudal** expansion, and have been adopted by a number of Tai speakers outside Thailand, such as the **Shan** in Burma, the **Lue** in **Sip Song Phan Na**, the **Lao** in Lan Xang, and the **Thai** in **Sip Song Chau Tai** in northwestern Vietnam, the extreme eastern limit of this expansion. Such an extensive area of influence makes the Tai script one of the most common indigenous scripts found in the massif, second only to **Chinese ideograms**, both ahead of the Latin transcriptions.

TAI YAI. *See* SHAN.

TAI-KADAI LANGUAGE FAMILY. One of the five main **language** families found in Asia (having over 20 language subgroups), all exclusive to and prevalent in mainland Southeast Asia and southwest China. Being part of the **Austro-Tai** superstock along with the **Austronesian** and **Miao-Yao** families, the Tai-Kadai family is believed to have been originally polysyllabic and nontonal. However, it is theorized that under the influence of neighboring Sinitic languages, it underwent a conversion to monosyllabism and tone-proneness, two of its fundamental features today. The **Tai** branch of this family is vastly more important in demographic terms than the **Kadai** one, the latter having only six recorded languages, found on the **Guizhou**-Guangxi border area in China and in small pockets in northern Vietnam, and possibly on **Hainan** Island. *See also* TAI LANGUAGES. (*See* figure 5.)

Note: All languages and sublanguages in this family are spoken in the Southeast Asian massif.

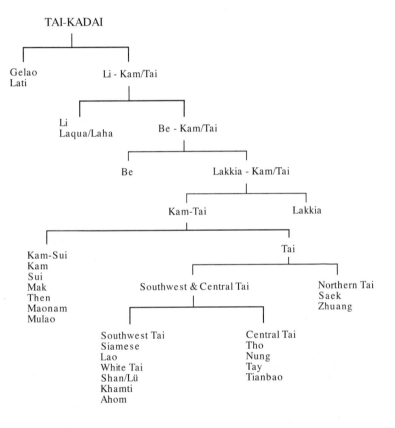

Source: Matisoff, James. "Genetic Versus Contact Relationship: Prosodic Diffusibility in South-East Asian Languages." *Areal diffusion and genetic inheritance: problems in comparative linguistics*, 291-347. In Aikhenvald, A., and R. M. W. Dixon (eds.) Oxford: OUP, 2001.

Figure 5.   The Tai-Kadai Language Family

TALIENG (TALIANG). In 1995, the 23,091 Bahnaric-speaking, **Mon-Khmer** Talieng were primarily located in southeastern Sekong province in Southern Laos. Early colonial literature named them Kasseng or Kaseng, and at the time, they were reported to be living in Saravane province. They are predominantly **swiddeners** and **animists**.

TAMBON. In Thailand, a territorial administrative unit generally translated as "subdistrict" or "commune." Each *tambon* subdivides into a varying number of *mooban* (villages), while several *tambon* together form an *amphoe* (district).

TA-OI (TAU-OI, TA OY). The Ta-oi are a **Mon-Khmer** group of the Katuic branch, probably speaking a Bruan dialect. They are found evenly spread across the Lao–Vietnamese border between Saravane province in Laos (30,876 in 1995), where they are officially named Ta Oy, and Thua Thien-Hue province in the *Tay Nguyen* of Vietnam (34,960 in 1999).

TASSENG. Throughout Laos, including its highlands, this is an administrative unit best translated as "subdistrict," grouping 10 to 20 villages (*ban*) together. Introduced by the French colonial administration, the *tasseng* was a territorial subdivision of the *muang* (district). Following the implementation of the New Economic Mechanisms in Laos in 1986, the *tasseng* were officially abolished, and the *ban* now report directly to the *muang*.

TAY. This is the most numerous national minority (*cac dan toc thieu so*) of Vietnam, with 1,477,514 members accounted for in 1999. The Tay form a key group within the Central **Tai** branch of the **Tai-Kadai language family**. They inhabit almost every valley of moderate elevation over the whole of northern Vietnam east of the Da (Black) River watershed, where the domain of their cousins the **Thai** starts. The Tay are particularly concentrated east of the Red River in the provinces of Lang Son (252,800 in 1999) and Cao Bang (208,822), where they regularly cohabit with their close relatives the **Nung**, as well as in Tuyen Quang (172,136), Ha Giang (152,829), Bac Can (149,459), Yen Bai (126,140), Thai Nguyen (106,238), and Lao Cai (81,666). They are also present in significant numbers in Quang Ninh and Bac Giang. The Tay are also numerous just across the northeastern border in the **Guangxi Zhuang Autonomous Region** of China, but their population there is unknown due to the Chinese authorities lumping them together with the larger **Zhuang** minority nationality (over 16 million). It is likely that their number there is in excess of 1 million. Encouraged to economic mobility by the Vietnamese government, since the early 1990s over 75,000 Tay from northern Vietnam seeking new economic opportunities have moved to the southern provinces of Dak Lak and Lam Dong in the **Central Highlands**, where they pursue farming activities.

In cultural, religious, political, and economic terms, the Tay bear a striking resemblance to their immediate neighbors, the Nung. Like them, they are highly Vietnamized, in particular as regards the growing importance of the Chinese version of Mahayana **Buddhism**. A powerful vector of this acculturation was the implementation by the Le Dynasty in the 15th century of the *tho-ti* system, by which **Kinh** mandarins were sent to various locations in the Tay mountains not only to rule in the name of the imperial state, but also to live, get married, and start establishing elite **lineages** among the Tay by passing the mandarin titles to their sons—a unique prerogative (see for comparison the *tu-si* **system** in China). The political alliance thus created between the Tay and the Kinh helps explain why it was in Tay areas that the anti-French "pirates" (**Flag armies**) were the most solidly rooted in the late 19th century, and why it is there that Ho Chi Minh and the Nationalist leaders took refuge during the war for independence.

A constant source of confusion regarding the identification of the Tay in French archives and scholarly publications is the fact that during the colonial era, the colonists and the Vietnamese used to call them "Tho," an ethnonym written with the same tone and diacritics as another group officially recognized today by Vietnamese ethnologists, the Vietic-speaking **Tho** of Nghe An and Thanh Hoa provinces. Colonial publications mentioning the ethnonym Tho must therefore be decoded accordingly.

TAY BAC AUTONOMOUS REGION. After 1954, in the new Democratic Republic of Vietnam (North Vietnam) the victorious communists wanted to consolidate the political gains they had made among the various and traditionally disunited highland **minorities** of the northern highland region. Borrowing from communist China's policy requiring the setting up of minority **Autonomous Regions**, but also in connection with the national project of agrarian reform and as a political alternative for the upper northern region, a **Tai**-Meo Autonomous Region (quickly renamed Tay Bac, "Northwest," to better represent the ethnic diversity it enclosed) was created in 1955 in the northwest to replace the short-lived and pro-French **Tai Federation**. This was an area equivalent to three provinces in the mountains between the Red River valley and the Laotian frontier. A year later the **Viet Bac Autonomous Region** in the northeast was set up, covering five upland provinces east of the Red River. Together, these two entities covered well over half the territory of the Democratic Republic of Vietnam.

As in the Chinese model, both enjoyed on paper important privileges in terms of cultural rights and self-government, and the 1960 Constitution brought additional precision to this creation by indicating that, along with the administrative division of the country into provinces and districts, these Autonomous Regions would be considered to be on the same level as urban hubs like Hanoi or Haiphong, and would thus fall directly under the authority of the central state. One cannot help but notice that this policy was clearly related to the French colonists, with their establishment in the 1890s in those same highlands of the Military Territories system.

There is little doubt about the underlying political ideology supporting this reorganization by North Vietnam of large chunks of the highlands. Most action plans implemented in the northern high region by the regime were double-sided. They contributed to "developing" these remote areas and their inhabitants, and to attaching these ethnicities to mainstream Vietnamese society, making the Marxist-Leninist revolution triumphant across Vietnam. The establishment of additional Autonomous Regions was also planned, but this project did not survive the turmoil of the **Second Indochina War** (1954–1975). After the communists' final victory and the country's reunification in 1975, Autonomous Regions were not considered necessary anymore and were abolished.

TAY NGUYEN. The "Western Plateaus." In south and central Vietnam, the term specifically refers to a substantial area of the highlands usually called the **Central Highlands** in English, which stretches from the Laotian border to the eastern slopes of the southern **Annam Cordillera** (*Day Truong Son*). In Vietnam, the Central Highlands include the provinces of Song Be, Dak Lak, Lam Dong, Gia Lai, and Kon Tum, as well as high grounds of many other adjacent provinces stretching from Tay Ninh in the south to Quang Binh in the country's center. As a geomorphologic and a social entity, however, the Central Highlands could benefit from being defined more broadly and reconnected to the related areas and populations across the borders. In Cambodia, the border provinces of Ratana Kiri and Mondul Kiri are drained by the same rivers as Vietnam, flowing into the Mekong in Cambodia, and these two provinces are home to representatives of several of the same ethnic groups found in Vietnam. In southeast Laos, the provinces of Attapeu and Sekong, as well as the highlands in the provinces of Champassack and Savannakhet, also embrace parts of the southern Annam Cordillera uplands and, again, shelter many similar ethnicities, just as do the adjacent Vietnamese and Cambodian highlands.

Throughout history, these highlands have never formed a political entity as such. Instead, several local chiefdoms and, at times, kingdoms have existed there. Language association suggests that the most important historical **feudal** rulers connected with these highlands were probably the **Cham**, their kingdom of Champa finally being taken over by Vietnamese troops invading from the north in the 18th century A.D. During the French colonial period (1858–1954) these highlands, then called in French *hauts-plateaux*, *plateaux centraux*, or *pays montagnard*, began to be considered a meaningful geographical and cultural entity, at least in the sense of being mainly inhabited by non-**Kinh** groups. French authorities were eager to control the colony's frontier, its populations, and its resources; to separate Kinh and non-Kinh populations for strategic purposes; and to develop industrial rubber and **coffee** plantations there, and the active support of Catholic **missions** on location was instrumental in this enterprise.

When the Republic of Vietnam (RVN, South Vietnam) was established in 1954, soon to be sponsored by U.S. intelligence and military, wartime policies prevailed for the next 20 years of combat against socialist troops of the Democratic Republic of Vietnam (DRV, North Vietnam) and their sympathizers in the south. Because of its strategic location, right at the southern end of the network of Ho Chi

Minh trails, and due to ethnic networks straddling the borders into Cambodia and Laos, the Central Highlands became a terrain of fierce ideological competition between the pro-RVN and pro-DRV forces. In the 1960s and early 1970s, military involvement in the highlands became important, and winning the **Montagnards**' (as central highlanders were to be generically named by the U.S. command, the troops in turn nicknaming them "Yards") allegiance became a major stake for all sides. The RVN leadership in Saigon devised and imposed an autocratic highland relocation policy called the **Strategic Hamlets** scheme, aiming at emptying the plateaus of potential supporters of the "Viet Cong" cause. This policy backfired because it contributed heavily to alienating the Montagnards from the southern cause. Caught in the crossfire, central highlanders had a miserable time, their families were torn apart, their villages were bombed, and the land was ruined by the massive use of chemical defoliants. Just making a living became nearly impossible, and resentment soared. Once the war was over and the communists were firmly in power, the government of the reunited Socialist Republic of Vietnam did little to soothe their pains, instead imposing on the local populations its **collectivization** scheme and its **New Economic Zone migration** program, bringing scores of lowlanders into the highlands. As a result, today the proportion of indigenous inhabitants in the *Tay Nguyen,* as well as their capacity to access agricultural land, keeps shrinking under growing demographic pressure.

In terms of linguistic classification, besides a growing number of outsiders who migrate into the *Tay Nguyen,* the chief source being the Kinh Vietnamese from the Mekong delta "spontaneously" migrating to seek economic opportunities or sent there through state-sponsored schemes, two main language families are historically found on these plateaus. Many belong to the **Austronesian** family, with approximately 700,000 speakers, including, in decreasing order of population size, the Giarai (**Gia-rai**), Ede (**E-de**), Raglai (Rag-lai), and Churu (**Chu-ru**); most inhabit Vietnam chiefly in the Kon Tum, Gia Lai, Dak Lak, Khang Hoa, and Ninh Thuan provinces. These Austronesian speakers are part of a very old settlement pattern—probably proto-Malay—preceding later waves of migrants who moved to the lowlands, such as the **Khmer**, the **Lao**, and the Kinh. The second family is represented by a variety of **Mon-Khmer** speakers totaling approximately 960,000, including the **Bahnar (Ba-na)**, Coho **(Co-ho)**, **Sedang** (Xo Dang), **Hre**, **Mnong**, **Stieng (Xtieng)**, **Bru-Van Kieu**, Cotu **(Co-tu)**, **Ta-oi**, Ma, **Gie-Trieng**, **Co**, Choro, **Ro-mam**, and **Brau**, found in all the Vietnamese, Cambodian, and Laotian provinces mentioned previously in this entry.

In cultural terms, both Mon-Khmer and Austronesian Central Highlands groups are territorial, in the sense that they have been dwelling in a particular area for a long time and consider the land theirs. They are also characterized by a rich material culture featuring elegant yet simple architecture, detailed basketry, and accomplished weaving. They are principally **animists**, although Christianity has secured a strong footing among certain groups. Vietnamese Mahayana **Buddhism** is also growing in popularity. Politically, since they are all **lineage societies**, there is traditionally no unity among ethnic groups under a common leadership, ethnic leaders acting locally instead, although they may decide to join forces at times when such a strategy appears promising or when they are left with no alternative. As a specific social and cultural space, the *Tay Nguyen* is becoming more and more ethnically mixed as migrants flock in, entering **cash cropping** and industrial agriculture, especially **coffee**. Many local groups resent what they perceive as an invasion of their domain, and they protest to the state.

Even with the wars over, the region is still the object of vigorous competition involving local populations, the Vietnamese state, diasporic representatives in the United States (in particular remnants of the **FULRO**), and Christian **missionary** organizations. The names by which all these groups call themselves often differ from those the outside world uses to call them. It is useful to note that the ethnonyms widely employed around the world for all these minority groups were most often devised by French colonial administrators. These were later taken up and promoted abroad by the American military and researchers who studied the French texts during the years of American involvement in the **Second Indochina War** (1954–1975).

TAYOK. *See* SHAN.

TERRITOIRES MILITAIRES **(MILITARY TERRITORIES IN FRENCH INDOCHINA).** For the French colonial administration in

Indochina during the last decade of the 19th century, the mountainous region of Tonkin along the China border—the extreme north of today's Vietnam—remained to be explored. Very little was known by the French administrators prior to their arrival in 1883 about the many highland societies living in these uplands. For the new colonial military establishment, based on their short experience, the northern mountains sheltered either rebels hostile to the French occupation, more or less organized looters harassing the local population, or massive groups of organized bandits involved in large-scale looting and trafficking. In 1890, only the **Viet** and Chinese ethnicities were acknowledged in the highland region, while "primitive" tribes people were known to be there, but were either not worth taking into account or were put in the same category as the looters. With this sketchy picture in mind, the colonial military command decided in 1891 to divide the whole of Tonkin into three areas in relation to the mode of composition and organization of the bands: the central Delta zone, which only included Viet bands; the Delta periphery zone, with mixed bands of Viet and Chinese; and the upland zone, with permanent or occasional Chinese bands.

In this way, the complete separation of the mountainous region from the delta was promulgated and a demarcation line was laid separating the mid- and highlands from the lowlands, equipped with blockhouses and permanent troops. Those uplands were then subdivided into five *Territoires Militaires*, or Military Territories, that spread along the Chinese border from the Gulf of Tonkin to Phongsaly province in Laos, the fifth and last Military Territory set up in 1916. These were given to the military high command to administer. The exact subdivisions of these territories varied constantly over the years, some sectors changing territory altogether, while others were further subdivided. Whole areas, such as the upper Red River valley around the town of Lao Cai, were at times given back to civilian administration, only to be declared military domain again when the political situation required it. On and off, this form of military administration in the highlands only ceased completely with the departure of the French from Indochina in 1954.

From an ethnological point of view regarding the **minorities** in the highlands of northern Vietnam, an important benefit from this military administration of the northern frontier was two successive periods of ethnography of the highland groups, launched and conducted in 1898 and 1903 at the request of the governors general of Indochina and executed by the military themselves. The second initiative in particular was put under the control of Commander Emile Lunet de Lajonquière, who published some of the results in his *Ethnographie des territoires militaires* [*Ethnography of the Military Territories*] (1904). The whole body of archives associated with those initiatives is the earliest and most comprehensive ethnographic portrait of the highland groups in that region produced during colonial times.

THAI. For most readers, following the common use in Western dictionaries, Thai applies to all inhabitants of Thailand—effectively written there in the vernacular script with an aspirated "th" (often formerly transposed as "T'ai" in English). For the authorities of Thailand, this "Thai" national category is all-encompassing. However, the Thai of Thailand who are also **Tai** speakers (83 percent of the national population) do not form a monolithic category. Major Tai subgroups, such as the Lao-speaking Isan in the northeast and the **Yuan** in the north, claim a distinctive linguistic identity, not to mention the fact that all other non-Tai speakers in the country are in this way simply forgotten.

Use of the word "Thai" as an ethnic name without an exclusive association with Thailand also exists. However, the word is not uniformly understood or consistently employed across countries and authors. It may refer to minority Tai-speaking groups in the massif, in particular in the official etymology of the White, Red and Black Thai as found in Vietnamese texts. The Vietnamese authorities' decision has been based on the aspiration in the pronunciation of the word among the said groups.

THAI. A Southwest **Tai**-speaking group and the second most numerous national minority in Vietnam. In 1999, there were officially 1,328,725 Thai in northwestern Vietnam, in the upper valleys of the Da (Black) and Ma Rivers, with extensions into the western Red River basin. The group occupies most of the midregion along the Laotian border from China to southern Nghe An province. More precisely, they are found in the provinces of Son La (482,985), Nghe An (269,491), Thanh Hoa (210,908), and Lai Chau (206,001), with substantial numbers in Lao

Cai and Hoa Binh. In colonial literature, as well as in current Viet-namese ethnological classifications, the Thai subdivide into several groups, often named after a color associated with their attire. There are thus the White Thai (Tai Khao, Tai Trang), centered around the town of Lai Chau in their ancient domain of **Sip Song Chau Tai**; the Black Thai (Tai Dam, Tai Den) around the town of Dien Bien Phu; and the Red Thai (Tai Deng, Tai Do) on both sides of the border between the provinces of Thanh Hoa and Nghe An in Vietnam, as well as Hua Phan in Laos, where some Black Thai are also found.

It is generally believed that the Thai of Vietnam migrated from China at least a thousand years ago and have inhabited northwest Vietnam ever since. Toponyms in the northwest highlands bear their mark, particularly the term *ban*, village, found everywhere on current Vietnamese maps. Many Thai **feudal *muang*** took shape over the centuries, pushing aside earlier and politically weaker **Mon-Khmer** and **Sino-Tibetan** groups in the highlands, while exerting their polit-ical and economic control over later migrants from the **Miao-Yao** family. The various Thai feudal kingdoms paid individual **tribute** to either Siam (Thailand), Lan Xang, Burma, China, or Vietnam de-pending on the circumstances, until a federated state called Sip Song Chau Tai came to encompass most of them. Though Siam's cultural influence was felt strongly, particularly through the adoption of a script derived from Siamese, Theravada **Buddhism** did not reach the Thai in Vietnam, who largely remained **animists**. In the late 19th cen-tury, the Thai were granted political favors by the French that ensured the colonial rulers of their indefatigable alliance against the Viet-namese communists and Nationalists. The Thai paid the price of this political choice after the communists took over in 1954. Its elite hav-ing largely fled abroad, the feudal system was abolished and **trade** networks profitable to the feudal lords were dismantled. Today, the Thai are under pressure with the building of dams on the Da River and the consequent relocation of large populations due to reservoirs being created and filled. The very town of Lai Chau, their former stronghold, is earmarked to be permanently flooded around 2006.

THAILAND, ADMINISTRATIVE DIVISIONS IN THE KING-DOM OF. In mountainous Thailand today, administrative divisions follow the same pattern as in all other rural areas in the country, with,

from top to bottom, the *changwat* (province), *amphoe* (district), *tambon* (subdistrict or commune), and *mooban* (village). The *mooban* can also be subdivided into smaller hamlets, each often inhabited by different ethnic groups—information that is not always registered in official statistics.

THAILAND, HIGHLAND MINORITIES IN THE KINGDOM OF. There are officially nine highland minority denominations listed in Thailand, where they are known as *chao khao*, "mountain people." These are the Kariang (**Karen**), **Hmong** (Meo), Musur (**Lahu**), Ikaw (**Akha**), **Mien** (**Yao**), Lisaw (**Lisu**), Lua (**Lawa**), **Khmu**, and Phi Tong Luang (**Mlabri**). Some official publications also add the Kha Tin (**H'tin**) and the Padaung. In 2002, all these groups numbered 923,722 individuals in total, with the Karen representing 47.5 percent of the total, and the Hmong 16.7 percent. Apart from the Karen, who have lived a sedentary life for over three centuries, all other highland **minorities** in the north were nonterritorial, at least until very recently. This meant that they lived for various periods of time in villages and hamlets located next to those of other groups to whom they were not related, all dispersed throughout the mountainous north. At the time of the 1995 census, these *chao khao* thus inhabited over 20 provinces sharing the northern highlands, with Chiang Mai (174,195), Chiang Rai (130,363), Mae Hong Son (94,347), and Tak (90,188) being the most important ones. This list of the *chao khao* in Thailand being a product of regional geopolitics of the 1960s, it only reflects the situation in the northern highlands. A few small groups of **Mon-Khmer** speakers, which Thailand shares with Cambodia, have been omitted. These groups, called in Cambodia the **Kui** and the Chong, dwell in the westernmost hills of the Cardamom range in Trat province, where their number is unknown. They are also found in the Dangrek Range (*Phanon Dongrak*) from southern Ubon to southern Buri Ram provinces. It has been estimated that there may be as many as 100,000 Kui in that region, although they have been heavily absorbed into mainstream rural **Thai** society.

With only 1.45 percent of its national population officially registered as *chao khao*, Thailand has understandably paid only limited attention to them. National unity in the country has long been, and still is, based on the three pillars of **Buddhism**, royalty, and the Thai na-

Table 5. "Hill Tribes" of Northern Thailand, 2002
9 official "Hill Tribes" (H.T.) (922,955) and two additional northern highland groups (767)

Ethnic Group	N	Percent of H.T.	Percent of Country
Kariang, Karen	438,131	47.5	0.69
Hmong, Meo	153,955	16.7	0.24
Lahu	102,876	11.1	0.16
Ikaw, Akha	68,653	7.4	0.11
Yao, Mien	45,551	4.9	0.07
H'tin	42,657	4.6	0.07
Lisaw, Lisu	38,299	4.1	0.06
Lua, Lawa	22,260	2.4	0.04
Khmu, Khamu	10,573	1.1	0.02
Padaung [1995]	485	0.1	0.00
Mlabri, Phi Tong Luang	282	0.0	0.00
"Hill Tribes"	**923,722**	**100**	**1.45**
COUNTRY (2000)	**63,484,000**	**—**	**100**

Source: Tribal Research Institute, 2002.

tion, leaving little room for drastically different highland peoples. Before the **Second Indochina War** in mainland Southeast Asia reached Thailand in the late 1950s, the Kingdom had no precise idea who these highland dwellers were, nor how many of them there were. American military pressure was applied to the Thai government and aimed at preventing the "domino effect" that could tip Thailand over to the communist side, due in particular, it was surmised, to the cultural similarity of many highland groups across the Thailand–Laos border. Around 1960, **Gordon Young**, the son of an American missionary family long established in upper Burma, was commissioned to locate and identify highland dwellers in Thailand. His report led to the government declaring in 1962 an official list of nine *chao khao* and setting up in 1964 in Chiang Mai a Tribal Research Center administered by the Ministry of Public Welfare. Until the end of the **Second Indochina War** in 1975, the main concern of the Thai government was to prevent the emergence within its population, including the *chao khao*, of communist sympathizers and guerrillas, a task that kept the Thai military intelligence busy until 1987, in the case of the Hmong.

Concurrently, **opium** growing in the uplands was also becoming a concern. In Thailand, as in neighboring countries, buying opium from highland producers had long been a state monopoly, with Thailand only officially banning it in 1959. The underground continuation of this **trade** after that date was directed at financing various "insurgent" activities, some connected with the wars, some simply having to do with plain trafficking and banditry. The final curtailing of opium production on Thai territory was also turned into a priority. Opium-growing eradication campaigns were conducted from the 1970s well into the 1990s with the active help of international development agencies, who contributed to turning highland farmers away from the poppy to replacement cash crops. Since the early 1990s, yet another concern, environmental protection in the northern highlands, has been brought to the top of the agenda. Highlanders have been labeled environmental hazards because of their practicing pioneer and rotational **swiddening**, which is targeted as the principal cause of highland deforestation and erosion. The ban on swiddening, the introduction of chemical additives into agriculture, and increasing connections to the market became the foundation of all policies addressing the *chao khao*.

Not surprisingly, new environmental problems swiftly developed, due in particular to the pollution of land and waterways resulting from the massive use of industrial farming chemicals in the highlands. Some lowland peasants and activists from all walks of life, including the Buddhist clergy and the Thai aristocracy, claimed that Thai peasants, who did not receive as many subsidies and were not allowed to farm in the highlands, were treated unfairly compared to highlanders, and protested with different degrees of violence. Perhaps the only country sharing the massif where freedom of speech is real, Thailand has become a social laboratory where the development of a dialogue among highland minorities, rural lowlanders, activist groups, experts, and the state on the hotly debated issue of protection of the environment versus protection of minority cultures seems to bear some promise.

THIN. *See* H'TIN.

THMAUN. A minority of 453 was officially listed under this name in Cambodia in 1995, one of four about which accurate linguistic information is unavailable.

THO. The group officially called Tho in Vietnam today numbered 68,394 in 1999. They are Vietic speakers from the **Viet-Muong** branch of the **Austro-Asiatic language family**. They all live in Vietnam, in the western portions of the northern provinces of Nghe An and Thanh Hoa next to the Laotian border, relatively close to their Vietic cousins the **Mone**. The Tho are believed to be a blend of ancient local populations and **Kinh** migrants who took refuge there in the late 17th century A.D. *See also* TAY.

THO (THU JEN). During colonial times in **Indochina**, the French, following a local habit, had assigned the name Tho to today's **Tay** of northeastern Vietnam. This usage came from the Cantonese pronunciation of the Chinese term *Thu*, which combined with the term *Jen* meant "Sons of the Soil" (*Thu Jen*),that is, **aborigines**. This also used to be the Chinese name for the vast **Zhuang** national minority in Guangxi, and by extension, other **Tai**-speaking groups in the vicinity, including the Vietnamese Tay found on both sides of the Sino–Vietnamese border.

TIBETO-BURMAN LANGUAGE FAMILY. One of the two subfamilies within the **Sino-Tibetan language family**. Tibeto-Burman comprises seven branches, four of which are found in the massif: Karenic in Burma and Thailand; Baic in **Yunnan**; Lolo-Burmese everywhere except Cambodia; and Kachinic in Burma and Yunnan. In China, where the largest number of Tibeto-Burman speakers live, there are officially 16 **languages** belonging to that language family, grouped in four branches: the Tibetan, **Yi**, **Jingpo**, and **Qiang**. Thirteen of these 16 languages thus fall within the scope of this book: **Yi**, **Lisu**, **Hani**, **Lahu**, **Jino**, **Naxi**, Jingpo, **Derung**, Qiang, **Pumi**, **Nu**, **Achang**, and **Bai**. The inclusion of the latter in this family is contested. Larger groups like the Yi (7.8 million) could be subdivided into a number of mutually unintelligible languages.

A huge variety exists within the Tibeto-Burman language family when it comes to summarizing social, political, and economic forms. Subsistence-oriented agriculture on rotational **swiddens**, with some additions from the market, is prevalent among the **lineage societies**, as with most **Mon-Khmer** and **Miao-Yao** speakers. Others, however, like the Yi, the Bai, and the Naxi of western Yunnan, have had the historical opportunity to develop complex social and political forms, in particular **feudalism**, and have produced original architecture, arts forms, and archives. Most Tibeto-Burman speakers have an **animistic** religious background, except when influenced to adopt **Buddhism** by their Tibetan and **Burman** neighbors, or Chinese religious practices when influenced by the **Han**. **Christianity** also reached several Tibeto-Burman groups during colonial times. (*See* figure 4.)

TINH. In Vietnam, the largest national territorial division, which translates as "province." The *tinh* further subdivides into ***huyen*** (districts) and *xa* (communes).

TONAL LANGUAGES. This refers to all **languages** that use tonality to mark syntactic differentiation. Tonality is the use of the voice to distinguish words by the different pitch attributed to syllables. Tonal languages are thus usually made of words with single syllables that do not modulate or aggregate in conjugation of verbs, forms of plural, or gender, such as is the case in most Indo-European languages. In East and Southeast Asia, tonality is found mainly within the Sino-Tibetan, **Mon-Khmer**, and **Tai-Kadai language families**. The tonal range spans from five to 15 tones and includes, among the most important languages, Sinitic, **Tai**, Vietic, and **Miao-Yao**. Linguists now believe that tonality is not a genetic characteristic, which means that it is not found across the board within one language family, but instead has been diffused from its Sinitic source through contact between neighbors over time. This explains why tonality is found among several language families, while none is exclusively tonal.

TOUBY LYFOUNG (TUBY LIFUNG) (ca. 1919–1978). An important **Hmong** dignitary of the Lao People's Democratic Republic. Born in Xiengkhuang province, Touby Lifoung's father (known as Ly Foung, from the Ly clan) was the son-in-law and secretary of the father of another prominent Hmong of Laos, **Faydang Lobliayao** (from the Lo clan). Touby's father sent one son from each of his three wives to school in Xiengkhuang town in the lowlands, including Touby, who was probably the first Hmong in Laos to receive formal primary education. In his case, this was followed by high school (*Lycée*) studies in Vietnam.

When Japanese troops entered Laos toward the end of World War II, Touby was arrested. He escaped, and helped by his brothers Toulia and Tougeu, he mobilized Hmong countrymen to support French resistance to the Japanese after March 1945. **Vang Pao**—the first Hmong to become a general in the Royal Lao Army (RLA)—also served in this guerrilla group as a young officer. In return for his service to the French, Touby was appointed in September 1946 to the position of *chao muong* (governor) for the Hmong of Xiengkhuang— a position he held until his promotion to a higher position in 1958. When the **First Indochina War** (1946–1954) broke out, Touby was asked by French General Raoul Salan to organize the Hmong resistance to the communist and Vietnamese advance in Xiengkhuang province, a responsibility he accepted despite the fact that taking sides in this way also entailed having to fight other Hmong allied with the Pathet Pao under the command of Hmong leader Faydang Lobliayao, his own cousin. To finance the pro-French Hmong resistance, Touby was allowed to impose a new **opium** tax on all Hmong producers and use these revenues to finance his militia.

Once the war was over, following the 1954 Geneva Agreements, Touby was directly involved in the tentative creation of successive royalist governments in Laos. In the 1958 general elections for the first **Lao** coalition government, in which both royalists and Pathet Lao participated, Touby Lyfoung and his brother Toulia were elected deputies to the National Assembly. In 1960, Touby was the first Hmong to gain cabinet rank, as minister for social welfare. In 1963, in the first years of official American involvement, Touby joined the King's Council and thereafter spent more of his time in Vientiane, away from major Hmong settlements and **refugee** centers. His influence back in the field was soon eclipsed by that of Vang Pao, whose position was greatly strengthened by the direct financial and logistical aid he was receiving from the American **Central Intelligence Agency** (CIA). In the Provisional Government of National Union formed in early 1974, Touby held the position of deputy minister for post and telecommunications. This was a short-lived appointment.

When the Lao Revolution triumphed in 1975, Touby had to face the consequences of having always fought against the advent of the now victorious communist regime in Laos. Former royalist supporters were demoted, and the Hmong anticommunist militia had to disband, some fleeing over the border into Thailand, the rest discretely staying behind and hoping for the best. Less fortunate than his brother Tougeu, who made it to France in 1975, Touby was taken away to Sam Neua as a detainee and forced, like all "enemies" of the regime, to undergo ideological cleansing by devoting all his time to strenuous manual labor. Very differently from his cousin and arch-enemy Faydang Lobliayao, Touby Lyfoung died a lonely death in that re-education camp in Sam Neua in 1978. His memory lives on in the minds of Hmong of the diaspora, especially in the United States, France and Australia, where he is considered a hero today.

TOULIA LYFOUNG. A **Hmong**, half-brother of **Touby Lyfoung**, and also an important figure in the modern history of Laos. Toulia is cred-ited with introducing to the Royal Lao Government the tri-tiered so-cial division of the country's population into **Lao Loum, Lao The-ung, and Lao Sung**, a categorization that lasted officially until 2001.

TOUM. A small contingent of 2,510 Toum were accounted for in central Loas in 1995. Like their cousins the **Mone**, they speak a Vietic dialect within the **Viet-Muong** language cluster. They are accordingly found just outside the Vietnamese border in eastern Borikhamxay province.

TOURISM IN THE HIGHLANDS. As a vector of social and eco-nomic change, tourism, both national and international, is playing an increasingly vital role in the **mainland Southeast Asian massif**'s highlands. In China, numerous highland destinations harboring "ex-otic" **minority** cultures in colorful attire, sometimes with an original architectural heritage, have been actively promoted over the last two decades as desirable destinations for nationals. The tourism industry in China is booming thanks to the growing spending power of the emerging middle class, for whom leisure-oriented consumption is both feasible and desirable. The Chinese state has designed a high-land development strategy counting on demand, among the lowland **Han** majority, for the "authentic" highland sites, that is to say, the surviving locales of ancient Han or pre-Han societies. In this strategy, the southwest highlands have become, in the Han psyche, the recipi-ent of pockets of preserved Chinese antiquity, such as in **Guizhou** province, standing in sharp contrast to and protected from the furious modernization process of coastal and lowland China. The town of Li-jiang, situated in northwestern **Yunnan**, is in this regard exemplary. In 1986, the old town center had been placed by Beijing on the list of

National Treasures to acknowledge the historical, artistic, and cultural value of this maze of canals and wooden shop houses, reminiscent of what was perceived as a vanishing traditional China. The beginnings were relatively slow, but a tourist boom was triggered by UNESCO's recognition of Lijiang, in 1997, as a World Heritage site. This head town of the **Naxi** Autonomous County offers national tourists today a chance to see enshrined ancient architecture, exotic minorities in their natural setting, stunning landscape, and an environment virtually exempt from industrial pollution, a rarity in China. The tourists may gaze on all this while renting rooms in modern concrete hotels now surrounding the old town.

Similarly, in Vietnam, where the emerging middle class is also the chief cause for a sudden increase in tourist demand, the ancient hill station of Sa Pa, in a predominantly **Hmong** and **Yao** district, has developed since 1993 into a major tourist destination for national as well as international tourism. Much the same can be said of the other important hill station, Dalat, in the **Central Highlands**.

Elsewhere in the **Peninsula**, highland tourism has been intimately linked to the development of what has been called adventure and nature tourism, best represented by its flagship activity, trekking. Northern Thailand led the way starting in the late 1960s by making its "**hill tribes**" the chief attraction in the northern mountains. This has proven effective to the point that there is today almost no tourist brochure promoting Thailand as an international tourist destination that does not include attractive pictures of exotic highland women and children. Recently Laos, which badly needed new ways of bringing in hard currencies, has also opened the door of its highlands to trekking tourism. Formerly remote and barely accessible provinces, such as Luangnamtha and Phongsaly, are now on the tourist circuit and are actively sought after by an eager "off the beaten track" crowd of young backpackers excited by popular guidebooks for independent travelers. Only Cambodia and Burma's highlands are on the whole left out of the tourist frenzy, the former for internal security reasons and lack of sufficient stretches of highlands, the latter due mostly to the troubled state of internal politics, which impairs the development of a tourist industry in the highlands beyond the sites of Pagan and Mandalay.

In all cases in the massif where highland tourism has developed in connection with the attractive exoticism of colorful highland minorities, the economic and political reins of this industry are held by outsiders, most of the time representatives of the lowland majorities or old midland dominant groups. These groups are better acquainted with the complexities of this sensitive industry, and they benefit from extensive networks developed in the lowlands, where the bulk of national tourists come from and where the most powerful economic actors in the tourist scene are based. For the highland minorities, economic benefits are nevertheless real in terms of accelerated local economic development, completion of transport infrastructure, **trade** opportunities, and a general increase in employment opportunities as labor. The cost for these minority hosts, as many observers also point out, has to be calculated in terms of cultural dilution to fit the formats of tourist demand, an invasion of economic actors from the outside, major disruption of tranquility, stress on local resources, multiple damage to the environment, and a disturbing influence on local youth.

In political terms, the national state sees it as its prerogative, as the main director of economic development within the national borders, to present to the other nationals and to the outside world the promotional image it considers fit for the market's demand. Especially in socialist countries, such as China, Vietnam, and Laos, the state insists on remaining the sole decision maker about the implementation of the most likely successful marketing strategy in a highly competitive regional market for this particular kind of tourist product. The end result most of the time is the creation and active promotion, locally and abroad, of a sketchy, distorted image of sanitized, exoticized, eversmiling highland minorities encapsulated in timeless traditions. Often such depictions also include the eroticization of highland women by lowland men, exemplified by the Mosuo's "Free Women" of Lugu Lake in northwestern Yunnan, or the Yao's "Love Market" in northern Vietnam. This whole public imagery stands in sharp contrast and in apparent paradox to the relentless efforts by the region's governments to sedentarize, modernize, and acculturate national minorities according to the standards of dominant lowland majorities.

TRADE. Trade and general exchange between peoples within the **mainland Southeast Asian massif**, but also with outsiders, has been operating for as long as can be traced. But to even occur in this relatively isolated part of the world, trade needed a number of favorable factors: a network of waterways, roads, **caravan** trails, and footpaths; several common vehicular **languages**; a balance between supply and demand over distance and time; and a political will to maintain the flow of goods and people. Consequently, the absence or the faltering of any of these factors was enough to cause major disruptions in the local trade systems. The many rebellions and the imperial wars of repression attached to them in southwest China in the late 19th century, for instance, caused such chaos in the production and trading of food that millions of people starved to death. With the arrival of European powers in the region, the ancient ideology of loosely controlled buffer zones was replaced by a new one founded on tight borders and exhaustive taxation, presenting a new and sometimes fatal obstacle to the pursuit of ancient trade links. More recently, political feuds between communist and noncommunist regimes have also forced many long, profitable exchange systems to adjust, or even disappear.

Whatever the specific conditions, at any time within a given society, essential goods had to transit from production sites to users, with a commensurate flow of goods, persons, or **currency** in the opposite direction. The most fundamental items traded in the whole massif included **subsistence** produce (**rice** in particular), commercial agricultural produce (with **opium** taking a leading role in the 19th and 20th centuries), local industries and handicraft (**blacksmithing, jewelry, alcohol**, cloth, etc.), **forest** products (both flora and fauna), various useful metals (chiefly iron and steel), a few precious metals (silver and, more rarely, gold), slaves (including prisoners of war), and more recently, an infinite list of industrial goods (in particular plastics, machinery, and agricultural implements).

Trade in the massif involved a division of activities founded on both ethnicity and geography. Broadly speaking, in the long-haul trading system, at one end the inhabitants of the highest lands, the **Miao-Yao**, many **Tibeto-Burman**, and some **Mon-Khmer** groups, had the role of providing forest products (and for a while, opium) for midland and lowland consumption. At the opposite end, the lowland majorities (**Han, Kinh, Lao, Khmer**, Kin, or **Burman**) put into circulation manufactured foods and agricultural surpluses. In between these two commercial poles, generally located at mid-altitude, the **Tai-Kadai**, some Tibeto-Burmans, and a few **Mon-Khmer** groups played the role of inevitable intermediaries in this three-tiered, functional trade structure. Nevertheless, with the development of infrastructures well into the remotest corners of the massif and the explosion of markets under the impetus of economic globalization, this division is now often bypassed and grows less and less relevant. *See also* TRADE ROUTES.

TRADE LANGUAGES. *See* LANGUAGES OF TRADE.

TRADE ROUTES. Trading within the **mainland Southeast Asian massif**, as well as between the massif and the lowlands surrounding it, has taken place from time immemorial. The amount of goods and numbers of persons transiting via these routes have, however, certainly increased gradually throughout history thanks to growing populations in and around these highlands. Long perceived by coastal powers chiefly as a buffer zone between lowland kingdoms, the massif's waterways have played the role of natural routes crossing it, while the actual highlands standing above those primary valleys would rarely be visited by outsiders. The **Doudart de Lagrée and Garnier expedition** up the Mekong River in 1866–1868, and the opening of the Haiphong-Kunming rail link in 1909, are typical examples of the transitory nature of the massif for outsiders. Today road construction is in progress to cross borders and link up the adjacent highlands of Burma, Thailand, Laos, Vietnam, and **Yunnan**, opening these formerly isolated regions and exposing their inhabitants to the full impact of international **trade** and circulation of people, including migrants and **tourists**.

Goods circulated through trade and the **currencies** used to pay for them have varied greatly over time in the massif and from one subregion to another. The massif being landlocked, this geomorphological limitation determined the type of trade routes that developed within and around it. Historically, for the long-haul trade, boats used all the major rivers and their tributaries draining the massif: the Irrawaddy and Salween in Burma; the Chao Phraya in central and northern Thailand; the Mekong in northeastern Thailand, Laos, Cambodia, and the south of Vietnam; the Red River in northern Vietnam, the headwaters of all of the above being in Yunnan; plus the Xi and Yangtse in southwest China. The lateral connection from one watershed to another was then made by **caravan** trails across ranges through mountain passes. This long-haul network was fed by a maze of local and regional capillary footpaths and trails, most just dirt, some paved with flat stones, used primarily among neighboring populations to exchange with one another. Together, this composite and intricate network ensured a steady flow of goods in times of peace; provided the state authorities with access to populations in order to tax them; and also opened a way to the remotest areas for the state military, war parties, and bandits. This network continues to be modernized and further expanded, confirming its role as the economic lifeline for all inhabitants in the massif.

TRI. Also called Brou Tri (20,906 in 1995), this group, found exclusively in Laos, is the smallest of four belonging to the **Brou** cluster within the Katuic language subfamily, part of the **Mon-Khmer language family**. The Tri dwell on the Vietnam border in highland Savannakhet province, in contact with close and more numerous relatives, the **Katang** in Laos and the **Bru-Van Kieu** in Vietnam.

TRIBUTE. Properly speaking, a tribute was a charge paid in **feudal** systems by one political entity to another, more powerful one, the former placing itself beneath the latter in a position of dependence or submission. Entering a tributary relationship was a pragmatic choice, a payment by a weaker or smaller state to obtain protection and favors from a dominant regional power using its dominance to extract wealth from its neighbors without having to bear the burden of invading and occupying them. In the massif, political submission was also used by the main powers to secure their mountainous margins with allies who could repel first line attacks by potent foes. This type of relationship was widespread in East and Southeast Asia in precolonial times. Vietnam, for instance, had for centuries been paying tribute to the Chinese emperor, who guaranteed his vassal protection while enriching his own empire.

Formal tributary relationships were attached to midaltitude **Tai**-speaking kingdoms (*muang*, or federations of *muang*), such as the **Sip Song Phan Na**, the **Sip Song Chau Tai**, and the **Shan** domain, all of which constituted large enough political and military entities for nearby empires to want to bring them into formal submission. Such relationships also affected some important **Tibeto-Burman** mountain kingdoms, such as Nan Chao and the **Yi**, **Bai**, and **Naxi** domains. In all these cases, the tribute was paid to either China, Tibet, Burma, Siam (Thailand), Lan Xang (Laos), Vietnam, or a combination of these, depending on historical circumstances and the balance of power among these regional giants. In the southern **Annam Cordillera** area, there are also records of highland **Jarai** "kings" paying tribute to the lowland **Cham** rulers. This was exceptional. Colonial observers have often recorded "tributary" relations linking small highland groups to larger ones, for instance some tribal Tibeto-Burman speakers in northern Laos having to buy protection from the dominant Sip Song Phan Na Tai Lue rulers. But in such cases the notion of tributary relationship is not really appropriate, as these smaller highland groups did not in fact have a state, or a centralized political organization, which also applies to all **lineage societies** in the massif. In such situations, it would be more accurate to qualify these hierarchical relations as exploitation, extortion, or simply protection.

TRUONG SON. *See* ANNAM CORDILLERA.

TUJIA. There were 8,028,133 individuals officially registered in China in 2000 as belonging to the Tujia *shaoshu minzu*. They are listed as living mainly in the Xiangxi Tujia-Miao Autonomous Prefecture, the Exi Tujia-Miao Autonomous Prefecture (set up late in 1983), and a few additional counties in southeastern Hunan and western Hubei, on the extreme northeastern fringe of the **mainland Southeast Asian massif**. The Tujia are located on the river route leading from the Chinese coastal plains to the **Sichuan** "rice bowl." This location contributed early on to a high degree of acculturation of the Tujia to **Han** culture, which in turn renders the Tujia's linguistic genealogy uncertain today. Despite their importance in numbers, it appears that their linguistic distinctiveness was overlooked until 1956. The prevalent hypothesis suggests a **Tibeto-Burman** connection with similarities to the **Yi**, while Chinese observers have also recorded an important drift toward **Miao languages**. The lack of uniformity among Tujia languages also suggests that the Tujia might actually form a composite of neighboring groups with few linguistic connections.

The Tujia (8 million), along with the **Zhuang** (16 million), the Miao (8.9 million), and the Yi (7.8 million), are all oversized clusters of languages that could benefit from being broken down into discrete and, sometimes, little-related language groups. Which speakers have been officially declared to be included in one or the other of these neighboring giants is more a matter of political and administrative convenience than the fruit of solid scientific consideration. The Tujia minority nationality could equally be an assemblage of languages with little connection, a remnant from an ancient political entity grouping various languages, or simply a convenient label in an over-crowded hill area on the immediate periphery of the densely popu-lated Han core.

TUMPOUN. The most numerous of the official highland minority groups of Cambodia, the Tumpoun numbered 15,861 in 1995. They live in Ratana Kiri province within the Cambodian section of the **An-nam Cordillera**. Like their neighbors the **Phnong** and the Steang, they are **Mon-Khmer** speakers, although who they are actually more closely related to remains uncertain.

TUNG-CHIA. *See* DONG.

TU-SI (TUSSI) SYSTEM. In non-**Han** settlements in all of southwest China where the Han Emperor wished to install his administration and accelerate the Sinicization of non-Han groups, the *tu-si* system was implemented. It consisted of appointing from among the indige-nous population hereditary local state officials who would then adopt Han surnames and receive their titles and privileges directly from the imperial administration. This system characterized the successive Ming and Qing dynasties (1368–1911) and started faltering during the Republican period. No new *tu-si* were appointed after 1931, and communist China abolished it altogether. See also the *tho-ti* system among the **Tay** in northern Vietnam.

– V –

VANG PAO (1931–). A **Hmong** military officer and leader in Laos who fought the communists and took refuge in the United States in 1975, where he lives today. Next to **Touby Lyfoung** and **Faydang Lobliayao**, Vang Pao is probably the best-known Hmong leader of modern Laos. Like them, Vang Pao was born in Xiengkhuang province. He attended the village elementary school of Nong Het. In 1945, at age 14, he joined the anti-Japanese resistance led by pro-French leader Touby Lyfoung. In 1947, during the **First Indochina War** (1946–1954), Vang Pao entered the French Gendarmerie and fought as a corporal, a sergeant, and then an officer with the French Union Army against the Viet Minh–backed communist guerrilla. By l959, he had been promoted to the rank of major in the Royal Lao Army (RLA), with soldiers of **Hmong**, **Lao**, and **Khmu** ethnicity under his command, and in December 1960 he was promoted to lieutenant-colonel in the RLA. In 1961, he was contacted by American and **Thai** military advisers to set up a defense line against neutralist and Pathet Lao forces in Xiengkhuang. Having earned the trust of his commissioners, in 1964 he was made general of the RLA by Prince Souvanna Phouma and commander of the Second Military Region in northeastern Laos along with four RLA colonels of Hmong ethnicity: Ly Nou, Blong Thao, Moua Pao, and Neng Yi.

From 1961 to 1973, in the midst of the **Second Indochina War** (1954–1975), General Vang Pao led a fierce resistance against the communists around the Plain of Jars, part of the "secret war" financed by the CIA. His position greatly strengthened by that financial and material assistance, he was able to impress the people with generous gifts made to supporters and to students or families in difficult circumstances. In the region under his control, he set up schools for the highlanders, paid the teachers, and organized nursing education through the U.S. Agency for International Development. One of only two radio stations in minority **languages** operated at the time from his headquarters and fortress in Long Cheng. Enjoying increased notoriety, Vang Pao soon overtook his elder, Touby Lyfoung, as the chief leader of the Hmong in Xiengkhuang. CIA largesse also provided him with the necessary resources to maintain a special army of more than 10,000 men (nine mixed "special battalions"), consisting mostly of Hmong, who joined in large part because of the salaries offered and the lack of employment opportunities in other fields. However, heavy casualties gradually reduced the number of Vang Pao's Hmong fighters, and by 1971, more and more Lao-**Tai** and Thai from Thailand were being enlisted. Meanwhile, tens of thousands of Hmong were not even involved in the war, except as victims or **refugees**.

At the time of the communist victory in 1975, General Vang Pao, along with many other Lao royalist leaders, was airlifted out of the country and eventually relocated to the United States with his family and thousands of his soldiers. He had the ambiguous privilege of being one among four condemned to death in absentia by the new LPDR. From his exile in the United States, Vang Pao was involved in 1980 in setting up a Lao government-in-exile—namely the National United Front for the Liberation of the Lao People—the principal aim of which was to free Laos from communism. In the meantime, those among Vang Pao's troops who had been left behind in Laos initially refused to back down or compromise with the new communist power. Anticommunist guerrilla operations were organized inside Laos, probably still with some support from the CIA. In the broader context of the China–USSR political feud of the early 1980s, this anticommunist guerrilla movement in Laos also operated with help from China. But by 1985 China had largely withdrawn its support, and guerrilla activity within Laos or based just outside its borders decreased considerably. By 1990, Vang Pao's supporters had to abandon their armed opposition to the Lao regime. In his American exile, Vang Pao today arguably remains the most prominent figure of the **Hmong diaspora**.

VIAL, PAUL (1855–1917). Father Vial arrived in China in 1880 as a French Catholic **missionary** with the *Missions Étrangères de Paris* (MEP). After traveling across **Yunnan** and upper Burma in 1881–1882 in the company of British explorer **Archibald Colquhoun**, who employed Vial as his guide, Vial was posted in Yunnan in 1885 and stayed there for the remaining 32 years of his life. He wrote several articles between 1888 and 1917 on the linguistics, history, and ethnography of the highland groups he was trying to convert. He also produced two language dictionaries and an ethnography: *Les Lolos: Histoire, religion, moeurs, langue, écriture* [*The Lolos: History, Religion, Customs, Language, Writing*] (1898).

VIET. *See* KINH.

VIET BAC AUTONOMOUS REGION. *See* TAY BAC AUTONOMOUS REGION.

VIET-MUONG LANGUAGES. A subgroup of the **Austro-Asiatic language family**, part of the **Mon-Khmer** branch. As its name indicates, this subgroup comprises the large Vietic cluster, which includes Vietnamese plus a few small affiliated languages (**Kri, Mone, Ngouan, Tho,** and **Toum**), and the Muongic cluster (the **Muong** of Vietnam). (*See* figure 2.)

VIETNAM, ADMINISTRATIVE DIVISIONS IN THE SOCIALIST REPUBLIC OF. Today in highland Vietnam, territorial administrative divisions follow the national model for rural areas, which includes, from largest to smallest, the *tinh* (province), *huyen* (district), *xa* (commune), and *ban* (hamlet). The notion of *ban,* however, is only used in the highlands. It is not considered in national statistics and does not appear in the decennial national censuses.

VIETNAM, HIGHLAND MINORITIES IN THE SOCIALIST REPUBLIC OF. Vietnam officially recognizes five indigenous linguistic families within its borders, each comprising several minority groups: **Austro-Asiatic**, with the **Viet-Muong** (4 groups including the **Kinh**) and Mon Kho-me (**Mon-Khmer,** 21 groups) branches; **Austronesian** (or Malayo-Polynesian, 5 groups); Thai Kadai (**Tai-Kadai,** 12 groups); Sino-Tibetan, with the Sinitic (3 groups) and the Tibetan-Burman (6 groups) branches; and Hmong-Dao (**Miao-Yao,** 3 groups). Of the 54 "nationalities" (*cac dan toc*) officially cataloged in the country, 53 are considered "national **minorities**" (*cac dan toc thieu so*). The 54th, the Kinh, also known as the **Viet,** forms the ethnic majority, with a population of 65,795,718 in 1999. The 53 national minorities of Vietnam represent 10,527,455 (1999) individuals, or 13.8 percent of the national population. However, four of these groups are merely overflow from lowland majorities in neighboring countries and should be subtracted from this total: the **Hoa** (Chinese), Kho-me (**Khmer**), **Cham,** and **Lao,** who together report a total of 2,062,029. The corrected total of highland minority representatives in Vietnam thus is 8,465,426, or 11.1 percent of Vietnam's population.

Of these 49 highland groups, the six largest in 1999 were the **Tay** (1,477,514), the **Thai** (1,328,725), the **Muong** (1,137,515), the **Nung** (856,412), the **Hmong** (787,604), and the **Dao** (620,538). Together, these six groups form exactly 70 percent of all the country's highland minority population. The largest linguistic family represented is the Tai-Kadai (Tay, Thai, Nung, **San Chay**, **Giay**, Lu, **Bo Y**, **La Chi**, **Co Lao**, **La Ha**, **Pu Peo**, plus the Lao), with 46 percent of all highland minority speakers, with the Hmong-Dao coming second at 16.7 percent. The provinces with the largest highland minority population are, in the north, Son La (728,431), Lang Son (587,718), Thanh Hoa (568,996), Hoa Binh (546,861), Ha Giang (529,551), Lai Chau (488,488), Cao Bang (467,379), and Lao Cai (397,475). In the south, they are Dak Lak (524,541), Gia Lai (421,902), Lam Dong (212,629), and Kon Tum (168,535).

Little is known about the highlanders in Vietnam's portion of the **mainland Southeast Asian massif** during imperial times, which means roughly until 1858, when the French conquest began. Studies of Vietnamese and Chinese archives show few traces of these marginal people, except when addressing ad hoc administrative or **trade** problems. Without indigenous written records, what is left of their early history in Vietnam is scarce. It is known that by the 19th century imperial Vietnamese military parties were occasionally sent into the mountains to restore order when **caravans** and **trading routes** were being threatened by banditry. This occurred especially in the north in the second half of that century, when wandering rebels appeared en masse, pushed out of the Chinese southwest by rebellious movements. For incoming French scholars, it was only through the early European testimonies, such as those left by Francis Garnier or **Émile Rocher** that the existence of **montagnard** groups in the **Indochina** massif began to be acknowledged.

In these mountain regions in French Indochina, a colonial divide-and-rule policy was soon applied, aimed at protecting metropolitan economic interests and keeping the highlands and their populations under loose but steady control. Of particular interest to the colonial administration was to make circumstances favorable for the growing of poppies and the production and trade of **opium**. To ensure the necessary level of stability, the Tonkinese highlands were put under a military administration separate from the civilian one in the lowlands. A similar strategy was later implemented in the south when dealing with the *montagnards* in the *hauts-plateaux*. This line of attack was guided by the fact that the Nationalist and communist factions were promoting their own projects among the highland populations.

Table 6. "National Minorities" of Vietnam, 1999
54 nationalities (*cac dan toc*), 53 being minorities (*cac dan toc thieu so*), 49 of which are found in the mainland Southeast Asian massif (Names of highland groups are in all capital letters.)

Ethnic Group	N	Percent of H.T.	Percent of Country
Kinh (Viet)	65,795,718	—	86.21
TAY	1,477,514	17.45	1.94
THAI	1,328,725	15.70	1.74
MUONG	1,137,515	13.44	1.49
Kho-me	1,055,174	12.46	1.38
Hoa	862,371	10.19	1.13
NUNG	856,412	10.12	1.12
HMONG	787,604	9.30	1.03
DAO	620,538	7.33	0.81
GIA RAI	317,557	3.75	0.42
E-DE	270,348	3.19	0.35
BA-NA	174,456	2.06	0.23
SAN CHAY	147,315	1.74	0.19
Cham	132,873	1.57	0.17
CO-HO	128,723	1.52	0.17
XO-DANG	127,148	1.50	0.17
SAN DIU	126,237	1.49	0.17
HRE	113,111	1.34	0.15
RA-GLAI	96,931	1.15	0.13
MNONG	92,451	1.09	0.12
THO	68,394	0.81	0.09
XTIENG	66,788	0.79	0.09
KHO-MU	56,542	0.67	0.07
BRU-VAN KIEU	55,559	0.66	0.07
CO-TU	50,458	0.60	0.07
GIAY	49,098	0.58	0.06
MA	33,338	0.39	0.04
CO	27,766	0.33	0.04
CHO-RO	22,567	0.27	0.03
XINH MUN	18,018	0.21	0.02
HA NHI	17,535	0.21	0.02
CHU-RU	14,978	0.18	0.02
Lao	11,611	0.14	0.02
LA CHI	10,765	0.13	0.01
KHANG	10,272	0.12	0.01
PHU LA	9,046	0.11	0.01
LA HU	6,874	0.08	0.01
LA HA	5,686	0.07	0.01
PA THEN	5,569	0.07	0.01
LU	4,964	0.06	0.01

Ethnic Group	N	Percent of H.T.	Percent of Country
NGAI	4,841	0.06	0.01
CHUT	3,829	0.05	0.01
TA-OI	3,496	0.04	0.005
LO LO	3,307	0.04	0.004
MANG	2,663	0.03	0.003
CO LAO	1,865	0.02	0.002
BO Y	1,864	0.02	0.002
CONG	1,676	0.02	0.002
SI LA	840	0.01	0.001
PU PEO	705	0.01	0.001
RO-MAM	352	0.00	0.000
BRAU	313	0.00	0.000
O DU	301	0.00	0.000
Foreigners	39,532	0.47	0.052
Not Stated	1,333	0.02	0.002
Highland Minorities	**8,465,426**	**100**	**11.09**
COUNTRY	**76,323,173**	**—**	**100**

Source: *National Census of Vietnam, 1999.*

After their victory in the north in 1954, the socialist state in the (then) Democratic Republic of Vietnam (DRVN, North Vietnam) maintained for a few years the division between highlands and lowlands by setting up **Autonomous Regions** in the north exactly where colonial military administrations had existed before, a plan abandoned in 1975 when national reunification was achieved. In the Republic of Vietnam (RVN, South Vietnam), minorities in the **Central Highlands**, generically called the Montagnards by American advisers and troops, became tragically entangled in the turmoil of the **Second Indochina War** (1954–1975). These highlands became the stage of fierce political and military confrontations. The RVN government tried to empty the land by forcing peasants to relocate in "**strategic hamlets**," while the communist guerrillas (Viet Cong) extended the southern end of the Ho Chi Minh trail network well into the highlanders' domain. Ultimately, in 1975, the DRVN prevailed, the nation was united under a socialist government, and economic and political measures enforced in the north since the 1950s were imposed on the south, including **collectivization** and migration from the lowlands to the highlands as part of the **New Economic Zones scheme**.

In a new country where the collective project had to be popular, national, and scientific, little room was left for the ways of the past. In the communist rhetoric, highlanders in Vietnam were considered to be at the lowest stage of economic development and in dire need of assistance, while the Kinh enlightened majority was entering socialism, the highest possible stage. The least "socialist man" could do for "traditional man," in the words of Vietnamese ethnologists of the time, was to help him relinquish his simplicity and reach as quickly as possible the superior levels of civilization of the lowlands. Vigorous plans for sedentarization, collectivization, and industrialization were implemented against an ideological background prioritizing the indivisible unity of country and nation, with active promotion of Kinh culture. Concurrently, ethnological studies of the national minorities gravitated almost obsessively to the issue of classification. A first exhaustive list of minorities in the DRVN was proposed in 1959 and included 64 ethnic groups. A second one followed in 1973, with 59. By 1979, the official total was finally established. All the efforts of the **Institute of Ethnology of Vietnam**, founded in 1968, culminated in Decree 121, which set the authoritative number of "nationalities" at 54 for all of reunified Vietnam, including the Kinh nationality. Much as is the case in China, and for comparable reasons, that figure has not changed since, despite the fact that dissatisfaction about it has been voiced internally as well as from outside the country.

The Economic Renovation (*Doi Moi*) that has been going on in Vietnam since 1986 has contributed to somewhat reducing the intensity of state authoritarianism in the highlands. A generally more liberal attitude regarding trade, religion, education, and cultural expressions has, however, has failed to completely dissolve the government's worries regarding highland security issues, such as Christian agitation in the Central Highlands, allegedly encouraged by outside agents—often referred to as **FULRO** sympathizers based in the United States.

The most hotly debated issue regarding the highlands is environmental protection. The highland people of Vietnam are blamed by their government for the deforestation occurring in the uplands. In fact, in the Central Highlands in particular, the massive migration of Kinh from the plains, officially launched under the New Economic Zones scheme, put immense additional pressure on the natural resources of that ecosystem. Economic immigration further unfolded at the end of the 1980s thanks to *Doi Moi*, and was soon encouraged by crop substitution schemes and extensive plantations, such as **coffee**, aimed at installing ever more farmers. This policy persists today, further compounded by economic migration of other minority peoples from the north, such as the Tay, Nung, and Hmong. This excessive stress on resources has caused social tensions triggering severe social unrest as well as a deterioration of the environment, most dramatically visible in rapid deforestation, lowering of the groundwater tables, and increasing severity of annual flooding in the lowlands.

In search of a sustainable solution, Vietnamese scholars are conducting research on such issues as customary law in relation to natural resource management, indigenous knowledge and indigenous strategies for improved fallow management, and community-based forest management institutions. In this process, preserving cultural identity is low on the national agenda. Following the Chinese example, a policy of **"selective cultural preservation"** among the national minorities has been implemented, in which the state decides unilaterally which aspects of a culture are sufficiently valuable—and politically acceptable—to be retained, and which should be actively discouraged. **Tourism**, booming in Vietnam since 1993, injects a new ingredient into this already complex equation.

– W –

WA. A **Mon-Khmer**–speaking group of the **Palaung-Wa** branch located on the China-Burma-Laos-Thailand border area. In China, 396,610 (2000) Wa dwelled in southwestern **Yunnan**, in particular in the **Xishuangbanna Dai Autonomous Prefecture**. Some believe that the group called **Lawa** in northern Thailand (15,711 in 1995) should also be included in the Palaung-Wa linguistic cluster, and the same applies to the **Samtao** of Laos (2,213 in 1995). In Burma, it is estimated that 108,367 (2004) Wa live disseminated in the higher reaches in the southeast of the **Shan** State. During British rule, Wa states were officially acknowledged, but after independence in 1947, their autonomy was no longer supported and they were slipped into in the larger, less culturally homogenous Shan State. Since then, the Wa have been battling both the Shan and the Burmese central state through their military arm, the United Wa State Army (UWSA). In particular, the UWSA has fought the Shan warlords' hegemony over gem and drugs trafficking in the region. In 1990, in a bold move, the UWSA allied with the Burmese military to defeat **Khun Sa**, the kingpin of Shan supremacy in drug processing and trafficking, and the UWSA has since taken over the lucrative business for its own profit. *See also* LAWA.

WANG GUOXING. Procommunist leader of the **Li** minority on **Hainan** Island, who contributed to defeating Kuomintang troops on the island in the 1940s. His 15,000 troops, called the "Li Column" in revolutionary historiography, were later held up by the authorities as a role model for other **minorities** in China.

WHITE THAI (TAI KHAO, TAI TRANG). *See* THAI.

WOMEN. *See* GENDER INEQUALITY.

– X –

XA. In Vietnam, the smallest territorial administrative unit, or "commune." In the highlands, a further subdivision, the *ban* (hamlet), is sometimes used, though it is not taken into account for census purposes. A few *xa* together form a *huyen* (district).

"XA" ("TSA"). See "KHA."

XA-PHO. *See* LOLO.

XIAN. In the People's Republic of China, an administrative area best translated as "county" or "district," a subdivision of the prefecture (*diqu*). In the PRC's southwest region, many counties are officially classified as "autonomous counties" (*zizhixian*).

XING MOUN. *See* XINH-MUN.

XINH-MUN. Two-thirds of this **Mon-Khmer**–speaking group dwell in northern Vietnam (18,018 in 1999) in the highlands of Son La province, in pockets isolated from each other along the Laotian border. The remaining third (5,834 in 1995) live in a few small hamlets in the Xaysomboun Special Region in Laos, northeast of Vientiane, where they have been relocated from farther north. In that country, their ethnonym is spelled Xing Moun. All are **animist swiddeners**.

XISHUANGBANNA DAI AUTONOMOUS PREFECTURE. *See* SIP SONG PHAN NA.

XO-DANG (SEHDANG, SEDANG). A **Mon-Khmer**–speaking group of the Bahnaric subfamily, formerly called **Sedang** by the French, officially known today as Xo-dang in Vietnam and Sehdang in Laos. Totaling approximately 128,000 individuals, 99 percent (127,148 in 1999) live in the provinces Kon-Tum, Quang Nam, and Quang Ngai in Vietnam's *Tay Nguyen*. The remaining 786 (1995) are just across the border in Attapeu province in southern Laos. Like the other Mon-Khmer groups in the **Central Highlands**, the Xo-dang have long been associated with this region and have developed a relationship to the land that translates into specific **animistic** rituals. A typical **lineage society**, the Xo-dang practice a rotational and sustainable form of **swiddening**.

XTIENG (STIENG). The Xtieng are part of the Stiengic branch of the **Mon-Khmer language family** and number approximately 70,000, straddling the border between Vietnam and Cambodia in the southern portion of the *Tay Nguyen* highlands. In Vietnam, where the vast majority live, there were 66,788 Xtieng officially registered in 1999, dwelling chiefly in the province Binh Phuoc, with some in Lam Dong province. In Cambodia, where they are called Steang, the group numbered 3,234 in 1995, all living in Mondul Kiri province. Like their main neighbor the **Mnong**, the Xtieng are longtime **animistic swiddeners**.

– Y –

YAI (TAI YAI). *See* SHAN.

YANG. A **Tai**-speaking minority in highland Laos (4,630 in 1995), an extension of the more numerous group found in Vietnam and there officially called **Giay** (49,098). Some confusion stems from the fact that some **Tibeto-Burman Karen** in Burma and Thailand are also called Yang, in this case a phonetic short for Kariang, one of their names there.

YAO (MAN). With the Miao, the Yao form the bulk of the **Miao-Yao language family**. They total a sizeable number of approximately 3.3 million across the **mainland Southeast Asian massif**. Originating from China, possibly in southern Hunan, the Yao have gradually dispersed westward under demographic pressure from the coastal **Han**. During at least the last four centuries, their movements have taken them to all countries sharing the massif except Cambodia, first into northern Vietnam, and from there into northern Laos, Burma, and Thailand. Possibly due to their late migration and the strong competition they met upon their arrival from older dwellers, particularly the **Tai**-speaking groups, the Yao in the **Peninsula** are generally found on higher ground in association with their linguistic relatives, the **Hmong**, who migrated south for similar reasons, although records suggest the Yao's diasporic movement into the Peninsula started earlier than the Hmong's. Formerly, the ethnonym *Man*, possibly a deformation of **Mien**, possibly also a derogatory term used generically in China, was widely used in place of Yao—such as in Wuling Man, Wuxi Man, Chang Sha Man, Man-ta-pan—and can be found in a majority of colonial reports and early ethnographies. In fact, the group was still formally listed as "Indochina Man" as late as 1964 in the compendium *Ethnic Groups of Mainland Southeast Asia* published by **Frank Lebar** et al. The Yao have long made use of **Chinese ideograms** to write their genealogies and ritual books, often accompanied by colorful paintings with a clear Chinese influence, highly prized by collectors around the world today.

In China in 2000, the Yao numbered 2,637,421. There, they constitute an official "minority nationality" spreading over most southern provinces, Guangxi being the most important, where they are present in 47 counties, with significant numbers in **Yunnan** (17 counties), Hunan (22 counties), **Guizhou** (6 counties), and northern Guangdong (11 counties). **Hainan** Island is the easternmost location where they can be found. The Yao **languages** in China, however, are extremely diverse, much like the various Yao subgroups' ethnonyms, to the point where linguists consider that only 44 percent of those the

Chinese officially label as Yao actually speak the main form of Yao language, Mien, the rest being divided between Pu Nu and Lak Kia. The eminent Chinese ethnologist **Fei Xiaotong** believes that of the languages officially clustered into the Yao category, Pu Nu shows astonishing similarities with parts of the **Miao** language branch, while Lak Kia shows similarities with **Tai languages** from the Kam-Sui branch, all possibly indicative of strong lateral linguistic diffusion between neighbors. A scholarly summary of the state of Yao studies in China was published in 1991 by coeditors Jacques Lemoine and Chiao Chien under the title *The Yao of South China: Recent International Studies*.

In Vietnam, where their name is misleadingly written *Dao*, the Yao numbered 620,538 in 1999. In Thailand, where the Yao are also known by their autonym Iu Mien, the group numbered 45,551 in 2002. They are found there in nine provinces, with concentrations in Chiang Rai, Nan, and Phayao. Laos officially accounted for 22,695 Yao in 1995, located in the northern Phongsaly, Luangnamtha, and Xayabury provinces. In Burma, their numbers were estimated to be a few hundred in 2004, in unclear locations.

Like the Hmong, the Yao in the Peninsula have been associated in the Western mind with dwellings in the highest locations, having an urge for political independence, practicing **animism**, and having a near emblematic involvement in the **opium** poppy cultivation and **trade**. During the **Second Indochina War** (1954–1975), they earned a reputation for fierce combativeness on all sides. However, beyond the clichés, throughout history these two cousin groups have also been systematically vassalized by midaltitude Tai-speaking groups, a condition they generally accepted but against which they could also rebel violently on occasion. Western powers have been adept at gaining political profit from this uneasy historical relationship.

"YARDS." *See* MONTAGNARDS.

YE. *See* JEH.

"YELLOW RAIN." In 1977, soon after the communist takeover of Laos in 1975, rumors began circulating among **Hmong refugees** in Thailand and in the United States that the **Lao** government was using a form of chemical warfare against Hmong Monarchist guerrillas on the Xiengkhuang Plateau, the chief anticommunist resistance group left behind after the departure of the American troops. A yellow powder that would cause serious illness, and sometimes death was reportedly being dropped from the air by planes (hence the "Yellow Rain"). Some American specialists have suggested that this substance could be linked to mycotoxins allegedly used by other communist regimes around the world. Substantial samples of this yellow powder from Laos proved difficult to obtain, and by 1987, Western investigators had concluded that there was no indisputable proof of such chemical agents having been used against the Hmong in Laos. The story appears to have died out since.

YI. Yi is the official name used in China for the group otherwise called **Lolo** or Lo Lo in the **Peninsula**. In China, the number of Yi officially accounted for in the 2000 national census was a considerable 7,762,272. With such demographic weight, the Yi are thus the most numerous and most widespread of the 16 **Tibeto-Burman**–speaking nationalities in China. Clearly, much as is the case with other oversize *shaoshu minzu* of China, such as the **Zhuang**, **Tujia**, and Miao, there would be a need to break down this artificial linguistic monolith into a variety of subgroups. In **Yunnan**, where the Yi are the most numerous minority nationality and form 18 percent of the total population, they have historically occupied the intermediate lands and, similarly to the **Tai** groups south and east, have acted as **feudal** lords in the exploitation of the land and of their highland neighbors.

The term *Yi*, like the terms *Man* and *Miao*, has been used in China for a long time as a generic label for untamed ("raw," "barbarian") highland populations in the southwest. Today, however, the use of the term has been narrowed down to this linguistic cluster only. The Yi live in southern **Sichuan**, western **Guizhou**, throughout Yunnan (in particular in the Honghe Hani-Yi and the Chuxiong Yi Autonomous Prefectures), and across the border in the Peninsula.

During the **Han** dynasty (202 B.C.–A.D. 222), the Chinese often lumped them into a generic category named Southwest Man (*Xi Nan Man*). They enjoyed a remote location in the mountains and developed a heavily stratified feudal political and economic organization sustained by a strong military. The Yi thus had the means to resist their other powerful neighbors, the **Naxi**, the **Bai**, and the **Lue**, as well as to refuse to bow to the Han imperial power, although paying **tribute** to China was unavoidable. Many anti-Han rebellions and revolts in which the Yi were active took place in the region during the 18th and 19th centuries. As late as between the 1920s and the 1940s, the Yi took advantage of the social turmoil in China to attack cities and terrorize government officials and Han settlers who had gradually moved in. Only in the mid-20th century did the Yi leaders make a final and peaceful submission to the communist Chinese. Eager to prove to the world that they had "liberated" the Yi and many other **minorities** from tyrannical feudal systems, the communists dismissed the old ethnonym "Lolo" as derogatory and inappropriate and replaced it with the current one, and in 1956 produced statistics stating that among the Yi who had just been "freed," the landlords amounted to 5 percent of the population, laborers 30 percent, and slaves a massive 65 percent, all figures that must be treated with circumspection.

The Yi have produced an aristocracy called Black Yi (Heiyi or Nosu), a social stratum that has received much attention from Western observers, especially Christian **missionaries**, such as **Paul Vial**, Alfred Liétard, and **Samuel Pollard**. The rest of the Yi were called White Yi and were an ethnically mixed group of serfs, some with slave ancestry or recently enslaved for unpaid debt, and all subordinate to the Black Yi. Intermarriage between Black and White Yi was not normally permitted.

Intercession with the supernatural among the **animistic** Yi has long been in the hands of the *pimu* (*peh-mo*) shaman, who used an indigenous form of pictographic script to write down and pass on incantations and various texts needed for divination, curing, and ceremonies. This script, long reserved for the exclusive use of priests, was simplified, made syllabic, and formalized by the Chinese government in 1975 to produce a standard writing system for all Yi.

YOUNG, GORDON O. (1927–). American author born in **Yunnan**, the third generation in a Baptist missionary family there. With his father, Young traveled extensively for several years in the highlands of Yunnan, Burma, and Thailand, in particular among the **Lahu** and **Wa** groups. Because of his knowledge of highland societies, Gordon Young received a commission from the government of Thailand and the United States Operations Mission to Thailand to investigate the **"hill tribes"** of Thailand. He authored the first official survey of non-Thai highland ethnic groups in Thailand. This seminal study, *The Hill Tribes of Northern Thailand: The Origins and Habitats of the Hill Tribes Together with Significant Changes in Their Social, Cultural and Economic Patterns*, first appeared in 1961 in limited circulation, and was published in 1962 by the Siam Society.

YUAN (TAI YUAN, LAN NA TAI). The few million **Tai** speakers inhabiting the northern basin of the Chao Phraya River and its tributaries in northern Thailand. Long sedentarized lowland dwellers, they speak a form of Siamese combining elements of **Lue** and **Shan**. Historically, they were subdivided among the kingdoms of Chiang Mai (**Lan Na**), Lamphun, Lampang, Nan, and Phrae, which all became vassals of Siam and have been incorporated into modern Thailand. In a historical sense, these ancient kingdoms can be seen as partaking in the same political and historical logic as the upland Tai kingdoms of Lan Xang, **Sip Song Phan Na**, **Sip Song Chau Tai**, and the Shan domain.

YUNNAN. "South of the Clouds." The southwesternmost province of China, Yunnan (population 42,880,000 in 2000) has common international borders with Vietnam, Laos, and Burma, as well as provincial borders with Tibet, **Sichuan**, **Guizhou**, and **Guangxi**. Geographically as much as culturally, Yunnan can be considered to lie at the very heart of the **mainland Southeast Asian massif**. It has a large number of highland minority populations (14.3 million, or 33.4 percent of the province's population) and is officially home to more than 25 of China's national **minorities**, including the **Yi**, **Bai**, **Hani**, **Dai**, **Zhuang**, Miao, **Lisu**, **Hui**, **Lahu**, **Naxi**, **Yao**, **Jingpo**, Bulang, **Achang**, **Nu**, Primi, **Jino**, and **Derung,** which are among the most important ones.

– Z –

ZHENG HE, ADMIRAL (1371–1433). Ma He, as he was originally known, was born in 1371 to a poor ethnic **Hui** family in Yunnan province, southwest China. In 1405, Zheng, who was enjoying a brilliant career as a navy officer, was chosen to lead the biggest series of naval expeditions in Chinese history. The Chinese navy of the time dwarfed the combined navies of Europe. Over the next 28 years, from 1405 to 1433, Zheng successively commanded seven fleets of hundreds of ships each, with tens of thousands of men, and visited nearly 40 countries throughout Southeast Asia, the Middle East, and Africa. These great expeditions created a vast web of trading links, from Taiwan to the Persian Gulf, under Chinese imperial control.

ZHOU (CHAU). In the People's Republic of China, an administrative division with a long and rich past as an administrative term bearing several possible meanings related to "region," "province," or "department." As an administrative entity today, the term *zhou* only survives in the form of ***zizhizhou***, or "autonomous prefectures." Many old toponyms in China and on its periphery in the **Peninsula**'s highlands still testify to this past, such as **Guizhou** and Guangzhou within the PRC, but also in the names **Sip Song Chau Tai** and Lai Chau in northern Vietnam. In the latter country, in late imperial times the peripheral and mountainous districts in the north all bore the specific name *châu* to differentiate them from the standard lowland districts, *huyên*. In theory, both were administered by **Kinh** mandarins sent to live on site, called respectively *Tri-huyên* and *Tri-châu*. In northern Vietnam in the late 18th century A.D., there were 44 such *châu* and 163 *huyên*, indicating that a fairly large proportion of the imperial territory was actually classified as "remote."

ZHUANG. (Pronounced "tchouang") China's largest minority nationality and the largest highland minority in the whole of the **mainland Southeast Asian massif**. The Zhuang officially number a staggering 16,178,811 individuals (2000), more than three times the total population of Laos, or equal to the populations of Laos and Cambodia put together. Such puzzling demographic disparity calls into question the very definitions of "**minority**" and "nation" in the massif.

Ninety percent of the Zhuang live in the western two-thirds of the **Guangxi Zhuang Autonomous Region**, of which they constitute one-third of the total population. They are plains or midland dwellers and practice wet **rice** agriculture. They are also found in adjacent portions of **Guizhou** and **Yunnan**, as well as in an enclave in northern Guangdong. The Zhuang language belongs to the Northern **Tai** branch of the **Tai-Kadai** family, but virtually all Zhuang can also speak the local form of Chinese. The Zhuang language proper is divided between a northern dialect, spoken by two-thirds of the population, and a southern one. With such a massive demography but little unity otherwise, the Zhuang as a discrete ethnic entity may make political sense from the Chinese government's viewpoint, but they are hardly viable as a linguistic or cultural unit. Meaningful subgroups could be "chipped off" the Zhuang mass and brought into the light in their own right. For instance, it is estimated that over 1.5 million **Nung**, and perhaps as many **Tày**, are categorized as Zhuang in China, while both ethnonyms exist as distinctive groups just across the border in northern Vietnam. Ancient Tai autonyms still in use among the Zhuang could also help in redefining subgroups.

Archeologists suspect that the Zhuang are related to the Haobinhian (9000–5600 B.C.) and Bacsonian (8300–5900 B.C.) cultures. This would potentially make them the **indigenous** group in Guangxi. In the third century B.C., the Chinese began permanent settlement in today's central and western Guangxi. Nowadays, the Zhuang, like their Tay and the Nung neighbors in Vietnam, are heavily acculturated to the dominant lowland group, in China's case the **Han**. To many observers, the Zhuang even appear to prefer to be considered Han. They have for long been farming like the Han, and they have adopted the main features of Chinese religion: **Buddhism**, Confucianism, and Taoism. Since ancient proto-Tai and Sinitic groups are known to have been markedly different in linguistic and cultural terms, today's high degree of Sinization among the Zhuang is explained by geographical proximity with the Chinese lowlands and the southern coastal plains. Sinization has probably also been further compounded by a desire not to have the wrath of the Han military inflicted on them in times of wars and rebellions in the second half of the 19th century, when Guangxi was prime terrain for important anti-Han revolts.

Since the 1950s, the Chinese communist state has made an effort to support the distinctiveness of the Zhuang ethnicity, arguably for fear of a separatist urge brewing among such an important and territorialized group. It made official the ethnonym Zhuang in place of various ancient Tai autonyms, such as Pu Tai, Pu Ban, Pu Nong, and Pu Yai, and it also replaced the ancient exonym of Tho Jen ("Sons of the Soil"), long used among the Han when referring to the Zhuang. China has granted the Zhuang homeland the status of **Au-**

tonomous **Region**, a grade equal to that of a province, a status only enjoyed by four other groups in China. Their language—that is, northern Zhuang—was given official recognition as one of China's most important minority **languages**, and a distinct Romanized script was designed for it in 1957. Primary school teaching in both Zhuang and Chinese is available in some places, and some of the rural Zhuang are encouraged to maintain their traditional way of life and **animism**.

ZIZHIQU. In the People's Republic of China, an "Autonomous Region," being a province-level division with a designated ethnic minority guaranteed particular rights under the constitution, at least in theory. For instance, each has a chairperson, while regular provinces have governors, and he or she must be of the ethnic group dominant in the autonomous region. In southwest China, the **Guangxi Zhuang Autonomous Region** is the only such entity. *See also* AUTONOMOUS REGIONS.

ZIZHIXIAN. "Autonomous counties." These are a special class of counties (**xian**) in the People's Republic of China, reserved for non-**Han minorities**. "Autonomous counties" are found all over China, in particular in the southwestern provinces and autonomous regions, and are given by law more legislative power than regular counties. They subdivide into prefectures, including the "autonomous prefectures," or *zizhizhou*.

ZIZHIZHOU. "Autonomous prefecture." An administrative entity in the People's Republic of China, a subdivision of the county (**xian** and **zizhixian**). The "autonomous prefectures" have been established as administrative areas for designated national **minorities**. In principle, more than 50 percent of their population is minority nationalities, or they have been historically inhabited by significant minorities. The official name of "autonomous prefecture" includes the dominant minority in that region, sometimes two, even three at times (e.g., the **Xishuangbanna Dai Autonomous Prefecture**, the Nujiang Lisu Autonomous Prefecture, the Honghe Hani Yi Autonomous Prefecture). *Zizhizhou* are not geographically or politically connected to the historical *zhou*.

Bibliography

INTRODUCTION

INTRODUCTION

Few books have been devoted to the whole range of highland societies that live in the Mainland Southeast Asian massif. It is with studies such as Lim's *Territorial Power Domains, Southeast Asia, and China: The Geo-Strategy of an Overarching Massif*, published in 1984, as well as Wijeyewardene's *Ethnic Groups Across National Boundaries in Mainland South-East Asia*, published five years later, that the massif started to be considered a geographical and political entity, and to some extent, a meaningful social space.

When Frank Lebar et al. (1964) were commissioned with the monumental task of taking stock of each and every ethnic group to be found in Southeast Asia at the time of the Second Indochina War, they were left with no choice but to produce a catalog trying to objectify each group and present its main characteristics. The result, *Ethnic Groups of Mainland Southeast Asia*, is a compendium compiled by hundreds of authors combined with the specific expertise of a dozen specialists of the region. Although useful as a typology, it leaves many questions unanswered about which criteria were applied to draw the frontiers between each groups, or how the authors could manage to merge accounts from quite different sources such as, say, French military ethnographers from the turn of the 20th century and American missionary accounts of the 1950s.

When, a few years later, in 1967, Peter Kunstadter took up a comparable challenge but from a more academic angle, he opted for a less exhaustive though more analytical stance. The two volumes of his *South-East Asian*

Tribes, Minorities, and Nations put together a selection of studies on political, economic, and historical issues discussed in the context of one given country, covering each country of the Peninsula plus South China. It is still the most serious attempt at examining the larger highland region and its inhabitants as a whole, while making space available for competent accounts of the cultural diversity; obviously it is now dated politically.

When editing his relatively short book (cited above) and focusing on the transnationality of the highlands groups, Wijeyewardene (1989) opted for an anthropological viewpoint. He did not aim at a thorough cultural and regional coverage, with most papers in the book somehow relating to Thailand and touching on lowland as well as highland situations. Although the end result is informative, it remains fairly narrowly focused.

The next academic publication on the massif and its societies was a special issue of the journal *Asia Pacific Viewpoint,* edited by geographer John McKinnon (1997a, 1997b), containing four articles and three research notes, whose coverage consequently remained modest. That same year, editors Don McCaskill and Ken Kampe published *Development or Domestication? Indigenous Peoples of Southeast Asia*, a critique of development covering chiefly Thailand but also venturing into Laos, Vietnam, and Cambodia. This was followed in 2000 by two more tightly focused books. The first, *Where China Meets Southeast Asia: Social & Cultural Change in the Border Regions,* was edited by Grant Evans, Chris Hutton, and Kuah Khun Eng, and included contributions from 15 authors, largely anthropologists, all addressing the border-crossing activities of particular ethnic groups. The second book, published that same year by Curzon Press, was edited by the author of this dictionary. Titled *Turbulent Times and Enduring Peoples: Mountain Minorities in the South-East Asian Massif*, its explicit aim was to depart from country-based studies of highland minorities and focus on the massif as a social space. With 10 contributors, mainly anthropologists, it put together case studies from each of the countries sharing the massif except Cambodia. Finally, the latest publication of significance covering the massif was edited by Christopher Duncan (2004) and is titled *Civilizing the Margins: Southeast Asian Government Policies for the Development of Minorities*. Although its subject is Southeast Asia as a whole, that is, including the archipelago, the book still provides an enlightening, critical presentation of national policies toward highland minorities in the massif outside China.

When it comes to country-based works, the volume of the literature on mountain minorities in the region can take on surprisingly large proportions. Let us consider Thailand, one of the better researched countries in the region for particular historical and political reasons. It is the Mainland Southeast Asian country that has had the greatest number of studies published on its "hill tribes" (as highlanders are known there). Over the last 40 years, important authors such as Young (1962), Schrock et al. (1970), McKinnon and Bruksasri (1983),

Walker (1986, 1992), and McKinnon and Vienne (1989) have contributed to drawing a fairly solid overall portrait of the mountain minority cultures in that country. In addition, a great many studies, including, among many others, Geddes (1976), Keyes (1979), Tapp (1989), Hutheesing (1990), and Symonds (2004), have been conducted and published on individual groups. If one considers also the hundreds of academic journal articles, theses and dissertations, and development and administrative reports—all in Thai or in one of the major Western languages, plus Japanese—the overall amount of scientific information for such a small cluster of highlanders, about half a million people, is impressive. In Cambodia, by contrast, little exists, partly because of the negligible demographic importance of highland minorities there, partly because of the difficult political circumstances endured by that country for most of the twentieth century. A similar case could be made for Burma, though in this instance the numbers of highlanders are dramatically higher, and there were many publications issued prior to independence in 1947, when it was the only British colony in the massif. One can cite, among others, works by Smeaton (1887) and Marshall (1997 [1922]) on the Karen, or Gilhodes (1996 [1922]) on the Kachin. After independence, important studies by Leach (1954) on the Kachin and Lehman (1963) on the Chin were followed up, despite political uncertainty, by a handful of recent work, such as Robinne's *Fils et maîtres du Lac: Relations interethniques dans l'Etat Shan de Birmanie* [*Sons and Masters of the Lake: Interethnic Relations in the Shan State of Burma*] (2000b).

China, Vietnam, and Laos, constitute a special case. Since the socialist regimes were put in place there in 1949, 1954, and 1975, respectively, local linguists and ethnologists have consistently published reports, surveys, and studies on their respective minority groups, which were considered a political priority. However, those hundreds of works are generally inaccessible to Western readership due to language constraints (this also applies, to a degree, to Thailand). Only a few locally produced works have been translated into a Western language, each time providing much-needed insight into the complexity of "minority affairs" under socialism. Prior to the socialist revolutions, China had seen numerous missionaries and explorers publishing their observations of highland societies, including works such as those by Vial (1898), D'Ollone (1912), and Pollard (1919), and their Chinese colleague Fei Xiaotong (HsiaoT'ung Fei). Since the gradual opening of China starting in the early 1980s, the West has shown a renewed interest in highland minorities of China's southwest. Chiao and Tapp's *Ethnicity and Ethnic Groups in China* (1989) and Lemoine and Chiao's (1991) on the Yao were early contributions. Then came Harrell's *Cultural Encounters on China's Ethnic Frontiers*, published in 1995, followed by solid monographs from authors such as Oakes (1998), Walker (1999), Schein (2000), Litzinger (2000), Tapp (2001), and

Mueggler (2001), with more works now appearing. In the case of French Indochina, several important, though little known, colonial contributions deserve consideration and have been listed in this bibliography. They include, among others, Lunet de Lajonquière (1904), Diguet (1908), Maître (1912), Bonifacy (1919), Savina (1930 [1924]), Abadie (1924), Sabatier (1940), Cuisinier (1946), and Roux and Tran (1954). After 1954 and the partition of Vietnam, the southern highlands were studied specifically, by competent scholars such as Condominas (1957), Dournes (1978), and Hickey (1982). Since the mid-1980s and the economic renovation in the reunified country, Western researchers are again studying Vietnam's highland societies, with recent works such as Salemink's *The Ethnography of Vietnam's Central Highlanders* (2003). In Laos, important pre-1975 authors include Lefèvre-Pontalis (1902), Lemoine (1972), and Yang Dao (1975). As in Vietnam, recent political opening there has allowed new studies to be conducted, including those of Taillard (1989) and Goudineau (1997).

Even with approximately 1,200 titles, this bibliography represents only a fraction of the existing publications on the highland societies in the Southeast Asian massif. Asian annals, in particular, have not been included due to language limitations and their unavailability to the general reader. The selection was made with the aim of providing a good, general, and serious sense of all the possible dimensions of highland cultural variety and lifestyle. A sign of the plurality of approaches in addressing these populations is that a significant number of titles here could have been classified under two or more different headings. However, in order to permit the inclusion of a maximum of references, no duplication has been allowed. The author has also decided against a classification by country to avoid reinforcing the existing bias toward associating groups with discrete political entities. A thematic structure has been used instead.

Websites have been left out of this bibliography because they are too numerous, often unrepresentative of the peoples they intend to describe or stand for, and most of the time politically biased. The most numerous and popular websites on the massif's populations currently available are those representing the views of the anti-junta minority groups of Burma (Kachin, Wa, Shan, Karen, etc.); those set up by the Laotian Hmong refugee diaspora in the United States, Australia, and France; and those initiated by anti-Vietnamese activists "representing" the Central Highlanders (such as FULRO) and vigorously lobbying the U.S. Congress; the last two display strong anticommunist overtones. A significant number of sites also exist that were opened by Christian missionary societies, often with an ethnological or a linguistic facade. From highlanders in Asia themselves, the millions in China, Laos, and northern Vietnam in particular, virtually nothing can be found in English on the Web. Finally, the enormous variation in transposing ethnonyms in the Roman alphabet causes a severe dispersion of information on the Web, often making it impossible to use. Such discrepancies confirmed the decision to refrain from attempting to include here a list of Web links. Nevertheless, it is suggested that readers search under those countries' names for websites, most of which will have a "minority" section.

For additional, complementary, and more detailed information on the history and culture of each of the six countries included in this dictionary, readers are invited to consult the country-based historical dictionaries, published by Scarecrow Press, that are devoted to each of them: on the People's Republic of China by Lawrence R. Sullivan, on Vietnam by Bruce Lockhart and William J. Duiker, on Burma (Myanmar) by Donald M. Seekins, on Laos by Martin Stuart-Fox, on Thailand by May Kyi Win and Harold E. Smith, and on Cambodia by Justin Corfield and Laura Summers.

1. GENERAL

Barnes, R. H., A. Gray, and B. Kingsbury, eds. 1995. *Indigenous Peoples of Asia*. Monograph and occasional papers series no. 48. Ann Arbor, Mich.: Association for Asian Studies.

Condominas, Georges. 1978. "L'Asie du Sud-Est." *Ethnologie régionale II. Asie, Amérique, Mascareignes*. Paris: Encyclopédie de la Pléiade.

Embree, John Fee, and William L. Thomas. 1950. *Ethnic Groups of Northern Southeast Asia*. New Haven, Conn.: Yale University Southeast Asia Studies.

Evans, Grant, ed. 1993. *Asia's Cultural Mosaic. An Anthropological Introduction*. NewYork-London: Prentice Hall.

Evans, Grant, Chris Hutton, and Kuah Khun Eng, eds. 2000. *Where China Meets Southeast Asia: Social & Cultural Change in the Border Regions*. New York: St. Martin's Press; Singapore: Institute of Southeast Asian Studies.

Harrell, Stevan, ed. 1995. *Cultural Encounters on China's Ethnic Frontiers*. Seattle and London: University of Washington Press.

Hayashi, Yukio, and Yang Guangyuan. 2000. *Dynamics of Ethnic Cultures Across National Boundaries in Southwestern China and Mainland Southeast Asia: Relations, Societies, and Languages*. Chiang Mai, Thailand: Ming Muang Printing House.

Keyes, Charles F. 1977. *The Golden Peninsula: Culture and Adaptation in Mainland Southeast Asia*. New York: Macmillan.

King, Victor T., and William D. Wilder. 2003. *The Modern Anthropology of South-East Asia: An Introduction*. London: Routledge.

Kunstadter, Peter, ed. 1967. *South-East Asian Tribes, Minorities, and Nations*. 2 vols. Princeton, N.J.: Princeton University Press.

Lebar, Frank M., Gerald C. Hickey, and John K. Musgrave. 1964. *Ethnic Groups of Mainland Southeast Asia*. New Haven, Conn.: Human Relations Area Files Press.

Lemoine, Jacques. 1978. "L'Asie orientale (les Chinois Han, les ethnies non han de la Chine, les Japonais, les Ainous)." In *Ethnologie régionale II. Asie, Amérique, Mascareignes*. Paris: Encyclopédie de la Pléiade.

Lewis, Paul, and Elaine Lewis. 1984. *People of the Golden Triangle*. London: Thames and Hudson.

Lim Joo Jock. 1984. *Territorial Power Domains, Southeast Asia, and China: The Geo-Strategy of an Overarching Massif*. Singapore: Institute of Southeast Asian Studies.

Michaud, Jean, ed. 2000. *Turbulent Times and Enduring Peoples: Mountain Minorities in the South-East Asian Massif*. Richmond, UK: Curzon.

Rigg, Jonathan. 2003. *Southeast Asia: The Human Landscape of Modernisation and Development*. London: Routledge.

Shen Xu. 1988. *Zhongguo xi nan yu dong nan Ya di kua jing min zu* [Border minorities of southwest China and southeast Asia]. Yunnan min zu chu ban she Yunnan sheng xin hua shu dian fa xing Beijing, China: Di 1 ban. Wijeyewardene, Gehan, ed. 1990. *Ethnic Groups Across National Boundaries in Mainland South-East Asia*. Social Issues in South-East Asia. Singapore: Institute of South-East Asian Studies.

Bibliographies

Dessaint, Alain Y. 1971. "Lisu Annotated Bibliography." *Behavior Science Note*, vol. 6(2):71–94.

Embree, John Fee, and L. O. Dotson. 1950. *Bibliography of the Peoples and Cultures of Mainland Southeast Asia*. New Haven, Conn.: Yale University Press. Southeast Asia Studies.

Guan Jian. 1992. *Tai Minorities in China*. Vol. 1, *A Select Bibliography*. Gaya, India: Centre for South-East Asian Studies.

Olney, Douglas P. 1983. *A Bibliography of the Hmong of Southeast Asia and the Hmong Refugees in the United States*. Southeast Asian Refugee Studies Occasional Papers no. 1. Minneapolis: University of Minnesota Press.

Pfeifer, Mark E. 2003. *Annotated Bibliography of Hmong-Related Works, 1996–2003*. Available at the Hmong Resource Center, www.hmongcenter.org.

Smith, J. Christina. 1988. *The Hmong: An Annotated Bibliography, 1983–1987*. Minneapolis: Southeast Asian Refugee Studies Project, Center for Urban and Regional Affairs, University of Minnesota.

Dictionaries and Encyclopedias

Corfield, Justin, and Laura Summers. 2002. *Historical Dictionary of Cambodia*. Lanham, Md.: Scarecrow Press.

Lockhart, Bruce, and William J. Duiker. 2006. *Historical Dictionary of Vietnam*. 3d ed. Lanham, Md.: Scarecrow Press.

May Kyi Win, and Harold E. Smith. 1995. *Historical Dictionary of Thailand*. Lanham, Md.: Scarecrow Press.

Olson, James S. 1998. *An Ethnohistorical Dictionary of China*. Westport, Conn.: Greenwood Press.

Seekins, Donald M. 2006. *Historical Dictionary of Burma (Myanmar)*. Lanham, Md.: Scarecrow Press.

Stuart-Fox, Martin. 2001. *Historical Dictionary of Laos*. 2d ed. Lanham, Md.: Scarecrow Press.

Sullivan, Lawrence R. 1997. *Historical Dictionary of the People's Republic of China*. Lanham, Md.: Scarecrow Press.

Teston, E., and M. Percheron. 1931. *L'Indochine moderne: Encyclopédie administrative, touristique, artistique et économique*. Paris: Librairie de France.

Country Studies

Bernier, D. W., et al. 1968. *Area Handbook for Thailand*. Washington, D.C.: Government Printing Office.

Chazée, Laurent. 1999. *The Peoples of Laos: Rural and Ethnic Diversities*. Bangkok: White Lotus.

Cima, Ronald J., ed. 1989. *Vietnam, a Country Study*. Washington, D.C.: Federal Research Division, Library of Congress.

Collective. 1996. *Interdisciplinary Research on Ethnic Groups in Cambodia*. Phnom Penh: Center for Advanced Study.

Dang Nghiem Van. 1993. *Ethnic Minorities of Vietnam*. Hanoi: The Gioi.

De Beauclair, Inez, and Lou Tsu-k'uang, eds. 1970. *Tribal Culture of Southwest China*. Tapei: The Orient Cultural Service, Asian Folklore and Social Life, Volume II.

Dessaint, Alain Y. 1980. *Minorities of Southwest China*. New Haven, Conn.: Human Relations Area Files.

Diran, Richard K. 1997. *The Vanishing Tribes of Burma*. New York: Watson-Gutpill.

Dudley-Buxton, L. H. 1929. *China: The Land, the People*. Oxford: Clarendon Press.

Goudineau, Yves. 2003. *Cultures minoritaires du Laos: Valorisation d'un patrimoine*. Paris: Éditions UNESCO.

Jack, Robert Logan. 1904. *The Back Blocks of China: A Narrative of Experiences among the Chinese, Sifans, Lolos, Tibetans, Shans, and Kachins, between Shanghai and the Irrawadi*. Westport, Conn.: Greenwood Press.

Keyes, Charles F. 1987. *Thailand. Buddhist Kingdom as Modern Nation-State*. Boulder, Colo. and London: Westview Press.

Lebar, Frank M., and Adrienne Suddard. 1960. *Laos: Its People, Its Society, Its Culture*. New Haven, Conn.: Human Relations Area Files Press.

Leitch LePoer, Barbara. 1989. *Thailand, a Country Study*. Washington, D.C.: Federal Research Division, Library of Congress.

Lewis, Judy, ed. 1992. *Minority Cultures of Laos: Kammu, Lua', Lahu, Hmong, and Mien*. Rancho Cordova, Calif.: Southeast Asia Community Resource Center.

Ma Yin. 1989. *China's Minority Nationalities*. Beijing: Foreign Language Press.

Mansfield, S. 2000. *Lao Hill Tribes: Traditions and Patterns of Existence*. London: Oxford University Press.

Salemink, Oscar. 2001. *Viet Nam's Cultural Diversity: Approaches to Preservation*. Paris: UNESCO.

Schliesinger, Joachim. 1997. *Hill Tribes of Vietnam*. 2 vols. Bangkok: White Lotus.

——. 2000. *Ethnic Groups of Thailand: Non-Tai-Speaking Peoples*. Bangkok: White Lotus.

——. 2003. *Ethnic Groups of Laos*. 4 vols. Bangkok: White Lotus.

Schrock, Joann L., et al. 1970. *Minority Groups in Thailand*. Ethnographic Study Series. Washington, D.C.: Headquarters of the Department of the Army.

——. 1972. *Minority Groups in Northern Vietnam*. Ethnographic Study Series. Washington, D.C.: Headquarters of the Department of the Army.

Steinberg, David J. 1959. *Cambodia: Its People, Its Society, Its Culture*. Rev. ed. New Haven, Conn.: Human Relations Area Files Press.

——. 2001. *Myanmar's Minority Conundrum: Issues of Ethnicity and Authority*. Tokyo: Japan Institute of International Affairs.

Tribal Research Institute. 1995. *The Hill Tribes of Thailand*. Chiang Mai, [Thailand]: TRI, Technical Service Club.

U Min Naing. 2000. *National Ethnic Groups of Myanmar*. London: Swift Winds Books.

Whitaker, D. P., H. A. Barth, S. M. Berman, J. M. Heimann, J. E. MacDonald, K. W. Martindale, and R. S. Shinn. 1985. *Laos, a Country Study*. Washington, D.C.: Foreign Area Studies, American University.

Young, Gordon. 1962 [1961]. *The Hill Tribes of Northern Thailand*. Bangkok: The Siam Society. (First published by the United States Operations Mission to Thailand.)

Zadrozny, Mitchell G., ed. 1955. *Area Handbook on Cambodia*. Subcontractor's Monograph No.21. New Haven, Conn.: Human Relations Area Files.

Explorers, Travelers, and Journalists

Boyes, Jon, and S. Paraban. 1992. *A Life Apart Viewed from the Hills*. Chiang Mai, [Thailand]: Silkworm Books.

Carey, Fred W. 1899. "A Trip to the Chinese Shan States." *Geographical Journal*, no. 14:378–394.

Collis, Maurice S. 1938. *Lords of the Sunset: A Tour of the Shan States*. London: Faber and Faber.

Colquhoun, Archibald R. 1883. *Across Chrysê: A Journey of Exploration through the South China Border Lands from Canton to Mandalay*. 2 vols. London, Sampson Low, Marston, Searle, and Rivington.

———. 1885. *Amongst the Shans*. London: Field.

Davies, John R., and Tommy Wu. 1990. *The Hill Tribes of Northern Thailand*. Wiltshire, UK: Footloose Books.

Garnier, Francis. 1873. *Album pittoresque du voyage d'exploration en Indo-Chine*. Paris: Librairie Hachette.

Garrett, W. E. 1974. "The Hmong of Laos: No Place to Run." *National Geographic Magazine* 145 (1):78–111.

Goodman, Jim. 1996. *Meet the Akhas*. Bangkok: White Lotus.

———. 1997. *The Akha: Guardians of the Forest*. Chiang Mai [Thailand]: Teak House.

———. 2002. *Children of the Jade Dragon—The Naxi of Lijiang and Their Mountain Neighbours the Yi*. Chiang Mai, Thailand: Teak House.

Grundeld, Frederic V. 1983. *Wayfarers of the Thai Forest: The Akha*. Amsterdam: Editors of Time-Life Books, Silver Burdett Press.

Lowy, Rennold L. 1947. "Adventure in Lololand." *National Geographic* [Washington, D.C.] 91 (1):105–118.

Medford, Beatrix. 1935. *Where China Meets Burma: Life and Travel in the Burma-China Borderlands*. London and Glasgow: Blackie.

Ollone, Henry M. d'. 1912. *In Forbidden China: The d'Ollone Mission, 1906–1909: China-Tibet-Mongolia*. Translated from the French by B. Miall. Boston: Small Maynard.

Orléans, Prince Henri-Philippe-Marie d'. 1894. *Autour du Tonkin*. Paris: Calmann-Lévy,

———. 1898. *Du Tonkin aux Indes, Janvier 1895—Janvier 1896*. Paris: Calmann-Lévy,

Pavie, Auguste, et. al. 1898–1919. *Mission Pavie Indo-Chine 1879–1895*. 10 vols. Paris: Ernest Leroux (English translation published in Bangkok by White Lotus, 1999–2000.)

Pitchford, V. C. 1937. "The Wild Wa States and Lake Nawngkhio." *Geographical Journal* 90:223–232.

Pretzell, Klaus A., ed. 1979. *Die Miao in Laos: eine Pressedokumentation.* Hamburg: Institut fur Asienkunde, Dokumentations-Leitstelle Asien.

Raquez, A. 1905. "Au Laos." *Revue Indochinoise*, 1225–1233, 1394–1406, 1481–1485.

Rocher, Émile. 1879. "La Province chinoise du Yün-Nan, tome 1." Paris: Ernest Leroux.

————. 1880. "La Province chinoise du Yün-Nan, tome 2." Paris: Ernest Leroux.

Smyth, Herbert Warington. 1898. *Five Years in Siam from 1891 to 1896.* London: John Murray.

Tucker, Mike. 2003. *The Long Patrol (with the Karen Guerrillas in Burma).* Bangkok: Asia Books.

Tucker, Shelby. 2000. *Among Insurgents: Walking Through Burma.* Bangkok: White Lotus.

Maps and Atlases

Bruk, Solomon Il'ch. 1959. *Karta Narodov Indokitaia* [Map of the Peoples of Indochina]. Moska: Glavnoe Upravlenie Geodezii I Kartografii MVD SSSR, Institut Etnografii imeni N.N. Miklukho-Maklaia Akademii Nauk SSSR.

Collective. 1992. *Zhongguo Lahu yu fang yan di tu ji = Cokawr Ladhof khawd fayer diqthurcir* [The Linguistic Atlas of Lahu in China]. Tianjin she hui ke xue yuan chu ban she Xin hua shu dian jing xiao. Beijing, China: Di 1 ban.

Michaud, Jean, S. Turner, and Y. Roche. 2002. "Mapping Ethnic Diversity in Highland Northern Vietnam." *Geo Journal* 57 (4):281–299.

Pluvier, Jan M. 1995. *Historical Atlas of South-East Asia.* Leiden, The Netherlands: Brill.

Service Géographique de l'Indochine. 1949. *Carte Ethnolinguistique de l'Indochine.* Paris: Ecole Française d'Extrême-Orient.

2. LANGUAGES AND LINGUISTICS

Afanassieva, Elena. 1998. "Baan and Muang as Polysemantic Expressions for Tai Key Conceptions." *International Review on Tai Cultural Studies* [Berlin], 3 (2):27–30.

Barker, M. E. 1968. "The Phonemes of Muong." *Studies in Linguistics* 20(1/4): 59–62.

Benedict, P. K. 1942. "Thai, Kadai and Indonesian: A New Alignment in Southeastern Asia." *American Anthropologist* 44:576–601.

———. 1975. *Austro-Thai Languages and Culture*. New Haven, Conn.: Human Relations Area Files Press.

———. 1943. "Studies in Thai Kinship Terminology." *Journal of the American Oriental Society*, no. 63:168–175.

Bliatout, Bruce. 1988. *Handbook for Teaching Hmong-speaking Students*. Folsom, Calif.: Folsom Cordova Unified School District, Southeast Asia Community Resource Center.

Bonifacy, Auguste Louis-M. 1905. "Étude sur les langues parlées par les populations de la Haute Rivière Claire." *Bulletin de l'École Française d'Extrême-Orient*, III–IV:306–27.

Bradley, David. 1997. "Onomastic, Orthographic, Dialectal and Dialectical Borders: the Lisu and the Lahu." *Asia Pacific Viewpoint* 38 (2):107–117.

———. 2001. "Counting the Family: Family Group Classifiers in Yi (Tibeto-Burman) languages." *Anthropological Linguistics* 43 (1):1–17.

Busnel, R.G., G. Alcuri, and B. Gautheron. 1989. "Sur quelques aspects physiques de la langue à tons sifflés du peuple H'mong." *Cahiers d'études vietnamiennes*, no. 26:39–52.

Cabaton, Antoine. 1905. "Dix dialectes indochinois recueillis par Prosper Odend'hal." *Journal asiatique*,10 (5):265–344.

Clark, Marybeth. 1980a. "Derivation between Goal and Source Verbs in Hmong." *Working Papers in Linguistics* [Honolulu] 12 (2):51–59.

———. 1980b. "Source Phrases in White Hmong (Laos)." *Working Papers in Linguistics* [Honolulu] 12 (2):1–50.

———. 1985. "Asking Questions in Hmong and Other Southeast Asia Languages." *Linguistics of the Tibeto-Burman Area* [Berkeley, Calif.] 8 (2):60–67.

———. 1989. "Hmong and Areal South-East Asia." *Pacific Linguistics. Series A*, no. 11:175–230.

———. 2000. "Deixis and Anaphora and Prelinguistic Universals [Vietnamese and Hmong]." In *Grammatical Analysis: Morphology, Syntax, and Semantics: Studies in Honor of Stanley Starosta*, ed. Videa P. De Guzman and Byron W. Bender. Oceanic linguistics special publication, no. 29. Honolulu: University of Hawaii Press.

Deaton, Brady, and Thomas A. Lyman. 1969a. "Types of Miao Hill-Rice." *Asia Aakhanee: Southeast Asian Survey* 1 (2):36–38.

———. 1969b. "Green Miao (Meo) Agricultural Terms." *Asia Aakhanee: Southeast Asian Survey* 1 (3):42–47.

Dellinger, D. W. 1968. "Ambivalence in Akha phonology." *Anthropological Linguistics* 10 (8):16–22.

Derrick-Mescua, Maria, Judith Berman, and Mary Beth Carlson. 1981. "Some Secret Languages of the Hmong." In *The Hmong in the West; Observations and Reports,* ed. Downing, Bruce T., and Douglas P. Olney. Papers of the 1981 Hmong Research Conference, University of Minnesota. Minneapolis: Southeast Asian Refugee Studies Project, Center for Urban and Regional Affairs.

D'Ollone, Henri. 1912. *Langues des peuples non chinois de la Chine: Mission d'Ollone 1906–1909.* Paris: Ernest Leroux.

Downer, Gordon. 1967. "Tone-Change and Tone-Shift in White Miao." *Bulletin of the School of Oriental and African Studies* 30 (3):589–599.

Eippinger, J, and D. Fippinger. 1970. "Black Tai Phonemes, with Reference to White Tai." *Anthropological Linguistics* [Bloomington, Ind.] 12 (3):83–97.

Enfield, N. J. 2001. "On Genetic and Areal Linguistics in Mainland South-East Asia: Parallel Polyfunctionality of Acquire." In *Areal Diffusion and Genetic Inheritance: Problems in Comparative Linguistics,* ed. A. Aikhenvald and R. M. W. Dixon. Oxford: Oxford University Press.

Enwall, Joakim. 1992. "Miao or Hmong?" *Thai-Yunnan Project Newsletter,* no. 17.

———. 1994. "In Search of the Entering Tone: The importance of Sichuanese Tones for Understanding the Tone Marking System of the Sichuan Hmong Pollard Script." In *Outstretched Leaves on His Bamboo Staff. Studies in Honour of Göran Malmqvist on His 70th Birthday,* ed. Joakim Enwall, Stockholm: the Association of Oriental Studies,

Fippinger, Dorothy Crawford. 1971. "Kinship Terms of the Black Tai People." *Journal of the Siam Society (Bangkok),* no. 59. pt.1:65–82.

Fippinger, Jay W. 1975. "Black Tai Sentence Types: A Generative Semantic Approach." In *Studies in Tai Linguistics in Honor of William J. Gedney,* ed. Jimmy G. Harris and James R. Chamberlain. Bangkok: Central Institute of English Language, Office of State Universities.

Gedney, William. 1999. *The Lue Language: Glossaries, Texts and Translations.* Ann Arbor: University of Michigan Centers for South and Southeast Asia,

Graham, David C. 1938. "Vocabulary of the Ch'uan Miao." *Journal of the West China Border Research Society* 10:53–143.

Hansson, Inga Lill. 1983. "A Phonological Comparison of Akha and Hani." *Linguistics of the Tibeto-Burman Area* 7 (1):63–115.

Harris, Jimmy G., and James R. Chamberlain, eds. 1975. *Studies in Tai Linguistics in Honor of William J. Gedney.* Bangkok: Central Institute of English Language, Office of State Universities.

Haudricourt, André Georges. 1951. "Introduction à la phonologie historique des langues miao-yao." *Bulletin de l'Ecole Française d'Extrême-Orient* XLIV, (1947–1950):555–576.

———. 1971. "Les langues karen et les langues miao-yao." *Asie du Sud-Est et Monde Insulindien* 2 (4):25–51.

———. 1974. "Le nom du champ sur brûlis et le nom de la rizière irriguée." *Études Rurales* 53–56:467–471.

Hutton, Christopher. 1998. "From Pre-modern to Modern: Ethnic Classification by Language and the Case of the Ngai/Nung of Vietnam." *Language & Communication* [Oxford] 18 (2):125.

Jones, Robert B., Jr. 1961. *Karen Linguistic Studies: Description, Comparison, and Texts.* University of California Publications in Linguistics, 25. Berkeley and Los Angeles: University of California Press.

Kun Chang. 1953. "On the Tone System of the Miao-Yao Languages." *Language* 29 (3):374–378.

Léger, D. 1974. "Vocabulaire comparé et recherche du vocabulaire dentaire bahnar-jolong." *Asie du Sud-Est et Monde Insulindien* 5 (1):123–131.

———. 1975. "Correspondances dialectales du parler bahnar." *Asie du Sud-Est et Monde Insulindien* 6 (4):81–91.

Lewis, Paul. 1968. "Akha Phonology." *Anthropological Linguistics* 10 (2):8–18.

———. 1973. "Tone in the Akha Language." *Anthropological Linguistics* 15 (4):183–188.

Li, Charles N. 1991. "The Aspectual System of Hmong." *Studies in Language* [Amsterdam] 15 (1):25–58.

Li Fang-kuei. 1959. "Classification by Vocabulary: Tai Dialects." *Anthropological Linguistics*, no. 1:15–21.

Lietard, Alfred. 1909. "Notes sur les dialectes Lo-lo." *Bulletin de l'Ecole Française d'Extrême-Orient* 9:549–572.

Long Yaohong, Zheng Guoqiao, and D. Norman Geary. 1998. *The Dong Language in Guizhow, Province, China.* Publications in Linguistics, 126. Arlington: Summer Institute of Linguistics and the University of Texas.

Luce, G. H. 1959. "Introduction to the Comparative Study of Karen Languages." *JBRS* 42 (1):1–18.

Lyman, Thomas A. 1978. "Note on the Name 'Green Miao'." *Nachrichten*, no. 123:82–87.

———. 1990. "The Mong (Green Miao) and Their Language: A Brief Compendium." *The Journal of the Siam Society* 78:63–65.

Ma Xue-liang, and Chen Ying. 1982. "Studies of the Antiquities of the Yi Nationality in Guizhou." *Wen Wu*, no. 4:24–34. 57.

Maitra, Asim. 1988a. *A Guide Book to Lisu Language.* New Delhi: Mittal Publications,

———. 1988b. "The Lisu Kinship Terminology: A Note." *Human Science*, no. 37:269–272.

Maspero, Henri. 1911. "Contribution à l'étude du système phonétique des langues thai." *Bulletin de l'Ecole Française d'Extrême-Orient* XI:154–169.

———. 1916. "De quelques interdits en relation avec les noms de famille chez les Tai Noirs." *Bulletin de l'Ecole Française d'Extrême-Orient* XVI (3):29–34.

———. 1930. "Langues." In *Un empire colonial français. L'Indochine. Tome 1: Le pays et ses habitants—l'histoire, la vie sociale*, ed. Georges Maspero. Paris and Bruxelles: Les éditions G Van Oest.

Matisoff, James. 1983. "Linguistic Diversity and Language Contact." In *Highlanders of Thailand*, ed. John McKinnon and Wanat Bhruksasri. Singapore: Oxford University Press.

———. 1991. "Sino-Tibetan Linguistics: Present State and Future Prospects." *Annual Review of Anthropology*, no. 20:469–504.

———. 1992. "The Lahu People and Their Language." In *Minority Cultures of Laos: Kammu, Lua', Lahu, Hmong, and Mien*, ed. Judy Lewis. Rancho Cordova, Calif.: Southeast Asia Community Resource Center.

———. 2001. "Genetic Versus Contact Relationship: Prosodic Diffusibility in South-East Asian Languages." In *Areal Diffusion and Genetic Inheritance: Problems in Comparative Linguistics*, ed. A. Aikhenvald and R. M. W. Dixon. Oxford: Oxford University Press.

Pederson, Eric. 1986. "Expressive Language in White Hmong." In *Proceedings of the Twelfth Annual Meeting of the Berkeley Linguistics Society, February 15–17*, ed. Vassiliki Nikiforidou et al. Berkeley, Calif.: Berkeley Linguistic Society.

Piat, M. 1962. "Quelques correspondances entre le Khmer et le Bru: langue montagnarde du Centre-Vietnam." *Bulletin de la Societe des Etudes indochinoises NS* 37 (3):311–323.

Purnell, Herbert. 1991. "The Metrical Structure of Yiu Mien Secular Songs." In *Yao of South China: Recent International Studies*, ed. Jacques Lemoine and Chiao Chen. Paris: Pangu.

———. 1992. "Lexical Tone and Musical Pitch in an Iu Mien Yao Wedding Song." *Selected Reports in Ethnomusicology* 9:61–80.

Ramsey, S. Robert. 1987.*The Languages of China*. Princeton, N.J.: Princeton University Press.

Ratliff, Martha. 1992. *Meaningful Tone: A Study of Tonal Morphology in Compounds, Form Classes, and Expressive Phrases in White Hmong*, Center for Southeast Asian Studies, Monograph Series on Southeast Asia, Special Report No. 27. DeKalb, Ill.: Northern Illinois University.

———. 1995. "Fine Granular Bits: 'Rice' and 'Grain' in Hmong-Mien." In *Papers from the Third Annual Meeting of the Southeast Asian Linguistics Society*, ed. Mark Alves. Tempe, Ariz: Program for Southeast Asian Studies, Arizona State University.

———. 1997. "Hmong-Mien Demonstratives and Pattern Persistence." *Mon-Khmer Studies* [Honolulu] 27:317–328.

Rispaud, J. 1937. "Les noms à éléments numéraux des principautés taï." *Journal of the Siam Society* 29 (2):77–122.

Sagart, Laurent. 1995. "Chinese 'Buy' and 'Sell' and the Direction of Borrowings between Chinese and Hmong-Mien: A Response to Haudricourt and Strecker." *T'oung Pao* 81 (4–5):328–342.

Smalley, William A., ed. 1976. *Phonemes and Orthography: Language Planning in Ten Minority Languages of Thailand.* Canberra: Department of Linguistics, Research School of Pacific Studies, Australian National University.

Svantesson, Jan-Olof. 1983. *Kammu Phonology and Morphology.* Lund, [Sweden]: CWK Gleerup.

Vidal, J. E. 1969. "Noms vernaculaires de plantes (Lao, Méo, Kha) en usage au Laos." *Bulletin de l'Ecole Française d'Extrême-Orient* 49 (2):560–562.

Language Dictionaries, Grammars, and Lexicons

Baccam, Don, et al. 1989. *Tai Dam-English, English-Tai Dam Vocabulary Book.* Eastlake, Colo.: Summer Institute of Linguistics.

Bertrais, Yves. 1964. *Dictionnaire Hmong-Français*, Vientiane [Laos]: Mission catholique.

Collectif. 2001. *Bouyei, Chinese, English, Thai Dictionary.* Bangkok: Mahidon University, Zhong yang min zu da xue [China].

Cushing, Josiah N. 1914. *A Shan and English Dictionary.* 2d. ed. Rangoon: American Baptist Mission Press.

Dai, Qingxia. 1992. *Jingpo yu yu fa = Jinghpo ga ladat* [The Grammer of Kachin]. Zhong yang min zu xue yuan chu ban she Xin hua shu dian Beijing fa xing suo fa xing. Beijing, China: Di 1 ban.

Diguet, Col. Edouard. 1895. *Étude de la langue Thaï, précédée d'une notice sur les races des hautes régions du Tonkin, comprenant grammaire, méthode d'écriture Thai et vocabulaire.* Hanoï: Schneider.

D'Ollone, Henri. 1912. *Écritures des peuples non chinois de la Chine; Quatre dictionnaires Lolo et Miao Tseu. Mission d'Ollone 1906–1909.* Paris: Ernest Leroux.

Enfield, N. J. 2003. *Linguistic Epidemiology: Semantics and Grammar of Language Contact in Mainland Southeast Asia.* London: RoutledgeCurzon.

Hanson, Ola. 1954. *A Dictionary of the Katchin Language.* Rangoon: Baptist Board of Publications.

Heimbach, Ernest E. 1969. *White Hmong—English Dictionary.* Linguistic series 4. Data paper 75. Ithaca, N.Y.: Southeast Asia Program, Department of Asian Studies, Cornell University.

Hope, Edward Reginald. 1974. *The Deep Syntax of Lisu Sentences: A Transformational Case Grammar.* Canberra: Department of Linguistics, Research School of Pacific Studies, Australian National University.

Hudak, Thomas J. 2002. *Bouyei-English Lexicon: Based on the Bouyei-Chinese Dictionary Compiled by the Chinese Academy of Sciences*. Tempe, Ariz: Monograph Series Press, Program for Southeast Asian Studies, Arizona State University.

Lyman, Thomas A. 1974. *Dictionary of Mong Njua: A Miao (Meo) Language of Southeast Asia*. Berlin: Walter De Gruyter.

Matisoff, James. 1982. *Grammar of Lahu*. UC Publications in Linguistics, 75. Berkeley: University of California Press.

———. 1989. *The Dictionary of Lahu*. University of California Publications in Linguistics Vol. 111. Berkeley: University of California Press.

Milne, Mary Lewis. 1931. *A Dictionary of English Palaung and Palaung-English*. Rangoon: Superintendent of Government Printing and Stationery.

Minot, G. 1940. "Dictionnaire Tay Blanc Français avec trancription latine." *Bulletin de l'Ecole Française d'Extrême-Orient* XL (1):1–237.

Mottin, Jean. 1978. *Éléments de grammaire Hmong Blanc*. Bangkok: Don Bosco Press.

Saul, Janice E. 1980. *Nùng Grammar*. Arlington: Summer Institute of Linguistics University of Texas.

Savina, François Marie. 1916. "Dictionnaire Miao-Tseu—Français." *Bulletin de l'Ecole Française d'Extrême-Orient* XVI (2):1–246.

Shimizu, Michio. 1981. *Shimizu Illustrated Dictionary, English-Hmong*. Minneapolis, Minn.: M. Shimizu.

Tharp, James A. 1980. *A Rhade-English Dictionary with English-Rhade Finderlist*. Canberra, Australia: Department of Linguistics, Research School of Pacific Studies, Australian National University.

Writing Systems and Scripts

Enwall, Joakim. 1995a. *Hmong Writing Systems in Vietnam: A Case Study of Vietnam's Minority Language Policy*. Stockholm: Center for Pacific Asia Studies at Stockholm University.

———. 1995b. *A Myth Become Reality: History & Development of the Miao Written Language*. Philadelphia: Coronet Books.

Jagacinski, Ngampit. 1986. "Tai Lue Scripts: The Old and New." *Crossroads* 3 (1):80–96.

Lafont, Pierre Bernard. 1962. "Les écritures 'Tay du Laos ('Tay Lü, Yuon, Lao, 'Tay Dam, 'Tay Deng, 'Tay Neua)." *Bulletin de l'Ecole francaise d'Extreme-Orient* 50 (2):367–394.

Stern, T. 1968. "Three Pwo Karen Scripts: A Study of Alphabet Formation." *Anthropological Linguistics* 10 (1):1–39.

Yang Wanzhi. 1991. "A Study of Hani Hieroglyphic Symbols." *Nationality-Studies (Honghe)* [in Chinese] 3:43–49.

Zhou Yu-dong. 1980. "Adoption and Propagation of the Yi Written Language in Yunnan." *Minzu Yanjiu* 6:65–68.

3. ANTHROPOLOGY, ETHNOLOGY, AND ETHNOGRAPHY

Colonial, Military, and Missionary Ethnography

Abadie, Maurice. 1924. *Les races du Haut-Tonkin de Phong-Tho à Lang-Son*. Paris: Challamel. (English translation, *Minorities of the Sino-Vietnamese Borderland with Special Reference to the Thai Tribes*, published in Bangkok by White Lotus in 2001).

Bacot, Jacques. 1913. *Les Mo-so*. Leiden, The Netherlands: E. J. Brill.

Beauvais, M. J. 1907. "Notes sur les coutumes indigènes de la région de Long Tchéou." *Bulletin de l'Ecole Française d'Extrême-Orient* 7:265–295.

Bernatzik, Hugo Adolf. *Akha und Meau*. Innsbruck, [Austria]: Wagner, 1947.

Bonifacy, Auguste Louis-M. 1904. "Les groupes ethniques de la Rivière Claire." *Revue Indo -Chinoise*, July, pp. 1–16. June, pp. 813–828.

———. 1907. "Étude sur les Thai de la Rivière Claire, au Tonkin et dans la Chine méridionale (Yunnan et Guangxi)." *T'oung Pao* ser. 2, vol. 8.

———. 1919. *Cours d'ethnographie indochinoise (professé aux élèves de l'Ecole supérieure d'Agriculture et de Sylviculture)*. Hanoi-Haiphong: Imprimerie d'Extrême Orient (Gouvernement général de l'Indochine, Enseignement supérieur d'Indochine).

Bourlet, Antoine. 1907. "Les Thay." *Anthropos* 2 (3):355–373.

Carrapiett, W. J. S. 1929. *The Kachin Tribes of Burma: For the Information of Officers of the Burma Frontier*. Rangoon: Superintendent of Government Printing and Stationery.

Clarke, Samuel R. 1911. *Among the Tribes in South-West China*. London: China Inland Mission.

Cordier, Henri. 1908. "Les Mosos." *T'oung Pao* 2 (9):663–682.

Cuisinier, Jeanne. 1946. *Les M'uong: Géographie Humaine et Sociologie*. Paris: Institut d'ethnologie.

Cushing, Rev. Dr. J. N. 2003. "Lecture on the Shan." *Rangoon Gazette and Weekly Budget via SOAS Bulletin of Burma Research* 1 (2).

Dam Bo (a.k.a. Jacques Dournes). 1950. "Les populations montagnardes du Sud-Indochinois." *France-Asie*, no. 5.

Department of the Army. 1970a. "The Meo." In *Minority Groups in Thailand*. Washington, D.C.: Government Printing Office.

———. 1970b. "The Yao." In *Minority Groups in Thailand*. Washington, D.C.: Government Printing Office.

Diguet, Col. Edouard. 1908. *Les Montagnards du Tonkin*. Paris: Librairie Maritime et Coloniale, Augustin Challamel.

Dodd, William Clifton. 1996 [1923]. *The Tai Race, Elder Brother of the Chinese*. Bangkok: White Lotus.

Fortune, Reo, ed. 1939. "Yao Society: A Study of a Group of Primitives in China." *Lingnan Science Journal* 18:341–455.

Gaide, Dr Laurent-Joseph. 1905. "Notice ethnographique sur les principales races indigènes du Yunnan et du Nord de l'Indo-Chine précédée de renseignements généraux sur la province du Yunnan et principalement sur la région des Sip-Song Pan-Na." *Revue Indo-Chinoise* 15 April (pp. 471–481), 30 April (pp. 544–553), 15 May (pp. 646–658), 30 May (pp. 707–717), 15 June (pp. 787–794), 30 June (pp. 838–855).

Girard, Henri. 1901. *Notes sur les Meos du Haut Tonkin, Notes anthropométriques et ethnographiques*. Paris: Imprimerie Nationale.

Guilleminet, Paul P. 1952. "La tribu Bahnar du Kontum (plateaux de l'Indochine centrale)." *Bulletin de l'Ecole Française d'Extrême-Orient* XLV(2):393–561.

Henry, Augustine. 1903. "The Lolos and Other Tribes of Western China." *Journal of the Royal Anthropological Institute of Great Britain and Ireland* 33:96–107.

Hudspeth, William H. 1937. *Stone Gateway and the Flowery Miao*. London: Cargate Press.

Hutchinson, E. W. 1934. "The Lawa in Northern Siam." *Journal of the Siam Society* 27:153–182.

Izikowitz, Karl G. 1951. *Lamet: Hill Peasants in French Indochina*. Ethnologiska Studier no. 17. Göteborg, [Sweden]: Etnografiska Museet.

———. 1969. "Neighbours in Laos." In *Ethnic Groups and Boundaries: The Social Organisation of Culture Difference*, ed. F. Barth. Bergen-Oslo: Universitets Forlaget-London, George Allen, and Unwin.

Jouin, Bernard. 1950. "Les traditions Rhadé." *Bulletin de la Société des Études Indochinoises* 25:357–400.

Lefèvre-Pontalis, Pierre. 1902. *Voyage dans le Haut-Laos et sur les frontières de Chine et de Birmanie. Introduction by Auguste Pavie*. Vol. 5 of *Mission Pavie Indo-Chine 1879–1895*, Géographie et voyages section. Paris: Ernest Leroux.

Lunet de Lajonquière, Étienne E. 1904. *Ethnographie des territoires militaires*. Hanoï-Paris: Ernest Leroux.

Macey, Paul. 1905. "Etude ethnographique sur diverses tribus, aborigènes ou autochtones habitant les provinces des Hua-Phan-Ha-Tang-Hoc et du Cammon, au Laos." *Actes du XIVe Congrès international des Orientalistes* [Alger] 1 (5):3–63.

Madrolle, Claude. 1906a. "La population de l'Indo-Chine." *Revue Indo-Chinoise* 30 août, pp. 1298–1315.

———. 1906b. "Les T'ai de la frontière sino-tonkinoise." *Revue Indo-Chinoise* 15 janvier pp. 1–8, 15 février pp. 103–110, 15 mars pp. 187–194.

Maître, H. 1912. *Les Jungles Möi*. Paris: Larose.

Marshall, Harry Ignatius. 1997 [1922]. *The Karen People of Burma: A Study in Anthropology and Ethnology*. Columbus: Ohio State University. (Reprint by White Lotus, Bangkok.)

Maspero, Henri. 1929. "Moeurs et coutumes des populations sauvages." In *Un empire colonial français. L'Indochine. Tome 1: Le pays et ses habitants—l'histoire, la vie sociale*, ed. Georges Maspero. Paris et Bruxelles: Les éditions G. Van Oest.

McCarthy, J. 1900. *Surveying and Exploring in Siam, Including Data on Meo and on Hau (Ho) Invaders of Laos*. London: Murray.

Michaud, Jean. 2004. "Missionary Ethnographers in Upper-Tonkin: The Early Years." *Asian Ethnicity* 5 (2):179–194.

Military Research and Development Center. 1969. *Meo Handbook*. Bangkok: Joint Thai U.S. Military Research and Development Center.

Milne, Leslie. 2001 [1910]. *Shans at Home: Burma's Shan States in the Early 1900s*. Bangkok: White Lotus.

Milne, Mary Lewis (Harper). 1924. *The Home of an Eastern Clan: A Study of the Palaungs of the Shan States*. Oxford: Clarendon Press.

Pinabel, Pierre-Charles. 1884. "Notes sur quelques peuplades sauvages dépendant du Tong-King." *Bulletin de la société de Géographie de Paris* 5:417–33.

Pollard, Samuel. 1905. *Miao Report*. London: Pollard Collection, Box 10 Reserve Collection, School of Oriental and African Studies, University of London.

Robert, Romain. 1941. *Notes sur les Tay Dèng de Lang Chanh*. Hanoï: Imprimerie d'Extême-Orient.

Rose, Archibald, and J.Coggin Brown. 1911. "Lisu (Yawyin) Tribes of the Burma-China Frontier." *Memoirs of the Royal Asiatic Society of Bengal* 3:249–276.

Roux, Henri. 1924. "Deux tribus de la région de Phongsaly (Laos septentrional) I: A-Khas or Khas Kôs, II: P'u Noi." *Bulletin de l'Ecole Française d'Extrême-Orient* 24:373–500.

Roux, Henri, and Can Chu Tran. 1927. "Les Tsa Khmu." *Bulletin de l'Ecole Française d'Extrême-Orient* 27:169–222.

Roux, Henri, and Tran Van Chu. 1954. "Quelques minorités ethniques du Nord Indochine." *France-Asie* 10 (93):135–419.

Sabatier, L. 1940. *Recueil des coutumes Rhadés du Darlac*. Hanoi: Imprimerie d'Extrême-Orient.

Schotter, P. Aloys. 1908, 1909, 1911. "Notes ethnographiques sur les tribus du Kouy-tschou." *Anthropos*, no. 3:397–425; no. 4:418–453; no. 6:318–344.

Seidenfaden, Erik. 1963. *The Thai Peoples: The Origins and Habitats of the Thai Peoples with a Sketch of Their Material and Spiritual Culture.* Bangkok: The Siam Society.

———. 1923. "The White Meo." *Journal of the Siam Society* 17 (3):153–199.

Siguret, Jean, trans. (from Chinese). 1971. *Territoires et populations des confins du Yunnan.* Taipei, Taiwan: Cheng Wen Publishing.

Silvestre, Capt. 1918. "Les Thai blancs de Phong Tho." *Bulletin de l'Ecole Française d'Extrême-Orient* XVIII (4):1–56.

Smeaton, Donald Mackenzie. 1887. *The Loyal Karen of Burma.* London: Kegan Paul Trench.

Stevenson, H. 1944. *The Hill People of Burma.* London: Green.

Stevenson, Paul H. 1932. "Note on the Human Geography of the Chinese-Tibetan Borderland." *Geographical Review* 22:599–616.

Stübel, Hans. 1938. "The Yao of the Province of Kwangtung." *Monumenta Serica* 3:345–84.

Vial, Paul. 1898. *Les Lolos. Histoire, religion, moeurs, langue, écriture.* Shanghai: Imprimerie de la Mission Catholique.

Monographs and Specialized Articles

Abrahams, Ray G. 1990. "Chaos and Kachin." *Anthropology Today* 6 (1):15–17.

An, Chunyang. 1985. *Where the Dai People Live.* China's Nationalities series. Beijing: Foreign Languages Press.

Andersen, J. P. 1923. "Some Notes about the Karens in Siam." *Journal of the Siam Society* [Bangkok] 17 (2):51–58.

Ayabe, Masao. 1996. "Ethnic Diversity among the Hill Tribes of Thailand: The Case of the Lisu." *Ethnic Studies Report* 14 (2):229–241.

Barney, G. Linwood. 1967. "The Meo of Xieng Khouang Province, Laos." In *Southeast Asian Tribes, Minorities and Nations*, ed. Peter Kunstadler. Princeton, N.J.: Princeton University Press.

Barua, S. N. 1991. *Tribes of Indo-Burma Border.* 1st ed. Columbia, Miss.: South Asia Books.

Berlie, Jean. 1988. "The Dai of China: A Preliminary Study of a National Minority." *Eastern Anthropologist* [Lucknow] 41 (4):325–342.

Bertrand, Henry. 1994. *Un peuple oublié: Les montagnards des hauts plateaux du Sud-Indochinois.* Paris: Sudestasie.

Blofeld, John. 1955. "Some Hill Tribes of North Thailand (Miaos and Yaos)." *Journal of the Siam Society* 43 (1):1–19.

Cauquelin, Josiane. 1997. *Au Pays des Buyi, une Ethnie du Berceau Thaie Province du Guizhou, Chine.* Paris: Les Cahiers de Péninsule, no. 4.

Chapman, Dean. 1999. *Karenni.* Stockport, UK: Dewi Lewis Pub.

Charusathira, Praphat. 1967. *Thailand's Hill Tribes*. Bangkok: Department of Public Welfare, Ministry of Interior.

Chazée, Laurent. 2002. *The Mrabri in Laos: A World under the Canopy*. Bangkok: White Lotus.

Chen Bin, and Li Minghui. 1995. *Azaleas in the Woods: The Yaos*. Women's Culture Series: Nationalities of Yunnan. Kunming, China: Yunnan Education Publishing House.

Cochrane, Wilbur Willis. 1981 [1915]. *The Shans*. New York: AMS Press.

Condominas, Georges. 1960. "The Mnong Gar of Central Vietnam." In *Social Structure in Southeast Asia*, ed. G. P. Murdock. Viking Fund Publications in Anthropology, no. 29. New York: Viking.

Condominas, Georges, Adrienne Foulke, Richard Critchfield, and Philip Turner, eds. 1994. *We Have Eaten the Forest: The Story of a Montagnard Village in the Central Highlands of Vietnam (Kodansha Globe)*. Reprint ed. Tokyo: Kodansha International.

Cooper, Robert G. 1998. *The Hmong: A Guide to Traditional Lifestyles*. Singapore: Times Editions.

Dang Nghiem Van. 1971. "Aperçu sur les Thai." *Études Vietnamiennes (Hanoï)* 32:163–225.

———. 1973. "The Khmu in Vietnam." *Vietnamese Studies* 36:62–140.

De Beauclair, Inez. 1956. "Culture Traits of Non-Chinese Tribes in Kweichow Province, Southwest China." *Sinologica* 5:16–30.

———. 1960. "A Miao Tribe of Southeast Kweichow and Its Cultural Configuration." *Bulletin of the Institute of Ethnology*, no. 10:127–205.

———. 1961. "Miao on Hainan Island." *Current Anthropology* 2:314.

———. 1986. "The Ta-Hua Miao of Kweichow Province." In *The Collected Papers of Inez de Beauclair*. Taipei, Taiwan: Ethnographic Studies (Translated reprint of "Die Ta-Hua Miao der Provinz Kweichou," *Gesellschaft für Natur- und Völkerkunde Ostasiens* 37 (1954):47–57).

Dessaint, Alain Y. 1992. "Lisu World View." In *The Highland Heritage: Collected Essays on Upland North Thailand*, ed. Anthony Walker. Singapore: Suvarnabhumi Books.

Dessaint, William. 1981. "The T'in (Mal), Dry Rice Cultivators of Northern Thailand and Northern Laos." *Journal of the Siam Society* [Bangkok] 69 (1–2):107–137.

———. 1995. "The Lisu, Highlanders of the Salween." *Bulletin of the International Committee on Urgent Anthropological and Ethnological Research* 37 (8):12–27.

Dinh Dang Dinh. 1967. *The Meo National Minority, North-West Vietnam*. Hanoi: Xunhasaba.

Dournes, Jacques. 1980. *Minorities of Central Vietnam: Autochtonous Indochinese Peoples*. Report no. 18. London: Minority Rights Group.

Durrenberger, E. Paul. 1982. "Shan kho: The Essence of Misfortune." *Anthropos* 77 (1/2):16–26.

———. 1983. "Lisu: Political Form, Ideology and Economic Action." In *Highlanders of Thailand*, ed. John McKinnon and Wanat Bhruksasri. Kuala Lumpur: Oxford University Press.

Gao Wenying. 1986. "The Survey of Akha (Branch of Hani) in Lanchang Prefecture." In *Nationality Studies*, 158–170. Kunming, China: Nationalities Publishing House.

Geary, Norman D., Ruth B. Geary, Ou Chaoquan, Long Yaohong, Jiang Daren, and Wang Jiying. 2003. *The Kam People of China: Turning Nineteen.* New York, London: Routledge.

Hanks, Lucien M., and Jane Richardson Hanks. 1975. "Reflections on Ban Akha Mae Salong." *Journal of Siam Society* [Bangkok] 63 (1):72–85.

———. 2001. *Tribes of the North Thailand Frontier.* Yale Monograph No. 51. New Haven, Conn.: Yale University Press.

Harvey, Godfrey E. 1957. "The Wa People of the China-Burma Border." *St. Antony's Papers.* Oxford University, St. Anthony's College, No.2. London: Chatto and Windus.

He Shutao. 1995. *A Myth Kept Alive the Nus.* Women's Culture Series: Nationalities in Yunnan. Kunming: Yunnan Education Publishing House.

He Zhengting. 1998. *Yunnan Zhuang Nationality.* Beijing: Foreign Press.

He Zhonghua. 1995. *Where the Goddesses Live: The Naxis.* Kunming: Yunnan Education Publishing House.

Hickey, Gerald C. 1964. *The Major Ethnic Groups of the South Vietnamese Highlands.* Santa Monica, Calif.: Rand, RM-4041–ARPA.

Hill, Ann Maxwell. 1983. "The Yunnanese [Haw] : Overland Chinese in Northern Thailand." In *Highlanders of Thailand*, ed. John McKinnon and Wanat Bhruksasri. Kuala Lumpur: Oxford University Press.

Hinton, Elizabeth. 1979. "Life and Love among the Pwo Karen." *Hemisphere* [Woden, Australia] 23 (6):348–351.

Howard, Michael C., and Wattana Wattanapun. 2001. *The Palaung in Northern Thailand.* Chiang Mai, [Thailand]: Silkworm Books,

Kunstadter, Peter. 1983. "Highland Populations in Northern Thailand." In *Highlanders of Thailand*, ed. John McKinnon and Wanat Bhruksasri. Kuala Lumpur: Oxford University Press.

Lafont, Pierre Bernard. 1967. "Notes sur les structures sociales des Mnong-Rlam du centre-Vietnam." *Bulletin de l'Ecole francaise d'Extreme-Orient* 53 (2):675–683.

Lam, Tam. 1973. "Coup d'oeil sur les Meo." *Etudes Vietnamiennes* 9e année (36):7–68.

Lemoine, Jacques. 1972. *Un village Hmong Vert du Haut Laos.* Paris: Centre National de la Recherche Scientifique.

Lemoine, Jacques, and Chiao Chen, ed. 1991. *The Yao of South China: Recent International Studies*. Paris: Pangu.

Lin Yue-Hua. 1940. "The Miao-Man peoples of Kweichow." *Harvard Journal of Asiatic Studies* 5:261–345.

Lin Yueh-hwa. 1947. *The Lolo of Liang Shan [Liang-Shan I-chia]*. Shanghai: Commercial Press. (Translation by Ju-shu Pan, published in New Haven, Conn., by HRAF Press, in 1961.)

Ling Zen-Seng (Johnson Ling). 1929. *Recherches Ethnographiques sur les Yao dans la Chine du Sud*. Paris: Presses Universitaires de France.

Lintner, Bertil. 1984. "The Shans and the Shan State of Burma." *Contemporary Southeast Asia* [Singapore] 5 (4):403–450.

Lowis, Cecil C. 1906. *A Note on Palaungs of Hsipaw and Tawngpeng*. Ethnographical Survey of India, Burma, no. 1. Rangoon: Superintendent of Government Printing and Stationery.

Luo, Rongfen. 1995. *Face-Tattooed Women in Nature: The Dulongs*. Women's Culture Series: Nationalities in Yunnan. Kunming: Yunnan Education Publishing House.

Mackerras, Colin. 1988. "Aspects of Bai Culture: Change and Continuity in a Yunnan Nationality." *Modern China* 14 (1):51–84.

Mao Youquan, and Li Qibo. 1989. *The Hani-People*. Honghe, Yunnan China: Jianshui Nationality Studies Institute. (First published in Chinese in 1989.)

Maurice, Albert-Marie. 1993. *Les Mnong des Hauts-Plateaux (Centre Vietnam)*. Paris: L'Harmattan.

Miller, Lucien. 1995. "The Ethnic Chameleon: Bakhtin and the Bai." *Comparative Civilizations Review* 32:26–45.

Millett, Sandra. 2001. *The Hmong of Southeast Asia*. Minneapolis, Minn.: Lerner Publishing Group.

Mole, Robert L. 1970. *The Montagnards of South Vietnam: A Study of Nine Tribes*. Rutland, Vt.: Tuttle.

Moninger, M. M. 1921. "The Hainanese Miao." *Journal of the Royal Anthropological Society, North China Branch* 52:40–50.

Mukhlinov, A. I. 1965. "Material on the Ethnography of the Highland Peoples in Nghe An Province (Democratic Republic of Vietnam)." *Sovietskaya Etnografiya* 5:45–56.

Naroll, R. 1968. "Who the Lue Are." In *Essays on the Problem of Tribes: Proceedings of the 1967 Annual Spring Meeting of the American Ethnological Society*, ed. J. Helm. Seattle: University of Washington Press.

Nguyen Dinh Loc. 1993. *Cac dan toc thieu so o Nghe An*. [Ethnic Groups in Nghe An]. Vinh, Vietnam: Nha Xuat Ban Nghe An.

Nguyen Duy Thieu. 1999. "Ethnic Groups Speaking Lao-Thay in Laos." *Vietnamese Studies* [Hanoi], no. 134:91–94.

Pathy, Jaganath. 1985. "The Muong: A North Vietnamese 'Tribe' in Transmutation." *Eastern Anthropologist* 38 (4):279–294.

Pham Nhu Cuong et al. 1987. *Môt Sô Vân dê Phát triên van hóa các dân tôc thiêu sô* [Some Problems Concerning the Cultural Developpement of Ethnic Minorities]. Hanoi: NXB Van hóa Dân Tôc.

Pismai, Wibulswasdi. 1982. "Hmong and Chinese Interaction with Thais in Thailand." In *Ethnicity and Interpersonal Interaction: A Cross Cultural Study*, ed. David Y. H. Wu. Singapore: Maruzen Asia.

Rock, Joseph F. 1963. "The Life and Culture of the Na-khi Tribe of the China-Tibet Borderland." In *Verzeichnis der orientalischen Handschriften in Deutschland*, 1–48. Supplementband 2. Wiesbaden: Franz Steiner Verlag.

Rossi, Gail. 1991. *The Dong People of China. A Hidden Civilization*. Singapore: Hagley and Hoyle.

Ruey Yih-fu. 1960. "The Magpie Miao of Southern Szechwan." *Social Structure in Southeast Asia*, ed. G. P. Murdoch. Viking Fund Publication in Anthropology, no. 29. New-York: Viking.

———. 1967. "A Study of the Miao People." In *Symposium on Historical, Archeological and Linguistic Studies,* ed. F. S. Drake, 49–58. Hong Kong: Hong Kong University Press.

Saimuang, Wirayasiri. 1986. *ChaoKhao nai prathet thai* [Hilltribes in Thailand]. Bangkok: Khurusapha.

Salemink, Oscar. 1996. "The Mnong in the Highlands of Central Vietnam." *Anthropos* 91 (1–3):278–279.

Sams, Bert F. 1988. "Black Tai and Lao Song Dam." *Journal of the Siam Society* [Bangkok] 76:100–120.

Schafer, R. 1964. "The Miao-Yao." *Monumenta Serica* 23:398–411.

Scott, George M. 1990. "The Shans of Burma." In *The Tai Khamtis of the North-east.* 2d ed., rev. and enl., ed. Lila Gogol. New Delhi: Omsons Publications.

Seitz, Paul L. 1975. "Des hommes debout: les Montagnards du Sud-Vietnam." Translated as *Men of Dignity: The Montagnards of South Vietnam.* Paris: C. Simonnet; Cambridge, UK: J. Jackson.

Sisawat, Bun Chuai. 1952. *Sām sip chāti nai Chaing rāi* [Thirty Nationalities in Chiengrai]. Bangkok: Outhai Press.

Tannenbaum, Nicola. 1990. "The Heart of the Village: Constituent Structures of Shan Communities." *Crossroads* 5 (1):23–41.

———. 1998. "Household, Villages, and Polities among the Shan of Maehongson Province, North-Western Thailand." *Tai Culture: International Review on Tai Cultural Studies* [Berlin] 3 (2):165–171.

Tapp, Nicholas. 1986a. *The Hmong of Thailand: Opium People of the Golden Triangle*. London: Anti-Slavery Society.

———. 1986b. "The Minorities of Southern China: A General Overview." *Journal of the Hong Kong Branch of the Royal Asiatic Society* 26:102–114.

Tapp, Nicolas, Jean Michaud, Christian Culas, and Gary Yia Lee, eds. 2004. *Hmong/Miao in Asia*. Chiang Mai, Thailand: Silkworm Books.

Tayanin, Damrong. 1994. *Being Kammu: My Village, My Life*. Southeast Asia Program Publications. Ithaca, N.Y.: Cornell University.

Tesler, Sherry. 2001. "The Akha of Thailand." *Athena Review* 2 (4):69–75, 81.

Thompson, Liz. 1998. *The Hmong of Vietnam*. Carlton, Australia: Heinemann Library.

Trier, Jesper. 1981. "The Khon Pa of Northern Thailand: An Enigma." *Current Anthropology* 22 (3):291–293.

Vang Tou-fu. 1979. "The Hmong of Laos." In *An Introduction to Indochinese History, Culture, Language, and Life*, ed. John Whitemore. Ann Arbor: University of Michigan, Center for South and Southeast Asian Studies.

Vargyas, Gabor. 1999. *À la recherche des Brous perdus, population montagnarde du centre indochinois*. Paris: Les Cahiers de Péninsule no. 5.

Walker, Anthony R. 1974. "The Lahu of the Yunnan-Indochina borderlands: An Introduction." *Folk Copenhagen*, nos. 16/17:329–344.

———. 1986. *Farmers in the Hills: Ethnographic Notes on the Upland Peoples of North Thailand*. Singapore: Suvarnabhumi Books.

———. 1992. *The Highland Heritage*. Singapore: Suvarnabhumi Books.

———. 1994. "'Ca Suh Aw_ Ca Ve': Eating the New Rice among the Lahu Nyi (Red Lahu) in North Thailand." *Contributions to Southeast Asian Ethnography* 10:63–90.

Wang, T'ung-hui. 1936. *Hua-lan Yao She-hui Tsu-chih* [The Social Organization of the Hua-lan Yao]. Shanghai: Special Government Research Publication.

Wang, Zhusheng. 1997. *The Jingpo: Kachin of the Yunnan Plateau*. Tempe, Ariz.: Arizona State University Program for Southeast Asian Studies.

Wu Che-Lin and Ch'en Kuo-chün. 1942. *Kuei-chou Miao-I She-hui Yen-chiu* [Studies of Miao-I Societies in Keichow]. Kweiyang, China: Wen-t'ung Book Co.

Xia Jian Feng. 1992. *From the Yues to the Thais*. Beijing: Foreign Press.

Xiao, Gen. 1995. *Love Through Reed-Pipe Wind and Mouth-String: The Lahus*. Kunming: Yunnan Education Publishing House.

Xiong, M., and N. D. Donnelly. 1986. "My Life in Laos." In the *Hmong World*, ed. Brenda Johns and David Strecker. New Haven, Conn.: Council on Southeast Asia Studies.

Xu Biao, Wang Yin-tao, and Ma Ji-kang. 2001. "Computerized Craniofacial Measurements Study of Bai Nationality in Yunnan." *Acta anthropologica sinica* 20 (2):125–129.

Yang Guocai. 1995. *Daughters of Mount Changshan and Erhai Lake: The Bais*. Kunming: Yunnan Education Publishing House.

Yang Shijie. 1995. *Ethnic Flavor in a Multi-Cultural World: The Yis*. Kunming: Yunnan Education Publishing House.

Zhao Jie. 1995. *The Restless Female Souls: The Junuos*. Kunming: Yunnan Education Publishing House.

Zheng Hai and Yin Haitao. 1995. *The Backbone of a Nationality: The Pumis*. Kunming: Yunnan Education Publishing House.

Zheng Xiaoyun Yu Tao. 1995. *Women Bathed in Holy Water: The Dais*. Kunming: Yunnan Education Publishing House.

Zhou Hong. 1995. *Rainbow Across Rivers and Lakes: The Shuis*. Kunming: Yunnan Education Publishing House.

Zhou Mingqi. 1995. *Women Not to Be Bound in Waistbands: The Deangs*. Kunming: Yunnan Education Publishing House.

Anthropological Analyses

Aroonrut, Wichienkeeo. 2002. " 'Lua Leading Dogs, Toting 'Chaek', Carrying Chickens': Some Comments." In *Inter-ethnic Relations in the Making of Mainland Southeast Asia and Southwestern China*, ed. Yukio Hayashi and Aroonrut Wichienkeeo. Chiang Rai, [Thailand]: Center for Ethnic Studies, Rajabhat Institute; Kyoto: Center for Southeast Asian Studies, Kyoto University.

Beauclair, Inez de. 1956. "Ethnic Group." In *General Handbook of China*, ed. Hellmut Wilhem. Subcontractor's Monograph no. 55. New Haven, Conn.: Human Relations Area Files (mimeographed).

Cam Trong. 1997. "What Has Been Achieved by Ethnology on the Tai Dam and Tai Khaao and How to Continue Research." *Tai Culture: International Review on Tai Cultural Studies* [Berlin] 2 (1):103–111.

Chesnov, Ya V. 1976. "On the Social Order of the Kachin [in Russian and English]; Comment on 'Situational Logic, Social Structure, and Highland Burma', by J. I. Prattis." *Current Anthropology* 17 (2):348–349.

Condominas, Georges. 1957. *Nous avons mangé la forêt de la Pierre-Génie Gôo*. Paris: Mercure de France.

Delang, Claudio, ed. 2003. *Living at the Edge of Thai Society: The Karen in the Highlands of Northern Thailand*. Routledge Curzon Studies on South East Asia. New York: Routledge Curzon.

Dournes, Jacques. 1978. *Forêt Femme Folie. Une traversée de l'imaginaire Jörai*. Paris: Aubier-Montaigne.

Durrenberger, E. Paul. 1977. "Lisu Etiological Categories." *Bijdragen tot de taal- land- en volkenkunde* 133 (1):90–9.

——. 1983. "Changes in a Shan Village." In *Highlanders of Thailand*, ed. John McKinnon and Wanat Bhruksasri. Kuala Lumpur: Oxford University Press.

Evans, Grant. 2000. "Transformation of Jinghong, Xishuangbanna, PRC." In *Where China Meets Southeast Asia: Social & Cultural Change in the Border*

Regions, ed. Grant Evans, Chris Hutton, and Khun Eng Kuah. New York: St. Martin's Press; Singapore: Institute of Southeast Asian Studies.

Formoso, Bernard. 2002. "Snake-Prince, the Impossible Metamorphosis: Bad Death, Kingship and Autochtony among the Lao and the Tai Lu. [in French]." *Archives de Sciences Sociales des Religions* 47 (119):127–145.

Friedman, Jonathan. 1975. "Dynamics and Transformations of a Tribal System: The Kachin Example [in French]." *L'Homme* 15 (1):63–98.

———. 1979. *System, Structure, And Contradiction: The Evolution of Asiatic Social Formations*. Walnut Creek, Calif.: Altamira.

Geddes, William R. 1976. *Migrants of the Mountains: The Cultural Ecology of the Blue Miao (Hmong Njua) of Thailand*. Oxford: The Clarendon Press.

Harrel, Stevan ed. 2001. *Perspectives on the Yi of Southwest China (Studies on China)*. Berkeley: University of California Press.

Harrel, Stevan, and Ma Erzi Bamo Oubumo. 2000. *Mountain Patterns: The Survival of Nuosu Culture in China*. Seattle, Wash.: University of Washington Press.

Hickey, Gerald C. 1958. "Social System of Northern Vietnam." Ph.D. dissertation, Anthropology Department, University of Chicago.

———. 1988. *Kingdom in the Morning Mist. Mayrena in the Highlands of Vietnam*. Philadelphia: University of Pennsylvania Press.

Hua, Cai, and Asti Hustvedt. 2003. *A Society without Fathers or Husbands: The Na of China*. Cambridge, Mass.: Zone Books.

Hubert-Bare, Annie. 1985. *L'alimentation dans un village Yao de Thaïlande du Nord: de l'au-delà au cuisiné*. Paris: Centre National de la Recherche Scientifique.

Iijima, Shigeru. 1965. "Cultural Change among the Hill Karens in Northern Thailand." *Asian Survey* 5 (8):417–423.

———. 1979. "Ethnic Identity and Sociocultural Change among Sgaw Karen in Northern Thailand." In *Ethnic Adaptation and Identity: The Karen on the Thai Frontier with Burma*, ed. Charles F.Keyes. Philadelphia: Institute for the Study of Human Issues.

Ishikawa, N. 1992. "Ethnography and Theory: Highland Burma and Anthropologies 1954–1982." *Japanese Journal of Ethnology* 57 (1):40–53.

Johns, B., and D. Strecker. 1986. *The Hmong World*. New Haven, Conn.: Council on Southeast Asian Studies, Yale Center for International and Area Studies.

Jones, Delmos J. 1971. "Social Responsibility and the Belief in Basic Research: An Example from Thailand." *Current Anthropology* 12 (3):347–350.

Jonsson, Hjorleifur. 2000. "Traditional Tribal What? Sports Culture and the State in the Northern Hills of Thailand." In *Turbulent Times and Enduring Peoples: Mountain Minorities in the South-East Asian Massif*, ed. Jean Michaud. London: Curzon.

———. 2001a. "Does the House Hold?: History and the Shape of Mien (Yao) Society." *Ethnohistory* 48 (4):613–654.

———. 2001b. "Serious Fun: Minority Cultural Dynamics and National Integration in Thailand." *American Ethnologist* 28 (1):151–178.

———. 2003. "Mien through Sports and Culture: Mobilizing Minority Identity in Thailand." *Ethnos* 68 (3):317–340.

Kandre, Peter. 1967. "Autonomy and Integration of Social Systems: The Iu Mien Mountain Population and Their Neighbors." In *Southeast Asian Tribes, Minorities and Nations*, ed. Peter Kundaster. Princeton, N.J.: Princeton University Press.

———. 1991. "Passing Through the Countries, Years and Life." In *Yao of South China*, ed. Jacques Lemoine and Chiao Chen., Recent International Studies. Paris: Pangu.

Kotaro, Matsumoto. 1985. "Social Adaptation of the Yao in Southwest China." *Japanese journal of ethnology* 50:52–66.

Leach, Edmund Ronald. 1969. "'Kachin' and 'Haka Chin': A Rejoinder to Levi-Strauss." *Man NS* 4 (2):277–285.

———. 1986 [1954]. *Political Systems of Highland Burma: A Study of Kachin Social Structure*. 4th ed. Monographs on Social Anthropology, No 44. London: Athlone Press.

Lefferts, H. Leedom, Jr. 1990. "The Cultures of Boxes: Information Flow and Social Organization among the Northeast Thai and Lao." *Crossroads* 5 (1):59–68.

Lehman, Frank K. 1963. *The Structure of Chin Society: A Tribal of Burma Adapted to a Non-Western Civilization*. Illinois Studies in Anthropology, No.3. Urbana: University of Illinois Press.

Litzinger, Ralph A. 2000. *Other Chinas: The Yao and the Politics of National Belonging*. Durham, N.C.: Duke University Press.

Moerman, Micheal. 1993. "Ariadne's Thread and Indra's Net: Reflections on Ethnography, Ethnicity, Identity, Culture, and Interaction." *Research on Language & Social Interaction* 26 (1):85–98.

Mueggler, Erik. 1998. "Procreative Metaphor and Productive Unity in an Yi Headmanship." *Journal of the Royal Anthropological Institute* 4 (2):235–253.

———. 2001. *The Age of Wild Ghosts. Memory, Violence, and Place in Southwest China*. Berkeley: University of California Press.

Robinne, François. 2000a. "Emergence of a Leading Group: A Case Study of the Inter-Ethnic Relationships in the Southern Shan States." In *Turbulent Times and Enduring Peoples: Mountain Minorities in the South-East Asian Massif*, ed. Jean Michaud. London: Curzon.

———. 2000b. *Fils et maîtres du Lac. Relations interethniques dans l'Etat Shan de Birmanie*. Paris: CNRS-Maison des Sciences de l'Homme.

Salemink, Oscar. 2003. *The Ethnography of Vietnam's Central Highlanders*. Honolulu: University of Hawaii Press.

Schein, Louisa. 2000. *Minority Rules: The Miao and the Feminine in China's Cultural Politics (Body, Commodity, Text)*. Durham, N.C.: Duke University Press.

Spiro, Melford E. 1977. *Kinship and Marriage in Burma: A Cultural and Psychodynamic Analysis*. Berkeley: University of California Press.

Tapp, Nicholas. 1989. *Sovereignty and Rebellion: The White Hmong of Northern Thailand*. Singapore, New York: Oxford University Press.

———. 2001. *The Hmong of China: Context, Agency and the Imaginary*. Leiden, The Netherlands: Brill Academic Publishers.

———. 2002. "Cultural Accommodations in Southwest China: The 'Han Miao' and Problems in the Ethnography of the Hmong." *Asian Folklore Studies* [Nagoya, Japan] 61 (1):77.

Trankell, Ing-Britt. 1995. *Cooking, Care and Domestication: A Culinary Ethnography of the Tai Yong, Northern Thailand*. Uppsala, Sweden: Uppsala University.

Yang, Dao. 1992. "The Hmong: Enduring Traditions." In *Minority Cultures of Laos: Kammu, Lua', Lahu, Hmong and Mien*, ed. Judy Lewis. Rancho Cordova, Calif.: Southeast Asian Community Resource Center, Folsom Cordova Unified School District.

Zheng Xiaoyun. 2002. "The Hua Yao Dai and the Upper Reaches of the Red River: Their Culture and Its Changes in the Contemporary Age." *Bulletin of the National Museum of Ethnology* [Osaka] 26 (3):449–472.

Identity and Ethnicity

Andrianoff, David I. 1979. "The Effect of the Laotian Conflict on Meo Ethnic Identity." In *Nationalism and the Crises of Ethnic Minorities in Asia*, ed. Tai S. Kang. Westport, Conn.: Greenwood Press.

Baranovitch, Nimrod. 2001. "Between Alterity and Identity: New Voices of Minority People in China." *Modern China* 27 (3):359.

Bradley, David. 1983. "Identity: The Persistence of Minority Groups." In *Highlanders of Thailand*, ed. John McKinnon and Wanat Bhruksasri. Kuala Lumpur: Oxford University Press.

Cheung, Siu-Woo. 2002. "Appropriating Alterity: Liang Juwu's Writings on Miao Identity." *Bulletin of the Department of Anthropology* [Taiwan] 59:42–71.

Chiao, Chien, and Nicholas Tapp, eds. 1989. *Ethnicity and Ethnic Groups in China*. New Asia Academic Bulletin Vol. 111. Hong Kong: University of Hong Kong.

Cohen, Erik. 1992. "Who Are the Chao Khao? Hill Tribe Postcards from Northern Thailand." *International Journal of the Sociology of Language* 98:101–125.

Fernando, Tissa. 1982. "Ethnic Adaptation and Identity: The Karen on the Thai Frontier with Burma." *Journal of Developing Areas* 17 (1):130–131.

Gladney, Dru C. 1997. *Ethnic Identity in China: The Making of a Muslim Minority Nationality*. 1st ed. Belmont, Calif.: Wadsworth Publishing.

Hamilton, James W. 1981. "Ethnic Adaptation and Identity: The Karen on the Thai Frontier with Burma." *American Anthropologist* 83 4:952–955.

Hayami, Yoko. 1993. "To Be Karen and to Be Cool: Community, Morality and Identity among Sgaw Karen in Northern Thailand." *Cahiers des Sciences Humaines* 29 (4):747–762.

Hinton, Peter. 1983. "Do the Karen Really Exist?" In *Highlanders of Thailand*, ed. John McKinnon and Wanat Bhruksasri. Kuala Lumpur: Oxford University Press.

Hsieh, Shih-Chung. 1995. "On the Dynamics of Tai/Dai-Lue Ethnicity." In *Cultural Encounters on China's Ethnic Frontiers*, ed. Harrell Stevan. Seattle and London: University of Washington Press.

Jonsson, Hjorleifur. 2000. "Yao Minority Identity and the Location of Difference in the South China Borderlands." *Ethnos* 65 (1):58–82.

Kammerer, Cornelia Ann. 1988. "Territorial Imperatives, Akha Ethnic Identity and Thailand's National Integration." In *Ethnicities and Nations*, ed. R. Rudieri, F. Pellizzi, and S. Tambiah. Houston: University of Texas Press.

Kandre, Peter. 1976. "Yao (Iu Mien) Supernaturalism, Language and Ethnicity." In *Changing Identities in Modern Southeast Asia*, ed. David J. Banks. The Hague: Mouton.

Keyes, Charles F. 1984. "Tribal Ethnicity and the State in Vietnam." *American Ethnologist* 11 (1):176–182.

——. 1995. "Who Are the Tai? Reflections on the Invention of Identities." In *Ethnic Identity: Creation, Conflict, and Accommodation*, 3d ed., ed. Lola Romanucci-Ross and George A. De Vos. Walnut Creek, Calif.: Altamira Press.

Keyes, Charles F., ed. 1979. *Ethnic Adaptation and Identity: The Karen on the Thai Frontier with Burma*. Philadelphia: Institute for the Study of Human Issues.

Kirsch, Thomas A. 1982. "Ethnic Adaptation and Identity: The Karen on the Thai Frontier with Burma." *International Migration Review* 16 (3):691–692.

Kiyoshi, H. 1998. "Cross-border Networks and Dynamics of Ethnicity: A Case of the Tai Lue in Xishuangbanna Dai Autonomous Prefecture, Yunnan Province." *Southeast Asian Studies* [Kyoto] 35 (4):620–643.

Kunstadter, Peter. 1979. "Ethnic Group, Category, and Identity: Karen in Northern Thailand." In *Ethnic Adaptation and Identity: The Karen and the Thai Frontier with Burma*, ed. C. F. Keyes. Philadelphia: Institute for the Study of Human Issues.

Lee, Maryjo Benton. 2001. *Ethnicity, Education and Empowerment: How Minority Students in Southwest China Construct Identities*. Hampshire, UK: Ashgate Publishing.

Litzinger, Ralph A. 1998. "Memory Work: Reconstituting the Ethnic in Post-Mao China." *Cultural Anthropology* 13 (2):224–255.

Moerman, Micheal. 1965. "Ethnic Identification in a Complex Civilization: Who Are the Lu?" *American Anthropologist* 67 (5, I):1215–1230.

Nguyen, Thi Mai Hong. 1994. "Ethnic Identity as Classificatory Criterium of the Yao Sub-groups." *Etnograficheskoe obozrenie* 3:41–50.

Peters, H. A. 2002. "Ethnicity along China's Southwestern Frontier." *Journal of East Asian Archeology* 3 (1–2):75–102.

Proschan, Frank. 1997. "'We Are All Kmhmu, Just the Same': Ethnonyms, Ethnic Identities, and Ethnic Groups." *American Ethnologist* 24 (1):91–113.

———. 2001. "Peoples of the Gourd: Imagined Ethnicities in Highland Southeast Asia." *Journal of Asian Studies* 60 (4):999–1032.

Santasombat, Yos. 2001. *Lak Chang. A Reconstruction of Tai Identity in Daikong*. Canberra, Australia: Pandanus Books.

Schein, Louisa. 1989. "The Dynamics of Cultural Revival among the Miao in Guizhou." In *Ethnicity and Ethnic Groups in China*, ed. Chiao Chien and Nicolas Tapp. New Asia Academic Bulletin, Vol. 111. China: University of Hong Kong.

Takatani, Michio. 1998. "Who Are the Shan?: An Ethnological Perspective." *Southeast Asian Studies* 35 (4):644–662.

Tefft, S. K. 1999. "Perspectives on Panethnogenesis: The Case of the Montagnards." *Sociological Spectrum* 19 (4):387–400.

Toyota, Mika. 1998. "Urban Migration and Cross-border Networks: A Deconstruction of the Akha Identity in Chiang Mai." *Southeast Asian Studies* 35 (4):803–829.

———. 2003. "Contested Chinese Identities among Ethnic Minorities in the China, Burma and Thai Borderlands." *Ethnic & Racial Studies* 26 (2):301–320.

Turton, Andrew, ed. 2000. *Civility and Savagery: Social Identity in Tai States*. London: Curzon.

4. HISTORY

In China

Beauclair, Inez de. 1946. "The Keh Lao of Kweichow and Their History According to Chinese Records." *Studia Serica* 5:1–44.

Cai, Kui. 1997. "Relationship Changes between Lowlander and Hill Tribes in Xishuangbanna, P.R. China [includes Dai, Hani and Jinuo communities]." *Asia Pacific Viewpoint* 38 (2):161–167.

Cheung, Siu-Woo. 1998. "'Miao Rebellion' and the Discursive Construction of Ethnic Identity." *Bulletin of the Department of Anthropology* [Taiwan] 53:13–56.

Collective. 1980. "Discussion of Problems on the History of the Yaozu and the Bouyei." *Minzu Yanjiu* 3:62–63.

Diamond, Norma. 1995. "Defining the Miao: Ming, Qing and Contemporary Views." In *Cultural Encounters on China's Ethnic Frontiers*, ed. S. Harrell. Seattle: University of Washington Press.

Edkins, J. 1870. "The Miao Tsi Tribes: Their History." *The Chinese Recorder and Missionary Journal* 3:33–36, 74–76.

Fabre, Guilhem. 2000. "La Chine des oubliés: voyage au centre du Guizhou." In *Où va la Chine? dix ans après la répression de Tien'anmen vingt ans après le lancement des réformes économiques*, ed. Jean-Jacques Gandini. Paris: Édition du Félin.

Feng Han Yi, and J. K. Shyrock. 1938. "The Historical Origins of the Lolo." *Harvard Journal of Asiatic Studies* 3:103–127.

Fitzgerald, C. P. 1972. *The Southern Expansion of the Chinese People*. New York: Praeger.

Gernet, Jacques. 1982. *A History of Chinese Civilization*. 2d ed. Cambridge: Cambridge University Press.

Gustafsson, Bjorn, and Li Shi. 2003. "The Ethnic Minority-Majority Income Gap in Rural China during Transition." *Economic Development and Cultural Change* [Chicago] 51 (4):805.

Harrell, Stevan. 1995. "The History of the Yi." In *Cultural Encounters on China's Ethnic Frontiers*, ed. S. Harrell. Seattle: University of Washington Press.

Harrell, Stevan, and Li Yongxiang. 2003. "The History of the Yi, Part II." *Modern China* 29 (3):362–396.

Jenks, Robert Darrah. 1994. *Insurgency and Social Disorder in Guizhou: The "Miao" Rebellion, 1854–1873*. Honolulu: University of Hawaii Press.

Kunstadter, Peter. 1967. "China: Introduction." In *Southeast Asian Tribes, Minorities and Nations,* Vol 1., ed. P. Kunstadter. Princeton: Princeton University Press.

Lemoine, Jacques. 1987. "Tai Lue Historical Relation with China and the Shaping of the Sipsong Panna Political System." In *Proceedings of the 3rd International Conference on Thai Studies, 3–6 July 1987*, Vol. 3. Part 1., ed. A. Buller. Camberra: Australian National University.

Lombard-Salmon, Claudine. 1972. *Un exemple d'acculturation chinoise: la province du Guizhou au XVIIIe siècle*. Publication de l'École Française d'Extrême-Orient, LXXXIV. Paris: l'École Française d'Extrême-Orient.

Ma Touan Lin. 1883. *Ethnographie des peuples étrangers à la Chine. XIIIe siècle, traduit du chinois et commenté par le Marquis d'Hervey de Saint-Denys*. Paris: Ernest Leroux.

Pollard, Samuel. 1919. *The Story of the Miao*. London: Henry Hooks.

Rock, Joseph F. 1947. *The Ancient Na-khi Kingdom of Southwest China.* 2 vols. Harvard-Yanching Institute Monograph Series, 8 and 9. Cambridge: Harvard University Press.

Sutton, Donald S. 2003. "Violence and Ethnicity on a Qing Colonial Frontier: Customary and Statutory Law in the Eighteenth-Century Miao Pale." *Modern Asian Studies* 37 (1):41–80.

Tapp, Nicholas, and Don Cohn. 2003. *The Tribal Peoples of Southwest China.* Bangkok: White Lotus.

Teng, Su Yu. 1971. *The Taiping Rebellion and the Western Powers: A Comprehensive Survey.* Taipei: Rainbow-Bridge.

Wang, Adine. 1933. *La Chine et le problème de l'opium.* Paris: A.Pedone Editeur.

Wiens, Herold J. 1954. *China's March toward the Tropics.* Hamden, Conn.: Shoe String Press.

Yan Liu, Wang Yi, Liu Biao, and Liu Pengtao. 1999. *An On-The-Spot Investigation into the Southernly Emigration of the Dai Race.* Kunming: Xishuangbanna Autonomous Prefecture Nationality Research Institute.

In the Peninsula

Adams, Nel. 2000. "Remembering the Tai of the Shan States." *International Review on Tai Cultural Studies* [Berlin] 5 (1):143–162.

Alleton. Isabelle. 1981. "Les Hmong aux confins de la Chine et du Vietnam: La révolte du 'Fou' (1918–1922)." In *Histoire de l'Asie du Sud-Est: Révoltes, réformes, révolutions*, ed. Pierre Brocheux. Lille: Presses universitaires de Lille.

Aung-Thwin, Michael. 1996. "The Myth of the 'Three Shan Brothers' and the Ava Period in Burmese History." *Journal of Asian Studies* [Ann Arbor, Mich.] 55 (4):881–901.

Bertrais, Yves. 1985. *Origins of the Hmong according to Vinai Confraternity* [in Hmong]. Javouhey, [Guyane Francaise]: Association Communauté Hmong.

Bourotte, Bernard. 1955. "Essai d'histoire des populations montagnardes du Sud-Indochinois jusqu'à 1945." *Bulletin de la Société des Études Indochinoises* 30:1–133.

Bruneau, Michel. 1974. "Ethnies, peuplement et organisation de l'espace en Thaïlande septentrionale." *Cahiers d'Outre-mer* 108:356–390.

Cam, Trong. 2000. "What Can We Learn from the Tai Ethnic Groups' Names about Their Origin?" *Tai Culture: International Review on Tai Cultural Studies* 5 1:8–17.

Cam, Trong, and Nguyen Huong. 2001. "Les Thai noirs du Viet-Nam: repères historiques." *Péninsule*, no. 42:81–143.

Carthew, M. 1952. "The History of the Thai in Yunnan." *Journal of the Siam Society* 40 (I):1–38.

Chapuis, Edouard. 1996. *L'adieu aux Thais*. Paris: L'Harmattan.

Christie, Clive. 2000. "The Karens: Loyalism and Self-determination." In *Turbulent Times and Enduring Peoples. Mountain Minorities in the South-East Asian Massif*, ed. Jean Michaud. London: Curzon.

Cupet, Captain Pierre. 2001. *Among the Tribes of Southern Vietnam and Laos. 'Wild' Tribes & French Politics on the Siamese Border*. Bangkok: White Lotus.

Dassé, Martial. 1993. *Les guérillas en Asie du Sud-Est*. Paris: L'Harmattan.

Deporte, Commandant. 1940. "Les origines de la famille de Dèo-Van-Tri." *Bulletin des amis du Laos* 4:65–94.

Descours-Gatin, Chantal. 1992. *Quand l'opium finançait la colonisation en Indochine*. Paris: L'Harmattan.

Dhamaraso, Bhikkhu, and Virojano Bhikkhu. 1977. *The Historical Background and Tradition of the Meo*. Bangkok: Sukhsa Samphan.

Du Perron, P. C. 1954. "Etudes d'un peuplement Man Xanh-Y." *Bulletin de la Société des Études Indochinoises* 29:23–42.

Durand, Maurice. 1952. "Notes sur les pays tai de Phong-tho." *Bulletin de la Société des Études Indochinoises* 27:193–231.

Eudey, Ardith A. 1988. "Hmong Relocated in Northern Thailand." *Cultural Survival Quarterly* 12 (1):79–82.

Fall, Bernard. 1956. *The Viet-Minh Regime*. Ithaca, N.Y.: Cornell University Press.

——. 1965. *Les guerres d'Indochine*. Paris: Robert Laffont.

——. 1967. *Hell in a Very Small Place: The Siege of Dien Bien Phu*. New York: Da Capo Paperback.

Falvey, L. 2001. "Early Origins of Agriculture in Thailand." *Asian Agri-History* 5 (1):23–38.

Fistié, Pierre. 1985. *La Birmanie ou la quête de l'unité. Le problème de la cohésion nationale dans la Birmanie contemporaine et sa perspective historique*. Publications de l'Ecole Française d'Extrême-Orient, 139. Paris: l'Ecole Française d'Extrême-Orient.

Forbes, Andrew D. W. 1988a. "Red, Black, Yellow and Striped Banners: The Siamese Military Expedition to Laos and Sipsongchuthai of 1884–85." *Journal of the Siam Society* 76:134–144.

——. 1988b. "The Role of Hui Muslims in the Traditional Caravan Trade between Yunnan and Thailand." In *Marchands et hommes d'affaires asiatiques dans l'Océan Indien et la Mer de Chine 13e-20e siècles*, ed. Denis Lombard and J. Aubin. Paris: EHESS.

Garnier, Francis. 1873. *Voyage d'exploration en Indo-Chine*. Paris: Librairie Hachette.

Geusau, Leo, and G. M. von Alting. 2000. "Akha Internal History: Marginalization and the Ethnic Alliance System." In *Civility and Savagery*, ed. Andrew Turton. Norwich, UK: Curran Publishing House.

Grandstaff, T. B. 1979. "The Hmong, Opium and the Haw: Speculation on the Origin of Their Association." *Journal of the Siam Society* 67 (2):70–79.

Guillemet, Docteur, and Capitaine O'Kelly. 1916. *En colonne dans le Haut-Laos*. Hanoi: Imprimerie d'Extrême-Orient.

Harmand, F. J. 1997 [1879]. *Laos and the Hilltribes of Indochina: Journeys to the Boloven Plateau, from Bassac to Hue through Laos, and to the Origins of the Thai*. Translated from French edition of 1879. Bangkok: White Lotus.

Hickey, Gerald C. 1982a. *Free in the Forest: Ethnohistory of the Vietnamese Central Highlands, 1954–1976*. New Haven, Conn.: Yale University Press.

———. 1982b. *Sons of the Mountains: Ethnohistory of the Vietnamese Central Highlands to 1954*. New Haven, Conn.: Yale University Press.

———. 1993. *Shattered World: Adaptation and Survival among Vietnam's Highland Peoples during the Vietnam War*. Philadelphia: University of Pennsylvania Press.

Hovemyr, Anders P. 1989. *In Search of the Karen King: A Study in Karen Identity with Special Reference to 19th Century Karen Evangelism in Northern Thailand*. Studia missionalia Upsaliensia, 49. Uppsala, Sweden: S. Academiae Upsaliensis.

Htoo, Aung. 2000. "Ethnic Issues in Burma: Part 1. the Fourth Burman Empire." *Legal Issues on Burma Journal (Burma Lawyers' Council)*, no. 5:1–12.

Jame, Raymond. 1904. "Les provinces du Tonkin: Le Chàu de Van-chan." *Revue Indo-Chinoise* 30 mai, pp. 717–725.

Johnson, Stephen T. 1993. "Laos in 1992: Succession and Consolidation." *Asian Survey, (A Survey of Asia in 1992: Part I)* 33 (1):75–82.

Kunstadter, Peter. 1967a. "Laos: Introduction." In *Southeast Asian Tribes, Minorities and Nations*, Vol 1., ed. P. Kunstadter. Princeton, N.J.: Princeton University Press.

———. 1967b. "Thailand: Introduction." In *Southeast Asian Tribes, Minorities and Nations*, Vol 1., ed. P. Kunstadter. Princeton, N.J.: Princeton University Press.

———. 1967c. "Vietnam: Introduction." In *Southeast Asian Tribes, Minorities and Nations*, Vol 2., ed. P. Kunstadter. Princeton, N.J.: Princeton University Press.

Le Thàn Khôi. 1971. *Histoire du Viêt Nam des origines à 1858*. Paris: Sudestasie.

Lebar, Frank M. 1967. "Observations on the Movement of Khmu' into North Thailand." *Journal of the Siam Society* 53:61–79.

LeFailler, Philippe. 1995. "Le 'coût social' de l'opium au Vietnam. La problématique des drogues dans le philtre de l'histoire." *Journal Asiatique* CCLXXXIII (1):239–264.

McAleavy, Henry. 1968. *Black Flags in Vietnam: The Story of a Chinese Intervention*. London: George Allen and Unwin.

McAlister Jr, John T. 1967. "Mountain Minorities and the Vietminh: A Key to the Indochina War." In *Southeast Asian Tribes, Minorities and Nations*, ed. Peter Kunstadter. Princeton, N.J.: Princeton University Press.

Michaud, Jean. 2004. "French Missionary Expansion in Colonial Upper-Tonkin." *Journal of Southeast Asian Studies* 35 (2):287–310.

———. 2000. "The Montagnards and the State in Northern Vietnam from 1802 to 1975: A Historical Overview." *Ethnohistory* 47 (2):333–368.

Mottin, Jean. 1980. *History of the Hmong*. Bangkok: Odeon Store.

Nguyen The Anh. 1993. "L'image de la piraterie tonkinoise dans la litterature coloniale." In *Rêver l'Asie: Exotisme et litterature coloniale aux Indes, en Indochine et en Insulinde*, ed. Denys Lombard. Paris: Ecole des Hautes Etudes en Sciences Sociales.

Nguyen, Trac Di. 1969. *Tim hieu phong-trao tranh-dau F.U.L.R.O. (1958–1969)*. Saigon: Bo Phat-trien Sac Toc.

Nugent, David. 1982. "Closed Systems and Contradiction: The Kachin in and out of History." *Man* 17:508–527.

Raquez, A. 1902. *Pages Laotiennes: le Haut-Laos—le Moyen-Laos—le Bas-Laos*. Hanoi: F.-H. Schneider.

Raquez, A., and Cam. 1904. "Mémoires de Déo-Van-Tri." *Revue Indochinoise*, no. 4:256–275.

Renard, Ronald. 1988. "Minorities in Burmese History." In *Ethnic Conflict in Buddhist Societies: Sri Lanka-Thailand-Burma*, ed. K. M De Silva, Pensri Duke, Ellen S. Goldberg, and Nathan Katz. London: Pinter.

Salemink, Oscar. 1991. "Mois and Maquis: The Invention and Appropriation of Vietnam's Montagnards from Sabatier to the CIA." In *Colonial Situations: Essays on the Contextualization of Ethnographic Knowledge*, ed. G. Stocking. History of Anthropology, 7. Madison: University of Wisconsin Press.

Savina, François Marie. 1930 [1924]. *Histoire des Miao*. Hong Kong: Imprimerie des Missions Etrangeres.

Trinquier, Roger. 1976. *Les maquis d'Indochine 1952–54*. Paris: Editions Albatros.

Wakin, Eric. 1992. *Anthropology Goes to War: Professional Ethics and Counterinsurgency in Thailand*. Center for Southeast Asian Studies, Monograph no. 7. Madison: University of Wisconsin.

Warner, Roger. 1995. *Back Fire: The CIA's Secret War in Laos and Its Link to the War in Vietnam*. New York: Simon & Shuster.

Winichakul, Thongchai. 1994. *Siam Mapped: A History of the Geo-body of a Nation*. Chiang Mai: Silkworm Books.

Zin, Min. 2000. "Karen History: In Their Own Words." *The Irrawaddy* 8 (10):1–4.

Migrations

Akira, Yoshino. 1998. "Migration by Swiddeners and Migration by Ancestors: The Ethnicity and Migration of the Mien of Northern Thailand." *Southeast Asian Studies* [Kyoto] 35 (4):759–776.

Ayabe, Masao. 1998 "National Boundaries and Ethnic Minorities: Migration and National Boundary Consciousness among the Lisu of Northern Thailand." *Southeast Asian Studies* 35 (4):777–802.

Bulk, Jac D. 1996. "Hmong on the Move: Understanding Secondary Migration." *Ethnic Studies Review: The Journal of the National Association for Ethnic Studies* [Tempe, Ariz.] 19 (1):7–28.

Chen, Lufan and Du Yuting. 1989. "Did Kublai Khan's Conquest of the Dali Kingdom Give Rise to the Mass Migration of the Thai People to the South." *Journal of the Siam Society* 77 (1):33–41.

Culas, Christian. 2000. "Migrants, Runaways and Opium Growers: Origin of the Hmong in Laos and Siam in the Nineteenth and Early Twentieth Century." In *Turbulent Times and Enduring Peoples. Mountain Minorities in the South-East Asian Massif*, ed. Jean Michaud. London: Curzon.

Culas, Christian, and Jean Michaud. 1997. "A Contribution to the Study of Hmong (Miao) Migrations and History." *Bijdragen Tot de Taal-, Land- en Volkenkunde* [Leiden] 153 (2):211–243.

Dessaint, Alain Y. 1971. "Lisu Migration in the Thai Highlands." *Ethnology* [Pittsburgh, Pa.] 10 (3):329–348.

———. 1972. "Lisu Settlement Patterns." *Journal of the Siam Society* [Bangkok] 60 (1):195–204.

Grundy-Warr, C., and Wong Siew Yin. 2002. "Geographies of Displacement: The Karenni and the Shan across the Myanmar-Thailand Border." *Singapore Journal of Tropical Geography* 22 (1):93–122.

Ito, M. 2003. "The Structure of Rural-Rural Migration of the Tay-Nung People: Ethnic Minorities' Networks in the Vietnamese Northeast Mountain Area." *Southeast Asian Studies* 40 (4):484–501.

Jonsson, Hjorleifur. 1999. "Moving House: Migration and the Place of the Household on the Thai Periphery." *Journal of the Siam Society* 87 (1–2):99–118.

Kacha-Ananda, Chob. 1983. "Yao Migration, Settlement and Land." In *Highlanders of Thailand*, ed. John McKinnon and Wanat Bhruksasri. Kuala Lumpur: Oxford University Press.

Mao, Youquan. 1989. *Inquiry on the Names, Identity and Migrations of the Hani*. Kunming, China: Yunnan Journal of Social Science.

Masao, A. 1998. "National Boundaries and Ethnic Minorities: Migration and National Boundary Consciousness among the Lisu of Northern Thailand." *Southeast Asian Studies* [Kyoto] 35 (4):777–802.

Platz, Roland. 1999. "Migration und ethnische Identitat der Sgaw-Karen und Lisu in Nordthailand." *Internationales Asienforum (International Quarterly) for Asian Studies* [Freiburg i.B.] 30 (3–4):295–312.

Ruey, Yih-fu. 1962. "The Miao: Their Origin and Southern Migration." *Second Biennial Conference Proceedings.* Taipei: International Association of Historians of Asia.

Sai, Aung Tun. 2000. "The Tai Ethnic Migration and Settlement in Myanmar." In *Dynamics of Ethnic Cultures across National Boundaries in Southwestern China and Mainland Southeast Asia: Relations, Societies and Languages*, ed. Yukio Hayashi and Yang Guangyuan. Chiang Mai, [Thailand]: Lanna Cultural Center, Rajabhat Institute Chiang Mai; Kyoto: Center for Southeast Asian Studies, Kyoto University.

Shi, Junchao. 1991. "Lowland and Highland Civilizations: Research on the Question of Migrations of the Hani." In *Research on Hani History.* Kunming: Nationalities Publishing House.

———. 1988. "On Ethno-History: Hani Oral History of Migration (Hania-Peizongpopo)." In *Nationality Studies.* Beijing: Nationalities Publishing House.

Waters, Tony. 1990. "Adaptation and Migration among the Mien People of Southeast Asia." *Ethnic Groups* 8 (2):127–141.

Refugees and Diasporas

Ajchenbaum, Yves, and Jean-Pierre Hassoun. 1980. *Histoire d'insertion des groupes familiaux hmong réfugiés en France.* Paris: ADRES.

Cha, Dia, and Cathy A. Small. 1994. "Policy Lessons from Lao and Hmong Women in Thai Refugee Camps." *World Development* [Oxford] 22 (7):1045.

Chan, Sucheng. 1994. "Hmong Life Stories." In *New Visions in Asian American Studies: Diversity, Community, Power*, ed. Franklin Ng et al. Pullman: Washington State University Press.

Chantavanich, S., et al. 1992. *The Lao Returnees in the Voluntary Repatriation Programme from Thailand.* Occasional Paper Series, no. 3. Bangkok: Indochinese Refugee Information Center, Institute of Asian Studies, Chulalongkorn University.

Chantavanich, Supang, and Bruce E. Reynolds, eds. 1988. *Indochinese Refugees: Asylum and Resettlement.* Asian Studies Monograph, No. 039. Bangkok: Institute of Asian Studies, Chulalongkorn University.

Condominas, Georges, and Richard Pottier. 1984. *Les réfugiés originaires de l'Asie du Sud-Est.* Coll. des Rapports Officiels. Paris, la Documentation Française.

Conroy, T. P. 1990. *Highland Lao Refugees: Repatriation and Resettlement Preferences in Ban Vanai Camp, Thailand.* Bangkok: T. P Controy.

Cooper, Robert G. 1986. "The Hmong of Laos: Economic Factors in Refugee Exodus and Return." In the *Hmong in Transition*, ed. G. L. Hendricks, B. T. Downing, and A. S. Deinard. New York: Center for Migration Studies of New York.

Donnelly, Nancy. 1994. *Changing Lives of Refugee Hmong Women*. Seattle: University of Washington Press.

Downing, Bruce T., and Douglas P. Olney. 1982. *The Hmong in the West: Observations and Reports: Papers of the 1981 Hmong Research Conference, University of Minnesota*, Minneapolis, Minn.: SARS Projects, CURA, University of Minnesota.

Dudley, Sandra. 1999. "Aspects of Research with Karenni Refugees in Thailand." *Bulletin of the International Committee on Urgent Anthropological and Ethnological Research* 39:165–184.

Hafner, J. A. 1985. "Lowland Lao and Hmong Refugees in Thailand: The Plight of Those Left Behind." *Disasters* 9 (2):83–91.

Hendricks, Glenn L., B. T. Dowring, and A. S. Deinard, eds. 1986. *The Hmong in Transition*. New York: Center for Migration Studies of New York.

Lanphier, C. M. 1993. "The Final Phase of Southest Asian Asylum? Some Unfinished Business." *Refuge*, September:3–7.

Lee, Gary Yia. 1990. *Refugees from Laos: Historical Background and Causes*. Available at http://hmongnet.org/hmong-au/refugee.htm.

Lemoine, Jacques. 1994. "Culture d'origine, culture d'accueil: À propos de l'intégration des réfugiés hmong et yao en France." *Péninsule* [Paris], no. 29:181–190.

Long, Lynellin D. 1993. *Ban Vinai: The Refugee Camp*. New York: Columbia University Press.

Salmon, S. 1990. "Transition from Refugee to Villager: An Experience with Hilltribes in Thailand." In *Back to a Future? Voluntary Repatriation of Indochinese Refugees and Displaced Persons in Thailand*, ed. L. Standley. Bangkok: Committee for the Coordination of Services to Displaced Persons in Thailand.

Ward, James T. 1967. "U.S. Aid to Hill Tribe Refugees in Laos." In *Southeast Asian Tribes, Minorities and Nations*, Vol. 1, ed. P. Kunstadter. Princeton, N.J.: Princeton University Press.

Tran, Peter. 2000. "Pastoral Response to Karenni Refugees." *Migration World Magazine* [Staten Island], 28 (3):33.

Vang, Pobzeb. 1991. *White Paper on the Murders and Persecution of the Hmong and Laotian Returnees in Laos: Submitted to the U.S. Congress and President*. Denver, Colo.: Lao Human Rights Council.

———. 1992. *White Paper on Forced Repatriation of Hmong Refugees from Thailand to Laos*. Denver, Colo.: Lao Human Rights Council.

———. 1993. *White Paper on Demonstrations of Hmong Refugees and Letters from the Napho and Ban Vinai Refugee Camps, Thailand to President Bill Clinton in 1993*. Denver, Colo.: Lao American Human Rights Council.

Waters, Tony. 1990. "Laotian Refugeeism, 1975–1988." In *Patterns of Migration in Southeast Asia*, ed. R. R. Reed. Berkeley: Centers for Southeast Asia Studies, International and Area Studies, University of California at Berkeley.

5. POLITICS

Acharya, Amitav, and Ananda Rajah, eds. 2004. *Reconceptualising Southeast Asia*. Portland, Oreg.: International Specialized Book Service.

Boudreau, Vince. 2004. *Resisting Dictatorship: Repression and Protest in Southeast Asia*. Cambridge, UK: Cambridge University Press.

Brown, David. 1988. "From Peripheral Communities to Ethnic Nations: Separatism in Southeast Asia." *Pacific Affairs* 61 (1):51–77.

Brown, David, and David B. Brown. 1993. *The State and Ethnic Politics in Southeast Asia (Politics in Asia)*. London: Routledge.

Colchester, Marcus, and Christian Erni, eds. 1999. *From Principles to Practice: Indigenous Peoples and Protected Areas in South and Southeast Asia*. 1st ed. IWGIA Document No. 97. Copenhagen: International Work Group for Indigenous Affairs.

Kang, Tai S. 1979. *Nationalism and the Crises of Ethnic Minorities in Asia*. Contributions in Sociology. Westport, Conn.: Greenwood Publishing Group.

Lim, Joo Jock, ed. 1984. *Armed Separatist Movements in Southeast Asia*. Singapore: Institute of Southeast Asian Studies.

Mayaram, Shail. 2003. *Against History, Against State: Counterperspectives from the Margin*. New York: Columbia University Press.

McCoy, Alfred W., et al. 1989. *The Politics of Heroin in Southeast Asia*. Singapore: Harper Torchbooks.

Sponsel, Leslie E., ed. 2000. *Endangered Peoples of Southeast and East Asia: Struggles to Survive and Thrive*. Endangered Peoples of the World Series. Westport, Conn., London: Greenwood Press.

Tonnesson, Stein, and Hans Antlov, eds. 1996. *Asian Forms of the Nation*. Nias Institute of Asian Studies, 23. London: Curzon.

Toshihiro, Y. 1998. "Maintaining the Link of Life into the Future: Relations between and within Ethnic Groups and between Ethnic Groups and the State in Northern Burma, Yunnan Province, China, and Northern Thailand." *Southeast Asian Studies* [Kyoto] 35 (4):874–897.

In China

Amat, Ismail. 1995. "The Ethnic Relations in China." In *Racial Identities in East Asia = Tung Ya chung tsu ren tung*, ed. Barry Sautman. Hong Kong: Division of Social Science, Hong Kong University of Science and Technology.

Bai, Yu. 1989. *The Cultural Drift of the Hani, Where Lords (Tu'ssi) Ruled*. Kunming: Nationalities Publishing House.

Berlie, Jean. 1998. *Sinisation*. Paris: Editions Guy Tredaniel.

Blum, Susan D. 2000. *Portraits of Primitives: Ordering Human Kinds in the Chinese Nation*. Lanham, Md.: Rowman & Littlefield Publishers.

Brown, Melissa J. 2002. "Local Government Agency: Manipulating Tujia Identity." *Modern China* 28 (3):362–395.

Brown, Melissa J., ed. 1996. *Negotiating Ethnicities in China and Taiwan*. China research monographs, no. 46. Berkeley: Institute of East Asian Studies; University of California, Berkeley, Center for Chinese Studies.

Connor, Walker. 1984. *The National Question in Marxist-Leninist Theory and Strategy*. Princeton, N.J.: Princeton University Press.

Croll, Elizabeth. 1993. "The Negotiation of Knowledge and Ignorance in China's Development Strategy." In *An Anthropological Critique of Development: The Growth of Ignorance*, dir. Mark Hobart. New York, London: Routledge.

Gjessing, Gutorm. 1956. "Chinese Anthropology and New China's Policy toward Her Minorities." *Acta Sociologica* 2:45–66.

Kaup, Katherine Palmer. 2000. *Creating the Zhuang: Ethnic Politics in China*. Boulder, Colo.: Lynne Rienner Publishers.

Lianjiang, Li. 2004. "Political Trust in Rural China." *Modern China* 30 (2):228–258.

McCarthy, Susan. 2000. "Ethno-Religious Mobilisation and Citizenship Discourse in the People's Republic of China." *Asian Ethnicity* 1 (2):107–116.

Moseley, G. V. R. 1973. *The Consolidation of the South China Frontier*. Berkeley: University of California Press.

Mueggler, Erik. 2002. "Dancing Fools: Politics of Culture and Place in a 'Traditional Nationality Festival'." *Modern China* 28 (1):3–38.

Oakes, Timothy S. 1999. "Bathing in the Far Village: Globalization, Transnational Capital, and the Cultural Politics of Modernity in China." *Positions* 7 (2):307–342.

Safran, William ed. 1998. *Nationalism and Ethnoregional Identities in China*. London: Franck Cass.

Sturgeon, J. C. 1997. "Claiming and Naming Resources on the Border of the State: Akha Strategies in China and Thailand." *Asia Pacific Viewpoint* 38 (2):131–144.

Tapp, Nicholas. 2000. "The Consuming or the Consumed? Virtual Hmong in China." *Asia Pacific Journal of Anthropology* [Canberra, Australia] 1 (2):73–101.

In the Peninsula

Andersen, Kirsten Ewers. 1979–1980. "Deference for the Elders and Control over the Younger among the Karen in Thailand." *Folk: Dansk Etnografisk Tidsskrift* [Copenhagen] 21–22:313–324.

Baffie, Jean. 1989. "Highlanders as Portrayed in Thai Penny-Horrible." In *Hill Tribes Today*, ed. John McKinnon and B.Vienne. Bangkok: White Lotus-ORSTOM.

Bernard, Patrick. 1988. *Karennis, les combattants de la spirale d'or*. Paris: L'Harmattan.

Bouchery, Pascal. 1988. "Les systèmes politiques Naga." *Journal Asiatique* 276 (3–4):285–334.

Bruneau, Michel. 1979. "Politique et stratégie du développement chez les Montagnards de la Thaïlande." *Espace Géographique* 8 (2):105–117.

Cam Trong. 1998. "Baan-muang: A Characteristic Feature of the Tai Social Structure." *Tai Culture: International Review on Tai Cultural Studies* [Berlin] 3 (2):12–26.

Chagnon, Jacqui, and Roger Rumpf. 1983. "Decades of Division for the Lao Hmong." *Southeast Asia Chronicle*, no. 91:10–15.

Chapman, Dean. *Karenni: Guerilla in Burma*. 1998. Neustadt, Germany: Umschau/Braus.

Checchi, F., G. Elder, M. Schafer, E. Drouhin,and D. Legros. 2003. "Consequences of Armed Conflict for an Ethnic Karen Population." *Lancet* 362 (9377):74–75.

Cheesman, Nick. 2002. "Seeing 'Karen' in the Union of Myanmar." *Asian Ethnicity* 3 (2):199–220.

Cohen, Erik. 1989. "International Politics and the Transformation of Folk Crafts—the Hmong (Meo) of Thailand and Laos." *Journal of the Siam Society* [Bangkok] 77 (1):69–82.

———. 1992. "The Growing Gap: Hill Tribe Image and Reality." *Pacific Viewpoint* 33 (2):165–69.

Collective. 1974. *The Montagnards of South Vietnam*. Minority Rights Group Report no. 18. London: Minority Rights Group.

Condominas, Georges. 1976. "Essai sur l'évolution des systèmes politiques thaïs." *Ethnos* 41:7–67.

Dang Nghiêm Van, et al. 1993. *Quan hê giua các tôc nguoi trong môt quôc gia dân tôc* [The Relation between Ethnic Groups in one National State]. Hà Nôi: NXB Chính tri quc gia.

Dournes, Jacques. 1977. *Pötao, une théorie du pouvoir chez les indochinois jörai*. Paris: Flammarion.

Durrenberger, E. Paul. 1975. "Understanding a Misunderstanding: Thai-Lisu Relations in Northern Thailand." *Anthropological Quarterly* 48 (2):106–120.

——. 1979. "An Analysis of Shan Household Production Decisions." *Journal of Anthropological Research* [Albuquerque, N.M.] 35 (4):447–458.

Durrenberger, E. Paul., and Nicola Tannenbaum. 1992. "Household Economy, Political Economy, and Ideology: Peasants and the State in Southeast Asia." *American Anthropologist* 94:74–89.

Evans, Grant. 1992. "Internal Colonialism in the Central Highlands of Vietnam." *Sojourn* 7 (2):274–304.

——. 1998. *The Politics of Ritual and Remembrance: Laos since 1975*. Honolulu: University of Hawaii,

——. 1985. "Vietnamese Communist Anthropology." *Canberra Anthropology* 8 (1–2):116–147.

Falla, J. 1991. *True Love and Bartholomew: Rebels on the Burmese Border*. Cambridge, UK: Cambridge University Press.

Fippinger, Jay W. 1972. "Black Tai Government." *South East Asia: An International Quarterly* [Carbondale, Ill.] 2 (1):71–76.

Geusau, Leo, and G. M. von Alting. 1992. "The Akha, Ten Years After." *Pacific Viewpoint* 33 (2):178–184. (Special edition on "Marginalisation in Thailand," edited by R. Lawrence, P. Morrison,and J. McKinnon, Department of Geography, Victoria University, Wellington, New Zealand.)

Gogoi, Padmeswar. 1956. "The Political Expansion of the Mao Shans." *Journal of the Siam Society* 44 (II):125–137.

Goudineau, Yves. 2000. "Ethnicité et déterritorialisation dans la péninsule indochinoise: considérations à partir du Laos." *Autrepart*, no. 14:17–31.

Gua, Bo. 1975. "Opium, Bombs, and Trees: The Future of the H'mong Tribesman in Northern Thailand." *Journal of Contemporary Asia* [Stockholm] 5 (1):70–81.

Gunn, G. C. 1990. *Rebellion in Laos: Peasant Politics in a Colonial Backwater*. Boulder, Colo.: Westview Press.

Hayami, Yoko. 2003. "The Decline of Founders' Cults and Changing Configurations of Power: Village and Forest among Karen in the Thai State." In *Founders' Cults in Southeast Asia: Ancestors, Polity, and Identity*, ed. Nicola Tannenbaum and Cornelia Ann Kammerer. Monograph 52. New Haven, Conn.: Yale Southeast Asia Studies.

Hayami, Yoko, and Susan M. Darlington. 2000. "The Karen of Burma and Thailand." In *Endangered Peoples of Southeast and East Asia: Struggles to Survive and Thrive*, ed. Leslie E. Sponsel. Endangered Peoples of the World series. Westport, Conn., London: Greenwood Press.

Hill, R. 1985. "'Primitives' to 'Peasants'?: The 'Sedentarisation of the Nomads' in Vietnam." *Pacific Viewpoint* 26 (2):448–459.

Hkawn, Marip. 1989. "War without End [Kachin]." *Cultural Survival Quarterly* 13:7–9.

Jonsson, Hjorleifur. 1996. "Rhetorics and Relations: Tai States, Forests, and Upland Groups." In *State, Power and Culture in Thailand*, ed. Paul E. Durrenberger. New Haven, Conn.: Yale University Center for Southeast Asia Studies.

Kalashnikov, B. 1991. "Kings of the Mountains." *Asia and Africa Today* [Moscow], no. 4:60–63.

Karniol, R. 1990. "Laotian Resistance Emerges from Mist." *International Defense Review* 23:269–272.

Kirkland, F. R. 2000. "Cultural Dynamics of Civic Action in the Central Highlands of Vietnam, 1967–1968." *Armed Forces & Society* 26 (4):547.

Kossikov, Igor. 2000. "Nationalities Policy in Modern Laos." In *Civility and Savagery: Social Identity in Tai States*, ed. A. Turton. Richmond, UK: Curzon.

Lambrecht, Curtis W. 2004. "Oxymoronic Development: The Military as Benefactor of the Border Regions of Burma." In *Civilizing the Margins. Southeast Asian Governement Policies for the Development of Minorities*, ed. Christopher R. Duncan. Ithaca, N.Y.: Cornell University Press.

Lee, Gary Yia. 2000. "Bandits or Rebels? Hmong Resistance in the New Lao State." *Indigenous Affairs* 4:6–15.

Lintner, Bertil. 1997. *The Kachin: Lords of Burma's Northern Frontier*. Bangkok: Teak House.

Litzinger, Ralph A. 1995. "Making Histories: Contending Conceptions of the Yao Past." In *Cultural Encounters on China's Ethnic Frontiers*, ed. S. Harrell. Seattle: University of Washington Press.

Duong, Mac. 1993. "The Issue of Nationalities in Southern Vietnam in the Process of Socialist Revolution." *Vietnam Social Science* 3 (37):3–10.

McCaskill, Don, and Ken Kampe, eds. 1997. *Development or Domestication? Indigenous Peoples of Southeast Asia*. Chiang Mai, [Thailand]: Silkworm Books,

McElwee, Pamela. 2004. "Becoming Socialist or Becoming Kinh? Government Policies for Ethnic Minorities in the Socialist Republic of Vietnam." In *Civilizing the Margins. Southeast Asian Governement Policies for the Development of Minorities*, ed. Christopher R. Duncan. Ithaca, N.Y.: Cornell University Press.

McKinnon, John. 1989. "Structural Assimilation and the Consensus: Clearing Grounds on Wich Rearrange Our Thoughts." In *Hill Tribes Today: Problems in Change*, ed. John McKinnon and B. Vienne. Bangkok: White Lotus-ORSTOM.

Moerman, Micheal. 1967. "A Minority and Its Government: The Thai-Lue of Northern Thailand." In *Southeast Asian Tribe, Minorities and Nations*, ed. P. Kunstadter. Princeton, N.J.: Princeton University Press.

Murdoch, J. B. 1976. "The 1901–1902 'Holy Man's' Rebellion." *Journal of the Siam Society* LXII:47–66.

Ngo, D. T. 2000. "Traditional Law of the Ede." *Asian Folklore Studies* 59 (1):89–107.

Ovesen, Jan. 1995. *A Minority Enters the Nation State. A Case Study of a Hmong Community in Vientiane Province, Laos*. Uppsala, Sweden: Uppsala Research Reports in Cultural Anthropology no. 14.

Po, San C. 1928. *Burma and the Karen*. London: Elliot Stock.

Post, Ken. 1989. *Revolution, Socialism and Nationalism in Viet Nam*. 4 vols. Aldershot, UK: Dartmouth Publishing.

Rajah, Ananda. 2002. "A 'Nation of Intent' in Burma: Karen Ethno-nationalism, Nationalism and Narrations of Nation." *Pacific Review* 15 (4):517–537.

Reynolds, C. J. 2003. "Tai-land and Its Others." *South East Asia Research* 11 (1):113–130.

Ritchie, Mark A., and Bai Yang. 2000. "Evicted and Excluded: The Struggle for Citizenship and Land Rights by Tribal People in Northern Thailand." *Cultural Survival Quarterly* 24 (3):32–3.

Rolly, Mika. 1989. "The Karenni and Pa-Oh: Revolution in Burma." *Cultural Survival Quarterly* 13:15–17.

Rujaya, Abhakorn. 1999. "The Fabrication of Ethnicity and Colonial Polity East of the Salween." In *Papers from the Myanmar Two Millennia Conference, Yangoon [sic], Myanmar, December 15–17, 1999*, 1–14. Yangon.

Salemink, Oscar. 1995. "Primitive Partisans: French Strategy and the Construction of Montagnard Ethnic Identity in Indochina." In *Imperial Policy and Southeast Asian Nationalism 1930–1957*, ed. H. Antlöv and S. Stonneson. London: Curzon.

———. 1997. "The King of Fire and Vietnamese Ethnic Policy in the Central Highlands." In *Development or Domestication? Indigenous Peoples of Southeast Asia*, ed. Don McCaskill and Ken Kampe. Chiang Mai, [Thailand]: Silkworm Books.

———. 2000a. "Ethnography as Martial Art: Ethnicizing Vietnam's Montagnards 1930–1954." In *Colonial Subjects: Essays on the Practical History of Anthropology*, ed. Peter Pels and Oscar Salemink. Ann Arbor: University of Michigan Press.

———. 2000b. "Sedentarization and Selective Preservation among the Montagnards in the Vietnamese Central Highlands." In *Turbulent Times and Enduring Peoples. Mountain Minorities in the South-East Asian Massif*, ed. Jean Michaud. London: Curzon.

Saw, Po Chit. 1947. *Karens and the Karen State*. Karen National Union Rangoon, India Office Record, IOR M//4/3023. pt. 1/1–206.

Schaeffer-Dainciart, Delphine. 1998. "Redistribution spatiale de la population et collectivisation au Nord-Vietnam: délocalisation des Kinh et sédentarisation des minorités." *Autrepart* 5:45–62.

Scott, George M. 1990. "Hmong Aspirations for a Separate State in Laos: The Effects of the Indochina War." In *Secessionist Movements in Comparative Perspective*, ed. R. Premads, S. W. R. de A. Samsarasinghe, and Alan B.Anderson. New York: St. Martin's Press.

Sompong, Witayasakpan. 2001. "Shan Customary Law." *Tai Culture: International Review on Tai Cultural Studies* [Berlin] 6 (1–2):209–216.

Stuart-Fox, Martin. 1986. *Laos: Politics, Economics and Society*. Boulder, Colo.: Lynne Rienner Publishers.

Taillard, Christian. 1989. *Le Laos: Stratégies d'un État-tampon*. Montpellier, France: Reclus.

Tapp, Nicholas. 1988. "Political Participation among the Hmong of Thailand." *Journal of the Siam Society* [Bangkok] 76:145–162.

Tawee, Swangpanyangkoon. 1991. "The Town System of the Tais in Vietnam." *Muang Boran* [Bangkok] 17 (3):36–41.

Taylor, K. W. 2001. "On Being Muonged." *Asian Ethnicity* 2 (1):25–34.

Tooker, Deborah E. 1996. "Putting the Mandala in Its Place: A Practice-based Approach to the Spatialization of Power on the Southeast Asian 'Periphery'—The Case of the Akha." *The Journal of Asian Studies* 55 (2):323–358.

Vandergeest, Peter. 2003. "Racialization and Citizenship in Thai Forest Politics." *Society and Natural Resources* 16 (1):19–37.

Walker, Anthony R. 1980. "Highlanders and Government in North Thailand." *Folk* 21–22:419–449.

Wekkin, Gary D. 1982. "The Rewards of Revolution: Pathet Lao Policy Towards the Hill Tribes since 1975." In *Comtemporary Laos. Studies in the Politics and Society of the Lao People's Democratic Republic*, ed. M. Stuart-Fox. New York: St. Martin's Press.

Yang, Dao. 1993. *Hmong at the Turning Point*. Minneapolis, Minn.: World Bridge Associates Ltd.

Yawnghwe, Chao Tzang. 1987. *The Shan of Burma, Memoirs of a Shan Exile*. Singapore: Institute of Southeast Asian Studies.

Education

Dai, Qingxia, and Yan Dong. 2001. "The Historical Evolution of Bilingual Education for China's Ethnic Minorities." *Chinese Education and Society* [Armonk, N.Y.] 34 (2):7–53.

Hansen, Mette Halskov. 1999. *Lessons in Being Chinese: Minority Education and Ethnic Identity in Southwest China.* Studies on Ethnic Groups in China. Seattle: University of Washington Press.

Long, Lynellen D. 1992. "Literacy Acquisition of Hmong Refugees in Thailand." In *Cross-Cultural Literacy: Global Perspectives on Reading and Writing*, ed. Fraida Dubin and Natalie A. Kuhlman. Englewood Cliffs, N.J.: Regents/Prentice Hall.

Postiglione, Gerard A., Regie Stites, and Edward R. Beauchamp, eds. 1999. *China's National Minority Education: Culture, Schooling, and Development.* Reference Books in International Education. New York: Garland Publishing.

Shih, Chih-Yu. 2001. "The Problem of Sluggish Enrollment in Ethnic Schools: The Case of One Dong Village in Shaoyang, Hunan." *Issues and Studies* [Taipei] 37 (2):177–198.

Shih, Chih-Yu. 2002. "Questioning the Meaning of Ethnic Education in Dong Villages." In *Negotiating Ethnicity in China. Citizenship as a Response to the State.* London, New York: Routledge.

Teng, X. 2002. "Bilingual Society and Bilingual Education of the Yi Ethnic Minority of the Liangshan Yi Ethnic Minority Autonomous Prefecture in China amid Cultural Changes. History, Present Situation, Problems, and Analysis." *Chinese Education and Society* 35 (3):65–86.

Zhou, Minglang. 2001. "The Politics of Bilingual Education in the People's Republic of China since 1949." *Bilingual Research Journal*[, 25 (1/2):147.

Gender Issues

Beyrer, C. 2001. "Shan Women and Girls and the Sex Industry in Southeast Asia; Political Causes and Human Rights Implications." *Social Science and Medicine* 53 (4):543–550.

Cooper, Robert G. 1983. "Sexual Inequality among the Hmong." In *Highlanders of Thailand*, ed. John McKinnon and Wanat Bhruksasri. Kuala Lumpur, New York: Oxford University Press.

Fuquan, Yang. 2001. "The Fireplace: Gender and Culture among Yunnan Nationalities." *Gender, Technology & Development* 5 (3):365–381.

Hayami, Yoko. 1998. "Motherhood Redefined: Women's Choices on Family Rituals and Reproduction in the Peripheries of Thailand." *Sojourn: Social Issues in Southeast Asia* [Singapore] 13 (2):242–262.

Hutheesing, Otome Klein. 1990. *Emerging Sexual Inequality among the Lisu of Northern Thailand: The Waning of Dog and Elephant Repute.* Leiden, The Netherlands; New York: E. J. Brill.

Litzinger, Ralph A. 2000. "Questions of Gender: Ethnic Minority Representation in Post-Mao China." *Bulletin of Concerned Asian Scholars* 32 (4):3–14.

Du, Shanshan. 2000. " 'Husband and Wife Do It Together': Sex/Gender Allocation of Labor among the Qhawqhat Lahu of Lancang, Southwest China." *American Anthropologist* 102 (3):520.

———. 2003a. *Chopsticks Only Work in Pairs: Gender Unity and Gender Equality among the Lahu of Southwest China*. New York: Columbia University Press.

———. 2003b. "Is Buddha a Couple? Gender-unitary Perspectives from the Lahu of Southwest China." *Ethnology* [Pittsburgh] 42 (3):253.

Symonds, Patricia V. 2004. *Calling in the Soul: Gender and the Cycle of Life in a Hmong Village*. Seattle, London: University of Washington Press.

Yoko, H. 1998. "An Ethnography of 'Ethnic Group' and Gender: Choices Made by Karen Women in Northern Thailand." *Southeast Asian Studies* [Kyoto] 35 (4):852–873.

Law

Boulbet, Jean. 1957. "Quelques aspects du coutumier (N'dri) des Cau Maa." *Bulletin de la Société des Études Indochinoises* 32:108–178.

Diamant, Neil J. 2001. "Pursuing Rights and Getting Justice on China's Ethnic Frontier, 1949–1966." *Law & Society Review* 35 (4):799–840.

Durrenberger, E. Paul. 1976. "Law and Authority in a Lisu Village: Two Cases." *Journal of Anthropological Research* [Albuquerque, N.M.] 32 (4):301–325.

Gerber, T. 1951. "Coutumier Stieng." *Bulletin de l'Ecole Française d'Extrême-Orient* 45:228–269.

Guilleminet, Paul P. 1952. *Coutumier de la tribu Banhar des Sedang et des Jarai (de la province de Kontum)*. Paris: École Française d'Extrême-Orient.

Lafont, Pierre-Bernard. 1963. *Toloi Djuat: Coutumier de la tribu Jarai*. Paris: École Française d'Extrême-Orient Publications.

Minority/Indigenous Policy and Aboriginal Issues

Batson, Wendy. 1991. "After the Revolution: Ethnic Minorities and the New Lao State." In *Laos: Beyond the Revolution*, ed. Joseph J. Zasloff and Leonard Unger, xix, 133–158. New York: St. Martin's Press.

Bhruksasri, Wanat. 1989. "Government Policy: Highland Ethnic Minorities." In *Hill Tribes Today*, ed. John McKinnon and B. Vienne. Bangkok: White Lotus-ORSTOM.

Blum, Susan D. 2002. "Margins and Centers: A Decade of Publishing on China's Ethnic Minorities." *The Journal of Asian Studies* 61 (4):1287–1310.

Cannon, T. 1989. "National Minorities and the Internal Frontier." In *China's Regional Development*, ed. D.S.G. Goodman London: Routledge.

Cheung, Siu-Woo. 2003. "Miao Identities, Indigenism and the Politics of Appropriation in Southwest China during the Republican Period." *Asian Ethnicity* 4 (1):85–114.

Chi Jen Chang. 1956. "The Minority of Groups of Yunnan and Chinese Political Expansion into Southeast Asia." Ph.D. thesis, University of Michigan. Ann Arbor, Mich.: UMI Dissertation Service.

Chou, Meng Tarr. 2001. "The Vietnamese Minority in Cambodia." In *Cambodia: Change and Continuity in Contemporary Politics*, ed. Sorpong Peou. Aldershot, UK, Burlington, Vt.: Ashgate.

Cooper, Robert G. 1979. "The Tribal Minorities of Northern Thailand: Problems and Prospects." *Southeast Asian Affairs* IV:323–332.

Courbage, Youssef. 2002. "Les minorités nationales en Chine: l'exception démographique?" In *La Chine au seuil du XXIe siècle. Questions de population, questions de société*, dir. I. Attané. Cahiers no. 148:215–254. Paris: Institut National d'Études Démographiques.

Deal, David Michael. 1971. *National Minority Policy in Southwest China, 1911–1965*. Ph.D. thesis, University of Washington. Ann Arbor, Mich.: UMI Dissertation Service.

Diao, Richard K. 1967. "The National Minorities in China and Their Relations with the Chinese Communist Regime." In *Southeast Asian Tribes, Minorities and Nations*, ed. P. Kunstadter. Princeton, N.J.: Princeton University Press.

Dreyer, J. T. 1976. *China's Forty Million. Minority Nationalities and National Integration in the People's Republic of China*. Cambridge, Mass., and London: Harvard University Press.

Duncan, Christopher R., ed. 2004. *Civilizing the Margins: Southeast Asian Government Policies for the Development of Minorities*. Ithaca, N.Y.: Cornell University Press.

Engelbert, Thomas, and Andreas Schneider, eds. 2000. *Ethnic Minorities and Nationalism in Southeast Asia*. Bern: Peter Lang Publishing, Festschrift.

Evans, Grant. 1995. "Central Highlanders of Vietnam." In *Indigenous Peoples of Asia*, ed. R. H. Barnes, A. Gray, and B Kingsbury. Monograph and occasional papers series no. 48. Ann Arbor, Mich.: Association for Asian Studies.

Furuie, H. 1993. "Rethinking the 'Chaau-Khau', or Hill Tribes—a Viewpoint on the Relationships of Hill Tribes in Northern Thailand." *Japanese Journal of Ethnology* 58 (1):29–52.

Ganguly, Rajat, and Ian Macduff, eds. 2003. *Ethnic Conflict and Secessionism in South and Southeast Asia: Causes, Dynamics, Solutions.* London: Sage Publications.

Geddes, William R. 1967. "The Tribal Research Center, Thailand: An Account of Plans and Activities." In *Southeast Asian Tribes, Minorities and Nations,* ed. P. Kunstadter Princeton, N.J.: Princeton University Press.

Gladney, Dru C. 1994. "Representing Nationality in China: Refiguring Majority/Minority Identities." *The Journal of Asian Studies* 53 (1):92–123.

———. 2004. "Ethnic Identity in China: The Rising Politics of Cultural Difference." In *Democratization and Identity: Regimes and Ethnicity in East and Southeast Asia,* ed. S. J. Henders. Lanham, Md., Oxford: Lexington Books.

Halpern, Joel M. 1960. "Laos and Her Tribal Problems." *Michigan Alumnus Quarterly Review* 47 (10):59–67.

Harrell, Stevan. 1990. "Ethnicity, Local Interests, and the State: Yi Communities in Southwest China." *Comparative Studies in Society & History* 32 (3):515–548.

———. 2002. *Ways of Being Ethnic in Southwest China.* Studies on Ethnic Groups in China. Seattle: University of Washington Press.

Harrell, Stevan, and Bamo Avi. 1998. "Combining Ethnic Heritage and National Unity: A Paradox of Nuoso (Yi) Language Textbooks in China." *Bulletin of Concerned Asian Scholars* 30 (2):62–71.

Heberer, T. 1989. *China and Its National Minorities: Autonomy or Assimilation?* New York and London: M. E. Sharpe.

Henders, Susan J. 2004. *Democratization and Identity: Regimes and Ethnicity in East and Southeast Asia. Global Encounters.* Lanham, Md.: Rowman & Littlefield.

Henin, Bernard. 1996. "Ethnic Minority Integration in China: Transformation of Akha Society." *Journal of Contemporary Asia* 26 (2):180–200.

Hsieh, Jiann. 1984. "China's Nationalities Policy: Its Development and Problems." *Anthropos* 81:1–20.

Jha, Ganganath. 2000. "Ethnic and Territorial Issues between Laos and Thailand." In *Southeast Asia: Security in the Coming Millennium,* ed. Ghosh Suchita, and Sen Rabindra. Ahmedabad, India: Allied Publishers.

Kahin, George McT. 1972. "Minorities in the Democratic Republic of Vietnam." *Asian Survey* 12 (7):580–586.

Kesmanee, Chupinit. 1988. "Hilltribe Relocation in Thailand." *Cultural Survival Quarterly* 12 (4):2–6.

Keyes, Charles F. 2002. "'The Peoples of Asia'; Science and Politics in the Classification of Ethnic Groups in Thailand, China, and Vietnam." *The Journal of Asian Studies* 61 (4):1163.

Kingsbury, Benedict. 1998. "Indigenous Peoples in International Law: A Constructivist Approach to the Asian Controversy." *The American Journal of International Law* 92 (3):414–457.

Laohoua, Cheutching. 2000. "The Situation of the Hmong and Minority Politics in Laos." In *Ethnic Minorities and Nationalism in Southeast Asia: Festschrift, Dedicated to Hans Dieter Kubitscheck*, ed. Thomas Engelbert, and Andreas Schneider. Frankfurt am Main, Germany: Peter Lang.

Lee, Gary Yia. 1982. "National Minority Policies and the Hmong." In *Contemporary Laos: Studies in the Politics and Society of the Lao People's Democratic Republic*, ed. Martin Stuart-Fox. New York: St. Martin's Press.

———. 1987. "Ethnic Minorities and National-Building in Laos: The Hmong in the Lao State." *Peninsule* 11–12:215–232.

MacKerras, Colin. 1994. *China's Minorities: Integration and Modernization in the Twentieth Century*. Hong Kong: Oxford University Press.

———. 2001. "China's Minority Cultures at the Turn of the Century: Issues of Modernization and Globalization." *Archiv Orientali* 69 (3):447–464.

MacKerras, Colin, dir. 2003. "Ethnic Minorities in China." In *Ethnicity in Asia*. London: New York : RoutledgeCurzon.

Manndorff, Hans. 1967. "The Hill Tribes Program of the Public Welfare Department, Ministy of Interior, Thailand: Research and Socio-economic Development [between 1950 and 1965]." In *Southeast Asian Tribes, Minorities and Nations*, ed. P. Kunstadter. Princeton, N.J.: Princeton University Press.

McKhann, Charles F. 1995. "The Naxi and the Nationalities Question." In *Cultural Encounters on China's Ethnic Frontiers*, ed. S. Harrell. Seattle: University of Washington Press.

McKinnon, John, and Jean Michaud. 2000. "Montagnard Domain in the South-East Asian Massif." In *Turbulent Times and Enduring Peoples: Mountains Minorities in the Southeast Asian Massif*, ed. Jean Michaud. Richmond, UK: Curzon.

McKinnon, John. 1997a. "Convergence or Divergence? Indigenous Peoples on the Borderlands of Southwest China." *Asia Pacific Viewpoint* 38 (2):101–105.

———. 1997b. "Ethnicity, Geography, History and Nationalism: A Future of Ethnic Strife for the Inland Border Peoples of Mainland South-East Asia?" In *Asia Pacific: New Geographies of the Pacific Rim*, ed. R. F. Watters, and T. G. McGee. London: Hurst and Company.

Mckinnon, John, and Wanat Bhruksasri, eds. 1983. *Highlanders of Thailand*. Kuala Lumpur: Oxford University Press.

Nguyen Khac Vien, ed. 1968. "Mountain Regions and National Minorities in the D.R. of Vietnam." *Vietnamese Studies*, no. 15:91–114.

Nong Quoc Chan. 1978. "Selective Preservation of Ethnic Minorities' Cultural Tradition." *Vietnamese Studies* (Special issue: Cultural Problems), no. 52:57–63.

Osborn, G.M.T. 1967. "Government and the Hill Tribes of Laos." In *Southeast Asian Tribe, Minorities and Nations*, ed. P. Kunstadter, 259–270. Princeton N.J.: Princeton University Press.

Ovesen, Jan. 2004. "All Lao? Minorities in the Lao People's Democratic Republic." In *Civilizing the Margins: Southeast Asian Governement Policies for the Development of Minorities*, ed. Christopher R. Duncan. Ithaca, N.Y.: Cornell University Press.

Ovesen, Jan, and Ing-Britt Trankell. 2004. "Foreigners and Honorary Khmers: Ethnic Minorities in Cambodia." In *Civilizing the Margins. Southeast Asian Governement Policies for the Development of Minorities*, ed. Christopher R. Duncan. Ithaca, N.Y.: Cornell University Press.

Pholsena, Vatthana. 2002. "Nation/Representation: Ethnic Classification and Mapping Nationhood in Contemporary Laos." *Asian Ethnicity* 3 (2):175–197.

Shih, Chih-Yu. 2001. "Ethnicity as Policy Expedience: Clan Confucianism in Ethnic Tujia-Miao Yongshun." *Asian Ethnicity* 2 (1):73–88.

Solinger, Dorothy J. 1977. "Minority Nationalities in China's Yunnan Province: Assimilation, Power, and Policy in a Socialist State." *World Politics* 30 (1):1–23.

Stewart-Cox, Belinda, and Margaret Hall. 1984. *The Restructuring of an Ethnic Minority in China:* Cambridge: Papers of the School of Hunlan Sciences.

Tapp, Nicholas. 1995. "Minority Nationality in China: Policy and Practice." In *Indigenous Peoples of Asia*, ed. R. H. Barnes, A. Gray, and B. Kingsbury. Monograph and occasional papers series no. 48. Ann Arbor, Mich.: Association for Asian Studies,

Thompson, Virginia, and Richard Adloff. 1955. *Minority Problems in Southeast Asia*, Stanford, Calif.: Stanford University Press.

Thomson, Curtis N. 1995. "Political Stability and Minority Groups in Burma." *Geographical Review* 85 (3):269–285.

Unger, Jonathan. 1997. "Not Quite Han: The Ethnic Minorities of China's Southwest." *Bulletin of Concerned Asian Scholars* 29 (3):67–76.

Viet Chung. 1968. "National Minorities and National policy in the DRV." *Vietnamese Studies*, no. 15:3–23.

White, Joanna. 1996. "The Indigenous Highlanders of the Northeast: An Uncertain Future." In *Interdisciplinary Research on Ethnic Groups in Cambodia.* Phnom Penh, Cambodia: Center for Advanced Study.

Wilkerson, James. 2003. "Disquiet on the Southwestern Front: Studies of the Minorities of Southwest China (review article)." *Pacific Affairs* 76 (1):79–91.

Wu, David Y. H. 1990. "Chinese Minority Policy and the Meaning of Minority Culture: The Example of Bai in Yunnan, China." *Human Organization* 49 (1):1–13.

6. ECONOMY

Basilico, Sandrine. 2003. *Mondialisation et Intégration des Minorités Ethniques au Viet-Nam: Le cas des Muong et des Thai.* Paris: L'Harmattan.

Binney, George A. 1971. *The Social and Economic Organization of Two White Meo Communities in Northern Thailand.* Washington, D.C.: Wildlife Management Institute.

Condominas, Georges. 1972. "Aspects of Economics among the Mnong Gar of Vietnam: Multiple Money and the Middleman." *Ethnology* 11 (3):202–219.

Cooper, Robert G. 1984. *Resource Scarcity and the Hmong Response: Patterns of Settlement and Economy in Transition.* Singapore: Singapore University Press.

David, S. 2003. "Premodern Flows in Postmodern China: Globalization and the Sipsongpanna Tais." *Modern China* 29 (2):176–203.

Dessaint, Alain Y. 1973. "Economic Systems of Northern Thailand." *Journal of Southeast Asian Studies* 3 (2):325–328.

Durrenberger, E. Paul. 1976. "The Economy of a Lisu Village." *American Ethnologist* 3 (4):633–644.

———. 1981. "The Economy of a Shan Village." *Ethnos Stockholm* 46 (1/2):64–79.

Kandre, Peter. 1971. "Alternative Modes of Recruitement of Viable Households among the Yao of Mae Chan." *Southeast Asian Journal of Sociology* 4:43–52.

Kesmanee, Chupinit. 1987. *Hill Tribe Relocation Policy (Is There a Way Out of the Labyrinth? A Case Study of Kamphaeng Phet).* Chiang Mai, [Thailand]: Tribal Research Institute.

Kunstadter, Peter. 2000. "Changing Patterns of Economics among Hmong in Northern Thailand:1960–1990." In *Turbulent Times and Enduring Peoples: Mountains Minorities in the Southeast Asian Massif,* ed. Jean Michaud. Richmond, UK: Curzon.

Ligh, Ivan H. T., and Steven Gold. 2000. *Ethnic Economies.* San Diego: Academic Press.

Luibrand, Annette, Franz Heidhues, and Joachim Von Braun. 2002. *Transition in Vietnam: Impact of the Rural Reform Process on an Ethnic Minority.* Development Economics and Policy. New York: Peter Lang Publishing.

Mckinnon, John, and Bernard Vienne, ed. 1989. *Hill Tribes Today: Problems in Change*. Bangkok-Paris: White Lotus-ORSTOM.

Michaud, Jean. 1997. "Economic Transformation in a Hmong Village of Thailand." *Human Organization* 56 (2):222–232.

Miles, Douglas. 1972. "Land, Labour and Kin Groups among Southeast Asian Shifting Cultivators." *Mankind* 8 (3):185–197.

Motoyoshi, S., and Y. Kiyoko. 2002. "Food Problems and Migration among the Hmong Tribe in Laos." *Southeast Asian Studies* 40 (1):23–41.

Odaka, Kunio. 1950. *Economic Organisation of the Li Tribes of Hainan Island*. Translated from Japanese by Mikiso Hane. New Haven, Conn.: Yale Southeast Studies.

Ovesen, Jan. 1993. *Anthropological Reconnaissance in Central Laos. A Survey of Local Communities in a Hydropower Project Area*. Uppsala, Sweden: Uppsala research reports in cultural Anthropology no. 13.

Robequain, Charles. 1929. *Le Thanh Hoa: Étude géographique d'une province annamite*. 2 vols. Paris et Bruxelle: G. Van Oest.

Stevenson, H. 1943. *The Economics of the Central Chin Tribes*. Published by order of the Government of Burma. Bombay: Times of India Press.

Tapp, Nicholas. 1988. "The Hmong. Political Economy of an Illegal Crop." In *Ethnic Histories and Minority Identities*, ed. J. G. Taylor and A. Turton. New York: Monthly Review Press.

Tayanin, Damrong, and Kristina Lindell Damrong. 1993. *Hunting and Fishing in a Kammu Village*. Richmond, UK: Curzon.

Thalemann, Andrea. 1997. "Laos: Between Battlefield and Marketplace." *Journal of Contemporary Asia* [Manila] 27 (1):85.

Van Roy, E. 1972. *Economic Systems in Northern Thailand*. Ithaca, N.Y.: Cornell University Press.

Demography

Berlie, Jean. 1992. "Economic Census of a Dai Neua Village in Dehong Autonomous Prefecture, Yunnan: Modernization and the Dai Socio-economic System." *Social Issues in Southeast Asia* 7 (1):123–141.

Halpern, Joel M. 1961. *Geographic, Demographic and Ethnic Background on Laos*. Laos Project Paper No. 4. Los Angeles: University of California.

Hutton, J. H. 1933. *Census of India, 1931*. 46 vols. Delhi: Manager of Publications.

Ireson, W. Randall. 1995. "Hmong Demographic Changes in Laos: Causes and Ecological Consequences." *Sojourn: Social Issues in Southeast Asia* [Singapore] 10 (2):198–232.

Khong Dien. 2002. *Population and Ethno-Demography in Vietnam*. Chiang Mai, [Thailand]: Silkworm; and Seattle: University of Washington Press.

Miles, Douglas. 1973. "Some Demographic Implications of Regional Commerce: The Case of North Thailand's Yao Minority." In *Studies of Contemporary Thailand*, ed. R. Ho and E. C. Chapman. Canberra: Australian National University,

Moréchand, Guy. 1952. "Notes démographiques sur un canton Meo Blanc du pays tai." *Bulletin de la Société Études Indochinoises* 27:355–361.

Poston, Dudley L., Jr., and Jing Shu. 1987. "The Demographic and Socioeconomic Composition of China's Ethnic Minorities." *Population and Development Review* 13 (4):703–722.

Agriculture, Swiddening, and Environment

Anchalee Phonklieng. 1998. "A Comparison of Karen and Hmong Environmental Values." In *Toward an Environmental Ethic in Southeast Asia*, ed. Peter Gyallay-Pap, Ruth Bottomley. Phnom Penh: Cambodia: The Buddhist Institute.

Chapman, E. C. 1978. "Shifting Cultivation and Economic Development in the Lowlands of Northern Thailand." In *Farmers in the Forest. Economic development and marginal agriculture in Northern Thailand*, ed. P. Kunstadter, E. C. Chapman, and S. Sanga, Honolulu: East-West Center, University Press of Hawaii.

Chen, Han-seng. 1949. *Frontier Land Systems in Southern Most China: A Comparative Study of Agrarian Problems and Social Organisation among the Pai Yi People [Tai Lue] of Yunnan and the Kamba People of Sikang*. New York: Pacific Relations.

Condominas, Georges. 1983. "Ecology of a Limited Social Space in Southeast Asia: The Mnong Gar of Vietnam and Their Environment. [French]." *Etudes Rurales* 89–91:11–76.

———. 1986. "Ritual Technology in Mnong Gar Swidden Agriculture." In *Rice Societies: Asian Problems and Prospects*, ed. Irene Norlund, Sven Cederroth, and Ingela Gerdin. Scandinavian Institute of Asian Studies Studies on Asian Topics series, no. 10. London: Curzon; Riverdale, Md.: Riverdale.

———. 1997. "Essartage et confusionnisme: à propos des Mnong Gar du Vietnam central." *Civilisations* 44 (1/2):228–252.

Coward, E. Walter, Jr. 1976. "Indigenous Organization, Bureaucracy and Development: The Case of Irrigation." *The Journal of Development Studies* 13 (1):92–105.

DeKoninck, Rodolphe. 1999. *Deforestation in Viet Nam*. Ottawa (Canada): International Development Research Centre.

——. 2000. "The Theory and Practice of Frontier Development: Vietnam's Contribution." *Asia Pacific Viewpoint* 41 (1):7–22.

Delang, Claudio. 2002. "Deforestation in Northern Thailand: The Result of Hmong Farming Practices or Thai Development Strategies?" *Society and Natural Resources* 15 (6):483–501.

Funakawa, S. 1997. "Ecological Study on the Dynamics of Soil Organic Matter and Its Related Properties in Shifting Cultivation Systems of Nothern Thailand." *Soil Science and Plant Nutrition* 43 (3):681–693.

Ganjanapan, A. 1998. "The Politics of Conservation and the Complexity of Local Control of Forests in the Northern Thai Highlands." *Mountain Research and Development* 18 (1):71–82.

Gravers, Mikael. 2001. "Karen Notions of Environment—Space, Place and Power in a Political Landscape." In *Forest in Culture—Culture in Forest: Perspectives from Northern Thailand*, ed. Ebbe Poulsen et al. N.p.: Research Centre on Forest and People in Thailand.

Guo, Yanchun. 1998. "The Thought and Techniques in the Preservation of the Environment: The Case of Tai Ethnic Group in Xishuangbanna, Yunnan." *Southeast Asian Studies* [Kyoto] 35 (3):465–488.

Harris, R. B., and M. Shilai. 1997. "Initiating a Hunting Ethic in Lisu Villages, Western Yunnan, China." *Mountain Research & Development* 17 (2):171–176.

Hayami, Yoko. 2000. "Challenges to Community Rights in the Hill Forests: State Policy and Local Contradictions, A Karen Case." *Tai Culture: International Review on Tai Cultural Studies* [Berlin] 5 (2):104–131.

Henin, Bernard, and M. Flaherty. 1994. "Ethnicity, Culture, and Natural Resource Use: Forces of Change on Dai Society, Xishuangbanna, Southwest China." *Journal of Developing Societies* 10 (2):219–235.

Hirsch, Philip, and Carol Warren. 1998. *The Politics of the Environment in Southeast Asia: Resources and Resistance*. London: Routledge.

Huihao Liu. 1994. "The Traditional Rice Culture of the Lahu (including Kucong) of Southwest China." *Contributions to Southeast Asian Ethnography* 10:37–62.

Ireson, Carol J., and W. R. Ireson. 1996. *Cultivating the Forest: Gender and the Decline of Wild Resources among the Tay of Northern Vietnam*. Working Papers, Indochina Series. Honolulu: East-West Center.

Jonsson, Hjorleifur. 1998. "Forest Products and Peoples: Upland Groups, Thai Polities, and Regional Space." *Sojourn: Journal of Social Issues in Southeast Asia*. 13(1):1–37.

Keen, F. G. B. 1973. *Upland Tenure and Land Use in North Thailand*. Bangkok: SEATO Cultural Program.

——. 1978. "Ecological Relationships in a Hmong (Meo) Economy." In *Farmers in the Forest*, ed. P. Kunstadter, S. Sabhasri, and E. C. Chapman. Honululu: University Press of Hawaii.

Kunstadter, Peter, and Sally Kundstadter. 1992. "Population Movements and Environmental Changes in the Hills of Northern Thailand." In *Patterns and Illusions: Thai History and Thought*, ed. G. Wijeyewardene, and E. C. Chapman. Canberra: Department of Anthropology and the Richard Davis Fund, Australian National University.

Kunstadter, Peter, E. C. Chapman, and Sabhasri Sanga, eds. 1978. *Farmers in the Forest. Economic Development and Marginal Agriculture in Northern Thailand*. Honolulu: University Press of Hawaii, East-West Center.

Le Duy Hung. 1995. "Some Issues of Fixed Cultivation and Sedentarization of Ethnic Minority People in Mountainous Areas of Vietnam." In *The Challenges of Highland Development in Vietnam*, ed. Terry Rambo, Robert R. Reed, Trong Cuc Le, and Michael R. DiGregorio. Center for Southeast Asian Studies (Berkeley), Center for Natural Resources (Hanoi), East-West Center, Honolulu, Hawaii.

Le Trong Cuc. 1995. "Biodiversity Conservation and Sustainable Land Use in the Da River Watershed." In *The Challenges of Highland Development in Vietnam*, ed. Terry Rambo, Robert R. Reed, Trong Cuc Le, and Michael R. DiGregorio. Center for Southeast Asian Studies (Berkeley), Center for Natural Resources (Hanoi), East-West Center, Honolulu, Hawaii (USA).

———. 1997. "Culture-Environment Relations: The Case of Vietnam's Northern Mountain Region." *Vietnam Social Sciences* [Hanoi] 6 (62):65–72.

Lohmann, Larry. 1993. "Thailand: Land, Power and Forest Colonization." In *The Struggle for Land and the Fate of the Forests*, ed. M. Colchester and L. Lohmann. Penang (Malaysia): Zed Books.

Lyman, Thomas A. 1969. "Miao (Meo) Slash-and-Burn Agriculture." *Journal d'agriculture tropicale et de Botanique appliquée* 16 (6, 7, 8):251–283.

Matras-Troubetzkoy, Jacqueline. 1983. *Un village en forêt. L'essartage chez les Brou du Cambodge. Préface de G. Condominas*. Paris: SELAF.

Nguyen Van Minh. 2000. "Agricultural Adaptation of the H'mong in Vietnam." *Vietnam Social Sciences* [Hanoi] 6 (80):75–95.

Nguyen Van Thang. 1995. "The Hmong and Dzao Peoples in Vietnam: Impact of Traditional Socioeconomic and Cultural Factors on the Protection and Development of Forest Resources." In *The Challenges of Highland Development in Vietnam*, ed. Terry A. Rambo et al. Honolulu: East-West Center Program on Environment.

Pei, Shengji. 1993. "Managing for Biological Diversity Conservation in Temple Yards and Holy Hills: The Traditional Practices of the Xishuangbanna Dai Community, Southwest China." In *Ethics, Religion, and Biodiversity: Relations between Conservation and Cultural Values*, ed. Lawrence S. Hamilton and Helen F. Takeuchi. Cambridge, UK: White Horse Press.

Rambo, Terry, and T. D. Vien. 2001. "Social Organization and the Management of Natural Resources: A Case Study of Tat Hamlet, a Da Bac Tay Ethnic Minority Settlement in Vietnam's Northwestern Mountains." *Southeast Asian Studies* 39 (3):299–324.

Schmidt-Vogt, Dietrich. 1995. "Swidden Farming and Secondary Vegetation: Two Case Studies from Northern Thailand." In *Counting the Costs. Economic Growth and Environmental Change in Thailand*, ed. J. Rigg. Singapore: ISEAS.

———. 1998. "Defining Degradation: The Impacts of Swidden on Forests in Northern Thailand." *Mountain Research and Development* 18 (2):135–149.

Shirasaka, Shigeru. 1996. "Slash-and-Burn Cultivation in the Southern Part of Yunnan Province, China: Sustainable or not Sustainable?" In *Geographical Perspectives on Sustainable Rural Systems: Proceedings of the Tsukuba International Conference on the Sustainability of Rural Systems*, ed. Hiroshi Sasaki et al., Tokyo: Kaisei Publications.

Tomforde, Maren. 2003. "The Global in the Local: Contested Resource-Use Systems of the Karen and Hmong in Northern Thailand." *Journal of Southeast Asian Studies* 34 (2):347–360.

Tungittiplakorn, W. 1995. "Highland-Lowland Conflict over Natural Resources: A Case of Mae Soi, Chiang Mai, Thailand." *Society & Natural Resources* 8 (4):279–288.

Walker, Andrew. 2001. "The 'Karen Consensus', Ethnic Politics and Resource-Use Legitimacy in Northern Thailand." *Asian Ethnicity* 2 (2):145–162.

———. 2002. "Ethnicity, Agriculture and Social Impact Assessment in Laos and Cambodia." *Asian Ethnicity* 3 1:109–113.

Walker, Anthony R. 1976. "The Swidden Economy of a Lahu Nyi (Red Lahu) Village Community in North Thailand." *Folk Copenhagen* 18:145–188.

Wezel, A., A. Luibrand, and L. Q. Thanh 2002. "Temporal Changes of Resource Use, Soil Fertility and Economic Situation in Upland Northwest Vietnam." *Land Degradation and Development* 13 (1):33–44.

Wezel, A., N. Steinmuller, and J. R. Friederichsen. 2002. "Slope Position Effects on Soil Fertility and Crop Productivity and Implications for Soil Conservation in Upland Northwest Vietnam." *Agriculture Ecosystems and Environment* 91 (1–3):113–126.

Yanchun, G. 1998. "Forest Utilization and Practice of 'Forest Creation' in Multi-ethnic Villages: Village Forestry and Agroforestry Cultivation in the Mountainous Area of Baoshan, Yunnan, China." *Southeast Asian Studies* 36 (3):379–426.

Opium

Cohen, Paul T. 1985. "Opium and the Karen. A Study of Indebtedness in Northern Thailand." *Journal of Southeast Asian Studies* 15:150–165.

———. 2000. "Resettlement, Opium and Labour Dependence: Akha-Tai Relations in Northern Laos." *Development & Change* 31 (1):179–200.

Cohen, Paul T., and Chris Lyttleton. 2002. "Opium-Reduction Programmes, Discourses of Addiction and Gender in Northwest Laos." *Sojourn* 17 (1):1–23.

Crooker, Richard A. 1988. "Forces of Change in the Thailand Opium Zone." *Geographical Review* 78 (3):241–256.

Culas, Christian. 2000. "L'opium chez les Hmong en Asie du Sud-Est: Tolérances et contraintes sociales." In *Opiums: les plantes du plaisir et de la convivialité en Asie*, ed. Annie Hubert and Philippe Le Failler. Paris: L'Harmattan.

Dessaint, William, and Alain Y. Dessaint. 1975. "Strategies in Opium Production." *Ethnos* [Stockholm] 40:153–168.

———. 1992. "Opium and Labor: Social Structure and Economic Change in the Lisu Highlands." *Peasant Studies* 19 (3–4):147–177.

Epprecht, Michael. 2000. "The Blessings of the Poppy: Opium and the Akha People of Northern Laos." *Indigenous Affairs* 4:16–21.

Geddes, William R. 1970. "Opium and the Miao: A Study in Ecological Adjustment." *Oceania* [Sydney] 41 (1):1–11.

Hinton, Peter. 1983. "Why the Karen Do Not Grow Opium: Competition and Contradiction in the Highlands of North Thailand." *Ethnology* 22:1–16.

Kesmanee, Chupinit. 1989. "The Poisoning Effect of a Lovers Triangle: Highlanders, Opium and Extension Crops, a Policy Overdue for Review." In *Hill Tribes Today*, ed. John McKinnon and B.Vienne. Bangkok: White Lotus-ORSTOM.

Renard, Ronald. 1994. "The Monk, the Hmong, the Forest, the Cabbage, Fire, and Water: Incongruities in Northern Thailand Opium Replacement." *Law & Society Review* [Denver, Colo.] 28 (3):657–664.

Saihoo, Patya. 1963. "The Hill Tribes of Northern Thailand and the Opium Problem." *Bulletin on Narcotics* 15 (2):35–45.

Economic Change and Development

Demusz, K. 1998. "From Relief to Development: Negotiating the Continuum on the Thai-Burmese Border." *Journal of Refugee Studies* 11 (3):231–244.

Department of Public Welfare of Thailand. 1963. *First Five Year Plan for the Development and Welfare of the Hill Tribes in Northern Thailand 1963–67.* Bangkok: Ministry of Interior of Thailand.

Eaton, Peter. 2004. *Land Tenure, Conservation and Development in Southeast Asia.* London: RoutledgeCurzon.

Giloggly, Kathleen. 2004. "Developing the 'Hill Tribes' of Northern Thailand." In *Civilizing the Margins: Southeast Asian Governement Policies for the Development of Minorities*, ed. Christopher R. Duncan. Ithaca, N.Y.: Cornell University Press.

Goudineau, Yves. 1997. *Resettlement and Social Characteristics of New Villages: Basic Needs for Resettled Communities in the Lao PDR*. 2 vols. Bangkok: UNESCO/PNUD.

Hickey, Gerald C. 1967. *The Highland People of South Vietnam: Social and Economic Development*. Santa Monica, Calif.: Rand, RM-5281/1.

———. 1971. *Some Recommendations Affecting the Prospective Role of Vietnamese Highlanders in Economic Development*. Santa Monica, Calif.: Rand, P-4708.

Huff, L. W. 1967. "The Thai Mobile Development Unit Programme." In *Southeast Asian Tribes, Minorities and Nations*, ed. P. Kunstadter. 2 vols Princeton, N.J.: Princeton University Press.

Ireson, Carol J., and W. Randall Ireson. 1991. "Ethnicity and Development in Laos." *Asian Survey* 31 (10):920–937.

Jian, Li. 2001. "Development and Tribal Agricultural Economy in a Yao Mountain Village in Northern Thailand." *Human Organization* 60 (1):80–94.

Kesmanee, Chupinit. 1994. "Dubious Development Concepts in the Thai Highlands: The Chao Khao in Transition." *Law & Society Review* [Amherst] 28 (3):673.

Kunstadter, Peter. 1984. "Cultural Ideals, Socioeconomic Change, and Household Composition: Karen, Lua', Hmong, and Thai in Northwestern Thailand." In *Household: Comparative and Historical Studies of Domestic Group*, ed. R. M. Netting. Berkeley: University of California Press.

Rambo, Terry, Robert R. Reed, Trong Cuc Le, and Michael R. DiGregorio, eds. 1995. *The Challenges of Highland Development in Vietnam*. Center for Southeast Asian Studies (Berkeley), Center for Natural Resources (Hanoi), East-West Center (Hawaii).

Renard, Ronald, P. Bhandhachat, G. L. Robert, M. Roongruangsee, S. Sarobol, and N. Prachadetsuwat. 1988. *Changes in the Northern Thai Hills: An Examination of the Impact of Hill Tribe Development Work 1957–1987*. Research and Development Center, Payap University, Research Report No. 42. Chiang Mai, Thailand,

Tapp, Nicholas. 1990. "Squatters or Refugees: Development and the Hmong." In *Ethnic Groups Across National Boundaries in Mainland Southeast Asia*, ed. G. Wijwyewardene. Singapore: Institute of Southeast Asian Studies.

Vienne, Bernard. 1989. "Facing Development in the Highlands: A Challenge for the Thai Society." In *Hill Tribes Today*, ed. John McKinnon and B.Vienne. Bangkok: White Lotus-ORSTOM.

Wongspraset, Sanit. 1988. "Impact of the Dhammacarik Bhikkus Programme on the Hill Tribes of Thailand." In *Ethnic Conflict in Buddhist Societies, Sri Lanka, Thailand, Burma*, ed. K. M. Silva et al. Boulder, Colo.: Westview Press.

Yang Dao. 1975. *Les Hmong du Laos face au développement*. Vientiane: Siao Savath,

Zhuge, Ren, and Clem Tisdell. 1999. "Sustainability Issues and Socio-Economic Change in the Jingpo Communities of China." *International Journal of Social Economics* [Bradford] 26 (1/2/3):21.

Tourism

Bartsch, H. 1997. *Trekking Tourism and Its Role in a Process of Socio-economic Change: A Karen Village in Northern Thailand as an Example*. Nijmegen, The Netherlands: Third World Center.

Berlie, Jean. 2001. "The Dai Minority and Prospect for Tourism in Yunnan Province." In *Tourism Anthropology and China*, ed. T. Chee-Beng, S. C. H. Cheung, and Y. Hui. Bangkok: White Lotus.

Chee-Beng, T., S. C. H. Cheung, and Y. Hui, eds. 2001. *Tourism Anthropology and China*. Bangkok: White Lotus.

Clastres, Geneviève. 1998. *Tourisme Ethnique en Ombres Chinoises. La Province du Guizhou*. Paris: L'Harmattan.

Cohen, Erik. 1979. "The Impact of Tourism on the Hill Tribes of Northern Thailand." *Internationales Asienforum* 10 (1–2):5–38.

———. 1983. "Hill Tribe Tourism." In *Highlanders of Thailand*, ed. John McKinnon and Wanat Bhruksasri. Kuala Lumpur: Oxford University Press.

———. 1989. "Primitive and Remote: Hill Tribe Trekking in Thailand." *Annals of Tourism Research* 16 (1):30–61.

———. 2001. *Thai Tourism: Hill Tribes, Highlands and Open-ended Prostitution*. Bangkok: White Lotus.

Dearden, Philip. 1991. "Tourism and Sustainable Development in Northern Thailand." *Geographical Review* 18 (4):400–413.

Dearden, Philip, and Sylvia Harron. 1992. "Case Study: Tourism and the Hill Tribes of Thailand." In *Special Interest Tourism*, ed. B. Weiler and C. M. Hall. London: Belhaven Press.

Forsyth, Timothy J. 1995. "Tourism and Agricultural Development in Thailand." *Annals of Tourism Research* 22 (4):877–900.

Hasegawa, Kiyoshi. 2002. "Ethnic Tourism and Cultural Change in the Border Region of Yunnan Province: A Case Study on Xishuangbanna Dai Autonomous Prefecture." In *Inter-ethnic Relations in the Making of Mainland Southeast Asia and Southwestern China*. ed. Yukio Hayashi and Aroonrut Wichienkeeo. Chiang Rai, Thailand: Center of Ethnic Studies, Rajabhat Institute; Kyoto: Center for Southeast Asian Studies, Kyoto University.

Kesmanee, Chupinit, and Kulwadee Charoensri. 1994. *The Impact of Tourism on Culture and Environment: A Case Study of the Mae Taeng Trekking Route in Chiang Mai*. Bangkok: Office of the National Culture Commission, Ministry of Education,

McKhann, Charles F. 2001. "Tourisme de masse et identité sur les marches sino-tibétaines. Réflexions d'un observateur." *Anthropologie et Sociétés* 25 (2):35–54.

Michaud, Jean. 1995. "Frontier Minorities, Tourism and the State in Indian Himalaya and Northern Thailand." In *International Tourism. Identity and Change*, ed. M. F. Lanfant, J. B.Allcock, and E. M.Bruner. Studies in International Sociology. London: Sage.

———. 1997. "A Portrait of Cultural Resistance: The Confinement of Tourism in a Hmong Village of Thailand." In *Tourism, Ethnicity, and the State in Asian and Pacific Societies*, ed. M. Picard and R. E. Wood. Honolulu: University of Hawaii Press.

Oakes, Timothy S. 1992. "Cultural Geography and Chinese Ethnic Tourism." *Journal of Cultural Geography* 12 (2):3–17.

———. 1995. "Tourism in Guizhou: The Legacy of Internal Colonialism." In *Tourism in China. Geographic, Political, and Economic Perspectives*, dir. A. A. Lew and L. Yu, ch. 12. Boulder, Colo.: Westview Press.

———. 1997. "Ethnic Tourism in Rural Guizhou: Sense of Place and the Commerce of Authenticity." In *Tourism, Ethnicity, and the State in Asian and Pacific Societies*, dir. Michel Picard and Robert E. Wood. Honolulu: University of Hawaii Press. Chapter 2.

———. 1998. *Tourism and Modernity in China*. London: Routledge.

Sofield, T. H. B., and Fung Mei Sarah Li. 1998. "Tourism Development and Cultural Policies in China." *Annals of Tourism Research* 25 (2):362–392.

Tan Chee-Beng, Sydney, C. H. Cheung, and Yang Hui, eds. 2001. *Tourism Anthropology and China*. Bangkok: White Lotus.

Walsh, E. 2001. "Living with the Myth of Matriarchy: The Mosuo and Tourism." In *Tourism Anthropology and China*, ed. Sydney Tan Chee-Beng, C. H. Cheung, and Yang Hui. Bangkok: White Lotus.

Xu Xinjian. 2001. "Developing China: Formation and Influence of 'Ethnic Tourism' and 'Ethnic Tourees'." In *Tourism Anthropology and China*, ed. Sydney Tan Chee-Beng, C. H. Cheung, and Yang Hui. Bangkok: White Lotus.

Trade

Cohen, Erik. 2000. *The Commercialized Crafts of Thailand: Hill Tribes and Lowland Villages*. Honolulu: University of Hawaii.

Hamilton, James W. 1963. "Effects of the Thai Market on Karen Life." *Practicing Anthropology* 10 (5):209–215.

———. 1965. *Kinship Bazaar Market: The Karen Development of a Dual Economy as an Aspect of Modernization*. Washington, D.C.: Washington State University.

Hill, Ann Maxwell. 1998. *Merchants and Migrants: Ethnicity and Trade Among Yunnanese Chinese in Southeast Asia*. New Haven, Conn.: Yale University, Southeast Asia Studies, Yale Center for International and Area Studies.

Michaud, Jean, and Sarah Turner. 2000. "The Sa Pa Marketplace, Lao Cai Province, Vietnam." *Asia Pacific Viewpoint* 41 (1):84–99.

Swain, Margaret Byrne. 1990. "Commoditizing Ethnicity in Southwest China." *Cultural Survival Quarterly* 14 (1):26–29.

7. RELIGION

Animism, Geomancy, Ancestor Worship, Buddhism, and Islam

Andersen, Kirsten Ewers. 1978. *Elements of Pwo Karen Buddhism*. Copenhagen: The Scandinavian Institute of Asian Studies,

———. 1981. "Two Indigenous Karen Religious Denominations." *Folk: Dansk Etnografisk Tidsskrift* [Copenhagen] 23:251–261.

Baba, Yuji. 1996. "Migration and Spirit Culture: The Case Study on the Tai-Lue Villages in Nan Province, Northern Thailand." *Proceedings of the 6th International Conference on Thai Studies* 2:27–47.

Bonifacy, Auguste Louis-M. 1915. "La fête Tay du Ho-Bo." *Bulletin de l'Ecole Française d'Extrême-Orient* XV (3):17–23.

Chob, Khacha-Ananda. 1986. "The Religious Life of the Yao People of Northern Thailand." *Contribution to Southeast Asian Ethnogrphy* 5:43–64.

Chindarsi, Nusit. 1976. *The Religion of the Hmong Njua*. Bangkok: Siam Society.

Culas, Christian. 2005. Le Messianisme Hmong Aux Xixe St. Xxe Siècles. Paris: CNRS Éditions.

Durrenberger, E. Paul. 1975a. "The Lisu Concept of the Soul." *Journal of the Siam Society* [Bangkok] 63 (1):63–71.

———. 1975b. "Lisu Occult Roles." *Bijdragen tot de taal- land- en volkenkunde* 131 (1):138–146.

———. 1975c. "A Soul's Journey: A Lisu Song from Northern Thailand." *Asian Folklore Studies* 34 (1):35–50.

———. 1977. "Of Lisu Dogs and Lisu Spirits." *Folklore* 88 (1):61–63.

———. 1980. "Belief and the Logic of Lisu Spirits." *Bijdragen tot de taal- land- en volkenkunde* 136 (1):21–40.

———. 1989. *Lisu Religion*. DeKalb: Northern Illinois University Center for Southeast Asian Studies.

Eberhardt, Nancy. 1993. "The Cultural Context of Moral Reasoning: Lessons from the Shan of Northern Thailand." *Crossroads* 8 (1):1–25.

Friedman, Jonathan. 1975. "Religion as Economy and Economy as Religion." *Ethnos* [Stockholm] 40 (1/4):46–63.

Geusau, Leo, and G. M. von Alting. 1983. "Dialectics of Akha Zang: The Interiorisations of a Perennial Minority Group." In *Highlanders of Thailand*, ed. John McKinnon and Wanat Bhruksasri. Kuala Lumpur: Oxford University Press.

Gilhodes, A. 1996 [1922]. *The Kachin: Religion and Customs*. Bangkok: White Lotus.

Graham, David C. 1941. "The Religion of the Ch'uan Miao." *Review of Religion* [Columbia University] 5 (March):276–289.

———. 1961. *Folk Religion in Southwest China*. Washington, D.C.: Smithsonian Miscellaneous Collections,

Hayami, Yoko. 2002. "Embodied Power of Prophets and Monks: Dynamics of Religion among Karen in Thailand." In *Inter-ethnic Relations in the Making of Mainland Southeast Asia and Southwestern China*, ed. Yukio Hayashi and Aroonrut Wichienkeeo, lxviii. Chiang Rai, Thailand: Center of Ethnic Studies, Rajabhat Institute; Kyoto: Center for Southeast Asian Studies, Kyoto University.

———. 1996. "Karen Tradition According to Christ or Buddha: The Implications of Multiple Reinterpretations for a Minority Ethnic Group in Thailand." *Journal of Southeast Asian Studies* 27 (2):334.

Henricks, R. G. 1998. "Fire and Rain—A Look at Shen-Nung (The Divine Farmer) and His Ties with Yen-Ti (The Flaming Emperor or Flaming God)." *Bulletin of the School of Oriental & African Studies-University of London* 61 (1):102–124.

Hinton, Peter. 1979. "The Karen Millennialism, and the Politics of Accomodation to Lowland States." In *Ethnic Adaptation and Identity: The Karen on the Thai Frontier with Burma*, ed. Charles F. Keyes. Philadelphia: Institute for the Study of Human Issues.

Kammerer, Cornelia Ann, and Nicola Tannenbaum. 1996. *Merit and Blessing in Mainland Southeast Asia in Comparative Perspective*. Yale Monograph No. 45. New Haven, Conn.: Yale University Press.

Kirsch, Thomas A. 1973. *Feasting and Social Oscillation: A Working Paper on Religion and Society in Upland Southeast Asia*. Data paper no. 92. Ithaca, N.Y.: Cornell University Press, Southeast Asia Program, Department of Asian Studies.

Lemoine, Jacques. 1983. "Yao Religion and Society." In *Highlanders of Thailand*, ed. John McKinnon and Wanat Bhruksasri. Singapore: Oxford University Press.

———. 1988. "The Turtle Symbol in Yao Kwatang and Tousai Ordinations." *Hong Kong Anthropology Bulletin* nos. 9–13:14–25.

Lewis, Paul. 1968. "The Role and Function of the Akha 'Village Priest'." *Behavior Science Notes* 3 (4):249–262.

Maurice, Albert-Marie. 2002. *Croyance et pratiques religieuses des Montagnards du Centre-Vietnam*. Paris: L'Harmattan.

Miles, Douglas. 1978. "Yao Spirit Mediumship and Heredity Versus Reincarnation and Descent in Phulangka." *Man* 13:428–443.

Ner, M. 1941. "Les Musulmans de l'Indochine française." *Bulletin de l'Ecole Française d'Extrême-Orient* 41:151–200.

Pranee Wongthes. 1991. "A Note on the Religion of the Black Tais." *Muang Boran* [Bangkok] 17 (3):50–54.

Rock, Joseph F. 1936. "The Origin of the Tso-la Books, or Books of Divination of the Na-khi or Mo-so Tribe." *Journal of the Western China Society* 8:39–52.

Simakin, S. A. 1988. "Kachin Animistic Beliefs (Concerning the Dialectics of Animism)." *Sovetskaya etnografiya*, 3:120–126.

Smalley, William Allen, Chia Koua Vang, and Gnia Yee Yang. 1990. *Mother of Writing: The Origin and Development of a Hmong Messianic Script*. Chicago: University of Chicago Press.

Soulié, George. 1909. "Les Musulmans du Yun-Nan." *Revue Indochinoise*, 30 septembre, pp. 1053–1062.

Srisakara, Vallibhotama. 1991. "The Belief in Taen of the Black Tais: The Primitive Religion of the Thais." *Muang Boran* [Bangkok] 17 (3):12–35.

Sumit, Pitiphat. 1980. "The Religion and Beliefs of the Black Tai, and a Note on the Study of Cultural Origins." *Journal of the Siam Society* 68 (1):29–38.

Svantesson, Jan-Olof. 1996. "Blessing among the White Hmong of Northern Thailand." In *Merit and Blessing in Mainland Southeast Asia in Comparative Perspective*, ed. Cornelia Ann Kammerer and Nicola Tannenbaum. Yale Southeast Asia Studies Monograph 45. New Haven, Conn.: Yale University Southeast Asia Studies.

Tadayoshi, M. 1998. "Intra-ethnic Relations among the Shan along the Border of Northern Thailand: A Case Study of Novice Ordination in Maehongson." *Southeast Asian Studies* [Kyoto] 35 (4):663–683.

Tannenbaum, Nicola. 1984. "Shan Calendrics and the Nature of Shan Religion." *Anthropos* 79 (4/6):505–515.

Tapp, Nicholas. 1986. "Geomancy as an Aspect of Upland-Lowland Relationships." In *The Hmong in Transition*, ed. G. L. Hendricks, B. T. Downing, and A. S. Deinard. Minneapolis, Minn.: Center for Migration Studies and the Southeast Asian Refugee Studies Center of the University of Minnesota.

———. 1988. "Geomancy and Development: The Case of the White Hmong of North Thailand." *Ethnos* [Stockholm], nos. 3–4:228–238.

———. 1989. "Hmong Religion." *Asian Folklore Studies* [Nagoya, Japan] 48 (1):59–94.

T'ien, Ju-k'ang. 1949. "Pai Cults and Social Age in the Thai Tribes of the Yunnan-Burma Frontier." *American Anthropologist* 51:46–57.

Tooker, Deborah E. 1992. "Identity Systems of Highland Burma: 'Belief', Akha Zan, and a Critique of Interiorized Notions of Ethno-religious Identity." *Man* 27:799–819; 28:801–803.

Vargyas, Gabor. 1996. "Ancestors and the Forest among the Brou of Vietnam." *Diogenes* 44. 2:117.

Yuji, B. 1998. "Being Lue, Not Being Lue: Guardian Spirit Cult in the Borderless Age." *Southeast Asian Studies* [Kyoto] 35 (4):716–737.

Shamanism

Cauquelin, Josiane. 1996a. "Eventail et grelot pour chevaucher dans le 'jardin des fleurs' (étude preliminaire du chamanisme nung du Guangxi—Chine)." *Bulletin de l'Ecole Francaise d'Extreme-Orient* 83:299–314.

———. 1996b. "The Flower-soul in Nung Shamanism (Guangxi province, China)." *Shaman* 4:27–44.

Chindarsi, Nusit. 1983. "Hmong Shamanism." In *Highlanders of Thailand*, ed. John McKinnon and Wanat Bhruksasri. Kuala Lumpur, New York: Oxford University Press.

Durrenberger, E. Paul. 1975. "Lisu Shamans and Some General Questions." *Journal of the Steward Anthropological Society* [Urbana, Ill.] 7 (1):1–20.

———. 1976. "A Lisu Shamanistic Séance." *Journal of the Siam Society* [Bangkok] 64 (2):151–160.

Hansson, Inga Lill. 1983. *Akha Shaman's Trance*. Copenhagen: East Asian Institute, University of Copenhagen.

Lemoine, Jacques. 1992. "Techniques of Direct Action: Miao-Yao Variations in Shamanic Healing." *Bulletin de l'Ecole Francaise d'Extreme-Orient* 79 (2):149–181, 376.

———. 1996. "The Constitution of a Hmong Shaman's Powers of Healing and Folk Culture." *Shaman* 4:143–165.

Lemoine, Jacques, and M. Eisenbruch. 1997. "The Practice of the Power of Healing by the Hmong Shamans and the Cambodian Traditional Healers of Indochina." *L'Homme* 37 (144):63–103.

Moréchand, Guy. 1955. "Principaux traits du chamanisme Meo Blanc en Indochine." *Bulletin de l'École Française d'Extrême-Orient* 47:509–546.

———. 1968. "Le chamanisme des Hmong." *Bulletin de l'École Française d'Extrême-Orient* 54:53–294.

Mottin, Jean. 1982. *Allons faire le tour du ciel et de la terre: le chamanisme des Hmong vu dans les textes*. Bangkok: White Lotus.

———. 1984. "A Hmong Shaman's Séance." *Asian Folklore Studies* 43:99–108.

Paja Thao. 1989. *I Am a Shaman: A Hmong Life Story with Ethnographic Commentary.* Translation by Xa Thao. Minneapolis: Southeast Asian Refugee Studies Project, Center for Urban and Regional Affairs, University of Minnesota.

Myths

Day, Nancy Raines, and Genna Panzarella. 2001. *Piecing Earth & Sky Together: A Creation Story from the Mien Tribe of Laos.* Fremont, Calif.: Shens Books.

Graham, David C. 1938. "The Legends of the Ch'uan Miao." *Journal of the West China Border Research Society* 10:9–51.

Johnson, Charles, ed. 1981. *Tus neeg txiav taws, nws tus gaib thiab nws poj niam* [The Woodcutter, His Rooster and His Wife: A Hmong Folk Tale in Hmong and Beginning ESL, level 2]. St. Paul, Minn.: Linguistics Department, Macalester College.

Lemoine, Jacques. 1987. "Mythes d'origine, mythes d'identification." *L'Homme* 101 :58–85.

Obayashi, T. 1964. "Myths and Legends of the Lawa and Karen in Northwestern Thailand." *Japanese Journal of ethnology* 29 (2):113–123.

Pa, Chou Yang, et al. 1985. *Myths, Legends and Folk Tales from the Hmong of Laos.* St. Paul, Minn.: Linguistics Department, Macalester College.

Rock, Joseph F. 1935. "The Story of the Flood in the Literature of the Mo-so (Na-khi) Tribe." *Journal of the Western China Society* 7:64–80.

Sutton, Donald S. 2000. "Myth Making on an Ethnic Frontier: The Cult of the Heavenly Kings of West Hunan, 1715–1996." *Modern China* 26 4:448–500.

Takemura, T. 1978. " 'Dog Ancestor' and 'The Crossing of the Sea': A Selection of the Mythical Cores of Yao Ethnic Identity." *Bulletin of the National Museum of Ethnology* [Osaka] 3 (4):615–681.

Tapp, Nicholas. 1982. "The Relevance of Telephone Directories to a Lineage-based Society: A Consideration of Some Messianic Myths among the Hmong." *Journal of the Siam Society* 70:114–127.

Walker, Anthony R., ed. 1999. *Mvuh Hpa Mi Hpa Creating Heaven, Creating Earth: An Epic Myth of the Lahu People in Yunnan.* Chiang Mai, [Thailand]: Silkworm Books.

Van, Dang Nghiem. 1993. "The Flood Myth and the Origin of Ethnic Groups in Southeast Asia." *The Journal of American Folklore* 106 421: 304–337.

Rituals

Bertrais, Yves. 1978. *The Traditional Marriage among the White Hmong of Thailand and Laos*. Chiang Mai, [Thailand]: Hmong Center.

———. 1992. "Pour obtenir l'Ombrelle: joute de mariage hmong, Laos." In *Chants alternés: Asie du Sud-Est*, ed. Nicole Revel. Paris: Editions Sudestasie.

Bliatout, Bruce Thowpaou. 1993. "Hmong Death Customs: Traditional and Acculturated." In *Ethnic Variations in Dying, Death, and Grief: Diversity in Universality*, ed. Donald P. Irish, Kathleen F. Lundquist, and Vivian Jenkins Nelsen. Washington, D.C.: Taylor, and Francis (Series in death education, aging, and health care.)

Bourotte, B. 1943. "Mariages et Funérailles chez les Meo blancs de la région de Nong-Het (Tranh Ninh)." *Bulletin de l'Institut pour l'Étude de l'Homme* [Hanoi] 6:33–56.

Cam Trong. 1996. "Black Tai Marriage Customs: A Life-long Process." *Tai Culture: International Review on Tai Cultural Studies* [Berlin] 1 (1):22–29.

———. 2000. "Le rôle de l'esprit mot (phi mot) chez les Tai Noirs du Viet-nam et quelques techniques de guérison élémentaires." *Aséanie*, no. 6:125–146.

Cuisinier, Jeanne. 1951. *Prières accompagnant les rites agraires chez les Muong de Man Duc*. Paris: Ecole Française d'Extrême-Orient.

Dzoedang, Phima Aghaw. 1979a. *Akha Death Rituals*. Translated by Inga Lill Hansson. Copenhagen: East Asian Institute, University of Copenhagen.

———. 1979b. *Akha Sickness Rituals*. Translated by Inga Lill Hansson. East Asian Institute, University of Copenhagen.

Graham, David C. 1937a. "The Customs of the Ch'uan Miao." *Journal of the West China Border Research Society* 9:13–70.

———. 1937b. "The Ceremonies of the Ch'uan Miao." *Journal of the West China Border Research Society* 9:71–119.

Hamilton, James W. 1976. "Structure, Function, and Ideology of a Karen Funeral in Northern Thailand." In *Changing Identities in Modern Southeast Asia*, ed. David J. Banks. The Hague: Mouton.

He, Shao-Ying. 2000. "An Exposition on the Funeral Rite and View of the Soul of the Dai Nationality in Jinping." In *Dynamics of Ethnic Cultures across National Boundaries in Southwestern China and Mainland Southeast Asia: Relations, Societies and Languages*, ed. Yukio Hayashi and Yang Guangyuan. Chiang Mai, [Thailand]: Lanna Cultural Center, Rajabhat Institute Chiang Mai; Kyoto: Center for Southeast Asian Studies, Kyoto University.

Hutchison Ray, and Miles McNall. 1994. "Early Marriage in a Hmong Cohorte." *Journal of Marriage and the Family* 56 (3):579–590.

Izikowitz, Karl Gustav. 1941. "Fastening the Soul: Some Religious Traits among the Lamet." *Göteborgs Högskolas Arsskrift* 47 (XIV):1–32.

King, William C. 1969. "Marriage and Its Dissolution among the Kachins of Burma." *Anthropologica* 11 (2):169–188.

Lehman, Frank K. 1970. "On Chin and Kachin Marriage Regulations." *Man* 5 (1):118–125.

Lemoine, Jacques. 1984. *L'initiation du mort chez les Hmong*. Bangkok: Pandora.

Lyman, Thomas A. 1968. "Green Miao (Meo) Spirit-Ceremonies." *Ethnologica* 4:1–28.

Mark, Lindy Li. 1967. "Patrilateral Cross-cousin Marriage among the Magpie Miao: Preferential or Prescriptive." *American Anthropologist* 69 (1):55–62.

Mottin, Jean. 1979. *Fêtes du nouvel an chez les Hmong Blanc de Thaïlande*. Bangkok: Don Bosco Press.

Nguyen Van Ku, and Luu Hung. 2003. *Nha Mo Tay Nguyen* [Funeral Houses in the Central Highlands of Vietnam]. Hanoi: The Gioi.

Rock, Joseph F. 1936. "Ha-la or the Killing of the Soul as Practiced by Na-khi Sorcerers." *Journal of the Western China Society* 8:53–58.

Tannenbaum, Nicola. 2002. "From Repairing the Village/Repairing the Country Ceremonies to Tree Ordinations: Changes in Political Ritual in a Shan Community in Northwestern Thailand." In *Inter-ethnic Relations in the Making of Mainland Southeast Asia and Southwestern China*, ed. Yukio Hayashi and Aroonrut Wichienkeeo. Chiang Rai, Thailand: Center for Ethnic Studies, Rajabhat Institute; Kyoto: Center for Southeast Asian Studies, Kyoto University.

Tannenbaum, Nicola, and Cornelia Ann Kammerer, eds. 2003. *Founders' Cults in Southeast Asia: Ancestors, Polity, and Identity*. Yale Monograph No. 52. New Haven, Conn.: Yale University Press.

Van Doanh Ngo. 1991. "Notes sur les cérémonies funéraires des Jarai et des Bahnar (centre Vietnam)." *Archipel* 42:39–45.

Walker, Anthony R. 1974. "Three Lahu Nyi (Red Lahu) Marriage Prayers: Lahu Texts and Ethnographic Notes." *Journal of the Royal Asiatic Society* 1:44–49.

———. 1976a. "Jaw te mehv jaw ve: Lahu Nyi (Red Lahu) Rites of Spirit Exorcism in North Thailand." *Anthropos* 71 (3/4):377–422.

———. 1976b. " Mvuhv nyi Nev caiv ve: A Lahu Nyi (Red Lahu) Rite to Propitiate the Sun Spirit: Ethnographic Notes and Lahu Texts." *Acta ethnographica Budapest* 25 (1/2):166–70.

———. 1977. "Propitiating the House Spirit among the Lahu Nyi (Red Lahu) of Northern Thailand: Three Lahu Texts with an Ethnographic Introduction." *Bulletin of the Institute of Ethnology Academy Sinica* 44:47–60.

———. 1978. "Lahu Nyi (Red Lahu) Funerary Chants: Two Lahu Texts with a Brief Ethnographic Introduction." *Journal of the Royal Asiatic Society* 2:163–170.

——. 1978/1979. "Lahu Nyi (Red Lahu) Farming Rites (North Thailand). 2." *Anthropos* 73 (5/6):717–736; 74 (5/6):697–716.

——. 1981a. "Chaw g'u K'ai leh hk'aw ne cai ve: A Lahu Nyi (Red Lahu) Rite of Spirit Propitiation: Lahu Text and Ethnographic Background." *Acta Ethnographica Budapest* 30 (1/2):196–200.

——. 1981b. "Shi nyi: Merit Days among the Lahu Nyi (Red Lahu), North Thailand." *Anthropos* 76 (5/6):665–706.

——. 1985. "'Sha Lao Te Ve': The Building of a Merit Shelter among the Lahu Nyi (Red Lahu) of the Northern Thai Uplands." *Asian Folklore Studies* 44:51–80.

Yang Guangyuan. 2000. "A Cultural Interpretation of the Religious and Sacrificial Rites of the Dai Personality." In *Dynamics of Ethnic Cultures across National Boundaries in Southwestern China and Mainland Southeast Asia: Relations, Societies and Languages*, ed. Yukio Hayashi. Chiang Mai, [Thailand]: Lanna Cultural Center, Rajabhat Institute, Chiang Mai; Kyoto: Center for Southeast Asian Studies, Kyoto University.

Ye, Dabing. 1993. *The Bridal Boat, Marriage Customs of China's Fifty-Five Ethnic Minorities*. Beijing: Foreign Language Press.

Christianity

Barney, G. Linwood. 1957. "The Meo—An Incipient Church." *Practical Anthropology* 4 (2):31–50.

Cheung Siu-Woo. 1995. "Milleniarism, Christian Movements and Ethnic Change among the Miao in Southwest China." In *Cultural Encounters on China's Ethnic Frontiers*, ed. Stevan Harrell. Seattle: University of Washington Press.

Covell, Ralph R. 1993. *Mission Impossible: The Unreached Nosu on China's Frontier*. Carol Stream, Ill.: Hope Publishing House.

——. 1995. *The Liberating Gospel in China: The Christian Faith among China's Minority Peoples*. Grand Rapids, Mich.: Baker Book House.

Diamond, Norma. 1996. "Christianity and the Hua Miao: Writing Power' in Bays." In *Christianity in China: From Eighteenth Century to the Present*, ed. Daniel H., Bays. Stanford: California University Press.

Fischer, Edward. 1980. *Mission in Burma: The Columban Fathers' Forty-Three Years in Kachin Country*. New York: Seabury Press.

Hayami, Yoko. 1994. "Buddhist Missionary Project in the Hills of Northern Thailand: A Case Study from a Cluster of Karen Villages." *Southeast Asian Studies* [Kyoto] 32 (2):231–250.

Kammerer, Cornelia Ann. 1990. "Customs and Christian Conversion among Akha Highlanders of Burma and Thailand." *American Ethnologist* 17 (2):277–291.

———. 1996. "Discarding the Basket: The Reinterpretation of Tradition by Akha Christians of Northern Thailand." *Journal of Southeast Asian Studies* [Singapore] 27 (2):320.

Leepreecha, Prasit. 2000. "Christian Conversion and Hmong Kinship Identity in Thailand." In *Globalization and the Asian Economic Crisis: Indigenous Responses, Coping Strategies, and Governance Reform in Southeast Asia*, ed. Geoffrey B. Hainsworth. Vancouver: Centre for Southeast Asia Research, Institute of Asian Research.

Lewis, Alison. 2000. "The Western Protestant Missionaries and the Miao in Yunnan and Guizhou, Southwest China." In *Turbulent Times and Enduring Peoples. Mountain Minorities in the South-East Asian Massif*, ed. Jean Michaud. London: Curzon.

Nguyên Xuân Nghia. 1989. "Thiên Chúa giáo và dao Tin lành các dân tôc thiêu sô Tây Nguyên" [Catholicism and Protestantism among the Ethnic Minorities of the Central Higlands]. *Tap Chí Dân Tâc Tâc Hoc* 4 (64):59–68.

Smalley, William A. 1956. "The Gospel and the Cultures of Laos." *Practical Anthropology* 3 (3):47–57.

Swain, Margaret Byrne. 1995. "Père Vial and the Gni-p'a. Orientalist Scholarship and the Christian Project." In *Cultural Encounters on China's Ethnic Frontiers*, ed. Stevan Harrell. Seattle and London: University of Washington Press.

Tapp, Nicholas. 1989. "The Impact of Missionary Christianity upon Marginalized Ethnic Minorities: The Case of the Hmong." *Journal of Southeast Asian Studies* 20 (1):70–95.

Tatsuki Kataoka. 1998. "On the Notion of 'the Lost Book' in the Early Mass Conversion to Christianity among the Lahu in Upper Burma." *Journal of Asian and African studies* [Tokyo] 56:141–65.

Tegenfeldt, Herman. 1974. *A Century of Growth: The Kachin Baptist Church of Burma*. Waynesboro, Ga.: Gabriel Resources.

Zhang Tan. 1992. *Zhai men "qian di shi men kan: Jidu jiao wen hua yu Chuan Dian Qian bian Miao zu she hui* [The Stone Threshold in Front of the "Narrow Door": Christian Culture and Miao People's Society of the Border Regions of Sichuan, Yunnan, and Guizhou Provinces]. Kunming, China: Yunnan jiao yu chu ban she Yunnan sheng Xin hua shu dian jing xiao.

8. CULTURE

Anderson, E. F. 1993. *Plants and People of the Golden Triangle: Ethnobotany of the Hill Tribes of the Northern Thailand*. Portland, Oreg.: Dioscorides Press.

Berlie, Jean. 1996. "A Preliminary Essay on Classification, Globalization, and New Frontiers: A Cultural Overview of the Tai." *Tai Culture: International Review on Tai Cultural Studies* [Berlin] 1 (2):24–49.

———. 1997. "Tai Nua in Laos and Yunnan (China): Tai-Lao and Tai-Nua." *Tai Culture: International Review on Tai Cultural Studies* [Berlin] 2 (2):46–56.

Betts, G. E. 1889–1890. "Social Life of the Miao-tsi." *Journal of the Royal Asiatic Society* [North China Branch] 33 (2):1–21.

Cooper, Robert G. 1978a. "Dynamic Tension: Symbiosis and Contradiction in Hmong Social Relations." *The New Economic Anthropology*, ed. John Clammer. London: Macmillan.

———. 1978b. "Unity and Division in Hmong Social Categorization in Thailand." In *Studies in ASEAN Sociology: Urban Society and Social Change*, ed. Peter S. J. Chen and Hans-Dieter Evers. Singapore: Chopmen Enterprises.

———. 1979. "The Yao Jua Relationship: Patterns of a Final Alliance and Residence among the Hmong of Northern Thailand." *Ethnology* [Pittsburgh, Pa.] 18 (2):173–181.

Dessaint, William. 2001. "Intangible Cultural Heritage: Tibeto-Burmese Peoples and Minority Groups in Viet Nam." In *Viet Nam's Cultural Diversity: Approaches to Preservation*, ed. Oscar Salemink. Paris: United Nations Educational, Scientific and Cultural Organization.

Diamond, Norma. 1988. "The Miao and Poison: Interactions on China's Southwest Frontier." *Ethnology* 27:1–25.

Giang, Ho Ly. 2000. "The Food Culture of the Hmong." *Vietnam Social Sciences* 6 (80):96–110.

Gu, Wenfeng. 1995. *Weavers of Ethnic Culture: The Miaos*. Women's Culture Series: Nationalities of Yunnan. Kunming: Yunnan Education Publishing House.

Hanson, Ola. 1913. *Kachins: Their Customs and Traditions*. Rangoon: The American Baptist Mission Press.

Houmphanh Rattanavong. 1994. "To Preserve the Cultural Heritage of the Multi-ethnic People of Laos." *Vietnamese Studies* [Hanoi] 42:107–111.

Hsu, Francis L. K. 1943. "Magic and Science in Western Yunnan." In *Sociological Change in Southwest China*, ed. F. L. K. Hsu. New York: Institute of Pacific Relations.

Huy, N. V. 1995. "The Particularity of Popular Beliefs among Ethnic Communities of the Hanhi-Lolo Linguistic Group." *Social Compass* 42 (3):301–315.

Khong, Kim Anh. 1997. "Material Culture of the Black Hmong in Paco Commune, Mai Chau District, Hoa Binh Province, in a Transitional Period." In *Methodological Issues in Ethnology—Social Anthropology*, [seminar in Hanoi, December 15–17. 1997]. Hanoi,

Lajoux, Jean-Dominique. 1977. *Le tambour du déluge: villages des montagnes d'Indochine*. Paris: Seuil.

Lewis, Paul W., and Bai Bibo. 2002. *Hani Cultures Themes*. Bangkok: White Lotus.

Li Yi. 2001. *Selected Cultural Relics of the Nationalities*. Kunming: Yunnan Provincial Museum.

Matras-Troubetzkoy, Jacqueline. 1978. "L'ordinaire et la fête: la cuisine chez les Brou (Cambodge-Province de Ratanakiri)." *Asie du Sud-Est et Monde Insulindien* [Paris] 9 (3/4):111–140.

Nong Quoc Chan. 1978. "Thirty Years of Cultural Work among Ethnic Minorities." *Vietnamese Studies*, no. 52:50–56.

Phan Huu Dat. 1962. "Materials on the Social and Family Organization of the Puok People of Northwest Vietnam." *Sovietskaya Etnografiya* 5:48–56.

Pinkaew, Laungaramsri. 1993. "Another Definition of Nature: An Example from a Karen Community." *Muang Boran* [Bangkok] 19 (3):21–40.

Pourret, Jess G. 2002. *The Yao, the Mien and Mun Yao in China, Vietnam, Laos and Thailand*. London: Thames and Hudson.

Renard, Ronald. 1990. "Taï Lü Self, House, Village and Moeng." *Crossroads* 5 (1):43–58.

Schein, Louisa. 1999. "Performing Modernity." *Cultural Anthropology* 14 (3):361–95.

Shiratori, Yoshiro. 1966. "Ethnic Configurations in Southern China." *Folk Culture in South-East Asia* 25:147–163.

Teng, Chi Yao, and Liu Chang. 1991. *The Festivals in the Mysterious Land of Yunnan: The Festivals and Traditional Ceremonies of the Minority Nationalities in Yunnan*. Kunming, China: Yunnan People's Publishing House.

Tsutomu, Kaneshige. 1998. "Creation of an Ethnic Symbol: Case of the Dong Nationality in Southwest China." *Southeast Asian Studies* [Kyoto] 35 (4):738–758.

Architecture

Léger, D. 1974. "La maison bahnar et ses dépendances d'après des documents inédits de P. Guilleminet." *Asie du Sud-Est et Monde Insulindien* 5 (2):25–87.

Ruan Xing. 1996. "Empowerment in the Practice of Making and Inhabiting: Dong Architecture in Cultural Reconstruction." *Journal of Material Culture* [London] 1 (2):211–237.

Tsutomu, Kaneshige. 2000. "Village Community and Public Architecture: 'Wagx' Concept and Drum Tower among Dong (Kam) People of Sanjiang in Guangxi Province, China." In *Dynamics of Ethnic Cultures across National Boundaries in Southwestern China and Mainland Southeast Asia: Relations, Societies and Languages*, ed. Yukio Hayashi and Guangyuan Yang. Kyoto: Center for Southeast Asian Studies, Kyoto University.

Zhu Liangwen. 1992. *The Dai or the Tai and Their Architecture and Customs in South China*. Bangkok: White Lotus.

Arts, Textile, and Ornamentation

Adams, Monni. 1974. "Dress and Design in Highland Southeast Asia: The Hmong (Miao) and the Yao." *Textile Museum Journal* 4 (1):51–66.

Boudot, Eric. 2003. "Miao Textiles from China, Guizhou Province." *Art Tribal* 2:130–149.

Chan, Anthony. *Hmong Textile Designs*. Owings Mills, Md.: Stemmer House, 1990.

Cohen, Erik. 1982. "Refugee Art in Thailand." *Cultural Survival Quarterly* 6 (4):40–42.

———. 1983. "The Dynamics of Commercialized Arts: The Meo and Yao of Northern Thailand." *Journal of the National Research Council of Thailand* 15 (1):1–34.

———. 1988. "From Tribal Costume to Pop Fashion: The "Boutiquisation" of the Textiles of the Hill Tribes of Northern Thailand." *Studies in Popular Culture* 11 (2):49–59.

———. 1990. "Hmong (Meo) Commercialized Refugee Art: From Ornament to Picture." In *Art as a Means of Communication in Pre-literate Societies*, ed. D. Eban, E. Cohen, and B. Danet. Jerusalem: Israel Museum.

———. 1996. "Temporal Ambiguity in Hmong Representational Textile Art." *Visual Anthropology* 9 (1):25–40.

Corrigan, Gina. 2001. *Miao Textiles from China*. Seattle: University of Washington Press.

Cresson, Michael, and R. Jeannin. 1943. "La toile Méo." *Bulletin de l'Institut pour l'Étude de l'Homme* [Hanoi] 6:435–447.

De Beauclair, Wolfgang S. 1986. "Dress and Ornamentation of the Pa Miao in the Anshun District of Kweichow Province." *Ethnographic Studies* 2:13–20. (Translation of "Tracht und Ornamentik des Pa Miao im Anshun Kreis des Provinz Kweichow").

Diep Trung Binh, and Barbara Cohen. 1997. *Patterns on Textiles of the Ethnic Groups in Northeast of Vietnam*, Hanoi: Culture of Nationalities Publishing House.

Feng, Hanji. 1985. *Zhongguo shao shu min zu yi shi* [National minority costume in China]. Beijing: Chu ban Edition.

Formoso, Bernard. 2000. "A Terraced World for an Armored Body: The Symbolism of Women's Costumes among the Yi of Yuanyang (Yunnan)." *Res* 37:89–105.

Gazzolo, Michele B. 1986. *Spirit Paths and Roads of Sickness: A Symbolic Analysis of Hmong Textile Design*. Evanston, Ill.: M. Gazzolo.

Gittinger, Mattiebelle, and H. Leedom Lefferts Jr. 1992. *Textiles and the Tai Experience in Southeast Asia*. Washington, D.C.: The Textile Museum.

Goldman, Ann Yarwood. 1995. *Lao Mien Embroidery: Migration and Change*. Bangkok: White Lotus.

Guanya, Zhu. 1985. *Clothings and Ornaments of China's Miao People*. Beijing: China Books and Periodicals.

Hinton, Elizabeth. 1974. "The Dress of the Pwo Karen of North Thailand." *Journal of the Siam Society* [Bangkok] 62 (1):27–34.

Howard, M. C., and B. K. Nhung. 1999. "Dress of the T'ai peoples of Vietnam." *Arts of Asia* 29 (1):93–105.

Howard, Michael C. 1999. *Textiles of the Hill Tribes of Burma*. Bangkok: White Lotus.

Hua, Wu Jin, and Long Zhi Yi. 1993. *Art of the Yi People in Southwest Guizhou: Illustrations from Nashi and the Ancient Documents in Yi Language*. Kunming, China: Foreign Language Press.

Izikowitz, Karl Gustav. 1943. "Quelques notes sur le costume des Puli-Akha." *Ethnos* (8):133–152.

Lefferts, H. Leedom, Jr. 1994. "Tai Textiles and Vietnam, 3 Landscapes." *Asian Art & Culture* 7 (1):62–77.

Lemoine, Jacques. 1985. *Yao Ceremonial Paintings*. Bangkok: White Lotus.

Liscak, Vladimir. 1991. "'Miao Albums': Their Importance and Study." *Cesky Lid* 78 (2):96–101.

Liu, Zhongyuan. 1998. "Ke zhi yi shu: Yi zu, Miao zu feng qing zhuan ji" [Art of Paper-carving: A Collection of Customs and Festivals of Yi and Miao Nationalities.] Guyang: Guizhou min zu chu ban she; Di 1 ban.

Lyman, Thomas A. 1962. "The Weaving Techniques of the Green Miao." *Ethnos* 27:35–39.

MacDowell, Marsha. 1989. *Stories in Thread: Hmong Pictorial Embroidery*. East Lansing, Mich.: Michigan Traditional Arts Program, Folk Arts Division, Michigan State Universtiy Museum.

Maxwell, Robin. 1990. *Textiles of Southeast Asia: Tradition, Trade and Transformation*. London: Oxford University Press.

McDaniel, Phila. 2001. "Miao Metal Weaving of China's Guizhou Province." *Ornament* 26 (1):74–77.

———. 2002. "Land of the Silk Dragon: Shidong Miao Embroidery." *Ornament* 25 (4):62–67.

———. 2003. "Folded silk Miao." *Ornament* 26 (3):58–61.

The Nationalities Affairs Commission of Guizhou Province. 1987. *Ethnic Costume from Guizhou: Clothing, Designs and Decorations from Minority Ethnic Groups in South West China*. Beijing: Foreign Languages Press, The Folk Art Gallery of Guizhou Province, and the Provincial Museum of Guizhou.

P'ang, Hsin-min. 1932. "Kwang-tung Pei Chiang Yao-shan Tsa-chi" [Miscellaneous Sketches of the Yao-shan of North Kwang-tung]. *Bulletin of the Institute of History and Philology, Academia Sinica* 2:473–514.

Peterson, Sally. 1988. "Translating Experience and the Reading of a Story Cloth." the *Journal of American Folklore* 101 (399):6–22.

Rossi, Gail. 1988. "Enduring Dress of the Miao, Guizhou Province, People's Republic of China." *Ornament* 11:26–31.

Xu Yixi. 1989. *Headdresses of Chinese Minority Nationality Women*. Beijing: Nationality Press.

Zhao Yuchi. 1985. *Clothing and Ornaments of China's Miao People*. Beijing: Nationality Press.

Kinship

Akira, Yoshino. 1995. "Father and Son, Master and Disciple: The Patrilineage Ideology of the Mien Yao in Thailand." In *Perspectives on Chinese Society: Anthropological Views from Japan*. ed. Suenari Michio, J. S. Eades, and C. Daniels. Kent, UK: Center for Social Anthropology and Computing, University of Kent at Canterbury.

Bradley, David. 1977. "Sound Symbolism in Jinghpaw (Kachin) [comment on 'The language of Kachin Kinship: Reflections on a Tikopia model', by E.R. Leach; with a reply by E.R. Leach]." *Man* 12 (2):336–339.

———. 1978. "Sound Symbolism in Jinghpaw (Kachin) [reply to comment by Sir E. Leach on 'Sound Symbolism in Jinghpaw (Kachin)', by D. Bradley; with a reply by Sir E. Leach]." *Man* 13 (4):659–663.

Ch'en, Tsung-hsiang. 1947. "The Dual System and the Clans of the Li-su and Shui-t'ien Tribes." *Monumenta Serica* 12:252–259.

Hanks, Jane Richardson. 1974. "Recitation of Patrilineages among the Akha." In *Social Organisation and the Applications of Anthropology: Essays in honour of Lauriston Sharp*, ed. R. J. Smith. Ithaca, N.Y.: Cornell University Press.

Hinton, Peter. 1984. "Matrifocal Cult Groups and the Distribution of Resources amongst the Pwo Karen." *Mankind* 14:339–347.

Kammerer, Cornelia Ann. 1998. "Descent, Alliance, and Political Order among the Akha." *American Ethnologist* 25 (4):659–674.

Lafont, Pierre Bernard. 1955. "Notes sur les familles patronymiques Thai noires de Son-la et de Nghia-lô." *Anthropos* 50:797–807.

Miles, Douglas. 1972. "Yao Bride-exchange, Matrification and Adoption." *Bijdragen tot de Taal-, Land-, en Volkenkunde* 128:99–117.

Rajah, Ananda. 1984. "'Au' Ma Xae: Domestic Ritual and the Ideology of Kinship among the Sgaw Karen of Palokhi, Northern Thailand." *Mankind* 14:348–356.

Ruey Yih-fu. 1958. "Terminological Structure of the Miao Kinship System." *Academia Sinica* (Taipei), 29:613–639.

Taillard, Christian. 1992. "Village, pouvoir lignager et société locale chez les Hmong du Laos." In *Habitations et habitat d'Asie du Sud-Est continentale: pratiques et représentations de l'espace*, ed. Jacqueline Matras-Guin and Christian Taillard. Paris: L'Harmattan.

Wei Hwei-lin. 1963. "Population and Genealogical Materials of Wu-Pau Lineage Group of Lolo, Ma-Pien, Szechuan Province." *Bulletin of the Ethnology Society China* 3:87–91.

Music

Baranovitch, Nimrod. 2003. *China's New Voices: Popular Music, Ethnicity, Gender, and Politics, 1978–1997.* Berkeley: University of California Press.

Becker, J. O. 1964. "Music of the Pwo Karen of Northern Thailand." *Ethnomusicology* 8 (2):137–153.

Catlin, Amy R. 1981. *Music of the Hmong: Singing Voices and Talking Reeds.* Providence: Rhode Island College Office of Publications.

———. 1982. "Speech Surrogate Systems of the Hmong: From Singing Voices to Talking Reeds." In *The Hmong in the West: Observations and Reports: Papers of the 1981 Hmong Research Conference*, ed. Bruce T. Downing and Douglas P. Olney. Minneapolis, Minn.: Southeast Asian Refugee Studies Project, Center for Urban and Regional Affairs, University of Minnesota.

———. 1985. "Harmonizing the Generations in Hmong Musical Performance." *Selected Reports in Ethnomusicology* 6:83–97.

———. 1992. "'Homo Cantens': Why Hmong Sing during Interactive Courtship Rituals." *Selected Reports in Ethnomusicology* 9:43–60.

———. 1997. "Puzzling the Text: Thought-songs, Secret Languages, and Archaic Tones in Hmong Music." *The World of Music* 39 (2):69–81. (Special issue, "Cultural Concepts of Hearing and Listening.")

Davis, Sara. 2002. "Snapshot: Dai Popular Music." In *East Asia: China, Japan, and Korea*, ed. Robert C. Provine, Yosihiko Tokumaru, and J. Lawrence Witzleben. The Garland Encyclopedia of World Music, 7. New York; London: Routledge.

Falk, Catherine. 2003a. "The Dragon Taught Us: Hmong Stories about the Origin of the Free Reed Pipes Qeej." *Asian Music* 35 (1):17–56.

———. 2003b. "'If You Have Good Knowledge, Close It Well Tight': Concealed and Framed Meaning in the Funeral Music of the Hmong Qeej." *British Journal of Ethnomusicology* 12 (2):1–33.

Francis, Marc. 1999. "Where Singing Is Food for the Soul [Dong Minority]." *China Review* [London], no. 13:20–21.

Graham, David C. 1954. *Song and Stories of the Ch'uan Miao*. Washington D.C.: The Smithsonian, publication no. 4139 .

Janpob, Jobkrabuonwan. 1991. "Tai Dum Rum Pan the Historic Song of the Black Tais." *Muang Boran* [Bangkok] 17 (3):62–65.

Khamleuy, Thao. 1980. "La cour d'amour de minuit chez les Hmong du Laos." *Péninsule* [Paris] (1):22–37.

Larsen, Hans Peter P. 1984. "The Music of the Lisu of Northern Thailand." *Asian Folklore Studies* 43:41–62.

Li Weibai. 1996. *Miao ling yue lun* [On Miao Ling music]. Guyang, China: Guizhou min tsuchu ban she; Di 1 ban.

Lindell, Kristina. 1982. *Kammu Year: Its Lore and Music*. Loughten, UK: Prometheus Books.

Ma Hexuan. 1995. *Leaves and Song as Matchmakers: The Buyis*. Kunming, China: Nationality Press.

Mackerras, Colin. 1984. "Folksongs and Dances of China's Minority Nationalities: Policy, Tradition, and Professionalization." *Modern China* 10 (2):187–226.

Mottin, Jean. 1980. *55 chants d'amour hmong blanc* [55 zaj kwv txhiaj hmoob clawb]. Bangkok: Siam Society.

Nguyen Van Huyen. 1941. *Recueil des chants de mariage Tho de Lang-Son et Cao-Bang*. Hanoi, Vietnam: École Française d'Extrême-Orient.

Rees, Helen. 2000. *Echoes of History: Naxi Music in Modern China*. Oxford, UK: Oxford University Press. (Book and CD edition.)

Schein, Louisa. 1994. "Love Songs of the Miao in China." *The Journal of Asian Studies* [Ann Arbor, Mich.] 53 (3):1030.

Stern, T., and T. A. Stern. 1974. "'I Pluck my Harp': Musical Acculturation among the Karen of Western Thailand." *Ethnomusicology* 15 (2):186–219.

Thao, H. 1995. "Hmong Music in Vietnam." *Nhac Viet, The Journal of Vietnamese Music* 4 (2): special issue.

Oral Tradition and Literature

Afanassieva, Yelena. 2000. "Folklore Origins and Evolution of the Narrative Poem Genre in Thailand and Laos." *International Review on Tai Cultural Studies* [Berlin], 5 (1):125–131.

Ahai, and Liuqia. 1989. *The Anthology of the Sipsongpanna Hani's Legends*. Jinghong, Yunnan: National Minority Committee.

Chaichuen, Khamdaengyotdai. 2001. "Tai Luang (Shan) Social Culture as Reflected in their Proverbs, Wise Sayings, and Folk Songs: An Introduction to Tai Wisdom Literature." *Tai Culture: International Review on Tai Cultural Studies* 6 (1–2):328–347.

Daoyong Li. 1992. "Motifs in a Kammu Story from Yunnan." *Thai-Yunnan Project Newsletter* 16:15–21.

Dessaint, William, and Avounado Ngwama. 1994. *Au sud des nuages. Mythes et contes recueillis oralement chez les montagnards lissou.* Paris: Gallimard.

Dournes, Jacques. 1977. *Akhan, Contes Oraux de la Forêt Indochinoise.* Paris: Payot.

Durrenberger, E. Paul. 1978. "An Interpretation of a Lisu Tale." *Folklore* 89 (1):94–103.

Giacchino-Baker, Rosalie, ed. 1995. *Stories from Laos: Folktales and Cultures of the Lao, Hmong, Khammu, & Iu-Mein.* Canberra, Australia: Pacific Asia Press.

Hansson, Inga Lill. 1984. *A Folktale of Akha in Northern Thailand.* Copenhagen: University of Copenhagen.

Lewis, Paul. 2002. *Akha Oral Literature.* Bangkok: White Lotus Ltd.

Lewis, Paul W., and Bai Bibo. 2002. *51 Hani Stories.* Bangkok: White Lotus.

Mottin, Jean. 1981. *Contes et légendes hmong blanc.* Bangkok: Don Bosco Press.

Proschan, Frank. 1992. "Poetic Parallelism in Kmhmu Verbal Arts: From Texts to Performances." *Selected Reports in Ethnomusicology* 9:1–31.

Shuter, Robert. 1991. "The Hmong of Laos: Orality, Communication and Acculturation." In *Intercultural Communication: A Reader*, ed. Larry A. Samovar and Richard E. Porter. Belmont, Calif.: Wadsworth.

Zezhong, Zhang, and Pan Nianying. 2000. *Littératures enchantées des Dong.* Paris: Bleu de Chine.

9. HEALTH

Beyrer, C., D. D. Celentano, S. Suprasert, W. Sittitrai, K. E. Nelson, B. Kongsub, and P. Phanupak. 1997. "Widely Varying HIV Prevalence and Risk Behaviours among the Ethnic Minority Peoples of Northern Thailand." *AIDS Care* 9 (4):427–439.

Chongvatana, N., and K. Wongboosin. 1989. *Family Planning Programs and Contraceptive Practice in Khao I Dang and Ban Vinai Refugee Camps: Resultats of the 1988 Survey.* Institute of Population Studies no. 164/89. Bangkok: Chulalongkorn University.

Conquergood, Dwight. 1988. "Health Theater in a Hmong Refugee Camp: Performance, Communication, and Culture." *TDR* [Cambridge] 32 (3):174–208.

Foggin, Peter, Nagib Armijo-Hussein, Céline Marigaux, Hui Zhu, and Zeyuan Liu. 2001. "Risk Factors and Child Mortality among the Miao in Yunnan, Southwest China." *Social Science & Medicine* 53 (12):1683–1696.

Huang W., G. Li, H. Yu, and F. Wang. 1997. "Infant Mortality among Various Nationalities in the Middle part of Guizhou, China." *Social Science and Medicine* 45 (7):1031–1040.

Ishida, T., S. Takao, W. Settheetham-Ishida, and D. Tiwawech. 2002. "Prevalence of Hepatitis B and C Virus Infection in Rural Ethnic Populations of Northern Thailand." *Journal of Clinical Virology*, 24:31–35.

Kunstadter, Peter. 1986. "Ethnicity, Ecology and Mortality in Northwestern Thailand." In *Anthropology and Epidemiology,* ed. C. Janes, R. Stall, and S. M. Gifford. Dordrecht, Boston, Lancaster and Tokyo: D. Reidel.

———. 1985. "Health of Hmong in Thailand: Risk Factors, Morbidity and Mortality in Comparison with Other Ethnic Groups." *Culture, Medicine and Psychiatry* [Dordrecht, Netherlands], 9 (4):329–351.

Kunstadter, Peter, et al. 1992. "Causes and Consequences of Increase in Child Survival Rates: Ethnoepidemiology among the Hmong of Thailand." *Human Biology* [Detroit] 64 (6):821.

Kunstadter, Peter, et al. 1993. "Demographic Variables in Fetal and Child Mortality: Hmong in Thailand." *Social Science and Medicine* [New York] 36 (9):1109–1120.

Li, Y., A. P. Shi, Y. Wan, M. Hotta, and H. Ushijima. 2001. "Child Behavior Problems: Prevalence and Correlates in Rural Minority Areas of China." *Pediatrics International* 43 (6):651–661.

Li, Y., G. P. Guo, A. P. Shi, Y. P. Li, T. Anme, and H. Ushijima. 1999. "Prevalence and Correlates of Malnutrition among Children in Rural Minority Areas of China." *Pediatrics International*, 41 (5):549–556.

Liao S. S., K. H. Choi, K. N. Zhang, T. L. Hall, B. X. Qi, Y. J., Deng, J. Fang, Y. Yang, J. Kay, Z. Qin, W. Liu, and J. S Mandel. 1997. "Extremely Low Awareness of Aids, Sexually Transmitted Diseases and Condoms among Dai Ethnic Villagers in Yunnan Province, China." *AIDS* 11 (Supp. 1):27–34.

Louisirirotchanakul, S., et al. 2000. "No Evidence of HTLV-I or HTLV-II Infection among the Hmong People of Northern Thailand or Injecting Drug Users in Bangkok." *Journal of Acquired Immune Deficiency Syndromes* 23 (5):441–442.

Miles, Douglas. 1973. "Prophylactic Medicine and Kin Units among Yao Ancestor Worshippers." *Mankind* 9:77–88.

Perngparn, Usaneya. 1992. *Impact of Health Development on Child Rearing of the Hilltribes: Karen and H'Mong.* Bangkok: Chulalongkorn University Print House.

Pranee Liamputtong. 1996. "Only When I Have Borne All My Children! The Menopause in Hmong Women." In *Maternity and Reproductive Health in Asian Societies*, ed. Pranee Liamputtong Rice and Lenore Manderson. Amsterdam: Harwood Academic Publishers.

———. 2000. *Hmong Women and Reproduction*. Westport, Conn.: Greenwood Publishing Group.

Symonds, Patricia V. 1996. "Journey to the Land of Light: Birth among Hmong Women." In *Maternity and Reproductive Health in Asian Societies*, ed. Pranee Liamputtong Rice and Lenore Manderson. Amsterdam: Harwood Academic Publishers.

———. 1998. "Political Economy and Cultural Logics of HIV/AIDS among the Hmong in Northern Thailand." In *The Political Economy of AIDS*, ed. M. Singer. Amityville, N. Y.: Baywood Publishing.

———. 2000. "Suivre les chemins culturels dans le cadre de la prévention du VIH/sida chez les Hmong de Thaïlande." In *Sociétés asiatiques face au sida*, ed. Marie-Eve Blanc, Laurence Husson, and Évelyne Micollier. Paris: L'Harmattan.

Westermeyer, Joseph. 1971. "The Use of Alcohol and Opium by the Meo of Laos." *American Journal of Psychiatry* 127:59–63.

———. 1974. "Opium Smoking in Laos: A Survey of 40 Addicts." *American Journal of Psychiatry* 131:165–170.

Westermeyer, Joseph, and Grace Peng. 1978. "A Comparative Study of Male and Female Opium Addicts among the Hmong (Meo)." *British Journal of Addiction* 73 (2):81–187.

Traditional Medicine

Chang-wen Yang. 1990. "A Further Discussion of Miao Medicine 1." *Thai-Yunnan Project Newsletter* 22–36:13–15.

Durrenberger, E. Paul. 1976. "Lisu Curing: A Case History." *Bulletin of the History of Medicine* 50 (3):356–371.

———. 1979. "Misfortune and Therapy among the Lisu of Northern Thailand." *Anthropological Quarterly* 52 (4):204–210.

Hansson, Inga Lill. 1984. *Akha Sickness Rituals*. Copenhagen: East Asian Institute, University of Copenhagen.

Jilek, W. G., and L. Jilek-Aall. 1997. "The Mental Health Relevance of Traditional Medicine and Shamanism in Refugee Camps of Northern Thailand." *Curare* 13 (4):217–224.

Lafont, Pierre-Bernard. 1959. "Pratiques médicales des Thai Noirs du Laos de l'ouest." *Anthropos* 54:819–40.

Long, C. 2004. "Ethnobotanical Studies on Medicinal Plants Used by the Red-headed Yao People in Jinping, Yunnan Province, China." *Journal of Ethnopharmacology* 90 (2):389–395.

Pake, Catherine V. 1987. "Medical Ethnobotany of Hmong Refugees in Thailand." *Journal of Ethnobiology* [Flagstaff, Ariz.] 7 (1):13–26.

Potter, Gayle Siscard, and Alice Whiren. 1982. "Traditional Hmong Birth Customs: A Historical Study." In *The Hmong in the West*, ed. Bruce T. Downing and Douglas P. Olney. Observations and Reports: Papers of the 1981 Hmong Research Conference, University of Minnesota, Minneapolis: Southeast Asian Refugee Studies Project, Center for Urban and Regional Affairs.

Westermeyer, Joseph. 1988. "Folk Medicine in Laos: A Comparison between Two Ethnic Groups." *Social Science & Medicine* 27 (8):769–778.

About the Author

Jean Michaud (Ph.D., Université de Montréal, 1995) is a social anthropologist and associate researcher with the *Centre d'Etudes de l'Asie de l'Est* at Université de Montréal and at the *Laboratoire Asie du Sud-Est et Monde Austronésien* in Paris. Between 1996 and 2002, he lectured at the Centre for South-East Asian Studies of Hull University, in the United Kingdom, and was visiting professor at Université de Paris-X, and visiting researcher at Otago University in New Zealand. Since 1987, he has conducted anthropological research in highland India, Thailand, Laos, and Vietnam on the topic of social change and adjustment to modernity among highland minorities in these countries. He is the editor of *Turbulent Times and Enduring Peoples: Mountain Minorities in the South-East Asian Massif* (Curzon, 2000), and coedited *Hmong/Miao in Asia* (Silkworm, 2004). His research articles include, among others, "Economic Transformation in a Hmong Village of Thailand." (*Human Organization,* 1997), "The Montagnards and the State in Northern Vietnam from 1802 to 1975: A Historical Overview" (*Ethnohistory,* 2000), and "French Missionary Expansion in Colonial Upper-Tonkin" (*Journal of Southeast Asian Studies,* 2004).